Praise for

THE REEL TRUTH

"This book is indispensable."
>—Tom Bernard, copresident, Sony Pictures Classics

"The path to the premiere and beyond of any feature film is a minefield. With *The Reel Truth*, Reed Martin has given new filmmakers the battalion of bomb detectors necessary for survival."
>—Ted Hope, producer of *The Ice Storm*

"The perilous and shifting independent-film business is notoriously difficult to pin down, but Reed Martin has done just that—he's created a brilliant how-to manual for tackling and mastering the industry. Comprehensive and entertaining, *The Reel Truth* is jam-packed with the experiences of some of the industry's most active filmmakers, whose successes, failures, and insights form an essential document for anyone attempting to break in."
>—Anthony Bregman, producer of *Eternal Sunshine of the Spotless Mind*

"There's an entire genre of books that exist to tell people how to make movies—how to make cheap movies, how to make horror movies, how to make independent movies, how to direct, how to write, how to storyboard, how to use a camera. And many of the books are either dry instructional reads or hopelessly out-of-date. Reed Martin has created a smart, engaging read that is also one of the most comprehensive and cutting-edge looks at the changing face of independent-film production and distribution today. So many potential filmmakers have found themselves stymied by simple, basic things: how to make a living off of filmmaking, how to approach the process, how to protect themselves legally and artistically. *The Reel Truth* not only offers current and crucial information, it does so in a way that suggests a realistic approach to the idea of a life in filmmaking while still managing to encourage. Tricky stuff, and well done—I learned volumes from this book.

"You can throw out that whole shelf of books about how to make movies, because from now on, this is the one book I would call essential for anyone who really wants to make a career out of filmmaking."

—Drew McWeeny, aka Moriarty, *Ain't It Cool News*

"Reed Martin's *The Reel Truth* is a must-have manual of knowledge and entertainment for beginning and experienced filmmakers. The stories within are hilarious, sad, and familiar. The chapter on postproduction catastrophes when nearing your finish line is worth the price of admission alone. To not have this information as a filmmaker is like scuba diving by yourself, skydiving without packing your own parachute, or practicing unsafe sex—why risk it?" —Chris Eyre, director of *Smoke Signals*

REED MARTIN
THE REEL TRUTH

Reed Martin has taught a course on film marketing, distribution, and exhibition at NYU's Stern School of Business since 2003, and he taught at Columbia Business School from 2001 to 2003. He recently worked as a research associate and casewriter in the Global Research Group at Harvard Business School. Martin is a graduate of the management trainee program at 20th Century Fox Film International in Los Angeles, and he received an MBA from Columbia and a second master's in business reporting from Columbia's Graduate School of Journalism. His two favorite films are *You Can Count on Me* and *The Bourne Identity*.

THE *REEL* TRUTH

EVERYTHING
YOU DIDN'T KNOW YOU NEED
TO KNOW ABOUT MAKING AN
INDEPENDENT FILM

REED MARTIN

FABER AND FABER, INC.
An affiliate of Farrar, Straus and Giroux
New York

For my parents and
my extended family of
aspiring filmmakers

Faber and Faber, Inc.
An affiliate of Farrar, Straus and Giroux
18 West 18th Street, New York 10011

Library of Congress Cataloging-in-Publication Data
Martin, Reed, 1969–
    The reel truth : everything you didn't know you need to know about
making an independent film / Reed Martin.— 1st ed.
        p.   cm.
    Includes index.
    ISBN-13: 978-0-571-21103-6 (pbk. : alk. paper)
    ISBN-10: 0-571-21103-8 (pbk. : alk. paper)
    1. Motion pictures—Production and direction.   2. Independent
filmmakers.   I. Title.

PN1995.9.P7M34 2008
791.4302'33—dc22

                                                           2008041266

www.fsgbooks.com

1   3   5   7   9   10   8   6   4   2

Contents

THE REEL TRUTH

Introduction

Do you dream of someday making an independent film? Can you picture your low-budget masterpiece debuting at Sundance next year? Can you see the poster for your indie feature under the lights of New York's Angelika Theater or L.A.'s Laemmle's Sunset 5? There has never been a better time to dream and achieve each of these goals if you know what to do and what pitfalls to look out for.

Today anyone hoping to make a terrific-looking narrative feature or full-length documentary can shoot in filmlike 24p digital video, assemble everything on a decent laptop using intuitive and affordable editing software, put a trailer up on YouTube and Facebook, and distribute the finished product on professionally replicated DVDs for only a dollar per disc. There are more avenues for getting independently financed shorts and feature films seen than ever before, allowing aspiring filmmakers who may or may not have gone to leading film schools to showcase their talents.

Developments that promised to revolutionize film production and democratize the industry have arrived, and all the tools anyone would ever need are available, affordable, and within reach. The technology needed to make independent films will only get cheaper and better, and the reasons to go through traditional middlemen will increasingly fall away, allowing filmmakers to self-publish and be totally independent from anywhere. In this environment, all that is needed is a passion for storytelling, a reservoir of perseverance, and a modicum of talent. Gone are the days when aspiring filmmakers had to spend thousands of dollars to have dozens of fragile MiniDV tapes digitized in real time before they could be edited on a slow-as-molasses computer. Today, many HD cameras record directly to memory cards or high-capacity hard drives, allowing each day's footage to be quickly imported into Avid or Final Cut Pro 6 as easily as copying a Word file from a pocket USB drive. Indeed, filmmakers can now make their editing "selects" immediately and start assembling a project in their living rooms in full, uncompressed HD, without having to wait for a lab to process their digital footage or their reels of 16mm or 35mm film.

On the theatrical front, new specialized distributors are expected to eventually take the place of those that folded in 2008. The Internet continues to provide avenues to get shorts and features in front of those eager to experience new voices, innovative stories, and fresh perspectives. There are several sites that showcase feature films online and new software applications such as Adobe's Media Player that aggregate content for mass consumption.

On the marketing side, new software widgets can be used to help aspiring directors and producers reach out to people who might invest in their projects and build a fan base by aggregating groups of consumers who appreciate a certain topic, all without hiring an ad agency or PR firm. For those pursuing festival acceptance—and after all, who isn't?—companies such as Withoutabox and its new competing service, B-Side, allow filmmakers to save time by paying a flat fee to have their films submitted to hundreds of festivals.

In just a few months, pocket still cameras available at any Radio Shack (such as the Kodak Zi6) and portable devices like the Flip from Pure Digital will be able to record higher quality video to internal standard drives or SD cards with improved sound, ushering in a new era of handheld indie filmmaking. Later this year, some intrepid filmmaker will debut a first film shot using store-bought gear and civilian actors, creating a sensation that merits an article in *Vanity Fair* and inspires a new generation of filmmakers. It could be you. The tools to pull it off are a fast laptop, a licensed copy of Final Cut Studio 3, StoryBoard Quick 5, an external Blu-ray DVD burner, and WordPress software to create the website—all are available for under $5,000, all-in. The newest HD and affordable 3K video cameras that record gorgeous filmlike images to swappable 64-gigabyte and 128-gigabyte memory cards can be rented for around $1,500 per week. Amazon's CreateSpace and the Tribeca Film Institute's Reframe Project can help filmmakers digitally master their projects and sell them online. Breakthrough Distribution can handle the DVD sales.

We already live in a world of amateur filmmakers, where the ubiquity of camera phone video, webcams, and cheap recording equipment has opened up opportunities for everyone to create something eye-catching and cool. Raw talent, an ear for dialogue, an eye for the perfect shot, and the passion to craft something that touches and inspires audiences are increasingly the only missing ingredient.

Yes, the best time to make an independent film is right now.

What won't ever change, however—with production budgets of $10,000, $100,000 or even $1 million—are the misperceptions about what can trip up aspiring filmmakers along the way and prevent their films from ever being completed. Because filmmaking is one of the most collaborative of the arts, a book focused on "101 Indie Production Pitfalls" would barely scratch the surface and could address just a tiny fraction of what can happen to make footage unusable, sound unrecognizable, editing impossible, and even the most compelling stories untellable. Indeed, one reason independent filmmaking can be so tough is that there is no single compendium on how to dodge the dozens of pitfalls, punji sticks, and land mines that are unavoidable on the way to celluloid glory. This book is that guide, providing everything in one place—including contracts to protect screenwriters from being ripped off—that all filmmaking stars of tomorrow need in order to avoid being blindsided, tripped up, or stopped cold.

Some parents believe that their children should make their own mistakes in life and learn their lessons from the school of hard knocks, but many aspiring filmmakers don't get a second or a third chance to try again and get it right. As a result, the country is filled with immensely talented but failed filmmakers who might have become the next Miranda July, Christopher Nolan, Kimberly Peirce, Kasi Lemmons, Alice Wu, or Darren Aronofsky.

Established filmmakers take pride in their suffering when recounting their stories from the podiums of festivals and other symposia. Those stories always get a laugh. But aspiring filmmakers in the audience think that an inordinate level of pain and tragedy is a rite of passage. The question going forward is "Should every filmmaker have to serve as his or her own crash-test dummy as an educational exercise?" Absolutely not. This book seeks to help new filmmakers avoid the obstacles that send so many first- and second-timers through the windshield of their own inexperience.

The good news is that many films produced today will be completed just in time for a coming wave of interest in user-generated content (UGC) and in novel forms of portable, short-form entertainment viewable on 3G iPhones, Samsung Instincts, BlackBerry handsets, Archos 805 or 905 portables, Sony PSPs, and the next batch of innovative 4G devices.

A convergence of other factors will well position aspiring independent filmmakers who start this year. According to recent estimates, the traditional movie download market, which doubled from $689 million in 2006 to $1.6 billion in 2008, is projected to reach $3.6 billion by 2014. Netflix is now offering more than ten thousand titles through its Watch Now service available through the Netflix Player by Roku and via Microsoft's Xbox LIVE service. Sundance short films in competition are now $1.99 a download and the festival may soon offer consumers the ability to buy distributor-less feature films and documentaries. In 2008, Motorola introduced full-length films to watch on its mobile handsets for the first time, offering downloads of *The Italian Job*, *Star Trek*, and *Team America: World Police* through Motorola's online store. Similarly, Sprint Nextel announced a new service to allow users to watch full-length movies, TV shows, concerts, and comedy specials. TiVo, Miglia TV Max, PlayStation Home, Sling Media, Xbox LIVE, VUDU, and AppleTV will no doubt provide new exhibition platforms for independent filmmakers.

Australian researchers have developed a prototype computer chip that will allow wireless links to a laptop that are twenty times faster than current chip architectures, allowing high-speed downloads of movies from data kiosks to portable handheld devices in less than a minute. At the same time, the global broadband boom will continue, doubling to

661 million households in 2012, according to a 16.4 percent compound annual increase.

Broadband penetration in the United States will reach 101 million households in 2012, a growth rate of 10.5 percent from 2008. There is also immense opportunity for a generation of content creators and filmmakers with an eye toward overseas markets. India's mobile phone industry, the second-largest market in the world with more than 280 million subscribers, is poised for the next big wave in the form of mobile value-added services. In mid-2008, China passed the United States to become the largest Internet market, with 253 million users compared to 230 million in the United States. To take advantage of these and other opportunities, Cinetic Rights Management was launched in 2008 to broker the online sale of films that make a splash on the festival circuit but might otherwise remain undistributed.

But as high-end tools have become more democratized, independent filmmaking is now far more competitive. Only about 120 films were accepted from the pool of 3,661 features submitted to the 2009 Sundance Film Festival, up from the roughly 3,624 features that were submitted for the 2008 festival, which in turn had been up from 3,287 submitted in 2007. More than 5,000 completed indie films are made each year—and probably three or four times that amount are attempted—but only 200 receive any kind of aggressive distribution effort by the major studios, and only 100 remaining show up in theaters through self-distribution and service deals.

The number of individual SKUs in big-box stores such as Wal-Mart, Target, and Best Buy has dropped from 4,500 to 2,500 in recent years, making things harder for independently financed films as box sets and episodic TV DVDs fill shelf space and squeeze out indie-film DVD sales. This has forced many aspiring indie filmmakers to investigate ways to fend for themselves, such as partnering with duplication and fulfillment houses like Breakthough Distribution to handle the replication and the "pick, pack, and ship" of their DVDs.

Given that the general movie-loving public has less and less time to watch movies on any platform, the biggest challenge for the independent filmmakers of tomorrow is probably in how to effectively market their films and attract significant audiences, whether by themselves or through traditional theatrical distribution deals. In 1928, when the U.S. population was 120 million, 65 million movie tickets were sold each week. Today, even with 300 million people living in the United States, fewer than 30 million Americans go to a movie theater in any given week, a decrease of more than 50 percent. Consumers are bombarded with choices from entire recorded seasons of *Mad Men*, *Dexter*, *Weeds*, *Nip & Tuck*, the new *90210*, classic episodes of *My So-Called Life*, DVDs from Netflix, or the latest box set of *Robot Chicken* or *Family Guy* purchased on Amazon. And because moviegoers no longer cut indie films any slack as far as production value goes—Kevin Smith disciples beware—specialized and low-budget indie-film projects now have to be as clever, entertaining, and visually coherent as everything else on offer.

The quality bar has been raised far above what used to qualify as watchable, given that even low-budget projects can now afford to shoot on 24p HD video rather than MiniDV. Aspiring filmmakers are expected to know more about film grammar and the craft and business of filmmaking than earlier generations, who defined the do-it-yourself movement with static camera shots and piecemeal financing.

New production shingles and Web 2.0 billionaires—beyond the reach of most civilian, middle-American indie filmmakers—continue to define the indie-film financing business model on the high side and have raised the level of sophistication of the projects that get made, which in turn has raised the bar for what average aspiring filmmakers need to spend and achieve with their first projects. And while the overall economy of recession, the housing downturn, bank liquidations, the credit crisis, and the wars in Iraq and Afghanistan have dampened the ability of friends and family to invest in indie films in recent years, many enterprising filmmakers are still finding ways to make their projects happen.

However, the dark secret of indie filmmaking is there are many grievous professional and personal injuries that are often risked and incurred. For example, screenplays that may have been polished for years can be stolen en route to production simply because aspiring indie producers aren't careful, handing them to anyone who will read them and e-mailing drafts as unlocked Word files all over town. Aspiring screenwriters often fail to officially register every new draft—or even their first draft—with the Library of Congress, opting instead to save $20 with a Writers Guild of America registration, despite the fact that a registration with the WGA provides no statutory protections to motion-picture screenplays whatsoever.

The reel truth is sometimes hard to swallow, but throughout these pages every assertion is backed up by an industry insider who hopes to help the next generation of screenwriters, directors, and producers avoid the years of pain and suffering that they themselves had quietly endured. This book is designed to show new filmmakers, including those who have attended elite film schools, where they are likely to run into trouble that can unravel years of preparation and sacrifice. Each chapter is set up to present to filmmakers and their film crews how to dodge the risks and dangers that keep even the most wildly talented filmmakers from achieving their dreams. It may surprise many, but sheer force of will—even on the level of James Cameron or Werner Herzog—is no longer enough to carry the day, especially since meteoric success is often determined by the mistakes film-makers *don't* make rather than the really smart decisions they do. Given that making it as a filmmaker today involves dozens of individual variables coming together with a bit of good luck at every step, ignorance can be fatal and for want of a shoe, the battle can be lost.

1. Many Famous Directors Struggled Famously

*R*egardless of the genre, production budget, or digital format, independent filmmaking is all about struggle. The sooner indie filmmakers realize that things are never going to be easy, the better equipped they will be to handle the setbacks and heartbreaks that go with every independent project. The struggle begins every time a new screenwriter types FADE IN or whenever an aspiring producer or director asks a sympathetic friend or family member for money. Struggle binds indie filmmakers together and makes them a brotherhood and sisterhood of fearless entrepreneurs whose product really is themselves. Given the number of moving parts and places where things can go wrong, nothing about independent filmmaking is ever simple, and those confident and daring enough to pursue their dream should know that they are about to enter the fight of their lives. Those who don't believe it can ask their favorite indie-film director or producer, since very few—if any—have had an easy road and most have suffered every indignity imaginable before becoming a household name. Many made first films that never saw the light of *day several years before debating what ultimately would become their "first" films in the minds of the public. Others had to work as caterers, baristas, waiters and temps, and nannies. While it may seem easy, few filmmakers will have their careers handed to them and it is rare that anyone hoping to make a film doesn't at some point feel lonely, defeated, crushed, abandoned, polluted, ripped off, sick, or everything all at once. Struggle is the silent badge of honor among those who choose to throw themselves into one of the most difficult and collaborative art forms, and as a result, filmmakers should never feel truly alone since they have an army of 300,000 fellow would-be filmmakers behind them. Even during their darkest moments of harrowing isolation, indie filmmakers are part of an extended family of unappreciated risk-takers and entrepreneurs following a well-worn path, trodden by many of the celluloid icons they cherish and admire.*

Even someone such as *The Dark Knight* director Christopher Nolan, whose second Batman film has now grossed more than $523 million in the United States and $978 million worldwide, was forced to endure years of poverty. "Around the time I finished *Following* [1998] I moved to L.A. and got a freelance job reading scripts," Nolan recalls. "I was getting $40 per script and I couldn't do more than a couple each day because I really felt a responsibility to try and do it well. A lot of people don't by the way, but I did, so I was really, *really* slow. Before that, I had spent a couple of years doing freelance video production in London, making absolutely no money. I had no personal entertainment budget for anything at all, and when I finally did get a salaried job in London, doing basically the same thing, my immediate response was: 'Well actually, now I can take half of what I'm making every week and buy film with it.' So as soon as I had regular money coming in—or what felt like steady income—I decided to use it to make *Following*. In L.A. I didn't give up my day job for a long time, even after *Following* started getting into festivals. You have to keep your day job a lot longer than you think, basically to pay the rent."

Many A-list auteurs whom everyone assumes were born successful and rich had it harder than today's struggling HD filmmakers could ever imagine. *Brothers* director Jim Sheridan, a six-time Academy Award nominee, mopped floors and cleaned toilets for years before he directed *My Left Foot* in 1989 and *In the Name of the Father* in 1993. "When I first moved to New York in 1982 I was an illegal alien and couldn't really get a job," Sheridan recalls. "I found a little stage where a guy taught opera and they paid $4.25 an hour to answer the phone and $6 an hour to clean the floors and the toilets. I preferred the cleaning. And whenever I was doing that stupid job, mopping up bathrooms, I would tell myself, 'Well, it can't get worse than this.' "

On top of struggling for his art, Sheridan had a family to support and couldn't pull himself along on Rice Krispies for breakfast, lunch, and dinner, or a steady diet of Two Boots pizza and ice water.

"I love New York but it's a city that's very easy to be poor in," Sheridan says. "At first we were living near Avenue B and then I found a place up in Hell's Kitchen. That was a great place and we lived there for about four or five years. Then we moved to Inwood, up at 218th Street, and that was like being in a rural Irish village. Y'know, when you're poor and just searching for a place to live, you have to go wherever you can."

Sheridan's early heartaches trying to make it in Manhattan and his humble living quarters would eventually inform one of his most personal projects, *In America*. "I don't think we played up what the apartment was like in *In America*," he says. "In reality it was even tougher in some ways and we had to start over a few times. I was a struggling director, just waiting for *The New York Times* to review me. Talk about a monopoly! You needed that newspaper to give you a good review to survive."

Many directors who today command six- and seven-figure salaries per film were so overwhelmed by early rejection that they considered quitting, even though doing so would have meant missing a wildly successful career.

"Right after *The Tic Code* I wanted to give up," remembers director Gary Winick, who would go on to direct *Bride Wars*, *13 Going on 30*, and *Charlotte's Web*, among others. "It was actually at the Hamptons Film Festival in 1998 and [*The Bridges of Madison County* screenwriter] Richard LaGravenese was there when I said, 'I'm done . . . I'm giving up.' I wasn't proud of *The Tic Code*, it wasn't coming out, I wasn't able to get any more work, I was raising money by myself for all my other films, and I was just thinking, 'You know, my life isn't going so well.' I didn't have a girlfriend at the time—all the personal stuff wasn't there—and I just thought: There's got to be a simpler way or something else that I'd be happier doing. The thing about independent filmmaking is you have to love it so much because it's so hard."

House of Sand and Fog director Vadim Perelman reportedly worked for several years as a dishwasher and gas station attendant before getting his first chance to direct at age forty. Writer-director Dylan Kidd tried his hand at all sorts of day jobs in and around New York City and wasn't happy doing any of them. "I was a doorman, I was a janitor in a tennis club, and I was a home-care attendant for a while," Kidd recalls ruefully. "Let me tell you, they were some grim years. I worked in a couple of video stores, I worked nights at a pool hall. I loaded cameras for [*Two Lovers* cinematographer] Joaquin Baca-Asay, who went on to shoot *Roger Dodger* and *P.S.* for me. I also worked in real estate for three years, which is how I made money for the first short that I did."

Kidd, who graduated from New York University in 1991,

says he scrupulously avoided getting too attached to any one day job because he didn't want to be defined as anything other than an aspiring director. "I think there was some voice in my head that said, 'You don't want to go and get a job that's going to make you too comfortable.' I had classmates who, right out of film school, got a job at a post house and ended up having that job for eight years. It actually became a curse, because they had health insurance and money, but they weren't able to write screenplays. It's the same as people who always say, 'I'm just going to grip on a shoot while I write my script.' Nobody in New York who thinks that they will have time for writing while they are working as a film technician actually ever does it because that lifestyle is just too exhausting. But there were definitely many years where I didn't do anything in film, where people would say, 'What do you do?' and I was too embarrassed to say I was a filmmaker because I wasn't doing it."

For some reason, many aspiring filmmakers in Los Angeles find it very hard to define themselves as screenwriters, producers, or directors, since without a credit on IMDb, such a statement might inspire nods of quiet pity or derision.

"I guess you just have to get into kind of a Zen thing of not taking people's opinions of your career choices personally," Kidd says. "You have to know that when you're trying to make it as a filmmaker, you're sort of guilty until proven innocent, and that people are going to doubt you until you make it. You just have to keep saying to yourself, 'I know that I am for real. I know that I'm a serious filmmaker. I know that this is a good script. Nobody else knows it, but someday they will.' And you just can't give up. I went to film school with plenty of people who had more talent than I did but I just happened to be more stubborn."

This is especially true for filmmakers hoping to raise financing for edgy or emotionally raw material. "I left New

York in January 2001 because I couldn't afford the overhead, and moved to Virginia, where I worked all these different odd jobs while I worked on the script for *The Woodsman*," says writer-director Nicole Kassell. "For a year I taught video filmmaking to two different local high school groups, I taught screenwriting to a group of adults, and I was also a wedding videographer. I constantly had all sorts of fears that it wasn't going to ever work out. There was definitely a very loud nagging voice in my head saying: 'What am I going to do if this doesn't happen?' "

Luckily, Kassell's producer on *The Woodsman* was someone who understood difficult storylines that focused on flawed antiheroes trying to make good. "My advice to filmmakers who are trying to make really challenging films is to embrace the struggle required to make them," says Lee Daniels, director of the Sundance Grand Jury Prize–winning *Push: Based on the Novel by Sapphire* and producer of *Monster's Ball*. "All great films come from a struggle. People said *Monster's Ball* shouldn't be made and even asked why I was working on such a film. But struggle puts hair on your chest. You fight so hard for these little movies that sometimes you feel like you must be crazy. Sometimes I think, 'Why don't I just buy into the system? Get myself a house and a decent car?' But when I see a result like *The Woodsman* and the effect the films have on people, it makes me feel like I'm not crazy, that I'm not alone, and that people do appreciate them. And that's why you do it."

The Wrestler director Darren Aronofsky went from being an unemployed screenwriter who frequently dined solo at Van Gogh's Ear in Venice, California, to being celebrated for his daring vision in films like *Pi*, *Requiem for a Dream*, and *The Fountain*.

"I was in film school at AFI [American Film Institute]

during my first year in Los Angeles so that kept me busy, but after that it was pretty tough," he recalls. "I think the loneliness and paranoia and isolation of Max Cohen in *Pi* is the most autobiographical part of that film because it's very much how my time in L.A. was for two and a half years. I had no one reading my scripts, and when I did finally send out a script I was working on, I think only one company responded out of the fifty I sent it to. But basically I found it a very hard place to be single and unemployed."

While aspiring filmmakers may speak disparagingly of "the suits," many specialized film distribution executives have shared their pain. "When I was in college at Penn State, I was so much poorer than any of the people trying to make movies," says Lionsgate Films president Tom Ortenberg. "I ate ramen noodles for a year and had to donate blood plasma twice a week for beer money. I ate a lot of mac and cheese and hot dogs for a long time. Some friends and I started our own political party while we were in college, and we showed movies like *Revenge of the Nerds* in the lecture halls on weekends to raise money for our political activities. That's how I got my start in film."

SHOW ME THE MONEY

The most common struggle shared by filmmakers, regardless of age, race, orientation, or education, is simply that of raising funds. Money is a lot harder to come by than most people realize, and any filmmaker who is secretly counting on an heiress friend or wealthy pal from childhood to finance his entire picture out of an ATM card, which she certainly could do, is in for a disappointing shock. Most aspiring filmmakers don't learn until it's too late that *very rich people do not typically invest in independent movies*, even if they dated or went to school with the director or aspiring screenwriter. Hedge funds aside, most people with huge cash reserves avoid the risk associated with speculative or illiquid investments with "high absolute-value beta."

Of course, the fantasy is hard for many independent film-makers to shake: the rich-person relationship they have nur-tured for years will pay huge dividends when it comes time to "green-light" their indie feature or short. Who can blame them? Oftentimes the idle words of encouragement from this wealthy friend will be wildly misinterpreted as some kind of future "call option" or offer to invest in the project. Other filmmakers simply hope to be introduced to a wealthy person's circle of high-net-worth friends at a party reminis-cent of a Dynamite Hack YouTube video. Until the right time to broach the subject presents itself, a filmmaker may work on a screenplay for years or endlessly rewrite a business plan at the exclusion of sleep, love life, personal finances, family visits, getting married, having children, and maintain-ing health insurance only to be terribly disappointed when it comes time to ask for the big check. Indeed, the most dan-gerous assumption a screenwriter or filmmaker can ever make is that any one individual wants to finance the entire project, or that any one person with amazing connections is the sole bridge to their film getting financed or produced. Even so, aspiring filmmakers are often shocked that rich friends from childhood or college might be insulted to dis-cover that they were the cornerstone of the filmmaker's nexus of funding sources. The truth is most wealthy people have familial obligations, wedding plans, hedge fund losses, trust covenants, company boards of directors, or other con-straints of an undisclosed nature that tie their hands and keep them from participating.

Even Oscar-winning actors, who know *plenty* of potential investors, often have a very hard time raising funds for movies they want to make, despite incontrovertible track records and every sort of connection under the sun. "I had difficulty raising money for *Albino Alligator*, I had difficulty raising money for *The United States of Leland*, I had difficulty raising money for *Beyond the Sea*," admits director and actor Kevin Spacey. "Don't make the assumption that just because an actor of a certain note is involved in a project that buckets of money are falling from the sky. It isn't true. It's just not the way movies are made."

Indeed, most independent filmmakers of any renown have had to crawl over broken glass at one point or another. "Everybody has a story," continues Spacey, who has served as the artistic director of the Old Vic Theatre in London since 2003. "If you go to any film festival and you listen to a director talk about how difficult it was to get a movie going, you'll hear how everybody has a tough time. I've had tough times, you know, and my story isn't any worse than anybody else's."

The secret is not to let everything good in a person's life unravel in the belief that chaos is part of the "tapestry" of getting an independent film made. Before quitting day jobs or risking relationships for a dream, filmmakers should remember that fund-raising can sometimes take *years*, not months, and that financing can fall out of a promised, green-lit, or "go" project even on the level of *Gods and Monsters*, *Pieces of April*, *The Caveman's Valentine*, the Diane Keaton–Sarah Jessica Parker indie *The Family Stone*, the Matthew McConaughey indie *Thirteen Conversations About One Thing*, *Young Adam*, Steve Buscemi's *Interview*, director Niki Caro's *The Vintner's Luck*, *Go*, and countless others.

Other indie productions require in excess of $300,000 just to complete reshoots and postproduction. "We got the initial financing for *Shallow Grave*, about one million pounds, which was about $1.4 million at the time, off of Film4, a source that has sadly gone to the wall now," recalls director

Danny Boyle. "But the funny thing was, we ran out of money. We were first-time filmmakers. They just gave us the money and they weren't going to give us any more. It wasn't like now where you can get some more money off people and things like that. That was *it*. We had four or five days left to shoot and we had no celluloid. So we sold off the set, bit by bit. It's all set in that one flat. We'd finish shooting in one room and then we'd sell all the props and furniture to members of the crew to raise money. They gave us money for the sofa and things like that, and we used the money to buy ourselves some more film for the last few days. We raised thousands of pounds because we sold a lot. It was great, though, because it's such a restriction on you, that you have to come up with other options. You don't have the solution of money as a low-budget filmmaker. And that's what we sort of did on *28 Days Later*, although we imposed the restrictions ourselves because we're lucky enough to be able to raise money now. We still set limitations on ourselves because they do make you more imaginative. It's an old cliché but it's true. When you can't solve your problems with money, you have to find a different way to do it."

Because productions are often not actually "cash-flowed" until the script revisions, shooting locations, cast, and sometimes key crew members have been approved, funds can be pulled by financiers unless certain contractual guarantees are in place. Indie filmmakers who don't think it can happen to them should know that it has happened to a number of well-known directors, including the late Oscar-winning writer-director Anthony Minghella, when 20th Century Fox famously dropped the financing for *The English Patient* in 1995, even though its director, cast, and crew were already on the set in Tunisia. Miramax stepped in and the film won nine Oscars, including Best Picture. But most aspiring indie filmmakers are not so lucky.

THE WRONG PRODUCER

More often than not, aspiring filmmakers are forced to struggle longer than they might have to simply because they have come across, tripped over, or gotten into bed with someone known as The Wrong Producer. This person talks a good game, seems to "get" the material, and puts the filmmaker at ease by promising to help get the film set up. TWP may even have a screen credit or some other credential— sometimes totally made up and rarely investigated—that makes him seem like he knows what he's doing. Unfortunately, The Wrong Producer is the last person in the world who a filmmaker should be talking to at this stage, as he will steer the project in the wrong direction and guarantee that the film never sees the light of day. The Wrong Producer is also easy to spot since he has usually left a trail of betrayed former friends, jilted investors, double-crossed colleagues, angry vendors, and unpaid actors in his wake. But aspiring filmmakers are the last to know because they never check references. Filmmakers may feel that asking a potential producer for a list of references (or culling their own list from Internet Movie Database) could be considered rude, but it can be the most important request a filmmaker ever makes. After all, few people would consider going into business with a total stranger without talking to *somebody* who has spent time working with that person.

Years before she met up with Christine Vachon and Eva Kolodner, who would be instrumental in backing her vision for *Boys Don't Cry*, director Kimberly Peirce ran into a TWP, and the experience almost prevented her from making *Boys Don't Cry*. By simply trusting a person who promised to follow through as producer, Peirce found her short-film project, "Take It Like a Man," almost derailed.

"I was in grad school [at Columbia] in 1992, working the

second and third night shifts as a paralegal and a computer consultant. The second shift was from six p.m. to two a.m., and the third shift was from ten p.m. to six a.m. The third shift paid the most. I had saved up twelve thousand dollars— that was everything I had in the world," Peirce remembers. "A guy who had line produced a few small films came recommended to me as a 'producer.' He said he was ready for the step up and my short film was the perfect opportunity, so I hired him. Everything seemed to be on course until one day, about ten days before shooting, he told me that he loved my movie but was very sorry, he would not be able to produce it because he got the opportunity of a lifetime and couldn't turn it down—producing a short film for an indie actress. I was in shock—I didn't have anyone else lined up to produce, I had already spent a great deal of money, and we were moving quickly to production. When I explained all this, he said he had a replacement. I wasn't thrilled with the idea but decided to meet this replacement—turns out it was a friend of his who also had never produced anything, but had done some coordinating. There was no way to stop production without losing everything, so I handed this girl—who shall remain nameless—my savings and hoped for the best. It was a rough road—we made it through the shoot but ran out of money before getting all the scenes shot—and by the time we were done I found out she had used all the money I had given her and racked up a number of debts under my name, including $8,000 in car rentals. I said, 'In car rentals? How is that even possible?' It was possible. I also found out I owed $2,000 in parking tickets from the city of New York. I called the City Parking Division and I told them I didn't know how to drive—I didn't even have a license."

Peirce, who had quit her job a month before to try and make a first attempt at *Boys Don't Cry*, was not able to pay the tickets in a timely fashion, which caused the parking fines to

double and later triple. She paid them off but still found herself hounded by creditors.

"I was terrified," she recalls. "I didn't answer my phone
sometimes because I had bill collectors calling. Then the bill
collectors would leave messages saying, 'We know you're
there! Kim, pick up the phone!' And if I happened to pick up
the phone, they would say, 'Is Kimberly Peirce there? THIS
IS KIMBERLY, ISN'T IT???' And they'd say, 'You owe us
money.' My phone would get shut off, then I'd pay the bill to
get it back on and it would get shut off again. My credit went
through a rough spot and I didn't have health insurance for
the longest time."

After losing $18,000, which could have paid for one year
of a master's program, a new car, or half a year's worth of
rent and groceries, most people would have called it a day
and given up. Peirce was devastated, but in retrospect she
says she should have seen it coming and asked for a reference
or two or three from the original producer. "Today I would
recognize that guy and this situation, but that's hindsight and
whatever wisdom comes from having made a few films. At
the time, even though I was coming out of a really good film
school and I had a lot of support, I wanted and needed to get
my movie made, so someone who had more experience than
I had and who seemed like he could get it done was appealing. When he took that other opportunity, he left me in the
hands of someone who wasn't up to the job—I could have
called it all to a halt right then and there, but then I wouldn't
have made the short and I wouldn't have had the footage that
led me to Christine Vachon in late 1995. The great thing
about Christine was that she had done this before, a lot. She
knew what she was doing. I don't think anyone other than
Christine could have gotten *Boys Don't Cry* made, in the way
we made it. So in the end it all worked out very well."

While many aspiring filmmakers think of film school and

the independent-film sector as gentle harbors or lagoons of integrity, free of the great white sharks that prowl Hollywood waters, even well-known indie filmmakers have stories of being chomped, dismembered, or nearly bled out when they least expected it. The truth is, the independent-film business is still the film business, and the film business is rough. "It happens every day and filmmakers need to know that getting hurt, sometimes badly, by someone they trusted but didn't really know is epidemic," explains Creative Artists Agency's Micah Green. "It's also very important not to jump into business with the first producer or financier you may meet when you're starting out. Filmmakers need to make sure they're consulting with experienced producers, attorneys, and agents before they enter into a legal relationship with someone. Unfortunately, people don't always do the homework of vetting the person they're about to trust with their project and a lot of them end up get taken advantage of." To avoid falling into this trap, filmmakers also need to recognize that there is never one single producer or line producer who can get their film made. Even in small towns, there is always more than *one person* who can be their game-changer.

It cannot be stressed enough that first-time directors and filmmakers about to spend thousands of dollars in production funds must take an hour or more out of their day to actually call and check references before hiring someone. Further, a lone enthusiastic recommendation amid several unreturned phone calls is not enough to trust someone to produce a short or feature. Of course, what most filmmakers do is rely on a single conversation in which they are snowed by The Wrong Producer's knowledge of one or more arcane aspects of digital filmmaking, such as the importance of white balance or the disastrous nature of a digital time-code break, as proof that The Wrong Producer knows his or her stuff and can be trusted. Still others mistake a shared love for the films of Wes Anderson, the ability to quote lines from *Pee-Wee's Big Adventure*, or insights into the shot complexity of the climactic confrontation at the end of *Buffalo '66* as some kind of production credential.

What many filmmakers also don't realize is that they can reasonably include separation or termination clauses triggered by "bad faith" into any production contract. In the face of this, The Wrong Producer may argue that he or she needs to receive full payment up front, but directors should consider whether they are acting rashly by granting this demand, since a separation clause should benefit the production and not unduly penalize the filmmaker. The argument The Wrong Producer will use is that he or she has already turned down a number of lucrative assignments to take this one and therefore should be paid in full, regardless of his or her incompetence or participation. This type of employment agreement should never be granted, and a producer who demands payment for the entire shoot on day one should be carefully vetted. Instead, a filmmaker would be far better off with even a neophyte film student who is inexperienced and enthusiastic rather than someone with more experience who is simply working for a day rate and not willing to go above and beyond what is necessary.

One of the best ways to suss out The Wrong Producer is to ask what his or her opinions are about postproduction. Self-described or wannabe producers usually know nothing about postproduction or have no opinion, even though it is where all the magic captured during the shoot can be completely undone. Indeed, because the post interval often dictates how certain scenes need to be shot, not having a position or list of suggestions about post is a huge red flag. Does The Wrong Producer want to choose a post house before the shoot begins? Does he want to have a conversation or two with the post supervisor? Does he even know what a post supervisor does? A knowledgeable producer or line producer doesn't have to be asked. Another question to help weed out The Wrong Producer is whether or not it's a good idea to use a "free" camera in an outdated or obscure digital format, such as JVC's D9, that anyone would know cannot be imported into Final Cut Pro 6 or Avid without a huge expense, since stand-alone decks to lay off obscure or exotic tape formats are often wildly expensive to rent. The answer is no.

DON'T QUIT YOUR DAY JOB

Given the ephemeral nature of financing, aspiring filmmakers should hold on to their day jobs and take paid vacation or sick days to work on their films until they are actually on set blocking out the first shot of a fully financed film. Peirce quit her day job when she was assured that the funds to finance an early version of *Boys Don't Cry* would be forthcoming, a misstep many aspiring filmmakers make.

"Getting *Boys Don't Cry* made was tough," she recalls. "I mean in some ways it was one struggle after another. Getting the money, getting the actors, and surviving the whole period of making it took five years—the walls were closing in all the time. But long before any of that, when I was still a floater at a law firm, I was told: 'We have a green light on the film. You need to quit your job and go out to Hollywood.'

"I had health benefits, which was a big deal, but I quit and we went to Hollywood in 1997," Peirce continues. "I say that because I had never been there before. So I went around 1997. I had a meeting at a studio and I remember saying, 'That's great! Thank you!' because it was apparently a done deal. Then I got this strange look from the executive. I came back to New York. We waited but nothing happened. They were interested, which meant they wanted to see what it might amount to, but it was going to be a long process. My lawyer at the time and I went out to lunch and he said, 'That project's DOA. You should move on.' "

Peirce was lucky in that the law firm where she had worked previously hired her back. "I had spent three years trying to put *Boys* together. I was brokenhearted. But the woman in charge of the office said she wanted to help me make my film, and she knew giving me the job would allow me to continue my pursuit," Peirce recalls. "A few more financing possibilities came and went. Then suddenly one day Christine called and said we had enough money to start preproduction, not *all* the money to make the movie, but enough to get far into it—it was a risk, but we weren't going to get all the money. She told me, 'I think this is the moment to make your movie and I think if you don't leap now you may never make it.' So I leapt. One of Christine's great assets as a producer is her instinct, knowing when to move forward, when to take the risk. She was right in this case. Young filmmakers often ask me what advice I would give them. Every situation has its specifics, but generally I would say make what interests you, what you like, stick with it, and bring people inside your process, people who love making movies and have done it before."

The lesson for filmmakers who are still working to make ends meet is that they must keep their day jobs and day-job mind-set for as long as possible, or at least until they receive a certified bank statement proving that the funds are actually in the production's bank account and cannot be revoked or otherwise pulled by investors. There's a reason people often say "Don't quit your day job," because in a difficult economy, it's good advice.

"Often what's holding you in it is your love of the story or the idea of being a filmmaker as opposed to the affirmation that you're not getting," says Peirce, who went on to direct *Stop-Loss*. "There were times during the five rejections from 1993 to 1998 that I just thought, 'Why am I persisting through all these rejections?' But maybe that's the course *Boys* needed to take. And if I had quit before the sixth time, the movie wouldn't exist. You're going to be very judgmental against yourself, but you have to realize that rejection doesn't actually mean anything. It's very hard to accept, but failing and rejection have little to do with how good a movie will be."

In some ways, long intervals of frustration and personal reflection can serve some benefit, says Vachon. "*Boys Don't Cry* took Kimberly a very long time to get made, but the film was ultimately better for it. All that time allowed her to keep working on the script, and as I've often said, 'The film gets made when it's ready to be made.' "

FAMILY COMES FIRST

The tug-of-war between the demands of filmmaking and the maintenance of family ties or romantic relationships can be extremely difficult, given the level of commitment production requires. Aspiring filmmakers often get it into their heads that their current girlfriends or boyfriends or their families are somehow keeping them from getting their screenplays or first films completed. This impression eventually gives rise to a manifesto—enunciated in an e-mail or expressed in a dozen passive-aggressive ways—that screenwriting or filmmaking requires a level of intensity, focus, concentration, and commitment they will never understand. Unfortunately, this destructive screed or letter will end up costing many filmmakers the one real thing many of them have in their lives. The truth is, indie filmmaking requires the emotional support of loved ones, who should not be spurned, talked down to, taken for granted, or ignored.

Unfortunately, the tension between the Ed Wood–ish lunatic optimism needed to make a film and the pragmatic realism required to support a family or just pay rent on time can easily break up relationships. Even the mere act of writing an independent-film script can have a devastating impact on a person's home life or marriage. The escalation of commitment that invariably kicks in makes every would-be Sundance superstar want to double down and risk the house, the car, the family, and the works: to safeguard all the sacrifices that went before, aspiring filmmakers feel they have to mortgage everything for that one shot at Sundance glory.

With that logic for justification, filmmakers often decide, as Ash does in *Alien* and as Burke does in *Aliens*, that everyone is expendable, a decision that has huge repercussions for years to come. The terrible thing is that they make this decision not knowing that only a dozen or so films accepted to Sundance each year actually get theatrical distribution and the other hundred *don't* wind up in movie theaters or on television. In fact, for the 2009 festival, there were an estimated 4,000 feature films submitted, an increase of 10 percent over the 3,624 feature films submitted to Sundance in 2008 and an increase of 21 percent over the 3,287 feature films submitted in 2007.

Filmmakers should also know that independent film is a mature sector of the entertainment industry and a notoriously low-margin business that in 2008 and 2009 was facing incredible pressure. According to longtime entertainment reporter Claude Brodesser-Akner, host of the popular podcast "The Business," the specialized film sector peaked in 2006 with grosses of $418 million, fell to $330 million in 2007, and still had not reached $200 million by October 2008. Overall box-office attendance was projected to be down by 5 percent in 2008 with projected revenues flat year after year at roughly $9 billion, despite the enormous popularity of *The Dark Knight* and *Sex and the City* that year.

Therefore, whenever possible, filmmakers need to temper their outlook and try to balance their topsy-turvy filmmaking reality with their real-world day-to-day. As Alec Baldwin's character pointed out in *The Departed*, being married (or at least being in a relationship) is an important part of getting ahead. Few video gamers would trade the people in their lives for an avatar they just met in World of Warcraft or Warhammer Online. Unfortunately, this is exactly what many independent filmmakers do even though their chances of getting into a festival are slimmer than they think, because the competition is shooting on 24p HD or 3k and because of the sheer volume of submissions.

"A lot of people don't realize just how many films are made each year—I really don't think they get it," says IFP president Michelle Byrd. "They don't get how many films are produced each year that are also vying for a slot in the same handful of festivals and that are trying to get on distributors' radar. There are also a lot of filmmakers who think they have made it once they've been accepted to a festival, when in fact there are *hundreds* of films each year that make it into a major festival but never receive distribution. It's a competitive, very aggressive marketplace."

And with consolidation hitting the specialized distribution sector particularly hard in 2008 leading to the closings of Paramount Vantage, Warner Independent Pictures, Picturehouse, and *Lord of the Rings* and *Austin Powers* producer New Line Cinema in a single year, there are fewer buyers attending screenings at Sundance in 2009 and 2010 with checkbooks in hand.

"There simply aren't enough distributors to handle all the

movies that get made each year," notes Fox Searchlight co-COO Nancy Utley. "When you think about all the independent films being made today, including the ones people never hear about, the truth is that very few independent films get distribution."

Indeed, getting accepted to Sundance remains an incredible long shot, something filmmakers often choose not to acknowledge. For 2009, there were more than 3,600 feature films submitted to the festival—up from 2,600 in 2005—with only the same 120 accepted in dramatic competition, a 3.3 percent acceptance rate that is far tougher than the acceptance rates at Harvard (7.1 percent), Princeton (7.8 percent), Yale (8.3 percent), Columbia (8.7 percent), or Stanford (9.5 percent).

Of course, some couples make it work. Laura Lau produced *Grind* and later *Open Water* with her husband, director Chris Kentis. Chris Nolan and his wife, Emma Thomas, together produced *Following*, *The Prestige*, and *The Dark Knight*. Similarly, Baz Luhrmann and his wife, the Oscar-winning costume designer Catherine Martin, have worked together on projects from *Strictly Ballroom* through *Australia*. Anna Boden and Ryan Fleck, another professional couple, collaborated on the writing, directing, and editing of both *Half Nelson* and *Sugar*.

For others, independent filmmaking is a lot like the monologue Michael Biehn gives Linda Hamilton in the first *Terminator*: "It can't be reasoned with, it can't be bargained with . . . it doesn't know pity or remorse." It doesn't care about aspiring filmmakers or their personal lives, or what bad things happen to them while they're trying to make their film. It's not a compassionate system. The business just wasn't set up that way, a situation that is difficult for many new filmmakers to reconcile with their view of how it should be.

Having one's filmmaking dreams wreck one's personal life may have been part of the process for many who have made it, but it should be a red flag to today's indie filmmakers that they might want to reconsider their approach and safeguard whatever finances, personal lives, and job opportunities they have left. "For all the success stories you read about, there are thousands of filmmakers who are still struggling to pay off credit card bills years and years later," says documentary filmmaker Marina Zenovich. "You shouldn't let your film-making dreams mess up your life. I spent five years working on *Polanski*, but during that time I worked other jobs to pay for life. Since 2004, I have made documentary shorts for a series on the Arts Channel, *Gallery HD*, so I worked consistently doing what I love. But the last three years were tough: I was making five of those shorts while working on *Polanski* and being a first-time mom. Fortunately, I have a fantastic husband and 'manny.' "

Indeed, persistence in the face of adversity is one of the most important traits a filmmaker can have, along with unflagging courage. Aspiring producers, screenwriters, and directors will have to endlessly pick up the phone and call whoever has received a copy of the script and ask if they are interested in buying it, investing in it, or helping to get it produced.

"Every successful person in the independent-film world, no matter what they do, whether they're writers—writing for magazines or screenplays—directors, producers, distributors, marketers, whatever they do, every person who has any level of success in the independent-film world has been told no a lot and yet kept going," explains Ortenberg. "I was told no a lot before I came on board with Lionsgate, and we have had the success we've had because we have been persistent. So you have to persevere and you have to be able to sustain yourself in the face of rejection. My advice to all struggling young filmmakers is 'Don't be discouraged by the word *no*."

WORKING THE SLIME LINE

Writer-director Chris Eyre, today a director of episodic TV such as *Law & Order* and PBS documentaries such as *We Shall Remain*, might have had the toughest road of all. Although he had written a first screenplay in college in Oregon, in 1991 he had no idea what to do next.

"I had just graduated with a BFA in media and I wanted to make a film I had written, but I had no money and I had no resources or network of any kind, so when I heard about a job in Alaska, I decided to move there to take a job cutting fish on a 'slime line,' " says Eyre, who is Cheyenne and Arapaho and who since directing *Smoke Signals* in 1998 has directed six films, two of which were produced by Robert Redford. "Most people, when they buy fish fillets at Citarella or Whole Foods or Vons, have no idea what goes into preparing that fish or what actually goes into getting fish in a can. They think it must be handled by machines or something, but it's not. What it actually entails is putting on a full-body rain suit and thick rubber gloves and grabbing a giant salmon or a black cod or a snapper by the tail, finding its anus and ripping it with a knife up to its gills, and standing next to one hundred other people doing the same thing as literally thousands of fish come down the slime line.

"The first person guts the fish and the second person cuts it and the third person makes sure that the blood line in the back of the spine is clean. The next person may be a quality control person who inspects the work," Eyre recalls. "Then the fish go through a whole other process, depending on whether they're going to be canned or cut into fillets or whether they're going to be frozen. So I did that in different capacities for about six months."

To avoid backing up the line or conjuring images of Lucy Ricardo working in the chocolate factory, Eyre and his fellow workers had to stand in place for literally twelve to eighteen hours at a clip and cut a new fish every few seconds. Harder still, however, was shouting down daydreams of directing films and someday attending Sundance, since indulging in flights of fancy could mean losing several fingers or even a hand.

"You could very easily cut your fingers off if you weren't careful, but it was actually more dangerous than that," recalls Eyre. "You got extra 'hazard pay' if you were doing the 'right' job, so at one point I graduated to working with chains on my wrists so my hands wouldn't go into a cutter that was slicing the heads off the fish—cutting through the heads of these giant king salmon—every two and a half seconds. So you're standing there for twelve hours or more on what's called a header. And you have these cables attached to your wrists to limit your range of motion so your hands won't get caught in the machine, because without exaggeration, if you got your finger stuck in there it wouldn't just take your hands off, it would pull you into the maw of this thing and take your arms off."

Rather than checking out the East Village nightlife or hanging out at Lola's on Fairfax or sampling the cool bars and clubs that run along Sixth Street in Austin, Eyre would simply try to stay awake so he could write screenplays in the modest apartment he shared with his coworkers. Every morning he would imagine a day when he might be able to sit in a director's chair—or sit at all in a day job—rather than cutting fish on his feet for double time and triple time. "The pay held out as long as you held out," recalls Eyre, who notes that state laws required workers to have six hours off in between shifts. "But after my roommate lost three fingers on one of the other machines and was fired, because it was somehow ruled to be his fault, I decided to get a job on a fishing boat in the Gulf of Alaska, which is just as dangerous but for different reasons.

"People watch *Deadliest Catch* on the Discovery Channel and they wonder if they could do that kind of work, but let me tell you when you have the cold frozen water blasting in your face and you're seasick day after day, it's a whole different story. The job of a fisherman on one of those boats is literally like running a marathon," continues Eyre, who in 2007 was named a USA Rockefeller Foundation Fellow. "I mean, you can handle it for a little while. People can handle it, but you know what they never show on TV is how all the fishermen get carpal tunnel syndrome from grabbing a fish tail one thousand times a day. You grab a fish tail over and over and over again, and the muscles at the base of your thumb and base of your index finger start to cramp up and get sore from the constant gripping motion. You're working fifteen hours a day, six or seven days a week on the boat if they'll let you, and it just wears you down and kills you. You can do it fine for a day or two, sure. You can handle the freezing water in the face and being cold and you can take falling down and getting seasick day after day, but when you're doing it week after week and starting to live it for two full seasons like I did, that's where you start to think, 'You know what? I don't think I'm cut out for this.' "

It would be six more years and several other grueling jobs in and around Alaska and Oregon before Eyre would get to direct *Smoke Signals* from a script written by bestselling author Sherman Alexie, who was himself an aspiring director and screenwriter at the time. "I learned two things from that experience," says Eyre. "I realized, number one, that I didn't want to do that kind of work. Ever again. And two, I remember this one day where I had worked an eighteen-hour day, after a series of eighteen-hour days, realizing that I *had* to get my first movie made come hell or high water."

THE SIEGE MENTALITY

The struggle that takes place during development, preproduction, production, and postproduction is often cast in military analogies by those who have been to the front lines and returned to tell the tale. "You have to have courage to be a soldier of cinema," explains Werner Herzog, director of *Rescue Dawn* and *Grizzly Man*. "You have to expect, as I did on *Fitzcarraldo*, that you are going to run into logistical problems, that you are going to run into this, that, and the other. Why should we as filmmakers be deterred from difficulties that come into our path en route? On some occasions I have not been able to get a film financed, but so what? It happens to everyone. I keep working all the time. I have never stopped working and I am not frustrated. And this is what I tell younger filmmakers who often ask me for advice. I tell them: 'If you have something of real substance, it will get made. You will manage somehow to do it.' And nowadays it has become easier to make films because the technical side has become much easier, much more lightweight, and much more inexpensive."

Spacey, who has seen his share of ups and downs as both filmmaker and theater director, echoes Herzog's advice to aspiring filmmakers: "The best advice I can give is: 'Don't give up. Don't ever give up.' Don't ever listen to anybody that tells you, 'You won't make your movie.' Don't listen to anybody. It doesn't matter how big they are, how important they are, how much money they have, walk away from people who are negative, and keep people around you that will help you make your movie. Because every film festival is filled each year with incredible stories about how people were able to pull it together, and that's perseverance. That's never giving up."

For Baz Luhrmann, one of the film industry's most innovative directors, this perspective not only served him through the lean years of working in theater but helped him raise the financing for *Strictly Ballroom*, the film that paved the way for *William Shakespeare's Romeo + Juliet*, which in turn allowed Luhrmann to resurrect the movie musical with *Moulin Rouge!* "The tagline of *Strictly Ballroom* is 'A life lived in fear is a life half-lived,' and in a sense that's what the lead character in that film and all struggling filmmakers have to keep saying," Luhrmann says by way of advice. "In the film, Scott Hastings unites with an outsider. She helps him confront the fear and together they overcome the all-powerful federation who says: 'There's only one way to cha-cha-cha.' I always felt that way, and even when people said I was crazy for even attempting it, I never stopped believing."

Miles Beckett, cocreator and codirector of *Lonelygirl15*, has some personal experience with taking big risks to follow his dream of becoming a filmmaker. "I spent six years languishing in a career that I really hated," he says. "And finally I reached a point where I realized that I could either look back on my life with regret or I could pursue my dream of becoming a filmmaker. I quit my surgery residency and hit the ground running in L.A." Some in Beckett's shoes might have been reminded of Brutus's speech to Cassius about "taking the current as it serves" or losing their ventures.

"The worst part for me was that 'doctor' carried a lot of prestige. I can't tell you how many times I heard, 'How wonderful . . . you're a doctor,' while inside I was yelling, 'But I hate it!' Aspiring filmmakers need to have the attitude that they must succeed *no matter what*, and if that means working seven days a week, fifteen hours a day for a year, then they need to be willing to do that. It's definitely a competitive business, so people need to make sure they are doing it for the passion and not for the money. I think the most important thing when assembling a team is to find people that you trust who are really good at what they do. A willingness to work all night helps also, but the number of people is less important than their talent and passion."

Of course, filmmakers who are in it for the long haul know when to dial the fervor back and reintroduce the concept of balance into their lives. "It's funny because I remember when I was making my baseball film that Pete Rose said, 'I would go through hell in a gasoline suit to play baseball,' and I feel that way about filmmaking," says the master of the documentary Ken Burns. "Fortunately, my family is very much involved in it. I make my films where I live, I make my films with my friends and my kids nearby."

2. Writing MBA-Style Business Plans ... *Or Not*

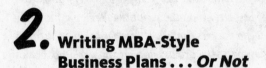

*I*n today's video game sector, a compelling business plan and a terrific new idea can potentially attract millions of dollars in financing from venture-capital firms in Menlo Park, California, or Manhattan's Silicon Alley. In the independent-film world, however, even the most bulletproof business plans often generate little more than a raised eyebrow and a vague promise to "get back to you . . . as soon as I get a chance to read it." Even so, one legacy of the first Internet boom and the Web 2.0 era is that many filmmakers believe they need to write—or hire someone to write—a stellar business plan before they can start fund-raising. Still others believe they need a business plan to prove that their projects are somehow closer to being made. A third group of filmmakers who never thought they'd ever have to write a business plan (since to them "the script is our business plan") find themselves dashing off to the bookstore to pick up how-to guides the minute a wishy-washy investor says, "That sounds great! I'd love to see your business plan!"—regardless of any measurable level of interest. As a result, business plans create major headaches for *indie filmmakers, since writing one requires a huge commitment of time and a skill set many do not possess. Many filmmakers think that a business plan has to be better than the script they're hoping to make before it will attract deep pockets that would rather invest in Web 3.0 start-ups or in programmers who are developing popular iPhone apps such as Loopt or Cowbell Plus. Other filmmakers believe that a business plan will magically grant them access to a level of investment that would not otherwise materialize, and that without one they will be forced to raise financing in paltry increments. But because business plans can be—and often are—endlessly improved, the producer, director, and/or screenwriter often struggle to polish their business plan for two, four, or even eight months rather than improving the screenplay, causing their momentum to stall and the project to fall apart. Certainly filmmakers shouldn't run out and get MBAs just to learn how to write a measured business plan, but would-be auteurs could use a degree of business savvy beyond the ability to negotiate heartbreak deals with equipment houses.*

FUND-RAISING IS SERIOUS BUSINESS

There was a time when potential investors would ask if there were speaking parts in the script for their favorite niece or nephew. Today many ask for something that can cause even bigger headaches: a well-crafted business plan explaining how and when investors might see returns on the level of *Pan's Labyrinth*, *Juno*, or *Open Water*. During severe economic downturns when cash is hard to come by, it's no longer enough to present a killer script and a terrific pitch. With high gas prices and thousands of bankers out of work on account of the mortgage crisis, those who still have cash to throw around want to hear about recoupment horizons, net present value, and internal rates of return.

And that's just on the executive summary page.

Call it the legacy of the housing bubble or the headlines

announcing the disintegration of major banks and insurance companies, but many investors are increasingly cautious about parting with capital. Before wallets or purse strings will open for indie filmmakers, they may have to present their projects as real businesses, even if the underlying content they hope to finance is numerically closer to *House of 1000 Corpses* than the S&P 500.

"Making any film is like starting a company from the ground up that is designed to make that one movie," says former Miramax acquisitions vice president Jason Blum, who later served as a producer on indie films such as Michael Almereyda's *Hamlet* and studio projects such as Griffin Dunne's *The Accidental Husband*. "Any time you make a film, you're creating a brand and you're running a business. Each movie should be thought of as its own little start-up company."

Indeed, filmmakers who aren't able to raise money from wealthy friends or family members may have to court private equity from high net-worth types who see a formal business plan as a sign of maturity, or at least as a signal that the project is more than just a pipe dream or a lark. There are so many things that can go wrong on the way to getting an independent film completed that having a business plan often shows that the people behind the project have thought through what they're attempting.

"As much as it's a pain in the neck, there are times when writing a business plan is really the only option," says Ira Deutchman, president of Emerging Pictures and associate professor of film at Columbia University. "If you can't tap into a small number of deep pockets or find money sources from industry connections, you may not have much of a choice."

Independent filmmakers may also need business plans because wealthy friends and family connections may opt out of investing even a token amount. So while writing a business plan can be a galling indignity, filmmakers are increasingly having to create them, as the sources of funding they were counting on fall through. Indeed, aspiring directors should never assume that the high-net-worth individuals they have known for years will invest a single dollar in an independent film. Even the richest contacts they have, people who could finance an entire indie film by selling off two shares of Berkshire Hathaway (BRK.A), will not invest or even lend an aspiring filmmaker money to finance the fundraising interval, business plan or no.

"Probably the biggest frustration is really the fact that it has to be done at all, that people don't just go with their gut when they read a script," explains *Boys Don't Cry* producer Eva Kolodner. "You don't really have to write a business plan if you're pitching to people who have experience in investing in films because they have their own models that they will run your project through. They've got their own metrics: 'Okay, this would work if you had this level of talent, and this budget, and were able to get video-only distribution if theatrical distribution wasn't possible.' "

With few exceptions, the idea of soliciting $20 or even $200 from everyone a filmmaker knows is a fool's errand, since the time it takes to court each investor over lunch or just a quick coffee equates to several months of pitching only to come away with three to four thousand dollars.

Even so, many filmmakers think they are keeping it real by emulating the approach famously taken in 1996 by Darren Aronofsky, who raised the bulk of the funds needed to shoot his groundbreaking debut, *Pi*, in increments of only $100 from friends and family. Although this now-mythic story is indeed true, what most filmmakers don't know is that this approach raised only $30,000 and that Aronofsky and his team did create a formal business plan which was crafted for wealthy investors who could afford to invest more than a C-note.

"We didn't put a business plan together for the people who were going to invest at the $100 level because to do that that would have cost more than the $100, but we *were* looking for larger investors and we did have a package with an explanation of how the finances could work," recalls Aronofsky. "We put together a nice spreadsheet and a well-designed package that we did on Adobe Photoshop and had it spiral-bound. I think we included a list of other independent films that had done well and we tried to educate the investors on how they can make money."

This is not to say that Aronofsky did not gain real traction from courting friends and asking for $100, but filmmakers hoping to follow this method should know that to raise the entire $60,000 shooting budget of *Pi*, Aronofsky and his team would have needed 600 individual investors to say yes and then actually come through with a check, a level of fund-raising conversion that could easily require contacting, courting, and brunching with 2,000 to 4,000 people. The aggravating reality of this approach is that it typically results in 100 to 200 coffee-and-bagel meetings with old friends who ultimately *do not* invest.

"The deal was, we sent out a form letter which we acknowledged was a form letter," recalls Aronofsky. "We made a joke right at the beginning: 'We know this is a form letter but don't think it's because we don't love you . . . It's because we're sending this to 300 friends with the hope of getting money from them.' We just put the whole concept out there: 'If you can help us we'll give you back $150 when the film makes money and you'll get your name in the cred-its.' Then we put together a list of names and addresses of people we thought would invest. But we didn't send a self-addressed, stamped envelope, just the form letter. Then we kept them updated about our progress. We kept it like a family."

Still, this approach can be costly and often requires a pre-liminary fund-raising effort to fund the fund-raising effort. The paper, toner cartridges, standard envelopes, and postage for a mass mailing to 1,000 people would cost somewhere in the neighborhood of $500 and take weeks for a small team of envelope-stuffing volunteers to actually mail out. Filmmakers hoping to save time by using ten-by-thirteen manila envelopes, Avery 5160 mailing labels, and self-addressed, stamped envelopes can expect to spend in the neighborhood of $1,500. Unfortunately, the response rate for direct mail solicitations is often less than 3 percent, regardless of whom the pitch is from. E-mail solicitation blasts typically have an even lower response rate.

"At that time a lot of our friends were just out of school and unemployed, but a lot of them came out and supported us and that was a really cool thing," Aronofsky says. "You know, people who you wouldn't think would invest or who didn't have $100 to spare gave us money, which was something we didn't expect. Two weeks before the film opened we sent checks out."

WHO'S GOT MY MIRACLE?

Before filmmakers kill themselves writing a business plan, they should know that no one investor will make their film happen or prevent it from happening. This is a fallacy that often inspires filmmakers to make self-destructive choices. The truth is, while many indie films have been financed by a single wealthy individual or a PayPal millionaire, filmmakers should never approach their fund-raising or business-plan writing from the perspective that all is lost if this person or that person doesn't invest. Often the potential investor who most wants to see the business plan is the one who is least likely to invest. Other interested parties may even secretly want to copy elements of it to generate interest in their own projects, which are likely to be more attractive Web-based ventures. Therefore, indie filmmakers who put their films on hold to throw themselves into a spasm of business-plan mania after hearing they need one may be heading in the wrong direction. A better approach may be to hire a coder to create an indie-film fund-raising widget that would link to Bank of America's iPhone widget.

SINGLE FILM OR SLATE

Some aspiring filmmakers wonder if their business plans should offer investors the chance to put money toward a portfolio of projects. Still others wonder if financing a development fund, which could allow the filmmakers to option a number of screenplays or provide finishing funds to a film nearing completion, might be more attractive.

And still others write two different business plans: one for an individual film and one for a production entity that hopes to finance a slate of films. This is not to say that one plan is optimistic and the other is realistic, but rather that the plan for a slate of projects could position the production shingle as a going concern that will not fold if the first project is not a resounding success. Kolodner advises filmmakers simply to write a single business plan, as she and her business partner and Salty Features cofounder, Yael Melamede, did in 2002.

"We didn't want to lose the time it would take to write two plans and then present them to people to see which one was more appealing to investors, so what we did was really focus on writing one plan and getting that one out there," says Kododner. "When we started out we were really trying to get a good plan written for a single film and get that one film financed and then hopefully gather some momentum. As a producer you're always talking to people and always trying to figure out ways to sell your slate and how you can go beyond just the slate to promote the company—who you are and what you can do and what we're trying to do—in a bigger way. But that's just a slower-going process." The job of being a film producer has expanded significantly over the past several years: "In the eighties, all you needed was a great script," says *The Ice Storm* producer Ted Hope. "In the nineties, you could say you had a really good script and that you could package it with a great cast and a director. But by the time the millennium rolled around, you had to say you had a really good script, you had packaged it with a great director and a great cast, *and* you had brought in a portion of the financing. Now that we turned the corner toward the end of the decade, you also need all four of those things, but today as a producer you also have to bring in part of the audience. And that basically means, I believe, maintaining an ongoing dialogue with a vast and varied audience, and the blog I maintain [letsmakebetterfilms.blogspot.com] is my little part of that."

This conservative approach may be more convincing, according to Sundance festival director Geoff Gilmore, since there is an increased level of sophistication among the investing community about independent-film economics. "The fact that many independent films will never see the light of day is a message that has gotten through loud and clear over the past few years," he says. "And as a result, I don't think you're seeing as much money being thrown up against projects 'just to watch it burn,' as it were. There's an awful lot of projects still being made that don't ever get distributed, but I don't think there's as much naïveté today as there once was—there used to be a lot more naïve enthusiasm—and there's not as much capital out there that's willing to be burned, particularly when you're talking about productions that are often in the $100,000 or $1 million plus range. As a result of growing investor sophistication, diminished minimum guarantees at the festival point-of-sale, fewer actual distributors buying films, and the current economic outlook, there is a school of thought that first- and second-time independent filmmakers should either make films for under $100,000 and limit their investors' losses or go all-out and make star-driven films for $1 million or more, with these known actors courting domestic and international TV sales. (See budgets in Appendix I.)

"Because there are a lot more places you can go for financing these days and because there are also a lot more investors who are knowledgeable," Gilmore continues, "filmmakers have to make a case not only for the creative aspects of what their film will be but also for what the business plan around that film needs to be. More filmmakers now are being as careful about their business plans as they are about what the creative exigencies of the production will be, and that involves what kind of a production they're putting together, who's going to be cast in it, how it's going to be produced, what the nature of it is, who they think the audience is for it, and what price it's being made for.

"Essentially there's more of a strategic sensibility in almost all the kinds of films that you see get put together today, and that means people are putting more thought into what they're going to do with the project," Gilmore concludes. "Now, they may not be able to execute it the way they had hoped to, but you don't get as much of that kind of naïveté as you used to. The bar for success has been raised higher over the last decade and the bar for what is required even to get projects made has also steadily gone up, so that overall you find a higher level of quality of work that's being submitted to us across the board."

For this reason, it is a good idea for all business plans to include a "competitive advantages" section in which producers detail how their projects will stand out, either by being shot on 24p HD, 35mm film, or by including well-known actors who may be able to raise the qualitative aspects of the production.

RETAINING CREATIVE CONTROL

Raising money with a business plan is also a way for filmmakers to cap or codify certain creative aspects of the production and keep the project true to its inspiration, ensuring that it doesn't devolve into a fun-in-the-sun beach party pairing stewardesses and ghosts. Instead of going with traditional funding sources like studios or established production companies that might require wholesale changes to the script, private funding in which investors become limited partners—that is, partners who are not given creative input—allows the production team to keep complete creative control.

Filmmakers can entertain helpful suggestions from investors—since everyone who puts money in the project is on some level buying the thrill of being a "producer"—but contractually, the business plan should spell out that the production team retains final say over what gets shot and what ends up on-screen. The last thing any filmmaker needs is a hundred (or more) chefs ultimately spoiling the soup. To that end, investors should be asked to sign an acknowledgment page certifying that they have read the synopsis of the story in the business plan and know what the film is about, that it includes scenes of graphic X or Y, and that it is rated R or PG-13. In today's climate it is possible that a sense of an underage character smoking could earn an R rating, since there is a push to toughen MPAA ratings.

While they had hoped to retain creative control, Heather Juergensen and Jennifer Westfeldt were initially offered a deal in which they would have had to sell the script to *Kissing Jessica Stein* and walk away from any involvement in the project. "That was not the route we were going to take with it, so basically we ended up financing the film through small equity investments," remembers producer Eden Wurmfeld. "When I say small, I mean a share in our company was $2,500. We had forty investors and the person who shared the producing credit put in $500,000. But we raised $450,000 through these $2,500 increments, which I call 'the uncles-and-orthodontists way' to make a movie. It's like asking every person you've ever known, a relative or otherwise, who you think might have a little extra cash if they want to get involved."

Over the summer of 2000, Wurmfeld, Juergensen, and Westfeldt, a production team which sounds like it could be a prestigious Beverly Hills law firm, raised the money for *KJS* with what they lovingly called their dog and pony show.

"We tailored our pitch depending on who the potential investors were," Wurmfeld continues. "We thought: 'Okay, do they want the sexy, fun energy of Jennifer and Heather? Or do they want someone like me, who's going to be a little more brass tacks?' And we strategized that way in terms of what we thought people would respond to best. Fortunately, with those two, you could wind them up and send them out and they were just like they were on-screen. So that chemistry helped our presentations."

This approach mirrored the way Vince Vaughn and Jon Favreau helped with the fund-raising for *Swingers* by acting out scenes, which they had been riffing together as friends for years, right on the spot for potential investors. Aspiring filmmakers who don't have cast members as part of the core production team may be able to achieve the same effect by shooting a compelling scene from the screenplay as a short and showing a five- to ten-minute DVD—what is known in special effects circles as a "proof of concept." Another approach is to stage and shoot a full trailer for a film that does not yet exist and send that along with the business plan.

Still, for every investor who asks for a business plan before one has been drawn up, there are a dozen film-industry veterans who caution against putting too much time—or faith—in such a document. "The problem with writing a business plan is that you're always tempted to improve it somehow and then you start to think, 'I sent the old version to this person and maybe it wasn't the perfect thing,'" explains Kolodner. "Then you start to think, 'Maybe I should send them a revised draft.'"

Others have come to dismiss indie-film business plans altogether. "People who work in the industry all have comical stories about some of the ones we've received," says Eamonn Bowles of Magnolia Pictures, a two-year veteran of Miramax. "They're usually filled with basic assumptions that are so erroneous that the business plans end up showing just how much the filmmaker who wrote it has no idea what's going on. A lot of them will say something like: 'We only have to sell out 40 percent of the seats in the theater—only 40 percent of the seats—to be guaranteed a $20 million gross on this film . . . as long as it plays in *this* many theaters!' Those kinds of statements are pretty legion. And you always hear the *Blair Witch Project* anecdote: 'If we can do just one-tenth of the business of *Blair Witch*,' which of course is already a foregone conclusion. That kind of thing in a business plan is pretty much a red flag. Right away you say to yourself, 'This person clearly has no idea what they're talking about.'"

Knowing how to avoid statements that undermine the credibility of a business plan in the eyes of savvy film investors and knowing how to enunciate goals that regularly appear in polished plans often determine who receives financing and who does not.

GETTING INTO A GROOVE

"The more you can learn to love the business side and the legal side and the logistics of the industry, the better off you are going to be as a filmmaker," says *November* director Greg Harrison, who wrote a business plan with *Waitress* executive producer Danielle Renfrew to finance *Groove*, their Sundance film shot in 1999 for $500,000. "These days the business side is really what supports the creative side."

Renfrew and Harrison formed a limited liability company—a form of incorporation that protects filmmakers and other entrepreneurs from personal liability should the venture go south—and courted Internet professionals in the San Francisco Bay Area who were still flush with cash prior to the 2001 Internet crash.

"As a filmmaker you need to speak the language of your potential investors, and we wanted to show serious businesspeople that we were for real," Renfrew says. "The approach we took was that we were a start-up company looking for venture capital, since that was a familiar paradigm to a lot of people in Silicon Valley."

The pair raised their production budget in one hundred $5,000 increments and ultimately sold *Groove*, shot in 16mm, to Sony Pictures Classics for $1.5 million. But long before the film entered preproduction, Harrison and Renfrew had to think about business-plan-type issues such as marketing, distribution, and Securities and Exchange Commission rules related to fund-raising.

"Originally, the business side wasn't my main focus—I wanted to make a film," Harrison remembers. "But it soon became apparent that the business side was going to be the bridge to becoming a filmmaker. At that point we had to put the script aside and begrudgingly become entrepreneurs."

The duo wanted the *Groove* business plan to stand out and represent their film—a night in the life of the San Francisco rave crowd—so they added a few nontraditional flourishes. "We didn't just send out photocopies of the plan," Renfrew says, "we tried to make it fun. We had it bound and sent it out in a cute little kit with a mix CD of songs we wanted to put in the movie. Doing whatever you can to make a business plan stand out is really important."

Crumb and *Juno* producer Lianne Halfon put together a similar pitch book to raise financing for *Ghost World* in 1998, before the film was fully bankrolled by United Artists for $6.3 million. "I had a screenplay which had a very subtle plot and a sense of humor that was lost on many studio executives," recalls Halfon. "And *Crumb* was seen as brilliant, but very dark. With *Ghost World*, I would send out large color copies of Daniel Clowes's comic—all of which somewhat belied the complexity of the work. But I was still battling the fact that Dan was not well known. After *Newsweek* called Dan a genius in a review.["A Certain Comic Genius: Daniel Clowes Wows 'Em with 'Ghost World,'" *Newsweek*, April 27, 1998], things got easier. We included a color blowup of the story and Dan used to joke that the xeroxed package I sent out was more expensive than the original comic, and it was true. At one point I had no money left for messengers, so I had to hand-deliver them myself." This situation is not uncommon as filmmakers often leave the costs associated with the fund-raising effort out of their business plans.

Despite any qualms aspiring producers might have, business plans need a frank discussion of the generally unavoidable "fixed" costs, such as printing, postage, and envelopes, that are related to the enterprise. Some savvy investors actually look for glaring omissions in prospectus offerings and investment documents as a red flag whenever they are weighing whether a deal or investment is worth pursuing.

"I constantly see business plans where entrepreneurs leave their own lives—and the related costs—out of the mix," says Columbia Business School professor Clifford J. Schorer, who has invested in low-budget film projects in the past. "I say, 'How are you going to pay your bills?' And they look at you with this blank stare. It's something they need to think about. There's the opportunity cost of not working, which is significant, especially since it can take several months to find a job if it doesn't work out, and then there is the cost of sustaining yourself while you're actually trying to make the film. Your apartment and everything in your life has to be considered an operational expense, and to keep the project going you're going to have to keep yourself going. A lot of people don't budget appropriately since they think they're getting a lot of things for free and listing the cost of only a few big-ticket items, but the real unavoidable costs can easily quintuple a proposed budget. People say, 'I'm going to use my apartment as my office so I don't have to worry about it,' and I say, 'Is your rent free?' And then it dawns on them that they're still going to have to pay rent somehow. When that kind of overly optimistic thinking breaks down, it shows me they haven't thought things through."

Indeed, many first- and second-time filmmakers don't think to pay themselves a salary while shooting their films, instead opting to put all the money they can raise "up on the screen," as the saying goes. "*Kong* was really much more about opportunity cost than it was about production cost, because I shot 90 percent of it, I edited it, and the bulk of the expense, at least in terms of the production and post actually, was just a couple of hotel rooms and the flights to get to Florida from Los Angeles," recalls Seth Gordon, director of *King of Kong: A Fistful of Quarters*. "So the out-of-pocket cost to the point where we got people to actually see the thing was really, really low, but the hard part was turning down other work and just living hand-to-mouth until the film saw the light of day."

Although it may seem counterintuitive, smart investors will respect the fact that the filmmaker has decided to include start-up costs and to pay himself or herself a reasonable salary. Filmmakers may be concerned that doing so will raise eyebrows with some investors, but real-life entrepreneurs who have invested in actual companies know that certain costs are integral to keeping any fledgling business afloat. "You don't have to put together an overly detailed description, but you can say, 'At the foot of my bed there is ten to twelve square feet of desk space that I'm leasing to the production company or to the production for $1,000 per month," explains attorney W. Wilder Knight III of Pryor Cashman LLP. "You put it in your business plan where everybody can see it and the cards are all on the table." Indeed, many potential investors, especially those who work in banking or management consulting, will turn straight to the pages of financials and fixed costs that all business plans should have before they will read even a word of the business plan's elegantly written and slaved-over prose.

But in the film business, where a short window of actor availability can make or break a production start, filmmakers need to be careful not to get sucked into the business-plan nebula. "I've been guilty of that myself," admits Columbia Business School professor of entrepreneurship Lawrence Sherman, who has launched several successful companies in the medical industry. "Some people spend eight to ten months writing the perfect bulletproof business plan—one with every appendix and financial projection you could think of—only to find themselves with a bloated forty-page document that nobody wants to read. That's not uncommon."

Other filmmakers spend so much time writing their business plans that several early sections—and possibly even the film itself—may become dated or obsolete by the time the document is completed. These filmmakers will spend forever writing a business plan over and over even though very few investors will actually end up reading it.

"Our business plan was barely looked at by our financiers," says *Roger Dodger* director Dylan Kidd. "We spent four months laboring over this thing, I mean we literally worked harder on our business plan than on the movie. Then after four months of working on it you finally go to a financing meeting, you hand over the business plan with trembling hands, and they look at it for three seconds and say: 'Oh, okay . . . Now tell me about your film.' I feel like the universe rewarded us for the energy we put into it, but the people who ended up giving us money for the film probably looked at the thing for about thirty seconds."

"That's why I suggest writing a short miniplan that won't take too much time away from the actual endeavor," says Sherman. "Very often a person will spend months writing an extensive proposal when they would have been better off setting up face-to-face meetings to try and get the effort moving forward."

Often what sells any entrepreneurial endeavor is an "elevator pitch," so named because it must be delivered quickly, during a fortuitous encounter with a CEO or venture capitalist in an elevator en route to the lobby.

As a result, Sherman suggests keeping any business plan between ten and twenty pages, including all appendices and financial projections. "Or what you can do is just draft a one-page letter that captures the appealing reason why an investor would want to meet with you in person," Sherman says. "The whole purpose of this letter will be to arrange a meeting where you can pitch your idea and see what issues they might have. Then if they ask for something more, you can provide what we call a 'back of the envelope' plan: a cursory summary that's quick and dirty and doesn't delve into unnecessary detail."

While many filmmakers can't resist the kitchen-sink approach, Harrison followed a less-is-more page-count doctrine. "You have to be as concise as possible because people don't want to read a thirty-page manifesto," he says. "Our whole business plan for *Groove* was only ten pages, and that included press clippings and an appendix explaining how the film industry works. The key was doing tons of research so we could distill it down to ten pages that read really well. It's like writing a good script: it has to be a page-turner."

Eden Wurmfeld said her plan struck a balance between a creative and a business orientation. "We put together a development kit—that was a little less formal than a business plan—with bios and a synopsis of the story," she recalls. "It also had a cover sheet of a budget and press we had gotten, that was related to any of us, that could be noteworthy. Our business plan wasn't one of those fat books, it was more like a glossy folder that said '*Kissing Jessica Stein* Investment Kit' on the front and had sections like Key Players, Project History, Profit, Context, and Plot Summary. It had the LLC investment papers in it, too, so it had the more user-friendly aspects to it, and then it had the legal, please-sign-on-the-dotted-line elements as well." This last component is critical because investors, like home buyers, often get cold feet between the pitch, the fine print, and the closing. Indeed, successful filmmakers follow the key roles of salesmanship: Always be closing, always pay attention to detail, and always follow up.

SHOW ME THE MONEY (THEY SPENT)

One of the reasons filmmakers in fund-raising mode always point to *My Big Fat Greek Wedding*, *Pulp Fiction*, and *Blair Witch* is that it is difficult to find hard data to create a return-on-investment matrix or "schedule," as Excel spreadsheets are sometimes referred to. Ideally this would be a comprehensive, easy-to-read spreadsheet that would contain data points on what films comparable to the one being proposed cost to make, what it cost to market them, what they actually grossed in each of their exhibition windows, and how much of that might have accrued to the filmmakers after prints-and-advertising costs and studio overhead were applied. This is maddening for filmmakers as they try to write business plans, since the best-, middle-, worst-, *and* Hurricane Katrina–case scenarios are what a lot of potential investors want to see in black and white before reading the more enthusiastic text, which they tend to discount anyway. Filmmakers who don't have numbers in their business plans might as well not even write one. But finding accurate figures can be difficult, especially when the numbers floating around are almost always impossibly low and often missing key expenses such as music clearances or the cost of the 35mm blowup. The truth is that published numbers associated with indie films are often inaccurate or even deliberately incorrect.

"First of all, nobody wants to say what the budget actually was because maybe they paid someone far below what they should've been paying them if the budget had been more," explains Kolodner. "That's an old trick. People are always trying to either undersell the budget to all the people they want to work with or to oversell what their budget actually was and what they spent on the film so they can get more money when it comes time to sell the film at a festival. In other instances it's the studio that wants to keep the numbers out of the spotlight since it may raise expectations for a film." For example, the Quentin Tarantino–Robert Rodriguez film *Grindhouse* reportedly cost $70 million to make and $30 million to market, but only grossed $25 million theatrically in the United States. Had it been produced for the same amount as *Pulp Fiction*, however, it would have been lauded as a modest hit that connected with the duo's core audience.

"Or the studio executive thinks, 'I really don't want the actual number we spent on this film to ever get out, especially what we spent on publicity or how much we saved by underspending on whatever it was,' because if the producer or the talent finds out, he or she may say, 'If you made X, and I know that you only spent Y, then I should be getting some piece of that.' It could be a problem," Kolodner continues. "So both of those things stand in the way of having any kind of accurate assessment of what a movie was made for, what it earned, and how much was spent to get it to earn what it did. And it is often hard to tell or to present to a potential investor what was spent and what the film actually earned so you can project a rate of return on investment in your business plan."

Another challenge filmmakers face is simply knowing what will draw in potential investors and not turn them off or make them lose interest. "That's the big question: What exactly will interest people with money?" says Kolodner. "What level of return will interest them, how do you talk about money so you don't come off as cavalier, uninformed, or just spinning a tale? And if you are going to try to spin a tale, do you know what the numbers are? Because even if you try to follow the box office, it's just incredibly hard to get real numbers. Producers fall back on the movies that they've made or have had personal contact with because everything else seems so false out there."

THE BUSINESS-PLAN GUMBO

What should go into a film business plan? Generally, every plan has an executive summary—a top sheet that lists the credits of the producers, director, and talent, and describes the budget, start date, and other key information in short, bite-size paragraphs. Next there might be a one-page synopsis of the story line followed by an investment merits section, which breaks down all the positive elements the project has going for it—whether it be established talent, distribution guarantees, large potential audiences, or simply the filmmaker's belief that the subject matter is timely and relevant.

There should be a marketing page that outlines the filmmaker's ability to reach a paying audience for the film and a risk factors section explaining the various ways the project could fail despite everyone's best intentions. Some filmmakers question the merit or the logic of including such a section, but they are required to do so for legal reasons and may save the production from substantial heartbreak at some future date should a nightmare investor claim that he or she had been duped and sue. Finally, an organization and operations section should contain bios of all key participants. An appendix can give a quick primer on how revenue is generated in the film business, or showcase supplemental material such as press clippings related to the project.

"My feeling is I'd rather have an investor tell me no right off the bat than to paint a rosy picture and have them pull their money two weeks before shooting begins, once they learn that exhibitors keep 50 to 60 percent of the gross receipts from theatrical ticket sales, [potentially delaying net profits]," explains Kidd. "Basically, you should assume the person reading your business plan has never invested in a movie before and explain what it means for a distributor to buy the film, how the money spent on printing and advertis-

ing has to be recouped, and how exhibitors actually keep half
of the ticket proceeds. The point is, you would rather have
the investor who thinks, 'This is really a long shot, but this is
money that I've got to lose anyway and I love the movies, so
I want to be a part of it.' You really don't want the person
who is mortgaging a house to invest in your movie. It's irresponsible to take his money."

Of course, if the film's budget is below $12,000, a business
plan probably isn't necessary. "Don't ask me about business
plans, man," says writer-director and now actor Mark Borchardt, best known for the documentary *American Movie* and
the horror sequel *Cabin Fever 2: Spring Fever*. "My business
plan is simple: every ten-minute roll of film—the stock and
the processing—costs $200, and that is straight-up serious,
dude. A roll of film is like a yellow legal pad and a Paper
Mate pen, and that's what you budget for. I'm straight-up
serious. My business plan is $200 at a time for another ten-
minute roll of film. I no longer try to raise money. Do you
try to raise money for a Paper Mate pen and a legal pad?
Hell no, man. Because it's only about two bucks for both of
them. I'm making a handful of films, dude—personal films—
and they do not require business plans."

Other filmmakers have succeeded with minimalist business plans that avoided flashy bells and whistles. "We actually didn't want to send the message that we were spending
a lot of money on basic administrative stuff. We wanted to
make sure people saw that all of our money was waiting to be
put on the screen," recalls Juergensen, cowriter and costar of
Kissing Jessica Stein and *The Hammer*. "We did have days
where we would put things in folders, like the ones you get
from Staples, and we tried to make them look as nice as we
could. But our prospectus and investment kits were pretty
straightforward affairs."

AVOIDING "HELLO KITTY" PLANS

Just as no actor wants to be considered a Hostess Twinkie, aspiring filmmakers should avoid writing overly precious or exceedingly clever business plans lest they not be taken seriously by "the money."

Kim Bangash of Orchid Ventures—who invested in well-known indies such as *You Can Count on Me*, *Sling Blade*, and *New Jersey Drive*—advises that taking the "cute" type of approach with their business plan works only with first-time film investors. He says that most established film financiers and bankers want to receive something far more formal known as "the package." This collection of sober preproduction documents includes the screenplay, a budget summary with projected above-the-line and below-the-line costs, a discussion of potential cast members, a one-page cover letter, and a short synopsis of the script that does not reveal the ending. "You don't discuss the ending in detail because if they're serious about investing, you want them to actually read the script," Bangash says. "Instead, end your synopsis or your cover letter saying something like: 'Our movie ends with a compelling and inspirational dance number that reunites the romantic leads, similar to the final sequence in *Dirty Dancing*.' You don't want to be overly optimistic, but you can reference films that did well and managed to connect with their audiences."

The package can also include professional head shots of cast members who have been signed and résumés of the creative and production teams. As for business plans, Bangash suggests sending one only if the potential financier likes the package. "I've only seen four business plans out of literally hundreds of packages," says Bangash, who typically invests in independent films with budgets of less than $3 million.

"Only one of the four was impressive: it was a business plan that was twelve to fifteen pages long, and it wasn't filled with ridiculous projections and aggressive assumptions. The film-maker acknowledged that it would be difficult to achieve distribution, but she said, 'If we get it, we can probably recoup based on the fact that my film will only cost $500,000 to make.' "

This winning business plan went on to explain how the filmmaker planned to achieve certain cost savings and how she would market the film using the Internet and traditional media. She also listed revenue-generating alternatives to theatrical distribution should the film be passed over by major distributors and how she planned to create buzz on her own. Finally, the plan included a budget breakdown and a list of freebies the production could count on.

"This plan was clearly compelling for first-time investors, because the filmmaker ended up getting the money from people who had never invested in films before," Bangash recalls. "She was able to raise $500,000 in $20,000 increments by explaining what is often a very nebulous business."

Business plans or pitch books with storyboards of certain sequences created in PowerProduction Software's Storyboard Quick for PC can make a financing presentation more compelling. But hard numbers, audience analysis, good comparables, and Excel spreadsheets will always trump fancy visuals. "To get *American Splendor* made, we put together a marketing book on how you could reach the huge audience that exists for Harvey Pekar and we really did our research," explains the film's producer Ted Hope. "HBO understood it and they said, 'Yes, we can reach this audience.' Maud Nadler [then vice president of indie productions at HBO] made the project happen for us. The film's directors [Shari Springer Berman and Robert Pulcini] had just left the pitch session when Maud called to tell me she had to do the film.

There probably was not another company in the world that we could have made that film with and have it come out as well as it did. HBO had confidence in the entire team, even though it was Bob and Shari's first narrative feature and Paul Giamatti's first leading role."

American Splendor was also a difficult film to pitch because it was a unique story told with innovative animation techniques in an era before Frank Miller's *Sin City*, *300*, *Waltz with Bashir*, *Watchmen*, and *The Spirit*, but showed that films emulating the aesthetic of graphic novels could be successful. "Very often the only film that will get financed is the one that you can describe in exact terms of the other movies that are just like it," says Hope. "It's such an expensive medium and there's just an enormous amount of risk, so companies are often seeking to buy some sort of insurance where none exists. And since the film business is really about repeating what has been done before—hopefully just the successes, not the failures—the job of a producer is to look at an orange and tell everyone that it's an apple: in other words, to present something commonplace as somehow unique and convince financiers that they too can be successful with it. That's the real challenge for independent-film producers—how to make it fresh, and if it can't be truly fresh, how to make everyone else feel the day-old bread is freshly baked."

KNOWING THE INDUSTRY IS KEY

Deutchman points out that first-time filmmakers should be well versed in the mechanics of the indie-film industry before trying to pass themselves off as experts in a business plan. The most common error many of them make, he notes, is to equate box-office success with massive returns for investors.

"The big bonanza for equity-financed films is not necessarily when they are successful in the marketplace," Deutchman says. "Return on investment really doesn't have anything to do with a film's success or failure in theaters, but merely the fact that it was sold for more than it cost to produce. That is good news that very few filmmakers leverage." In other words, while a $4 million purchase such as *Grace Is Gone* may have received only a token release and failed theatrically in 2008, its investors likely recouped the project's $3 million production cost. Similarly, even though *Son of Rambow* failed theatrically, grossing only $1.8 million in 2008, its $7 million purchase price allowed its investors to make money.

Positioning the acquisition as the "liquidity event" and not the film's performance shows that the filmmakers are not trying to dazzle investors with outsize promises of returns on the level of *Greek Wedding*, since many savvy investors know that small independently financed films rarely if ever share in theatrical gross. Legally, filmmakers must warn investors of the likelihood of the total loss of 100 percent of their investment. In practice, this means alerting investors that the project's return on investment could very well be zero, since a theatrical distribution deal is never guaranteed.

"There's always the possibility that you get into a film festival and nobody wants to distribute your film," explains Wurmfeld. "You just never know and you never have any guarantee. The upside potential can be significant, but the ability to truly predict that is zero. With *Kissing Jessica Stein*, the investors did very well and made 125 percent of their investment after we sold the film to Fox Searchlight," at the Los Angeles Independent Film Festival for approximately $1 million.

Today's far more modest acquisition prices averaging $200,000 or less haven't stopped many would-be directors and producers from regaling potential investors with stories of how *Pulp Fiction* cost $8 million to make and went on to earn $108 million in the United States and an additional $112 million abroad. The suggestion is that investors in the project now being proposed will be eligible for a big chunk of the theatrical distributor's grosses after it follows the path of the 1995 Tarantino phenomenon. The problem for filmmakers citing this example in their business plans and fundraising materials is that savvy film investors tend to know that (1) advances paid at the festival point-of-sale or shortly after are typically the only funds ever paid to an independent production; (2) investors typically do not share in the theatrical upside; (3) exhibitors keep half or even 60 percent of the theatrical grosses of specialized films; (4) the specialized film business is now a mature sector facing heavy consolidation, evidenced by the closings of New Line Cinema, Paramount Vintage, Warner Independent Pictures, and Picturehouse in 2008 alone; (5) *Pulp Fiction* was *not* equity-financed by individual investors as is widely believed, but was wholly financed by Miramax; (6) the film was developed by a major studio, TriStar Pictures; (7) *Pulp Fiction* was not purchased at Sundance after a heated bidding war for a huge multiple of its production cost; (8) theatrical attendance is in steady decline year after year, despite the performance of *The Dark Knight* and more recent hits; and (9) few films in the specialized or independently financed arena have connected with the global zeitgeist and performed on the level of *Pulp Fiction* since its release way back in 1994.

Of course, almost every aspiring filmmaker clings to the *Pulp Fiction* model and can't help but mention it as a shorthand for an independent-film business model, even though doing so sets expectations impossibly high among potential investors who don't know any better.

Reservoir Dogs producer Lawrence Bender, who would later produce *Pulp Fiction* and *An Inconvenient Truth*, advises today's filmmakers not to use early Tarantino movies as data points in fund-raising materials or as a shorthand for getting rich off an independent film. "If I were making a small movie I would not use that business model or pitch people the *Pulp Fiction* model," he says. "*Pulp Fiction*, honestly, was one of those movies that was good and bad for independent cinema. It was great because it was a big success and that encouraged a lot of people in the business and made them realize you could make money with independent movies. All the studios began creating their own independent or specialized divisions. But on the other hand, everybody also began looking for their own grand slam of an independent movie and looking for huge upside from small films. It used to be that if you made an independent movie and it grossed more than ten million bucks, you were in amazing shape. But today people are looking for much more than that. I know when I try to make a small movie like *The Chumscrubber*, the chances of it being a grand slam like *Pulp Fiction* are one in a million. Even though I happen to have made that one-in-a-million film, that doesn't mean it happens very often or even a second time."

BUSINESS-PLAN LIABILITY ISSUES

While many filmmakers believe that copying someone else's existing business plan will save time, it can also potentially lead to big trouble later on if there are glaring omissions or other common errors somewhere in the document.

"There are several places in business plans where the people writing them make themselves extremely vulnerable to securities law violations," explains Knight. "It's an area where you could be dealing with fraud, so you really want to have a law firm review whatever documents you're sending out. I wrote a business plan years ago for Todd Haynes's film

Poison and rewritten versions of it landed on my desk for years afterward. People just swapped in their names and the title of their films, but the typos from the original document are still in there more than nine years later. And of course the laws have changed and some of those provisions are outdated. It's very dangerous to simply copy a document."

Charles H. Googe, Jr., an attorney with the Manhattan firm Paul, Weiss, Rifkind, Wharton & Garrison, also advises hiring a lawyer to evaluate all written materials before the plan goes to investors. "If you're planning to solicit funds only from sophisticated, accredited investors—people with substantial assets or substantial business backgrounds—you don't need to provide detailed disclosures," he says. "There are different disclosure requirements depending on the type of offering and the investor being courted."

But no matter what type of potential investors are on someone's hit list, material omissions in a business plan can still get filmmakers into big trouble and open them up to unwinnable lawsuits from people who rightly or wrongly Rickrolled. Omissions can include forgetting to mention that the screenwriter suddenly gets a $60,000 or $100,000 deferred payment if the film is sold at Sundance, or that the filmmaker has contractually guaranteed first-position payments to an earlier stable of investors—or perhaps that the director's girlfriend's apartment is doubling as a production office and her rent and groceries are included in the film's budget as craft service.

"If it's a legitimate expense and you're paying yourself $1,000 per month to use the biggest room in your apartment in New York City, that's the market rate. But you're opening yourself up to an investor coming in and saying you're self-dealing," says Knight. "And on a practical level, people may just get angry because they lost their money when the film didn't get distribution or wasn't completed and yet you man-

aged to get your rent paid. They might say, 'If you lose
money and I lose money, I feel fine. But you didn't lose
money. Maybe you should have had a little more skin in this
thing.' "

Knight advises filmmakers to always use sober prose and
to avoid making any outsize promises that might come back
to haunt them later on. Thus anything that might be inter-
preted as a surprise once the project is under way, such as the
fact that the director plans to cast his girlfriend in a pivotal
role—as *Purple Violets* director Edward Burns did with Max-
ine Bahns in *The Brothers McMullen* and *She's the One*—
should be clearly and explicitly spelled out, lest an investor
feel duped. The business plan should also explicitly spell out
that it is superseding all conversations, intimations, and projections that may have been made in e-mails, in person, or
by phone, since some investors can interpret optimism
and nonverbal cues as a promise or as a goal that can be
easily met.

"You always want to have a statement in the paperwork
that says that everything related to the deal and everything
related to the investment is based on what's in the written
contract," Knight says. "No oral representations, which basically means that your investor is acknowledging that she is
going into the deal based on what's written right here and
not based on what she may have heard or what she thinks
she's heard somewhere. You want to make a statement in the
business plan that says: 'I, the investor, am not going into
this deal based on anything I've heard someone say,' and that
the business plan represents the entire agreement."

Of course, having such a clause or other disclaimers in the
business plan does not allow a director or producer to make
grandiose promises when they pitch, or intimate that their
project is a sure thing. "You can't make a statement like: 'We
are certain we will make $100 million in theatrical box-office

revenue,' " Googe cautions. "There are state 'blue sky' laws that protect investors from con artists promising them the sky, if not the moon."

In fact, laws governing the promotion of securities require filmmakers raising more than $1 million to have all investors sign a formal private-placement memorandum prepared by an attorney. Such a document will scrupulously list the risk factors and relevant tax laws germane to the investment. Of course, there is often a disconnect between the harsh reality of the legal memoranda and the bullish pitch letters and wildly optimistic business plans that filmmakers throw around, resulting in a kind of sticker shock for investors who are close to cutting a check.

On the other hand, independent filmmakers might just decide to skip the business-plan rigmarole altogether. "I would suggest using the five months you're probably going to spend writing a business plan to write another script or to get your first script read by people in the film industry," says *Donnie Darko* producer Adam Fields. "At the end of the day, scripts are the currency we deal in. Regardless of how good a business plan may look, the only thing that's going to matter to me is the script, a filmmaker's potential talent as a director, and the actors who will star in the film. Use the time to get the screenplay out to established producers, established talent, or people who have experience raising production funds. They're the ones who are going to get your movie made."

3. First You Get the Money

FINANCING WOES

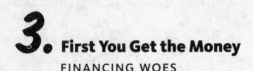ilm financing evolved heading into 2009 and beyond, expanding the definition of what qualifies as an independent film. Even the terminology has changed, making old labels no longer accurate. What used to be known as art-house films graduated into mainstream theaters. Art-house films became big business, and there was a rush of interest in what became known as independent or "indie" films. Soon the studios and studio-owned specialized divisions began financing projects that defined the indie sensibility. While huge Sundance sales still grabbed headlines and captured aspiring filmmakers' imaginations, more and more indie films began arriving at festivals with distribution already in place. The traditional financing model evolved as well. With a major star's commitment, filmmakers could raise funds from overseas television presales based on what the star's drawing power was in that region, and for a time, international financing was the wellspring of American independent film financing. Specialized divisions of major studios were created to compete with Miramax at the Academy Awards and to take advantage of the

attractive economics that lower-budget films could provide. The term specialized films came to describe a certain type or genre of film regardless of its financing, but this moniker also became outdated. Billionaires who had survived the dot-com bubble of the 1990s were attracted to filmmaking and began competing with the specialized divisions, pushing the budgets of independent films to new heights. Today the correct term is no longer "indie film" but "independently financed films," since they are just that regardless of the size, budget level, or star power, as long as they are paid for by nonstudio, independent financiers. The former "indie" tag is today a marketing term used to describe a genre of film with a certain risk-taking sensibility, that offers an antidote or counterpoint to the traditional portfolio of mainstream, general-audience "popcorn" films that are the studios' bread and butter. Dozens of these projects were financed by studio specialty divisions while others are financed by independent financiers who multiplied as Wall Street hedge funds came in to provide fresh capital. Leading talent agencies in Los Angeles recognized that there was a need to help structure the financing of what previously qualified as an indie film, and then advanced the business model further to where even the best scripts that had once been snapped up by the major studios and their largesse could be developed by outside financing with "smart money" willing to give the filmmaking teams behind each project more creative control, bigger budgets, and greater financial participation. This meant that the studios' specialized divisions were able to buy a higher class of indie films that appealed to an increasingly sophisticated audience while the films' financiers actually made money and in some cases won Academy Awards. It was a democratization of the previous Miramax model, albeit among billionaires who could afford to underwrite quality films such as Crash, An Inconvenient Truth, *or* Good Night, and Good Luck.

Today, there are still more potential sources of independent financing than there were during the original heyday of indie film that blossomed during the mid- to late-1990s. The sector is now drawing interest and no longer solely the domain of outsiders, mavericks, and iconoclasts who don't fit into the studio system. Smaller films financed by friends and family are also easier to make as technology continues to put the tools of filmmaking within easy reach of anyone with access to a few thousand dollars, a decent 24p HD camera, and a high-end computer to edit their project. As a result, the only thing preventing a waiter, a barista, or an unemployed dreamer from becoming a filmmaker is the money needed to shoot a film. Money attaches cast, secures locations, attracts talented crew, and generally separates actual filmmakers from the thousands of wannabes who will not end up at Sundance or Cannes, and never get a chance to chat up Charlie Rose, Mark Kermode, Elvis Mitchell, or Creative Screenwriting's Jeff Goldsmith. But aphorisms aside, financing is the single most important goal of any filmmaker, since it often determines everything else: the shooting format, the lighting package, the level of cast, the start date, and whether a film will make it through postproduction. Indeed, aspiring writer-directors may want to put the time spent fund-raising ahead of the endless rewrites that can leave a project in limbo, since the ones who get films made are those able to get cash in the bank, and not necessarily those with the best scripts, the most enthusiastic coverage, or a knockout business plan. Of course, the problem is, as a result of the mortgage meltdown, the bank failures of 2008, the stock market's devaluations, investor migration to Treasury Bills, the price of oil and hedge fund losses, ongoing economic uncertainty, and what economists call "the law of inefficient markets," those who have money don't need it, and those who need money can't get it.

If the precursors to today's do-it-yourself indie films were John Cassavetes's influential *Faces* and *Husbands*, then it is surprising to many that nearly forty years later, there is still no public organization providing qualified first-timers with financing in the United States. And although Congress and President Bush approved a taxpayer-funded $700 billion bailout package for Wall Street in late 2008, there is still no bank, NEA, or government-sponsored grant for struggling student or indie filmmakers who desperately need help. Renew Media, a nonprofit organization established in 1990 by the Rockefeller Foundation, does offer media-arts fellowships, but most first and second films are still typically financed by "former friends and now-distant relatives," as the saying goes—the implication being that the filmmaker burned every bridge, spent the money unwisely, or was crushed to a pulp by the Sundance Dream Wrecking Ball.

"If you're making a first film you will probably have to rely on financing from people who have some connection to you, whether they're your relatives or people who have known you all your life," suggests Cinetic Media founder John Sloss. "It's not always the case. You can find someone who wants to be in the game, but it can take a long time to find that person. And as a result the lion's share of first films are financed by family and friends and credit cards while most subsequent films are often financed by the conventional means, because if you're successful and have the ability to pay back your family and friends, or if you evinced clear talent in making your first film, you're going to get noticed and have the ability to go through conventional channels the next time around, which is a much easier route than raising equity financing from private individuals. Of course if you're not successful with your first feature, you probably won't have the conventional means available *or* your family and friends because you won't have sold your film or paid back your investors."

Because the filmmakers who make it have such varied personal stories of how they got there and because there are few surefire approaches to raising hundreds of thousands, if not millions of dollars, those just starting out are often left to their own devices and forced to walk down blind alleys. "There's not one prescribed route, which is what makes it so confusing for people," says *The Hammer* and *Kissing Jessica Stein* producer Eden Wurmfeld. "There are so many things in life where there's a formula of some kind, where you know that if you do X, Y, and Z you'll get from point A to point B. But it's not like that in the film business, so your motto really has to be: 'Try everywhere.' "

Of course, one of the biggest questions filmmakers have surrounds just how much cash they actually need to start shooting and when they can stop soliciting the funds they need. Starting down the runway with just enough cash to get the project aloft could lead to a mad scramble for finishing funds just when the production team should be focused on completing the film. On the flip side, any filmmaker trying to raise $3 to $5 million may have to pound the pavement for years and risk missing his or her window of opportunity to actually make the film. Regardless, it often surprises aspiring filmmakers just how long it can take to raise financing.

"In most cases filmmakers shouldn't expect anything less than a six- to eight-month window from when they begin their fund-raising to the start of principal photography," says Cinetic Media senior executive Matt Littin. "Unfortunately most of them don't realize how long it can take to elicit director, cast, and financier interest; to structure and close financing deals, and then get cash actually flowing in time for preproduction. Filmmakers and producers would have a much better chance of succeeding if they kicked things off earlier than they typically think is necessary."

For one thing, even if a filmmaker gets a financial commitment from a wealthy friend or high-net-worth individual, actually collecting a check is another matter entirely. To see this dilemma vividly played out, aspiring producers and directors need only to recall the scene in *Ed Wood* where the title character is unable to collect a production-financing check he was absolutely sure would be forthcoming.

In other instances, an aspiring producer who has an established director seemingly committed can find the project suddenly dead in the water if the director waffles, delays, or decides to squeeze in an already fully financed project in the meantime. Then when the director drops out, any financing based on his or her participation—along with the participation of the name actors who had hoped to work with the director in a small, intimate project—can also fall away forever.

"Since most projects can't make up-front financial guarantees to talent, the best you can hope is that the actor agrees to be attached, which is only a loose agreement to appear in the film subject to the deal working out and subject to continuing availability," Littin goes on. "The challenge then is trying to secure financing fast enough so you *can* lock in the actor's participation before they drop out and take another job. Similarly, a director may have a preference for your particular film, but if you can't lock in the financing by a certain date, the director may go elsewhere. Unless you can secure participation with pay-or-play offers or hold fees, you risk losing that actor or director to another project."

Unfortunately, new filmmakers often don't give themselves enough of a window to let chicken-or-the-egg issues related to casting and financing fully play out and end up missing their window of opportunity to actually make the film with those elements.

THEY DID IT FOR LESS

For those on the low end of the spectrum, the original inspiration to go for it may be *Filmmaker* magazine articles or Wikipedia entries celebrating Shane Carruth, who reportedly spent $7,000 to make the techno-thriller *Primer*, or perhaps the $218 pegged to director Jonathan Caouette's iMac-assembled documentary *Tarnation*. The truth is, using those projects as a point of reference is totally unrealistic because they were both miracle projects that received theatrical distribution where tens of thousands of films in the same budget range did not. Today's aspiring filmmakers have to be far more realistic and practical when it comes to setting a level of financing that fits the needs of their stories, taking into account the hidden and unforeseen costs that push most budgets past the breaking point. The truth is, despite what anyone may have said on a festival panel, *Primer* did not cost $7,000 and *Tarnation* did not cost $218. Indeed, once *Tarnation* was picked up, clearance costs raised its budget from $218 to $230,000, a significant outlay that specialized film distributors are rarely willing to cover. In fact, most filmmakers who try to shoot their films using figures repeatedly cited online and in *Filmmaker* and *MovieMaker* magazines find themselves dead in the water at the halfway point—frantically begging friends and relatives for the rest of the funds and then brazenly hitting them up a *third* time because they are unable to finish their shoot, let alone afford postproduction.

At the time of its release, Robert Rodriguez's *El Mariachi* was widely reported to have cost $7,000, but Columbia Pictures put $1 million into postproduction to get the film to a stage where it could be exhibited. Many of the famous production figures—such as the $33,000 cobbled together to get *The Blair Witch Project* shot, Neil LaBute's budget of $25,000 to shoot *In the Company of Men*, Darren Aronofsky's $60,000 to make *Pi*, the reported $100,000 budget of *Once*, or Laura Lau and Chris Kentis spending $150,000 of their own savings (over a three-year period) to make *Open Water*—may not be enough to cover principal photography *and* postproduction, since small indie projects always cost far more to shoot and finish than aspiring indie filmmakers realize. Additionally, since the bar is always being raised, filmmakers who are serious must at least shoot in 24p MiniDV or preferably 24p HD to make a first film that can qualify for a spot at a major festival in 2010 and beyond.

The good news is that the money is out there somewhere. "There *are* high-net-worth individuals who definitely seem to be interested in putting money into movies," says *Kill Bill* and *An Inconvenient Truth* producer Lawrence Bender. "There are definitely people interested in indie film these days, but you know every time you make a small movie it's an incredibly difficult process because you never have enough money and you never have enough time. Many times the investors have not been in the film business very long and that creates its own problems in terms of what their expectations are. And many times the financing comes from multiple people or multiple companies, so the ability to hold the money together from many different sources takes an enormous amount of effort and time. And it's just a really hard thing to do."

One thing filmmakers often hear while shopping their screenplays and trying to get their films financed is that a mini-major's distribution executives are interested and would love to help out in some way but cannot because in their or their studio's estimation the project is "execution dependent."

"When you're in the independent arena, the actors are often not a guarantee at the box office and the scripts aren't usually high concept, so distributors or film executives may read the script and say, 'Yes, the script is beautiful but if the director can't deliver what I see on the page, then the script is execution dependent,'" explains *Juno* producer Lianne Halfon, who later produced Rebecca Cammisa's feature documentary *Which Way Home*. "It's a term that people will use when they are passing on the project. It's kind of like someone in a breakup who says, 'It's me, not you,' or the kind of thing the studio executives used to say, which was: 'I would absolutely go see this movie myself, but my company would not make it.' That used to be the way people would say no thank you. Today the line I often hear is: 'It's the kind of thing we would buy in a minute as an acquisition.' In other words: 'If you can raise the money independently, and the film is as good as it looks on paper, then I'll buy it from you as an acquisition when it's done.' It leaves the door open, risk free."

Once filmmakers start the fund-raising process and see how tough it is to get to a yes, many ask themselves: "How long should I keep at this before I decide to lower my expectations and try to reimagine the project in the vein of Richard Linklater's *Tape* with all the action taking place in one room or as some kind of *Xavier: Renegade Angel*–like video game Machinima?" Given the challenges inherent in raising money, filmmakers are advised to create two or even three production budgets, one representing the Escalade version and another envisioning the project along the lines of a Jetta or a Passat. Established filmmakers often swear that the limitations related to their low-budget first or second features actually forced them to be far more imaginative about solving problems during the shoot.

"The reality is that *Swingers* was a much better movie because we weren't able to raise the million and a half we were originally shooting for," says the film's director Doug Liman. "I'm a big believer that for most filmmakers, including myself, you need some limitations in order to force your creativity. I'm just a big believer that giving yourself limitations, whether you're artificially imposing them or, as was the case with *Swingers*, they were being imposed on me, you're forced to be more creative."

Gritty films such as *Personal Velocity* or *Half Nelson* might not have felt as immediate or affecting if they had been made with a bigger budget and a glossier look, as with *Crash*, whose Bob Yari–financed budget was reportedly closer to $8 million. "For us, making our first movie with a budget of just under $1 million was like a huge amount of money," says *Half Nelson* cowriter and editor Anna Boden. "We didn't know what to do with $1 million. We had made movies with three or four people and a video camera before that. We shot our documentary *Young Rebels* and all of our short films on no budget at all, so $1 million seemed luxurious. Instead of having to double as wardrobe, props, art, and craft service, as we did on our short *Gowanus, Brooklyn*, we were able to have a real crew of people who had specific jobs that they knew how to do better than we ever would. Having a budget of that size afforded us an amazing group of talented people to collaborate with on *Half Nelson*."

Because many first films don't get distribution, some regular film financiers recommend keeping the budget of a debut project on the low end. "For a first-time director I would almost always recommend making the film for less than $1 million, or even at a microbudget level," says Kim Bangash. "Sure, you'll be fighting and scraping and up all night cutting corners and begging people for support and trying to get all your equipment for free if you go that route. It's a terrible life during your shoot, but those are the filmmakers I really want to talk to, the ones who can make their films for $100,000 like *Once* or for $300,000 like *Napoleon Dynamite*. The ones who can still come up with good production values despite their budgets."

While budget information is often hard to come by, filmmakers can use the *Variety* or the *Hollywood Reporter* websites to track down published budget figures related to projects similar in tone to the ones they are about to make and use that level as a guideline. "Two of the most important ques-

tions filmmakers need to ask themselves before starting out
are: 'Who is my audience?' and 'If I execute this film correctly or execute it as I envision it, is that audience big
enough to justify whatever the cost is?' " says Sloss, whose
Cinetic Media brokered the sale of *Napoleon Dynamite*, *Little
Miss Sunshine*, and *Under the Same Moon* to Fox Searchlight.
"Finally, they should ask themselves, 'Do I have a way to
actually reach that audience?' You know it seems moronically
simple and obvious, but it's incredible how many filmmakers
don't ever think about that. And it's not even about test marketing. It's just doing comparables in your head, saying,
'Okay, I can envision this film a certain way. Now, where
would it play? And who's going to go see it?' Filmmakers
need to reverse-market from the potential audience and
budget accordingly so that their film, if successful, will
appeal to an audience large enough to support that budget.
It's a distributor's job to recognize that a filmmaker has been
successful and to actually connect the film to that audience,
but it's the filmmaker's responsibility to think in those terms.
None of this is a substitute for good, old-fashioned talent
and attention to story, but it is a necessary component."

To arrive at an appropriate budget level, filmmakers must
balance the needs of their production with the latest average
purchase prices for worldwide rights, which are far lower
than the headline-grabbing sales figures such as the $4 mil-
lion paid for *The Wrestler* in 2008, the $10 million paid for
Hamlet 2 in 2008, the $7 million paid for *Son of Rambow* in
2007, the $10 million paid for *Little Miss Sunshine* in 2006,
the $8 million paid for *Thank You for Smoking* in 2005, or the
$9.3 million paid for *Hustle and Flow* in 2005. Most indie-
film distribution minimum guarantees now fall into a range
somewhere between $200,000 and $3 million. Because savvy
film financiers know this, filmmakers trying to raise $6 to
$9 million without a star actor's commitment in place are

tipping their hand and revealing that they are ignorant of the current acquisitions climate.

SOMETIMES LESS MONEY IS MORE

Of course, there is some argument for eschewing international presales altogether and simply making the film with whatever funds are available by a certain target date within a set six- to nine-month window. "There are a lot of people who set out to raise whatever they think their budget should be who come up with a lot less than they expect," says Liman. "And there's no shortage of filmmakers walking around with commitments for a part of their budget but no way to raise the rest of it. That's why I advise people to just go for it with what they've got. With *Swingers* we were looking for $1.5 million but all we were able to raise was $200,000 and that's what we went with.

"Most sane people are emboldened by the fact that they were able to raise the first $200,000 and so they keep going with the fund-raising to try to get more money," Liman continues. "Maybe they're confident they'll be able to raise the rest of it as opposed to thinking, 'We were looking for $1.5 million and we've got $200,000. What about just making the film for $200,000? What about making the film for the money we have, rather than for what we're hoping to get? What about just doing it now?' Obviously that approach made all the difference with *Swingers*. If I had waited to get the rest I'd probably still be waiting, trying to raise that other $1.3 million. Along the way I would've found somebody else willing to write a $200,000 check and then years later, I'd be saying, 'I have $400,000 or maybe $600,000 raised. All I have to do now is find the other $900,000.' So many films languish or just never get off the ground because filmmakers are stuck with one way to do things. But it's important to figure out what you have and see if you can make the movie for that.

"I was only able to find one person willing to write a check for $125,000," Liman recalls. "It doesn't seem like a very smart investment: a film about a guy whining about his ex-girlfriend and waiting for her to call for two hours, and starring a bunch of unknown actors. It's just not a great sales pitch. And even though Jon [Favreau] and Vince [Vaughn] would actually perform scenes from the script for investors, that's all I was able to raise initially. I ultimately raised another $75,000. So what happened was we had the $200,000 and I turned to my producer-partner, Nicole LaLoggia, who was also my housemate at the time, and said, 'If we can come up with a budget that's under $200,000, we can make this film right now.' And of course, her initial answer was: 'It's impossible.' But then I was like: 'Well, let's reevaluate every assumption that you would normally make and then just start over.' Because in the movie world, $200,000 is nothing, but in the real world, that's a lot of cash. If I had $200,000 in a suitcase in my car right now, people would be like: 'Holy shit! Where'd you get all that money?' So that was literally the way I approached it and sort of got people to rethink their perspectives: 'You mean by walking in with a suitcase full of $200,000 we can't go make a movie?' And we said, 'Fine, we're actually making the movie.' "

But filmmakers who hope to emulate the *Swingers* business model should know that Liman took big risks and unconventional shortcuts—such as serving as director and cinematographer—that all managed to pay off. "On *Swingers* I had to level the playing field. A normal set has grips and electrics and lights and a generator. There are usually about forty people in your crew, but on *Swingers* we had twelve," Liman explains. "We had a production assistant whose job it was to put in larger-wattage consumer-grade lightbulbs in existing fixtures, and that is how we lit the sets. I wanted to be totally free with the camera, so I said, 'I'm just going to use normal lights,' which is something I hadn't seen before and had no idea whether it would really work. It just seemed like it would. We could have ended up with a film that looked awful. In fact I had said to Jon Favreau, 'This film's not going to look great but it's going to have great performances and great energy but I have to compromise something and I'm compromising the lighting.'

"After I decided to go for it with just regular old household lightbulbs, it took us a couple of days to get the dailies back," Liman remembers. "We started shooting on a Wednesday and Friday night I got the dailies. One of the first scenes we shot was with Jon on the phone with Vince Vaughn, where Vince is trying to convince him to go to Vegas. It's a really complicated shot because I gave Jon a cordless phone. Normally he would just be static but I told him to wander all over the apartment. I designed this fairly complicated shot: it's 360 degrees and the camera is going all around him while he goes in the kitchen and turns on the lights, then opens the refrigerator and turns off the lights. For a film where we had an hour and a half to shoot that scene, I basically made it a lot more complicated than it needed to be. And when I watched the dailies on Friday night, I literally cried, because I had taken a huge risk and it had actually paid off."

Since it worked the first time, Liman took the same approach but raised the stakes considerably with his sophomore effort. "With *Swingers* under my belt I went off to do *Go*, an independent film, and it was budgeted at $3 million, with a car chase set in Vegas in the script," Liman continues. "And the producers were like: 'You can't do the car chase if your budget is only $3 million.' So I said, 'Well, I did *Swingers* for $200,000, so if we shoot the rest of *Go* for

$200,000 we can have $2.8 million for the car chase,' which
is basically how we did it. It wasn't that dramatic a difference
but we were really cheap on a lot of things so we could spend
more on other things."

Producer rep, consultant, and adviser Peter Broderick is
another advocate of the "just do it" approach. "These days if
people can find a movie they are passionate about that can be
made for $100,000 to $200,000, then there are actually lots
of places they can find the money, particularly if they've
already made a film that impresses people or shows they have
talent," he explains. "I think there's less reason than ever for
filmmakers who want to end up making movies they're really
passionate about to go through conventional channels.
When you see the amazing stuff that's being done on tiny
budgets where there is creative risk-taking and where—for
better or worse—it's actually the film the filmmaker wanted
to make rather than someone else's idea of what's marketable
or what's packageable, then I think those are the filmmakers
who are going to find the resources one way or another to
keep making movies."

Even with major names attached, filmmakers working
with edgier scripts need to err on the conservative side and
try to keep a lid on costs. "We deliberately embraced low-
budget filmmaking on *Trainspotting* because we knew that
normally nobody goes to see drug films, nobody," says *Slumdog Millionaire* director Danny Boyle. "But we had this idea
that we would do it differently, we would approach it differently and that it would be more of a carnival. Film4 gave
us the money but they rightly limited it to 1.6 million
pounds. And we kept the budget low rather than looking for
'the rest of the financing' elsewhere. We didn't finance it
through family and friends because it is not much of a tradition in Britain and because the film culture is not the same.
It's not embedded in Britain the way it is in America.

Although you hear the odd stories of people financing films themselves, we didn't with *Trainspotting*. We had a very good relationship with Film4 in that particular case so we didn't need to."

This ethos follows what many working filmmakers and specialized film distribution executives advise, which is that just because a filmmaker or production team suddenly has access to capital, boosting the production budget is not always in the best interests of the project. "The tougher the material, the more you want to keep an eye on the budget," says Stephen Gilula of Fox Searchlight. "A perfect example of that was *Boys Don't Cry*. We bought worldwide rights for $5 million and people thought that was a high price at the time. But since it was produced for just $2.5 million, the film went on to be successful for everyone."

Indeed, Hilary Swank won an Oscar for her performance and the film grossed $11.5 million theatrically in the United States. "In some ways, the reason *Boys Don't Cry* was as good as it was, in my opinion, was because we kept the budget low enough that we could take really gigantic creative risks, like putting Hilary Swank in the lead and giving Kimberly [Peirce] her first shot at directing a film," recalls Christine Vachon of Killer Films. "I don't think at a higher budget of $4 million or $5 million we would have been able to make the film that we did. It would have been a different movie. It worked at the amount of money we had and I think there was a reason the movie got made that way."

RUNNING OUT OF MONEY

The tension between making an indie film for as little as possible and running out of money in the middle of a shoot is a serious problem for a lot of filmmakers, including many names that would surprise people. However inspirational their stories may be, running dry and having the film shut down—often for good—is one of the major pitfalls that can derail a production and prevent even the most talented directors and producers from finishing their films.

Liman experienced major financing hiccups on his second film, *Go*. "For *Swingers* I raised the money, but I didn't personally raise the money for *Go*," he says. "Producer Mickey Liddell raised the money. I never really asked where the money came from—I think it was from [French distributor] Pathé. We spent four and a half months casting the movie. We cast the entire film with Sarah Polley, Katie Holmes, Jay Mohr, Scott Wolf, William Fichtner, and Taye Diggs—a great cast. But about six weeks out from shooting, Pathé said, 'Y'know what? We don't like the cast,' and they yanked our budget. That happened on a Friday afternoon and Mickey didn't tell us. Without telling me that had happened, he secretly sent the script to Miramax, figuring that since they distributed *Swingers*, maybe they'd just step in, but on Monday morning Miramax passed. So on Monday, Mickey called us and said, 'Don't bother coming in, we're shutting down.' Because if anyone was going to pick up 'a Doug Liman film' at that point, it would be Miramax, so it wasn't even worth going to the other studios if they wouldn't do it.

"But Paul Rosenberg, who was one of the other producers of *Go*, said, 'No, we're not giving up.' So John August [the writer], Paul, and myself sat in the office on Monday calling everyone we knew at whatever studio. It was more dramatic than anything that's ever been in any of my films because we were desperate, we were fighting for our lives. Paul would call up some executive at Sony and talk for about a minute and then say, 'Here, I'm going to give you John August,' since we were all in the same room, and John would take over that phone call and pitch the movie. Then Paul would be on the phone with somebody else and after a minute he'd hand me the phone and I would be pitching the movie to another executive."

Their frantic efforts call to mind the scene in *The Bourne Identity* where the entire roster of Treadstone assassins is activated by Chris Cooper's character, Alexander Conklin. "The office production assistants were just frantically xeroxing the screenplay and delivering them all over town. And by Tuesday morning we had half a dozen studios interested in doing the movie. And by Tuesday afternoon we were in a conference room at Creative Artists Agency—they were my agents—and one by one, heads of studios were coming in with their executives and pitching why their studio should be the home of the movie. It was a really dramatic turnaround. And we picked TriStar on Tuesday night and were back in production Wednesday morning. Then Miramax called Wednesday afternoon and said they wanted to make an offer for the movie. But there was some hostility in the office for Miramax for having put us through all that and now, just because everybody else was interested, they were interested."

The lesson to aspiring filmmakers of unbonded projects is to escrow all funds until the entire amount is in place and to keep the fund-raising effort going even after they are actually in production and the shoot is well under way, since this situation can happen to even the best producers.

"The toughest time I can remember was when I produced *Lock, Stock and Two Smoking Barrels*," remembers *Layer Cake* director and Guy Ritchie's longtime producer Matthew Vaughn. "We had no money, and two weeks before filming, the financing we *did* have collapsed. Any little bit of money I had put into the film was gone. And a few actual gangsters we had cast in it said they were going to break my legs if it didn't happen because they had told all their friends they were going to be in a movie. I've only ever had one panic attack in my life and that was the time I had it, when I thought, 'I'm broke. I'm going to have two broken kneecaps, and I'm not going to have the chance to make my movie.' "

While Vaughn's 2007 Paramount Pictures–financed *Stardust* budget approached $70 million and starred Robert De Niro, Michelle Pfeiffer, Claire Danes, and Sienna Miller in a special effects–driven fantasy, the initial *Lock, Stock* budget had started out at $3 million before the project fell apart. "I just sat down and rolled up my sleeves and got the budget down to $900,000," recalls Vaughn. "Then I begged, borrowed, and stole and managed to get it. But try raising nearly one million dollars in a pinch."

Many first-time filmmakers who find themselves in need of $300,000 in completion funds after their films have been shot are often shocked to learn that the last investors to come in at this level hold all the cards and can demand 100 percent of the upside in exchange for providing the money. Filmmakers should not assume that they can get finishing funds as a flat loan or at 15 percent interest. The deal in these situations requires filmmakers to subordinate or even *burn* the project's initial investors and give up ownership of the film and possibly even the copyright. The only thing the filmmakers get out of the transaction is the ability to get the project finished and entered into a festival. There are no favors in indie film when it comes to money. Believe it.

Long before he established his directing credentials with *William Shakespeare's Romeo + Juliet*, Baz Luhrmann came extremely close to having his financing pulled from his first film, *Strictly Ballroom*, in 1992. It was a close shave that might have prevented the director of *Australia* and *Moulin Rouge!* from becoming a filmmaker, and a cautionary tale for aspiring filmmakers: until the funds are actually in the bank and irrevocable, they should not be considered a sure thing.

"Sadly the man who was my producer on *Strictly Ballroom*, and who had put up $1 million to finance the film and stand alongside me on that one, died just as we were about to roll cameras," he recalls. "And we just thought the film was over. His family wanted to pull the money and they told his widow that she should have nothing to do with filmmaking. But she stood in and said, 'My husband could tell when something was going to work and I'm going to honor his vision.' And that film, by the way, went on to make $18 million worldwide and won the *Prix de la Jeunesse* at the 1992 Cannes Film Festival and many awards throughout the United States. We had to overcome impossible odds to follow our vision and invent our own way over our obstacles."

HOW MUCH IS EACH SHARE?

As the fund-raising rolls into action, one question filmmakers often have is how much each share in the project should be worth. Setting the price too high may limit the number of interested or full-share investors, but setting the price too low could leave the project at risk of never reaching critical mass. Filmmakers should not expect that they can revisit their first-in investors for a second round of financing. Nearly all investors will look askance at the prospect of having their shares diluted or having to re-up because the filmmakers didn't do their math correctly.

"When we first decided to make *Kissing Jessica Stein* I said, 'We're never going to be able to put together the money we need to make this film with shares of $2,500. It's just not going to be enough to solve the problem,' " recalls producer Wurmfeld. "But when you're dealing with small fish—which in some cases we really were—they're not going to be able to put in big money. They don't have $10,000 or $25,000 or $50,000 lying around. We did have investors that were coming in at a higher figure than $2,500, but the majority of our investors were actually coming in at a smaller number.

"One of the things we had happen, which was actually quite moving, was that a group of Heather Juergensen's high school friends got together to buy one share, so we had eight people who had put together $2,500 in little drabs and dribbles," Wurmfeld continues. "It turned out to be a total pain logistically because of the structure of the fund-raising deal and how you have to issue a K-1 to each member of a limited liability company for their tax returns. I think we had forty members and I think you are allowed one hundred all together. We had a total of forty at varying rates."

Kissing Jessica Stein was half financed by a single dot-com investor whom the production team had met late in the fund-raising process. But filmmakers today should not count on such serendipitous encounters or miracle investments, especially not from the one high-net-worth individual they know or roomed with in college. Many filmmakers secretly base their entire business model and all the years of sacrifice and hardship it takes to write a script on the assumption that when the time comes, they can ask the one wealthy individual they know for 50 to 100 percent of a multimillion-dollar indie-film production budget. They feel they only have to wait for the right time to pop the question and the money will be forthcoming—since this college buddy or family friend could easily afford to finance an entire slate of low-budget films. But filmmakers should know that this is a flawed and extremely dangerous assumption. People's lives can change, and the millionaire or billionaire who was supportive and encouraging at one point will eventually get married or divorced, have children, create trusts for their kids that tie up significant capital, change his or her personal priorities, spend a large portion of his or her portfolio on wind farms or Maseratis, lose money in a housing crisis, or simply fall out of touch. For these reasons, filmmakers should never base a business model on the assumption or delusion that one rich person is going to come through once the script is in good shape. Chances are it won't happen.

THE STOCK MARKET'S IMPACT

Just as the lunar orbit affects the tide, the run-up or deceleration of the equity markets—which includes the New York Stock Exchange, NASDAQ, the American Stock Exchange, and other regional and foreign stock exchanges—often affects the average person's willingness to jump into illiquid investments such as indie films. Strangely enough, the best time to raise production funds may not be when Google's share price hits $600 again, when Boeing reverses its slide, or right after Time Warner finally unwinds AOL, but when the market begins to level off from a high or a dramatic low. Because there were dozens of terrific, always more conservative investments to consider, many filmmakers trying to get their projects off the ground in the late 1990s and early years of the twenty-first century were actually hampered by the first dot-com bubble and, later on, the booming home equity markets that crashed in 2007, triggering bank failures and some of the steepest single-day market declines in history in late 2008. However, it remains an open question just how recessionary forces—the bursting of a credit bubble, a banking liquidity crisis, commodity devaluations like those seen in early 2008, the dissolution of two pillars of the investment banking world, Merrill Lynch and Lehman Brothers, in late 2008—or a possible depression in 2009 and the Madoff hedge fund scandal will impact filmmakers' ability to access capital from private equity in 2010 and beyond.

Indeed, the best time to raise independent-film financing from private sources may be when the stock market is flat or even falling and when interest rates aren't offering appealing returns, since there are few places where cash will appreciate at an aggressive level and the threshold for taking money out of equities and treasuries is lower.

"There's a potential paradox in that when the stock market is going through the roof and people feel like they're doing well, it's actually harder to find money for films because they just can't bear to have their money out of the market," says Sloss. "Arguably, when the market isn't doing well, then provided someone has money, a film investment isn't going to be taking cash away from any huge returns, and symbolizes just another risk investment in a portfolio. So the argument could be made that when the stock market isn't advancing in double digits—provided people haven't lost all their money—those who have taken profits may feel more comfortable investing in films. It hasn't been my experience that economic hard times or even recessions have negatively impacted or discouraged people from trying to make films, though very few people consider a first film to be a savvy economic investment. Typically friends and family invest in someone's first film because they have some income they can afford to part with and they want to be supportive."

Los Angeles–based filmmakers with connections to Menlo Park's Sand Hill Road, where most of today's blue-chip dot-com companies and several video game publishers were first financed, may be able to access rich entrepreneurs living among 30 percent of the country's independent venture-capital firms, but those companies do not typically put money in one-off projects such as film productions. Those living in New York can troll for dot-com millionaires and hedge fund managers who cashed out of the equity markets before the gas, housing, credit, and banking crises of 2008. Of course, in uncertain times, these individuals may be looking for a more conservative place to park their net worth, something that filmmakers should always address head-on.

"One of the first times we raised private equity funds for a series of movies in 1996 a guy said to me, 'Look, I'm making a 40 percent return on my money in the capital markets right now. Why should I be in the movies?' And I said, 'You shouldn't! If you're looking for money you shouldn't be in this business,' " recalls longtime indie-film producer Ted Hope. "I recently got a call from a fairly new producer who has had the good fortune and smarts to be involved with a couple of hits. One of his films was a low-budget Sundance hit that got picked up for distribution and won some awards. It was by all accounts a hit, but when he and the other producer were going through the revenue, they still were in the hole. He wondered how the business could work when even small films don't earn their money back. All I could tell him was that it is a crazy business and you have to find people who want to be in it for other reasons than making money. And there never is a shortage. But as smart as most of this money that is creating today's product glut is, a lot more people will still *lose* money than will make it."

So where is the smart money? Following the dissolution of several leading banks in 2008 and the ongoing mortgage crisis, filmmakers can look to high-net-worth individuals with holdings in the Web, video game, and technology sectors and to software engineers.

"Before you call your uncle or your dentist looking for money, I would somehow scout around for people who still have dot-com money burning a hole in their pockets. Those are the people you have to find," explains director Dylan Kidd. "There are a lot of people who actually did get out before the bubble burst: thirty-five-year-old billionaires who never have to work again, are living in New York, and are into film. These are interesting, committed, passionate people trying to figure out what to do with all their money and I think they are an untapped resource."

TOUGH PROJECTS, TOUGH PROSPECTS

Many aspiring indie filmmakers think they are staying true to their stories by making their screenplays and their finished films relentlessly, even punishingly downbeat without so much as a single breather for script readers or audiences to pause and reflect. "You have filmmakers who say, 'I want to make a movie about the most depressing thing you could possibly think of, but I think it's interesting, and by the way, I'm not going to have a happy ending, an uplifting message, or a scene where the protagonist gets to win even for a moment, because it's cooler or because that's keeping it real,' " says Marian Koltai-Levine of Picturehouse. "But the questions they should ask themselves are: 'What movie are you comparing yours to that worked that way? What films do you know of in that style that got distribution and connected with audiences?' I mean, look at what the real grosses are. You want to make a film just like *The Squid and the Whale*? Fine. It made $3 million, because remember, exhibitors often keep more than half of the box-office grosses on specialized films. So the question is: 'Do you really think people are going to go see your film?' "

Uplifting scenes or at least a glimpse of the possibility of happiness, romance, humor, or victory, however remote, are critically important to the marketing of independent films, since trailers and television ads cannot be made up only of discouraging, depressing, or disturbing images. While a studio marketing department would never want to position something as gritty as *Requiem for a Dream* or *Buffalo '66* as a laugh riot, challenging films such as *Half Nelson* and *The Div-*

ing Bell and the Butterfly had moments of humor and triumph of the spirit to mitigate what might otherwise be tough-to-market material.

"*The Diving Bell* was a very difficult film to get made," recalls Miramax president Daniel Battsek. "If you were looking at it in a very hard-hearted, factual way, there were many things about it that made it *impossible* to make, and then impossible to make it a commercial success. But what literally gave *The Diving Bell* its lifeblood was that it was about a man who despite everything discovered a joie de vivre, the desire to live, and everything about the human existence that he still wanted to experience. What really connected to people was that someone even in that devastating moment still had this incredible soul and this incredible heart and the will to live, which is very different from being in that position and wanting to die. Jean-Dominique Bauby didn't want to die. He thought he did and then he realized he really didn't."

Rather than giving the marketing department an uplifting scene to include in the trailer or a PG-rated sequence that can be shown on E!, *Entertainment Tonight*, or NYT.com, many independent filmmakers refuse to budge since they are keeping it real. In staying true to their stories, which are often unflinchingly autobiographical, filmmakers make it impossible for their films to get a distribution deal. Others worry that adding moments of happiness or hopefulness will somehow reveal their secret that not everything in their script is *true* or will violate the truth of the story. As a result, when they receive suggestions from a producer to lighten the mood of at least a handful of scenes to give the audience at least one moment of lightness, they defiantly object. What these filmmakers need to realize is that narrative fiction is different from autobiographical documentary or the cinematic retelling of a personal diary, and that the lives of their characters must have at least a few moments of optimism and hope.

"We thought a lot about suggestions to make the character and the story lighter than what people who had read the script imagined it was going to be," explains *Half Nelson* editor and cowriter Anna Boden. "Throughout the process, particularly when we were looking for financing, there was a lot of fear that this was going to be a really dark movie, but we had never pictured it like that. We always imagined it with the ending that it has, which we think gives a lot of hope. And also I think the character of Drey adds a real light to the film, as do the moments of humor that Dan Dunne has. So we never pictured it as this incredibly dark film, but when people would read the script, that's kind of what would come to mind.

"We spent two years looking for financing for *Half Nelson* before we made the short, *Gowanus, Brooklyn*, and another year and a half before meeting our producer-financier Jamie Patricof, who ended up making the film with us," recalls Boden. "We shot *Gowanus, Brooklyn* in May 2005 for less than $1,000 on MiniDV to get it in the can, and then once it got into Sundance we ended up spending another $3,500 in post and we got a really nice deal to go to 35mm. We had already written *Half Nelson*, but wanted to capture its story and spirit in twenty minutes so we could show people what we wanted to do with the full-length feature. It was also a great way to workshop the characters and practice the craft of filmmaking without having the stakes be very high."

The short tied with another short film for the Grand Jury Prize in short filmmaking in 2004 at Sundance, and Boden and Ryan Fleck were able to raise $1 million with the help of their agent Craig Kestel, of the William Morris Agency, who introduced them to producer-financier Patricof of Hunting Lane Films.

The pair stayed true to their vision, however, and didn't soften Dan Dunne's story, believing that the inherent decency of its central character and his relationship with Drey would outshine his numerous personal demons and challenges. "When we finally found the people who ended up producing the film they really got on board," Boden recalls. "I think that there was sometimes a little bit of concern about certain scenes and making sure that they weren't reading too dark, but ultimately they were really supportive of what we had in mind. And once we were actually on the set and shooting it, and they were feeling the character and feeling those moments, they were kind of okay with everything."

Confidence in a script's merits and the passion to see the project through regardless of the setbacks en route to production are critical to any fund-raising effort, but even more so with challenging or offbeat material, such as Todd Haynes's *Safe* or John Cameron Mitchell's *Shortbus*.

"Passion is still the main thing that brings money to a project and makes a movie great," explains Hope. "Filmmakers should go back and figure out why their movie really has to get made and not give some sort of cynical pitch but learn to really talk about it from the heart. When I try to get any movie made I talk about the movies I love, why I love them, why this film fits into that category, and why I'm willing to put in my time with this filmmaker and this particular script. It takes the average indie at least five years to get made, so you'd better love the film and the filmmaker if you are going to invest that much of your life into a single project."

Surprisingly, even Hope, an icon in the independent-film world, has repeatedly experienced the same disappointment and heartache as the armies of unknown filmmakers who are just getting started. "Along the way, we've had scripts that agencies banned, or I've heard time and time again, 'You're making that film? Well, good for you, Ted! Good for you, staying with it for four years . . . *sucker!*' It's just what you hear," he says. "And then hopefully when it gets made, people will wake up. But I keep hoping that one day the industry will change so people will say, 'Yeah! This really should get made.' "

Hope's determination, resolve, and unshakable belief in the projects he backs may draw skepticism from certain circles, but it has led to films such as *American Splendor*, *The Savages*, and *The Ice Storm*, among others. For that reason, Hope believes that confidence in the worthiness of a script and an infectious drive to see the project through are critical to any fund-raising effort. "Every time I set out to make a film I have to get really worked up and convince people, even with my track record. Every time!" he adds. "I make films that people don't want to see made, and once they are, audiences don't want to go to them until they've actually heard good things from somebody they trust, and then it's like: 'Oh, it was such a great idea.' "

FINANCING TODAY'S HIGH-DEFINITION PROJECTS

Today, keeping the budget below $200,000 usually means shooting on "prosumer" digital-video (DV) either on 24p MiniDV or high-definition (HD) cameras. (For theoretical indie-film budgets that may be used as a reference point for readers' own productions, please see Appendix I.) "The savings from shooting digitally comes more in the size of the crew that is necessary because you need to do less in terms of lighting and you're able to get into practical locations you would never be able to get into with a normal film crew," explains Ira Deutchman, founder of Emerging Pictures. "That reduces your budgets substantially and allows you to find all sorts of real locations that require less prep from set dressing and set building. If you're going to film in a tiny kitchen with a normal film crew, you usually have to either build it or just shoot it from a single angle, but DV allows you to shoot several angles in a real kitchen."

A viable business model for today's low-budget HD filmmakers was established by Independent Digital Entertainment (InDigEnt), which blazed a trail in the early years of this decade with individual production budgets below $300,000 and a blueprint for democratizing whatever profits come in from the sale of the completed film for distribution.

"In essence the InDigEnt model was to make a film for as little as legally possible and provide gross participation to everybody who works on the film, from the cast to the crew," explains Micah Green. "The financing for InDigEnt came from the Independent Film Channel, which acted as the equity financier. They took a basic cable window on all films produced by InDigEnt, but what it means is that the initial investment is in essence recouped when the film is made, so that any money that comes into the film after that goes to a gross participant, and anyone who worked on the film generally is a gross participant. So people saw money whether the film was sold for $100,000 or $10 million.

"Generally this means that the cast can go into the project knowing that if the film makes money and the producer makes money, they too will get something and usually they know exactly how much that's going to be," Green continues. "And in the case of *Tadpole*, which Miramax bought for $5 million in 2002, people who worked on the film received sizable checks that were higher than they would have earned via the traditional model."

Indeed, for those who worked on *Tadpole*, a single point in the film was worth $50,000 regardless of what position they filled during the production. "The idea was that a huge chunk of all revenue would be given to the filmmakers to allocate among the people who make the film, and that everybody who works on it gets some piece of first-dollar gross," adds Sloss, whose Cinetic Media represented and sold InDigEnt films in the marketplace. "This means that without any deduction, if a dollar came in from the exploitation of the film, anyone with a point of first-dollar gross got a penny. One of the primary goals behind InDigEnt was to combat the cynicism of back-end accounting in Hollywood where people felt it was nonexistent."

After eight years, InDigEnt closed its doors in January 2007 and had its final release, Andrew Wagner's May-December love story *Starting Out in the Evening*, distributed late that year. Looking back, Sloss said he was pleased with the company's successes and its legacy. "I think the business model combated some of the cynicism in the creative world about whether there can be a real back end. I'm very happy with that model: I think it lasted as long as it should and it did its job. And I think we made some cool movies."

While the InDigEnt model is easily applicable to today's low-budget productions hoping to defer new salaries and shift much of the financial risk to the filmmakers themselves, getting name actors to sign on for the promise of gross points in a MiniDV or HD feature may be a challenge, since the fact that most independently financed projects never get theatrical distribution is well known.

"After *Tadpole* was bought at Sundance I found that a lot of producers—many of them in New York—were trying to imitate the InDigEnt model and were focusing more on the digital format than on the fact that it was the deal structure that enabled the film to get made the way it did," says Green. "It's actors who bring inherent value to a project, and they are willing to work in low-budget movies but aren't willing to be taken advantage of financially by producers. That's why there have been very few producers who have been able to sell that model."

Digital is a viable format for making an independent film as long as by "digital" today's filmmakers mean 24p HD and not the blurry MiniDV of *Blair Witch* or *Tarnation*. Tomorrow's Sundance and Slamdance stars can feel okay about not shooting on 16mm or 35mm film. "There's the obvious benefits of not having to yell 'Cut' anymore because now the 'film' is cheap. But what I was excited about and what I got other filmmakers excited about was working with the smaller digital cameras," says director and InDigEnt cofounder Gary Winick. "When you work with the smaller digital cameras, you can do huge things creatively. My idea with InDigEnt was to give experienced filmmakers a chance to work with these little cameras and make stories in a very different way than they would when making a 35mm movie. Part of what they can do, which you can't easily do in 35mm, is to rework scenes as you're going, to have two or three cameras going simultaneously, to be able to sneak into subways and go wherever you want with the camera, and to have crews of only ten to twelve people.

"Once people started doing it, they got converted pretty easily," Winick continues. "And in terms of the distribution side, I think this still stands true, a good film is a good film. If the film is working, then people are not really questioning the merits of the format. Of course, what's great is that the quality is getting better as we speak, so from the blowups to the cameras to the facilities, everything is getting better on a level where it's really exciting. With InDigEnt we weren't trying to make the digital video look like film, we were trying to give it a new aesthetic. And the directors of photography, like Maryse Alberti and Tom Richmond and Ellen Kuras, have been interested in pushing that aesthetic, not to make it look like film but to make it fit the story. That's really what we were trying to offer filmmakers, a new creative way of doing things."

Sloss, who cofounded InDigEnt with Winick and whose company Cinetic Media acted as sales agent for all InDigEnt projects, believes that as HD-camera technology catches up with traditional film—if it hasn't already with the introduction of the 3K RED Scarlet and the 5K RED Epic—a new business model will further democratize the indie-film sector. "Within a couple of years there are going to be 24p HD video cameras that are the size of the MiniDV cameras used at InDigEnt," Sloss says. "And so it's really just going to be about whether filmmakers want to use 24p HD cameras in terms of the ease of motion and other benefits you get, while the look will eventually be almost identical to film." One of the newer cameras that may be a game-changer for indie filmmakers is the RED Scarlet, a tiny ⅔-inch 3K camera that will provide enormous chip resolution from a small form factor.

LOW-BUDGET INDIE VS. HIGH-BUDGET BLOCKBUSTER

"How much your film should be made for is an almost impossible question to answer, but the reality is that all films, be they big-budget studio blockbusters or low-budget indies, have to fit into viable economic models," explains Lionsgate president Tom Ortenberg. "Whether it's due to cast or production value, the script or a certain director, foreign sales or a project's inherent ancillary value based on genre, the real answer is that films shouldn't cost more than they need to. And independent films have to cost even *less* because the economic models of the business won't support anything more than that. Most domestic-rights acquisitions cap out near $5 million and often far less.

"The good news is that movies made for a few hundred thousand dollars like *Open Water* can sell for several times that amount," Ortenberg continues. "We bought worldwide rights for $2.5 million and ended up grossing $30 million domestically, and the film did terrific business in many foreign territories as well. The producers made a lot more than the $2.5 million we originally paid them, so of course you could argue that they might have been able to spend a little bit more making the film. But they didn't need to and it paid off hugely for everyone involved."

"If you're going to work with experimental-type filmmaking with an unknown cast, you'd better be making it for $500,000 or less," suggests Cassian Elwes of William Morris Independent, who with Rena Ronson sold Courtney Hunt's *Frozen River* to Sony Pictures Classics in 2008. "For projects with cast, filmmakers should remember there is a cap for what a distributor will pay to acquire even a hit film at Sundance. So I think that making an independent film for more than $5 million without American distribution in place is probably the top range filmmakers should be gambling in."

First- and second-time filmmakers shouldn't peg their budgets to the $5 million it cost to make *Greek Wedding*, the $8 million spent on *The Good Girl*, the 6 million pounds it took to make *28 Days Later*, the $15 million reportedly spent on *Sideways*, or the $20 million that gave *The Brothers Bloom* its ambitious production values and impressive cinematography. The problem with production budgets in this range is that they are far above what most unconnected people could ever hope to raise from friends and family, and they require the participation of major stars and the deal-brokering prowess of major agencies, international sales agents, or established production entities stepping in to handle financing.

WHAT IS GAP FINANCING?

Most aspiring filmmakers have heard or read about gap financing but are unclear what it actually is or how to go about securing it. Gap financing is a form of bridge loan from a bank—and being a loan it must be repaid—that covers budget shortfalls on films that are partially financed by overseas presales. These budget gaps, which can reach as high as 20 percent of a film's budget, are often financed by banks such as Comercia, U.S. Bancorp, Natixis, Imperial Capital Bank, Union Bank of California, Royal Bank of Ireland, Royal Bank of Scotland, Barclays, and others that provide the financing to make the film until remaining overseas distribution rights can be sold by international sales agents.

At that point, the bank loan is repaid with interest from incoming revenues. Banks that do gap financing typically lend at aggressive rates and at terms that aren't particularly favorable to the filmmakers, but few independent producers are in a position to argue, since the risk involved with financing movies is significant. Some filmmakers erroneously believe that they can skip the presales step and secure gap financing based on a name actor's commitment alone, but in fact gap financing is triggered only after a bank's analysis and approval of firm presale or distribution contracts that a filmmaker's sales agent or representative has secured.

"Banks are generally not a good source of film financing because, except for a small portion of low-risk gap financing, they are involved only insofar as lending against contracts where distributors agree to pay producers upon delivery of the movie, but that's only at the very last stage in the financing," explains Sloss. "In a 'negative pickup,' a filmmaker would use a contract from a distributor that promises to pay the production company a promised amount if the film's producer delivers a movie made in accordance with the screenplay, with the actors the producer has promised. The producer can then take that promise to a bank and borrow against it, using the loan to fund the production budget and actually make the film."

"When considering a gap loan, lenders look for certain minimum criteria to be fulfilled. For a typical senior loan—up to 20 percent of a film's budget—international sales estimates from a reputable source must show 200 percent coverage of the loan in a conservative, or 'low,' scenario," explains Cinetic Media's Matt Littin. "Most banks—such as Comerica or Bank of Ireland—also require one or two pre-sales to be in place prior to funding. Filmmakers can sometimes save time by connecting with a sales company that doubles as a buyer. Integrated companies such as Maximum or Wild Bunch, or even specialized divisions of the U.S. studios, can trigger loans by simultaneously providing sales estimates and licensing rights in certain territories. In some cases, nimble lenders such as CinemaNX will consider gap loans without any presales, or larger loans—up to 40 percent of a budget—sometimes called 'supergap.' "

The influx of billionaire investors into the arena of independent-film financing has changed the nature of gap financing since 2005 and has shifted the meaning of the term somewhat, since there is now often far less of a gap to cover. "The bigger independently financed films, the more commercial films, the films with stars, films with commercial genres today are often backed by billionaires or large film funds," explains Green. "The current model, which was not the model even two years ago, for how these movies are often getting financed is that one of these financiers commits the financing before the film is cast and then works with a foreign sales agent and an agency, like CAA or one of the others, to package the film with actors that help offset the production risk, to a point at which, based on projections alone, they feel they're covering anywhere from 60 to 100 percent of the budget out of foreign presales. Then they'll cash-flow the entire movie and fully finance it with no presales, based on a presale model, in partnerships that allow them to service the film through a foreign sales agency. Then they'll sell North American distribution at some point before production, during production, or as a completed film.

"Now, frequently, on the high-end material, major-talent-interest projects, you can get these movies fully financed with Groundswell, the Winchester Fund, River Road, Steve Samuels, and Endgame," continues Green. "These companies will fully finance movies without having sold any territories. And because they are working only with high-end talent and are confident that they will get the numbers they need to out of foreign presales, they don't need to wait for sales to happen in order to prove that it's a viable project. We work hand in hand with these companies to bring them into projects, to help them package their projects in a way that we all believe is going to cover their risk significantly, or a chunk of it."

Most independent filmmakers don't know any billionaires or leading talent agents they can call to arrange financing, but it is important for directors and producers working with lower budgets to know how these deals are increasingly assembled. "The situation is much better than it used to be," says Green. "It used to be that your only resource was friends and family, or a studio. The bigger movies that found their way to independent financiers were films that studios refused to make, that got put into turnaround, or that were never in development, and then they find their way eventually to some consortium of amateur investors. Today what is happening frequently is that when an agency recognizes high-end material, it will take the film to a financier, who will agree to fully finance the film with no sales, and that could be a budget as high as $3 million or more. So this is only a good thing. And it's also the reason we have so many more big movies being made today without distribution."

Given the recent cascade of financial shocks, hedge fund losses, and bailout plans for car manufacturers, banking firms, and insurance companies reeling from the mortgage crisis, private equity's interest in film financing may dry up in 2009, 2010, and possibly into 2012. Even so, enterprising independent filmmakers will always find a way, despite the rejection, toil, and privation.

"However you do it, whether you write a business plan and go back to your hometown to get the money from a consortium of dentists or whether you go trotting around from studio to studio, it's always tough," says *Sideways* director Alexander Payne, whose first feature, *Citizen Ruth*, was financed by Miramax for $3.5 million. "When you're just starting out they're both hard roads to follow and neither implies greater freedom or hardship."

4. Seeking Legal Advice
CHEAPER THAN YOUR LIFE

Independent filmmakers think of lawyers the way college students think of doctors in the student health clinic. They know they may end up having to talk to one if they engage in risky behavior such as drinking too much or having unprotected sex, but they pray nothing bad will happen to them. And just like college students, independent filmmakers also wait too long to talk to someone, until things go from bad to worse and they're really in trouble. For this reason and others, no casual conversation or book on independent filmmaking should ever stand in lieu of a formal conversation with a qualified attorney. From eschewing production insurance to inventing their own employment contracts, filmmakers put themselves on the line in ways that risk not only their projects but their credit ratings and future finances. On any occasion, not talking to an attorney about a major decision can prove disastrous. Indie filmmakers who think it's all about art and passion and "doing whatever it takes to make the film," rather than about contracts and lawyers and protecting their own interests from people who will hose them if given the chance, are

in for a series of unpleasant surprises. What people will discover far too late is that the indie-film world is not a lagoon of integrity, that everyone they thought they could trust will not necessarily act in the best interests of the project, and that lawyers are critical to every type of filmmaking. It is a completely naïve approach to think that even the lowest of low-budget indie films can be assembled on a promise and a handshake instead of with official contracts and sound legal advice from a qualified attorney. The only thing aspiring filmmakers need to know about lawyers is that they can talk to them now or they can talk to them later, after everything goes haywire, but rest assured they will need to talk to them eventually. Attorneys are the $54 rental-car insurance people waffle on opting for: no one thinks they need it until a fender bender ends up costing thousands of dollars or until a head-on collision leaves them lying mangled in the hospital for months.

In *Sex, Lies, and Videotape*, James Spader's character, Graham Dalton, claims that lawyers are the lowest form of life on Earth. Sooner or later, however, every independent film-maker needs one. Lawyers should be considered members of the crew, as integral to the process of filmmaking as the people who know how to operate cameras and set lighting.

And while many indie filmmakers have no problem dropping $6,000 for a Sony EX1 or $5,000 for a Mac Pro tower or $2,500 for a top-end Aja or Black Magic Design card, many wrongly think allocating $450 an hour for legal advice is either extravagant or dumb. Still others fear that once they sit down with an attorney, they'll end up spending twenty times what they planned and have nothing to show for it.

The truth is that filmmakers regularly need legal advice and protection in the form of written contracts, from many common and uncommon threats. The producer may not realize that the screenplay is secretly based on a real person who has not released his or her life rights. The director may not realize that by shooting the film "run-and-gun" he or she will forget to secure location rights that need to be cleared. Or the production may not actually own or have secured the rights or official chain of title to the book that a writer has adapted into a screenplay. And though it may seem far-fetched while eating cold Thai food in a tiny walk-up with 120 pages, a box of screenplay brads and a dream, lawsuits from disappointed investors, shifty vendors, opportunistic crew members, do-nothing line producers, furious actors, and various advisers who suddenly demand producer credit and net profit participation can all cost tens of thousands of dollars in settlement fees or court costs.

What many directors and producers don't realize is that *everyone* associated with a film—even a poorly lit digital-video movie—is a potential litigant, especially if the film eventually lands a distribution deal and becomes a huge hit. Actors and extras can sue if they are in a slip-and-fall accident or a crew member injures someone on the street with faulty gear or hot lights costing the filmmaker tens of thousands of dollars in legal fees. For that reason and others, forging ahead without legal counsel—even on a six-minute short—is an extremely risky proposition.

"There are a million legal problems with your average independent film," says Sony Pictures Classics copresident Tom Bernard. "So much so that it often becomes a deal point or deal breaker for the distributor. Legal problems can create a very complicated situation when you're trying to sell the movie at a festival, and you can bet we've heard and seen it all."

Contrary to popular belief, distributors with deep pockets rarely step in and make intractable legal problems go away. More often it is the distributor who walks away, since a protracted dispute or court battle can cost more than the film. "Whenever a distributor buys a film, the money is not disbursed until the producers can prove they have clear chain of title and ownership of all the necessary underlying rights," explains Mark Gill, chief executive at The Film Department, who distributed *A Scanner Darkly* and *A Very Long Engagement* as president of Warner Independent Pictures. "For starters a distributor needs to know that the filmmakers have the rights to the material they've produced, especially if it's based on a book or a person's life story. If the film was shot in a certain location, do they have all the required clearances, releases, and signatures? Did all their actors and extras sign releases? Do they still have all the signatures? There are often a gazillion legal issues that can trip you up, which is why sometimes only *10 percent* of a film's advance is paid up front. The biggest chunk of the purchase price is held back not only for delivery items like your sound elements and film negative but for proof that all of the required clearances and licenses exist. The big check isn't cut until all of those important questions have been answered."

Lawyers are therefore a crucial part of the production team since they are needed to form limited liability companies (LLCs), conduct background checks on investors, negotiate contracts with actors and crew, clear copyrights, keep records of important documents, check business-partner references *before* they join the project, and broker deals with vendors and distributors on behalf of the film.

"The biggest place people make a mistake is in thinking, 'Lawyers cost $300, $400, $500 per hour: I don't want to call them now—they're too expensive. I don't want to call them yet,' " says Wilder Knight, of the New York law firm Pryor Cashman LLP. "But all I need to do is uncover one fatal mistake and I've justified my fee. The mistake could be in the choice of investor, partner, vendor, or service provider, or it could be a technical legal issue. Major studios can make mistakes and then cover the cost of fixing those problems or simply write off an entire project. Independent filmmakers have budgets so tight that one mistake may be fatal." The tragedy, of course, is that the legal problems indie filmmakers run into time and time again are usually avoidable.

"Filmmakers need to be smart and hire someone early on to protect them before they either grant rights or legally obligate themselves in some way," says John Sloss, founder of Cinetic Media. "You really do need a very competent lawyer on your team, because a lot of what needs to be done to iron out a deal is relatively technical stuff."

For that reason, filmmakers need to arm themselves with the best legal aid their money can buy. "Just as you would rather hire an experienced cinematographer or experienced actors, you also want experienced legal counsel," says attorney Steven C. Beer, who runs the film division in the New York offices of Greenberg Traurig. "It's one of the most important aspects of your team from the time you acquire underlying rights to when you're raising money, making the film, and negotiating a distribution deal. There are numerous contracts for each along the way that require painstaking levels of detail, and a filmmaker's willingness to cut corners on the legal front will come back to bite him every time."

LEGAL ISSUES RELATED TO FUND-RAISING

The first important legal issue most filmmakers do not—or choose not—to understand is that raising money without including specific warnings and investment language in a prospectus or business plan (or in the registration documents) can violate state and federal statutes designed to protect widows and orphans. These laws are important to the public since there is nothing to stop a charlatan indie filmmaker from raising hundreds of thousands of dollars or even millions of dollars and then never actually making the film.

According to *Federal Securities Law* by Thomas Lee Hazen, the term "security" is defined as "any note, stock, treasury stock, security, debenture or bond, or evidence of indebtedness, collateral-plus certificate, certificate of interest, subscription, investment contract, transferable share, 'put,' 'call,' 'straddle,' 'option,' or privilege on any security or certificate of deposit." By this definition, any filmmaker asking people for money, with the implication or hint that returns are a possibility, is in fact selling securities and courting trouble if registration documents are not filed and the appropriate legal terms are not spelled out.

"Investors who lose money on movies file lawsuits all the time, and many throw in allegations of securities fraud when they do," says Sloss. "Lawsuits filed by disappointed investors who say the filmmakers failed to properly advise them of the risks are legion. You just don't hear about them because they are usually person-to-person affairs that settle out of court."

"State 'blue sky' laws are designed to protect people from fraudulent investment opportunities, so any time you're soliciting funds, compliance with state and federal regulations is required," says New York–based entertainment attorney Emerson E. Bruns, who served as production counsel to the Polish brothers on *Twin Falls Idaho*. "Just because you're raising money from friends and family does not exonerate you, it just means that your disclosure requirements are different. Raising funds from friends and family does limit the probability that someone will file a complaint with the attorney general's office or the Securities and Exchange Commission [SEC], but you can still run afoul of state and federal regulations. The problem is that most filmmakers don't really concern themselves with these issues."

By now most aspiring filmmakers have heard about how producer Eric Watson, actor and cowriter Sean Gullette, and director Darren Aronofsky cobbled together $60,000 to make *Pi* in 1997. "It's a true story," says Aronofsky. "We were sort of desperate, we needed money, and someone on the team came up with the idea of asking every person we knew for $100 each because if you got 300 people, then you'd have the $30,000 we were looking to raise in the beginning. At that time, though, a lot of our friends were just out of school and unemployed, but a lot of them came out and supported us." Aronofsky's updates to friends and diary entries during that interval would provide the basis of his inspirational 1998 paperback, *Pi: Screenplay and the Guerilla Diaries*.

This inspirational tale has since launched a thousand ships, but unless a form-letter solicitation is structured as a no-interest loan, those looking to emulate Aronofsky's business model could arguably be in violation of Rule 144A, Regulation A. "If the securities bureaus had wanted to come down on Darren, he could've theoretically been thrown in jail," says Bruns. "He didn't do it 'right,' they just didn't hear about it or didn't elect to go after him because they had bigger fish to fry and other things to worry about. But a lot of these myth stories about Darren Aronofsky or Ed Burns—people who raised money this way and it was fine—are problematic because filmmakers could end up exposing themselves to civil or even criminal liability."

Offering an investment as a "loan" with a wink and a nudge in the deal memo may not get indie-film producers off the hook if a frustrated "contributor" decides to complain to the newly energized SEC.

"You can't give an investment all the attributes of equity and then say, 'But it's not really an equity stake, so I don't have to do any of the compliance registration,'" explains Bruns. "You could do it as a straight loan, but the people giving you money wouldn't be able to hold an equity stake in the picture and you would have to put real language in their contracts to support that. The problem with blue sky laws is: 'What constitutes a security?' It's not black and white. Having an ongoing interest in an enterprise constitutes a security, so if I give you $100,000 and you pay me back $100,000 with 5 percent interest, well, wham, you're into a security."

Even if everything is aboveboard and the filmmakers are actually setting out to make the film described in their prospectus, the minute one investor complains, the fundraising effort could theoretically be shut down by the weight of enforcement action.

"Our advice is always that if you're going to raise any money—there isn't really a threshold cutoff level—you should have a preliminary conversation with an attorney to at least get a road map of where you can and definitely cannot go," says Bruns. "There are different degrees of danger, but for anything except the most guerrilla film, it's usually worth spending the money to get a qualified attorney to advise you about securities laws and draw up the appropriate documents."

HOW TO HIRE AN ATTORNEY

As for finding the right attorney for a feature, short, or documentary, Knight suggests checking prices before formal discussions begin.

"You should talk to three different lawyers but don't waste their time," he says. "Just say, 'I'm thinking about doing a private placement and I'd like to know what you would charge for putting together an LLC and the offering documents,' and see what they say. There are many boutiques in New York and L.A. that do it for a lot less than the big firms. My firm is expensive and I am not offended if someone who speaks with me elects to go with a boutique. There are advantages to using documents vetted by tax attorneys and litigators who have extensive experience in this area. But many independents cannot afford the additional cost for this level of expertise."

The benefit of working with high-end lawyers—by making their fees a priority—is that they often have access to capital and/or connections in the film industry that can help get projects financed or cast up. But low-budget filmmakers do not need to retain fancy or expensive lawyers. "If investors see the name of a leading law firm on your documents, it's going to give them some comfort, but if you're only raising $100,000 for a DV film I don't think you should be paying $10,000 to $15,000 for your documents," says Knight. "If the budget is too low, I'll sometimes recommend a colleague in another firm who can do the securities work less expensively."

Blood, Guts, Bullets and Octane executive producer Peter Broderick, himself an attorney, warns against hiring the first barrister put forward by friends or relatives. "The selection of a lawyer is something most laypeople have a difficult time with—in terms of interviewing more than one and also in trying to make a decision about who to go with," he says. "In choosing a lawyer you need to find one who not only has experience but has some passion for your project. They're very busy people making more money doing other things, and getting them on the phone to deal with the kind of deadlines filmmakers often have to operate under requires a fundamental commitment."

Of course, it can be a delicate balance between access and expertise. Like craft service or lighting packages, filmmakers usually get what they pay for when it comes to counsel. "The advice I always give is that while legal advice is expensive, cheap legal advice is more expensive," says Knight. The fee for setting up a full-blown investment—one where more than seven or eight investors live in different states—could begin at $25,000 to $30,000, not counting the production legal work, a figure that typically exceeds the budget for legal services of a lot of independent films.

Then, one way to keep costs down may be to have a heavy-duty attorney steeped in financing issues review the LLC and other legal documents and have a second "friend" attorney handle all the day-to-day issues. "I negotiated our lawyer down to $12,000 and gave him a share in the movie so he actually made some money, which is nice," explains *Kissing Jessica Stein* producer Eden Wurmfeld. "He basically worked on every single contract, including our operating agreement for our LLC filing. He was a young lawyer who saw working on our film as an opportunity, but the funny thing now is when I get my legal bills—because I just did a deal on a screenplay—I see how much I get charged for things and realize what a great deal we had back then."

Probably the most important question filmmakers should lead with is whether the serious discussion or casual conversation now under way is on the clock or part of a flat fee, rather than playing billable-hour roulette and getting socked with a $1,000 total for a preliminary consult. The second-most crucial inquiry is whether the deal memo or legal agreement being drawn up represents an equitable arrangement or one that potentially benefits investors, actors, vendors, or distributors more than might be necessary. An entertainment attorney may have allegiances the filmmaker is unaware of or may be using outdated figures in a standard document that is far more generous than it needs to be.

LEGAL PROBLEMS WITH DOCUMENTS—SETTING UP LLCS

Before the fund-raising process gets under way, many struggling auteurs don't see the wisdom in putting $500 toward an hour of counsel. Indeed, at that point, legal advice may seem like a pipe dream given that monthly credit card payments are late and rent is due. As an early step, filmmakers can acquaint themselves with some of the issues they will face and many of the contracts they will need by buying Mark Litwak's terrific primer, *Contracts for the Film & Television Industry*. But filmmakers who try to wing it and take matters into their own hands, something Litwak explicitly discourages, can end up in hot water.

"Financing agreements are notoriously troublesome, especially when they have been improperly crafted," warns Beer. "Producers can run afoul of securities laws and in so doing guarantee that they never make another film. If things aren't done right, investors can open a filmmaker up to all sorts of accusations and liabilities of civil fraud. And where there's a finding of fraud, litigants can circumvent corporate-liability restrictions and attack a producer personally and go after his or her personal assets."

Similarly, cribbing someone else's professionally drafted LLC registration, even if it looks and sounds official, is also ill-advised. "It's extremely dangerous to cobble together your own legal documents or memoranda without having an attorney take a look at them," says Knight. "Can you do it? Sure. But I never recommend that clients wing something like that on their own because I have seen too many cases where things have gone wrong. If you make one mistake you may be opening yourself up to a raft of unwinnable lawsuits. Also, many of the documents that people obtain from friends may come from old deals that had their own idiosyncrasies and may have been heavily negotiated. Taking the deal-terms contained in those documents may put you in a worse position vis-à-vis your deal. Attorneys know what deal points are important, but a layperson can easily miss one or two major points."

To limit personal exposure, the first step filmmakers will

need to take is to form an LLC that enables any and all liabilities and financial upside to reside within a legal entity.
"Typically the safest way to do things is with an LLC that
costs roughly $3,000 to do the internal organization,"
explains Bruns. "For a short film that's a pretty significant
amount of money, so most people do their shorts under the
auspices of their production companies. If you don't have a
production company, that means you're doing it individually,
and that puts you, as an individual, on the line.

"In that instance the best thing to do is form a corporation for roughly $1,500, which allows you to use an ongoing
banner or production company, rather than a one-off formed
for a single project. That way when the next film comes
along you can work under that production banner. If it's a
full-blown film and you have the resources, you do it as
a one-off LLC, which is the most recommended route
whether it's a short, a television program, or anything, in
almost every instance.

"Filmmakers who tell themselves it's too late to do things
the right way because production is about to begin are 100
percent wrong. The minute you write the check, an attorney
can form an LLC and file it the next day and the state will
process it over the course of the following week," Bruns
explains. "It's a pretty easy process."

LEGAL PROBLEMS WITH CLEARANCES

Having a lawyer handy or even on set to discuss clearances
can be as important as hiring someone to do script supervi-
sion and continuity. Many filmmakers assume they don't
need attorneys until (or unless) they are being sued, and even
then many think they can smooth things over.

"So many filmmakers I know—it's astounding—will say
something like: 'Let's put this neon Coca-Cola sign in the

shot . . . Coke will be happy to get the free publicity,' " says producer Gill Holland, who produced the 2008 Sundance documentary *Flow*, focusing on the global water crisis. "I've heard that so many times from student filmmakers. And I say, 'Do you realize you're talking about a multibillion-dollar world conglomerate? Do you really think that you're doing them a favor? This is a brand and a trademark protected by hundreds, maybe even thousands of lawyers. I mean, step back from your grandiose perspective about your film! The last thing they want is a Coke can showing up in some drug-related, anomie-ridden indie that looks like crap.' "

Clearances also require careful scrutiny when filmmakers are adapting material with some foot in reality, such as a newspaper or magazine article about a real family or person. "You can end up getting sued if you infringe upon someone's life story or if someone feels they have been defamed," explains producer Laura Lau. "Because *Open Water* was based on a true story, I wanted to make sure that we were not opening ourselves up to any problems. We also wanted to respect the privacy of all the actual persons and their families, so we completely changed the characters, the locations, and many other details—from the kind of boat to the gender of the boat captain. If we had written something closer to the actual persons and not cleared it, we could have gotten into trouble. And because *Open Water* was shot guerrilla style, where we were frequently taping real people, I always carried around personal release forms to make sure we obtained permission to use their image and likeness."

Filmmakers are in for an unpleasant surprise if they think that shooting "run-and-gun" on a public street or in a bustling restaurant allows them to forgo getting signed releases from every person who ends up in the film.

· Issues with actors and extras are probably among the most frequent but avoidable legal headaches. "We were shooting a scene of *Hurricane Streets* in the schoolyard in Asher Levy School in the East Village and we had all these little kids as extras and we realized we needed a kid to say a line to Brendan Sexton," recalls Holland, the film's producer. "The kid was supposed to be buying something from Brendan and say something like, 'Hootie and the Blowfish! Cool!' But we didn't have releases there and we just thought we'd get it later. A year down the road we were selling the movie and somebody said, 'So who's that actor?' And we said, 'No, he wasn't an actor.' And then we looked at each other: 'Ohhhhh, shit. We don't have a release for him.' So we had to call Asher Levy and ask for the names of all the Korean and Asian American kids and then all the Asian kids in general to track him down. We pulled a still from the film and were showing it to the principal and he said, 'This kid doesn't go here, he's not even a student at this school.' It was an absolute nightmare. It took *two months* to track him down because no one knew who this kid was. We finally found him and his parents and he signed our release and that was that, but it took us two months to get something that should've taken two seconds.

"You can bet that distributors who want to buy a film at a festival will ask to see all the releases before cutting a check. Documentaries are much looser because you have to catch the world as it happens, but technically on a feature film the director is controlling everything in the shot and everything in the frame," explains Holland. "So if you have a FedEx truck passing by during a take, you're supposed to get a release from the company."

Often filmmakers have no concept that logos on soda cans, cell phones, and even hood ornaments for BMW, Jaguar, and Mercedes-Benz are trademarked. The solution is not to wing it but to spend time prepping each location so that all clearly visible products are positioned so their labels are obscured. "A lot of people have an incorrect sense of what is and what is not fair use, and that can often get them into trouble," explains Sloss Law Office attorney Paul Brennan. "Fair use is a somewhat vague area of the law that can be difficult to determine. It is based on a weighing of several factors and is therefore never clear-cut. It's a judgment call. When filmmakers dress a set, they can't just throw up a bunch of signs, movie posters, or copyrighted artwork. These items must be cleared ahead of time. And clearance problems have increased with the Internet. So many images and materials are readily available and inexperienced filmmakers just pull images or artwork from the Web, don't bother to clear them, and it causes big trouble later on."

"Fair use," as defined by Richard Stim in his book *Getting Permission*, is any use of "copyrighted material done for a limited and 'transformative' purpose, such as to comment upon, criticize, or parody a copyrighted work." However, the way courts and juries interpret fair use can diverge widely from this definition and from the perception aspiring filmmakers have of the concept.

"There are myths circulating out there, such as: If you use something for less than three seconds, then it's automatically fair use," explains Brennan. "Or: Use of copyrighted material in a documentary is automatically fair use simply because the filmmaker believes the film has some significant, social, or educational import. The decision to use material based on the fair use exception should always be the result of a careful legal analysis. Even then, there is some potential risk."

In almost every case these theories end up crashing into the unforgiving reality of copyright law, something *Bad Santa* director Terry Zwigoff learned firsthand when he made *Ghost World* in 2000.

"Apparently legal clearances have gotten much harder over the last couple of years," he says. "For *Ghost World* I'd say I couldn't use about 50 percent of the stuff I wanted to put in Seymour's room, even though they were things that already belonged to me personally. A lot of it hadn't been cleared and the production lawyers just would not go for it. They went around the day before we shot and started taking stuff down off the walls, saying, 'Nope. Can't use this, can't use this, can't use this.' We had people working on our clearances for six months but there were still a lot of things I wanted to use that we couldn't clear. And the lawyers just kept saying, 'Nope, can't use it.' It was heartbreaking. The problem is that once they start taking choices away from you it really does start weakening the film. It's often hard to capture anything truthful because of all of these rights and clearance problems."

Clearances also apply to stills taken by private individuals and posted on Flickr.com and film footage from old movies that may be playing on a TV during a scene. Steven Soderbergh's use in *The Limey* of footage from Ken Loach's 1967 film *Poor Cow* or the stock shots of seventies-era Manhattan toward the end of Alexander Payne's *Election* both had to be cleared.

Clearances are particularly relevant to documentaries and segments of low-budget narrative features shot documentary style. "For some reason filmmakers are a lot more casual when it comes to getting clearances for documentaries," says Brennan. "We've had documentary-filmmaker clients who just went ahead and included photographs and music that they never cleared. Documentary filmmakers should be particularly aware of music that is embedded in their footage, such as a radio playing in the background. We had a film that essentially lost distribution over that issue. Also if you're reading text—maybe a poem or something like that—it has to be cleared as well. People don't necessarily realize it, but if you're filming someone in a room and there's artwork all over the walls—like a scene in an art gallery, such as in *Basquiat* or *Factory Girl*, you have to clear all the paintings and photographs that are copyrighted works."

Smart filmmakers know to purchase an E&O (errors and omissions) insurance policy from a company such as Chubb to guard against unforeseen lawsuits related to clearance issues. "E&O insurance covers certain intellectual-property issues such as copyright infringement, defamation, and personal privacy," explains Brennan. "But when a producer obtains an E&O policy, he or she basically makes a representation to the E&O insurer that customary clearance procedures have been followed and that the producer has in fact properly cleared everything in the film. The errors and omissions insurers watch your film, and then they look at all your contracts and have to decide whether you might get sued or not. For that reason, E&O is cheaper if you're a more experienced producer who has delivered movies before because they know that you are responsible for controlling what is in frame and that if a FedEx truck drove by during the last take, you should shoot another one. They also will know how to get the clearance and licensing contracts right. The policy really is supposed to cover only red herring claims or situations where a genuine dispute exists. It's not designed to absolve a filmmaker from clearance obligations.

"If a claim occurs and the E&O carrier determines that it derives from the producer's failure to follow customary clearance procedures, coverage protection may be denied."

For this reason, set design often catches the eye of potential distributors, but not for the reasons filmmakers might imagine. "Very often we'll be interested in an independent film and we'll have to ask ourselves, 'Did they clear the Miller Beer bottles and the Coca-Cola cans and that bus going by with an ad for Poland Spring water on the side of it?'" says Bernard. "We need to know they have permission to use all those things in the film because in many cases someone is going to have to pay to get the rights, but who's going to pay for that? It's the same thing as seeing a movie with great music and finding out that it has $700,000 worth of music rights that haven't been cleared."

Being a part of a scrappy little independent-film-that-could cuts no slack with copyright holders, especially now that the rags-to-riches Tarantino myth is so well ensconced.

"Assuming you haven't cleared it at the outset, what usually happens is the copyright owner sends you a cease-and-desist letter and then you have to work toward a settlement," says Brennan. "Hopefully you don't get to a point where a lawsuit is actually filed against you, but you'll still end up having to pay them off. The problem with that is, if you're talking about an independent film made on a low budget or a documentary made on no budget, having to shell out $5,000 here and there to settle claims can turn into real money very quickly."

Independent-film budgets are tight to begin with, but filmmakers should consider allocating or raising extra funds for legal issues, say $10,000 to $100,000 to address legal problems and/or demand letters should any arise.

One of the things filmmakers can do to address the clearance challenge is to hire a firm that specializes in rights clearances, such as Wendy Cohen Production Resources in New York. "The best-case scenario would be to have an experienced clearance person working with legal counsel to clear things in advance and use those items as set dressing," suggests Brennan. "If you have people on your team who can point out some of these pitfalls and either remove certain things from the set or get permission for the things you absolutely want to use, that can save you a lot of headaches later on."

Filmmakers who struggle to track down the appropriate

party may or may not be able to establish good faith in court if they use a copyrighted item or element without a signature. "Sometimes we've had clients who have said, 'Look, we have used all of our efforts to try and locate the rights holder and we can't find them,' " explains Brennan. "Say they have a character reading from a book that is long out of print or they're using a photograph from a magazine that went out of business years ago . . . they say, 'We can't find the artist anywhere.' Sometimes you use your best efforts and you can't locate someone, and while there's still a risk in going ahead with it, we sometimes tell clients, 'Use your best efforts but if you can't find someone, at least you've demonstrated good faith.' However, filmmakers may run into a situation where the rights holder simply refuses to grant a clearance under any circumstances and the material has to be cut from the film. That can be a real problem," adds Brennan.

Indeed, the fastest way to find out who actually still holds the rights (and to end up getting a cease-and-desist order in the process) is to use copyrighted material without any clearance. In 1995 artist Lebbeus Woods filed a successful lawsuit against director Terry Gilliam for the appropriation of Woods's illustration *Neomechanical Tower (Upper) Chamber*, which was used in *12 Monkeys*. The artist's logic is that the reason a film succeeded at the box office is because of the intangible benefit the filmmaker received from the cachet of their (or their now-dead relative's) labor.

"Clearances just kill you," says Zwigoff. "Clearance lawyers are very conservative and in many cases you have to find heirs to the artist's estate or the heirs to companies that have long since gone out of business in order to get their approval."

Without this exhaustive search, *Ghost World* might not have opened with one of its signature moments that helps instantly establish the milieu and the personality of the main character. "Dan [Clowes, creator and screenwriter of *Ghost World*] had a bunch of old video and audiotapes that hipsters pass around, stuff like Dean Martin and Jerry Lewis swearing off-mic, that kind of thing," Zwigoff remembers. "These underground tapes get passed around and he was showing me some oddball stuff on a videotape he had with a bunch of things on it, but among them was a really bad, tenth-generation copy of this Indian musical sequence. We only had about thirty seconds of it and we couldn't figure out where it had originally come from, but when I saw it I said, 'We gotta have that in the film!' And Dan said, 'Well, how's that gonna fit?' And I said, 'Well, we gotta think of something!'

"The hardest part was tracking down the people who had the rights because it was made in 1965 in another country and we didn't even know the name of the film," says Zwigoff. "The only lead we had to go on was the name—a fake name—on the drum kit that said: Ted Lyons and His Cubs. We had people searching for nine months and it was really hard to find.

"The two sons of the original producer of *Gumnaam* were still alive living in Calcutta or Bombay, I forget, and we eventually tracked them down. They were really nice guys and they were so cooperative they actually hand-carried the original negative over from India for us to use. We gave them a licensing fee but it was very, very reasonable. We never could have afforded a normal fee for such a thing but they were just great about it."

LEGAL PROBLEMS WITH ACTORS

Negotiating with name actors is yet another area where low-budget filmmakers can get into big trouble if lawyers aren't on hand to stave off disaster. Because filmmakers often pay big money (even if it is still well below an actor's studio quote), the expectation is that the star will make time for festivals, press junkets, and marketing efforts once the film is completed. However, this is a major misperception that often leaves first- and second-time filmmakers feeling betrayed and stung.

"I don't think I've ever seen an actor 100 percent locked in to doing publicity or having to attend film premieres," explains Holland. "If they're not doing something better and you offer to fly them out and they like the movie and think it's good for their career, they'll do the premiere. But the clause in the contract usually says 'according to availability' or 'subject to availability,' so they can always have their agent say, 'She has an audition for something big, so she can't come,' which gives them an easy out. That's just the harsh reality. If actors think a film is good for their career, they will promote it, period. It doesn't matter if they're paying their own way, it doesn't matter what the contract says. But if they think the film sucks and it's not good for their career, forget it."

Frequently, actors' agents and managers will insist their client is not available for press because they are legitimately working on another film that is paying full freight or because the scope of the role in the indie film does not warrant promotional participation or a dilution of their client's "brand" image.

Indeed, signing on for a battery of round-robin print interviews and sit-downs with AICN, *Access Hollywood*, *MTV News*, MovieWeb.com, and *Entertainment Tonight* is surprisingly low on many actors' lists of favorite things, but it is often critical to building a groundswell of interest in an independent film.

"Being willing to get on the road and promote your

movie, whether you're the director or an actor, is really important to the marketing," says Fox Searchlight's Nancy Utley. "There's nothing like actually getting out there and promoting a film in person. Filmmakers and actors need to see the promotion of their film as a political campaign and remember that Barack Obama and John McCain didn't stay in their offices in New York or Washington, D.C., when they were running for president. They were everywhere, and that's really the level of dedication and foot-soldiering that's required to get the word out about independent films. It's great when people are willing to give up their creature comforts, and in some cases get on a tour bus, and live not the most comfortable life for six weeks.

"In April and May of 2007, we put Glen [Hansard] and Markéta [Irglová] on a concert-size tour bus and went all over the country and had them show [Once] to people in a word-of-mouth screening program that included a Q&A and a short performance," Utley recalls. "There was definitely a push to market Once, but the film itself was so beloved [by people who had seen it] that they kind of took it from us and in many ways made it their own. Then they made it their business to e-mail everyone in their address book to say: 'Go see this movie.' So, in that way, sprinkling the market with those first little seeds of a talent tour and screening program created a huge fervor later on for people to go see the movie. We talent-tour a lot of our directors, since a lot of times the director and the actors may not be known or the director may be the real story for a movie because he or she is a new voice the public hasn't really heard before."

Utley witnessed the shift in the public's perception of Once firsthand during the summer of 2007. "We were walking around the streets of New York with Glen and Markéta in the beginning of the film's release in June when we were first trying to get it noticed," she says. "Back when we were screening for critics in New York and doing some museum screenings, you could just walk everywhere with them and no one would recognize them. Then six months later we went back to New York, and the amount of passion about the film was really incredible. Everywhere we went, people wanted to come up and talk to them and shake their hand— even in the very same area we had been to earlier.

"People were so taken with Glen and Markéta and so involved with the movie emotionally that they couldn't help but come up and start telling their own stories about the time they got their first guitar or about how much they loved the film. There were a lot of people who wanted to tell us about the date they went on the night they saw the film or how they had gone back and taken family members to see it. Or they wanted to know when the DVD was coming out. It was really kind of stunning to see the change in people's reactions just a few months later, after the film had connected with audiences even without a lot of advertising. That was the movie doing all the work by itself."

While not touring sounds less than generous, consider that an actor or actress would theoretically have to leave the set of a studio-produced period film in Morocco to participate in a low-budget indie press junket or attend a lesser festival to support an independent film they may have completed a year ago. Still other name actors may have fewer ties to an indie either because they did it on a lark or because they got the dash of street cred they needed to land a coveted studio role. The upshot is, if press commitments are not spelled out in writing, appearances are very unlikely to occur.

Often when it comes time to promote a low-budget film at a festival or in newspaper interviews an actor may say: "Hey, I gave at the office. You should be happy I agreed to be in your film." Filmmakers wrongly assume that press-junket participation is probably in the contract somewhere or that press and publicity participation is implied. After all, what actors wouldn't want to promote a movie they spent several months working on? Wouldn't a refusal to appear make them look bad? The truth is, if deal points are not clearly spelled out in the short-form memorandum, it may be a tough negotiation when it comes time to hammer out the long-form deal memo with the actor's agent, who could very easily negotiate an additional payment or some other deal point when it comes time to sell the film to distributors or when the long-lead marketing and publicity cycle begins.

"The reason you may have courted a particular actor in the first place was so you could use his or her name and star power in the credits," suggests Knight. "You might have wanted to put his or her name on the marquee or above the film's title but now you can't because there are limitations in your contract that you didn't notice. In fact, you may not even be able to use the actor's name in radio spots or television commercials at all. Or say you want to show your big-name actor kissing an unknown starlet in your film, but his agents won't give you permission to do that. They only want him in press shots next to A-level talent. Well, now you may have hurt your investors' ability to recoup their investment. Distributors will be upset at these limitations and this could affect what they are willing to pay for the picture. And that's just one example of a thousand missteps people make. Again, the reason you go to a lawyer is so they can spot these land mines that are very important to every filmmaker and their investors but easy to overlook."

Of course, many first- and second-time filmmakers worry that they might risk upsetting an actor by asking for any assurances in writing, and fear scaring them away from the project. These optimistic souls keep their fingers crossed that everything will work out for the best, but name actors have been known to disassociate themselves from films they dislike and even to decline to have their likenesses used in the promotional materials of certain lower-budgeted films.

Other filmmakers may be so eager to land a major star that they are willing to give up all their leverage, promising anything short of a film's copyright or ownership of the original negative. Worse still, many aspiring filmmakers offer or sign intractable pay-or-play agreements because they mistakenly believe that an actor's participation will elicit funds from distributors overseas. The problem with this concept is that (1) the actor may not be as much of a draw abroad as the filmmaker thinks; (2) international presales are based on the health of the overseas television market, which has dried up in recent years; and (3) aspiring filmmakers without track records don't always attract international financing simply by adding recognizable actors to the cast. The truth is that there are so many indie films looking for financing these days that international distributors can afford to wait until a project is completed or sign deals that are execution dependent.

Even so, filmmakers cling to the notion that with a signed letter of intent in hand, it will be a piece of cake to attract millions of dollars in financing. So an actor signs a pay-or-play agreement "subject to execution or approval," which gives him an out in case he doesn't like the budget level, the rest of the cast, or the look on the assistant director's face. But the producer is now facing the same problem Detective Sergeant Alonzo Harris had in *Training Day:* come up with $1 million by a set date or be gunned down by a carload of Russian hit men, or in this case the pay-or-play actor's entire desk of agents armed with a cadre of lawyers and a ton of bricks.

LEGAL PROBLEMS WITH CREW

Lawyers can also draft employment agreements ensuring that the right people are in charge once the production gets under way. "Without a good attorney, you could wind up giving more control to your creative team than your investors deem appropriate," explains Greenberg Traurig's Steven Beer. "If a producer were to give a first-time director final cut—when most first-time directors don't get that privilege—investors might feel wronged and claim that because agreements with the writer and the director were not handled properly, an additional 'burden of risk' was placed on their money. The concern for the producer as a fiduciary agent for the investors is that the writer and/or the director could hold the film hostage, paralyzing the project and infuriating investors, who then decide to sue. So the producer needs to ensure that his or her hands stay firmly on the steering wheel, and to do so he or she must clearly delineate the rights, obligations, and limitations of the creative team." The ways a lunatic or auteur director can hold a project hostage include insisting on expensive songs in the soundtrack or end credits, turning in a cut that is more than two hours long, including explicit content that merits an NC-17 rating, or simply absconding with the hard drives being used to edit the film itself.

Sometimes the director of photography or line producer attached to a project at its inception will not or should not actually work on the film. Unfortunately, many filmmakers hire the first or second person they meet and are stuck with them for the duration of their shoot. Still others get into trouble with crew members they want to keep on the project because no contracts were drawn up before the production began. "Even if it's a simple thing where you scratch someone's name on a piece of paper, you should have some kind

of contract or written understanding with people—especially
the ones you care about—that spells out what the rules are
and what's going to happen," says Wurmfeld. "Signed contracts also go a long way toward saving and preserving your
friendships with colleagues, since every film has its relationship casualty. I am a believer in that advice be-cause I've
experienced it myself."

Independent filmmakers who follow this advice, using
contracts every step of the way and setting down every single
conversation in writing (and in an e-mail that can subsequently be printed and saved in a secure location), are going
to be seen not as sellouts or "Hollywood types" but as intelligent, professional filmmakers who are only being careful
and responsible and doing things by the book. "You need
to put everything in writing, because everyone always starts
out as the best of friends with the best of intentions, but if
there is any lack of clarity about credit or compensation or
anything else, that's when it can get ugly, especially in
instances of a film that is successful where there is real
money at stake," Brennan says. "You never want to be in a
situation where you are relying on your recollection of a
conversation as your agreement. So many disasters begin
with: 'We're good friends and I know we would be able to
work it out without a contract.' This applies as much to relationships with fellow producers—if you're coproducing the
project with someone—as it does to relationships with your
investors."

Preemptively consulting an attorney may raise eyebrows
among the core production team, which may include best
friends or a longtime girlfriend or boyfriend, but their initial
shock is preferable to what can happen after a shoot gets
under way and disagreements spring up under "combat conditions." Claiming and counterclaiming can get even more
heated after a low-budget film is purchased at a festival for

millions of dollars. When big money is involved, friendship dynamics can change overnight and forever.

"On my first film, *Grind*, I ran into trouble with both the cast and crew wanting to renegotiate during the shoot," says Lau. "Around halfway through the shoot, I had an actor who decided he wanted more back-end money and threatened to stop working. I can tell you I will never work with him again. And even though I had deal memos with the crew, it was a nonunion shoot and the deal memos were loose and vague about overtime compensation. As a first-time producer I really didn't know how to handle it.

"You don't want people to be able to come up to you after you've begun shooting and demand more money or producer credit or whatever, which is why you have to have signed deal memos in place before you hire anybody," Lau continues.

Instead, however, aspiring filmmakers are often so grateful to have anyone helping them that they promise back-end points to a documentary's subject or to the first competent actor who tells them their narrative feature film script may actually be viable. "Rather than giving everything away, filmmakers should negotiate from a position of strength," says Lau, "especially if they have a good project, because people will want to work on it." Or, just as disastrous, filmmakers don't ask for contracts as long as everyone is getting along and the project is coming together. Then, when it comes time to apply to festivals and divvy up credits and ownership of the project, fights and legal battles ensue.

In some cases directors and producers might be better off firing an actor or crew member and paying them a small severance fee rather than allowing them to stay on and sabotage the production or to put in only a minimal effort. This action should not be taken lightly, threatened, or bandied about, and once a crew member *is* fired, they should stay fired. This is simply because the opportunity to retaliate will always be a temptation for someone who feels embarrassed or spurned.

"The bottom line is you have to have deal memos with absolutely *everybody* you work with," Lau warns. "Don't ever do things on a handshake. If you're working with your friends and it's great, you still have to be really clear *on paper* about who's going to get what in terms of credit, who's going to get what payments, and who's going to have what participations down the line. So whomever it is that you're working with—be it crew, be it actors, be it agents, be it above-the-line personnel—make sure everything is spelled out and that you have deal memos and legal documents in place. Be clear up front and avoid headaches and heartaches later."

Producers also need to be sparring with bonuses. Savvy investors may get cold feet once they see that huge percentages of a film's upside are already promised to members of the production team or to others who helped the filmmakers in the past. Thus, a deal that seems equitable and fair among those who signed on first may prevent the project from attracting the budget it needs to draw name talent and indie-film distributors because so few profit corridors are left to justify significant investment.

"Again, filmmakers tend to not think about what is going to happen next, because it's so hard to get a film made and even harder to get distribution," says Lau. "But they need to think about the best-case scenario. If your film gets picked up, there may be a lot of money involved. You need to think about what you're promising people or potentially granting them in light of the best possible outcome down the road, and a lot of filmmakers don't do that."

Huge deferred payments or a lack of legally codified limits on gross and net participations for those most likely to lobby for deferred payments may also give investors pause.

"Where you run into trouble is in instances where the screenwriter or others claim they were entitled to some kind of producer or coproducer credit and a commensurate cut of the money," explains Brennan. "When it comes to optioning the script from your best buddy the screenwriter, you want to make sure you have all the rights properly cleared. The Screen Actors Guild requires that you have chain of title tied up before you go into production, but sometimes filmmakers go ahead without it."

With stories of the crew earning money after the sale of InDigEnt projects such as *Pieces of April* or *Tadpole*, crew members on other projects shooting today may assume every indie film follows the same model, entitling them to a cut of the sale price or to any overages realized from its distribution. After all, they helped make the film that's now getting all sorts of acclaim. "In some cases you may get crew members saying they were promised a bonus or some kind of net-profit points; they may think they are entitled to be paid sooner or have a share in the project itself, and those misunderstandings can get you into trouble," Brennan explains. "A filmmaker should always be clear with everybody in writing and not rely on conversations. People often have a different interpretation of what was said at different times." Again, all contracts should include a line that specifies that the agreement being signed supercedes all previous conversations, promises, assurances, and/or oral contracts that may or may not have been formed.

LEGAL PROBLEMS WITH INVESTORS—LOSING THEIR MONEY

Filmmakers will often pore over cinematographers' reels for weeks before choosing a director of photography, but rarely will they do anything to find out more about their investors, such as who they are and what they are like to do business with. "As long as their money's green," the thinking goes, "they're all right with me." Unfortunately nothing could be further from the truth. A lot of investors come with strings attached. For some, taking their money requires taking their calls in the middle of the night. Other investors think their money entitles them to be on set every day, while still others believe that since their money is making the film happen, they should be given production responsibilities.

Just as getting references before hiring a director of photography or a line producer is a critical part of the production process, so too is vetting investors before taking their money. "Many investors who are all smiles at the outset can grow fangs and bite. There are a lot of litigious individuals out there, people who will threaten you with lawsuits if they don't get their money back," explains Knight, "regardless of how careful and sincere you have been in the production of your film which for whatever reason has not been commercially successful. People who become physically threatening when you lose their money are actually the least of anybody's worries. The bottom line is, if you bring in a certifiable 'bad guy,' that person may in fact sue at some point, and regardless of the fact that it is a meritless case, you will end up writing a check for $50,000 simply to get rid of him because it will cost $100,000 for your lawyer to win the case. It's simple arithmetic. Even though it may be a nuisance lawsuit, you're going to end up paying someone one way or another. When vetting your investors it can be useful to find out whether they have ever been involved in litigation. Some people are actually proud of how many people they have sued. If your potential investor brags about all the people he or she has taken to court, beware."

Brennan agrees. "Some investors end up sending cease-and-desist letters or a letter alleging some kind of a breach of obligation all the time and costing a production money, because to make them go away you've often got to throw them a few thousand dollars," says Brennan. "It's not worth your time, effort, and money to try to litigate against someone who really has no basis for a claim. Most claims end up settling anyway, but short of an actual lawsuit being filed, filmmakers can face claims that require a cash settlement."

This is not a rare occurrence in the industry or something that aspiring filmmakers should just not worry about and go forward with their fingers crossed. "On almost every project I've worked on someone has threatened me with a lawsuit," admits *Kid Stays in the Picture* codirector Nanette Burstein, whose documentary *American Teen* was acquired by Paramount Vantage for $1 million at Sundance in 2008. "Sometimes they tell you they're going to sue you and sometimes you just get a letter in the mail from somebody's lawyer, but either way you have to be ready for it."

Indie directors and producers are typically smart enough to steer clear of sketchy types who may be laundering drug money, but many don't realize that normal-looking, level-headed investors are routinely party to litigation. "Even if you've done everything aboveboard and you've dotted the i's and crossed the t's, it is frequently the case that the returns or the timetable of returns doesn't match up to the timetable that investors—especially those from the finance community—are used to, which means you're a sitting duck for a lawsuit," Beer explains. "It wouldn't be the first time a film investor was dissatisfied with how things turned out."

The best defense is to not bring any bad apples into the mix in the first place, even in cases where a deep-pocketed investor's last-minute check seems like a miracle. Lawyers can use LexisNexis, Westlaw, and Fastcase to do legal background checks on investors and protect the production team from disasters waiting to happen.

WARNINGS ARE WARRANTED

"It may scare some potential investors away, but you want language in all your documents that puts all investors on notice that this is an extremely risky investment. The investors should also acknowledge that their investment will be illiquid," says Knight. "It's not a bad idea to advise potential investors that horse races—where three out of fifteen horses win, place, or show—are better investments than independent films, where fifteen out of fifteen projects may fail. In your prospectus you want statements signed by everyone that say, 'I am a qualified investor: not only did I earn in excess of $300,000 last year, not only is my net worth in excess of $2 million [or whatever the minimum figures currently are] but I recognize that I may lose 100 percent of my investment.'

"I don't think any investor should be risking more than 5 percent of their net worth or more than 10 percent of their liquid net worth," advises Knight. "As long as they have $2 million in total assets they can probably afford to play with and lose $100,000. I find when investors lose a small piece of their net worth, they tend to lick their wounds and move on. But if you find someone with $300,000 in the bank and he puts $200,000 of it into your movie, he may be devastated if he doesn't get his money back. Consider the fact that this individual has lost $200,000. If a contingency-fee attorney were to take on this case for a third of the amount recovered, you might now be faced with the combination of a sympathetic plaintiff—since small investors who lose more than half of their life savings tend to be more sympathetic than people who live on Park Avenue—and an aggressive (and free) attorney."

5. Casting Up and Cashing In
LANDING BIG NAMES

*I*t is often said that 90 percent of directing is simply good casting. As a result, it's also one of the areas where novice directors often shoot themselves in the foot. Casting presents special challenges for independent films since it often drives the budget, the interest level of potential distributors, and the timing of the production. Casting can also completely change the texture of an indie film in ways that don't always benefit the production, even though having a certain name may attract more capital and allow the director to shoot in 35mm. What would Hard Candy have been like had its director David Slade been forced to cast Harry Potter's Emma Watson instead of a then-unknown Ellen Page? Or if Little Miss Sunshine codirectors Jonathan Dayton and Valerie Faris had been forced to cast Pepsi girl Hallie Kate Eisenberg or The Ring's raven-haired Daveigh Chase over relative newcomer Abigail Breslin to get financing? Indeed, while misplaced casting can get an indie project off the ground, it can also derail its prospects and its original intent. But even as recognizable stars such as Glenn Close star in The Chumscrubber, Heights, and

Nine Lives, and other well-known faces are open to acting in lower-budgeted projects, it is not that easy to get commitments. Indeed, first- and second-time filmmakers who have managed to scratch and claw their way to raising $200,000 to $2 million in production funds often find themselves facing another seemingly impossible hurdle: getting name stars to appear in their projects. While it may seem like every film accepted to Sundance or Toronto has a major star these days—Sundance even publishes the number of films with stars attached that were rejected each year—the reality is that most aspiring indie filmmakers don't have major Hollywood connections and cannot necessarily get their scripts, no matter how well written, into the hands of a star who could help get the film made. But given declining theater admissions and ever-spiraling marketing costs, casting has become a critical element to indie films seeking national distribution. And while filmmakers can point to Napoleon Dynamite, Open Water, and 28 Days Later as evidence that plenty of films succeed without big names, "casting up" is increasingly important given the enormous marketing costs required to open specialized films, the glut of movies now released each week, the cocooning of older audiences, and the number of competing entertainment options.

A question that often haunts many aspiring indie directors and producers is: "Should we actually make this film if we can't get at least one recognizable actor in the cast?" Given the number of films with famous faces in competition at Sundance, and given how tough it is to get a serious distribution deal—only six narrative features were sold for more than $1 million at the festival in 2008—the realist's answer would be no. In fact, specialized distributors argue that there are already too many independent films being made and that it is simply too risky to bet millions of dollars on a film with unknown actors in it.

Stephen Gilula of Fox Searchlight underscores why stars are important. "You need recognizable elements, and a name actor helps give a film some distinction in a very tough and unforgiving marketplace," he explains. "Unfortunately, people don't go to movies because the filmmakers put in a good effort. And with smaller independent films made by filmmakers who are not known, with cast members who are unknown, the odds of getting distribution are long. The odds of being successful are long as well. So many movies open and don't get very much traction. They get some good notices, and then just like that they're gone. They disappear."

Of course, the never-say-die indie-film cheerleader argument would be that first films without a name cast, like *Following*, lead to second or third films with name casts, such as *Memento* and *Insomnia*, which in turn lead to directing *The Prestige*, *Batman Begins*, and then *The Dark Knight*. Nobody should abandon their directing or producing dreams for want of a familiar face. Indeed, the argument could be made that the second-highest grossing film in 2008 starred four of the most challenging-indie-arthouse-keeping-it-real actors: Aaron Eckhart (*In the Company of Men*), Christian Bale (*The Machinist*), Maggie Gyllenhaal (*Secretary*), and Gary Oldman (*Sid and Nancy*), not to mention Eric Roberts (*The Pope of Greenwich Village*) and Heath Ledger (*Brokeback Mountain*). "I don't think everyone sets out to make a really polished first movie, and a lot of people just make what they can with the tools and resources that are in front of them," says John Sloss of Cinetic Media. "We still see so many films with a production value on the level of *Clerks*—with apologies to Kevin Smith, a Sloss client—which speaks to the fact that a lot of people make the film they can make with the camera and the actors they know."

Most independent filmmakers are not connected to actors, actors' agents, or even friends of friends in "the biz" who can broker an introduction to a working actor, and are therefore unlikely to be able to attract leading names to their projects. Furthermore, the naïve approach of sending unsolicited copies of a script to actors' agents or production companies, using *The Hollywood Creative Directory*, IMDbPro, or WhoRepresents.com to divine the correct mailing address, not only instantly telegraphs a misunderstanding of how things actually work but is simply a fool's errand guaranteed to trigger a rejection letter.

While this is true, there are many who argue that any filmmaker realistically hoping to get a distribution deal after being accepted to a major festival needs to consider cast as a fundamental aspect of moving forward, especially when producing an independent film with a budget above $200,000. The ability to recoup a budget that high for investors almost necessitates a name cast member so that filmmakers can at least have a shot at selling the completed project and paying investors back.

"A-list talent provides a security blanket and a bridge to foreign, home-video, and cable sales, which distribution companies calculate and rely on before making a commitment," says New York–based attorney Steven Beer of Greenberg Traurig. "The classic Sundance no-budget independent film that succeeded years ago invariably does not succeed today. Almost every film that gets distribution has some level of pedigree that typically comes from its cast."

Indeed the top three films bought at Sundance 2008 for $10 million, $5 million, and $3 million starred Steve Coogan, Sam Rockwell, and Luke Wilson, respectively. The only other narrative feature purchased at the festival that year in the $2 million ballpark starred Ben Kingsley and *X-Men*'s Famke Janssen. And while 2008 may have been an off year for acquisitions—by some estimates buyers spent $27 million, about 49 percent less than the $53 million spent in 2007, to acquire films—more often than not, the films that sell for more than $1 million at festivals usually have somebody recognizable in them.

Synecdoche, New York producer Anthony Bregman has seen the trend evolve. "When we're putting together films and showing them to distributors, the biggest priority for a lot of them is often who's in it," he explains. "They won't come out and say that necessarily, but they will say, 'It sounds like a great project! When you fully put it together, come and talk to us,' with the implication being that if you get Edward Norton, the film will suddenly become very interesting in a way that it wasn't before."

Even directors who historically never had to worry about cast are feeling pressured. "For me casting issues started to become more essential around 1999 or 2000," recalls *Fay Grim* writer-director Hal Hartley. "The distributors who would pre-buy my films before that weren't insisting on a certain level of talent or a certain level of visibility. It was based on my reputation and my scripts, but that's different now. That doesn't get my films financed now. Today my actors don't have to be super-visible because I still make very small films, but I do have to cast a certain level of visibility."

This necessity regularly creates a tension between what is best for the film in terms of making it believable and compelling and what might help the film get fully financed or picked up should it get into a festival. "Sometimes a certain actor will seem like the right person as far as marketing or drawing an audience is concerned, but casting them can be shortsighted because once the audience is in their seats, they are unconvinced of the appropriateness of the choice," says *Juno* producer Lianne Halfon. "On the other hand, if audiences believe that the actors are those characters and that belief is consistent in the supporting roles as well, the result is a sense of truthfulness that has a tremendous effect on the audience because it makes the fiction resonate."

Halfon, who also produced genre-defining independent films such as *Ghost World* and the iconic documentary *Crumb*, says this is something first- and second-time filmmakers overlook during the casting interval. "The intent is not to cast someone who makes the film seem 'real' or like you're watching a documentary," she says. "Moviegoers don't need reality—they don't rely on fiction for that—but they do need truthfulness, and audiences have a remarkable sensitivity to it on the screen. It's not as if people see *The Philadelphia Story* and think it's realistic. But it touches you, because it is truthful. And that truthfulness has an enormous power that transcends accuracy. It's why we respond to Katharine Hepburn's Tracy Lord, decades after most of the details of setting and character have disappeared from the audience's frame of reference." From that perspective, the casting process for *Juno* is instructive for many directors and producers. "People often will say they can't imagine anyone else in a certain role, and that especially happens after you see a finished film, but when you're having early discussions with studios, there are actually a lot of discussions about cast and they can imagine a lot of people in the various roles. It's part of the juggling that you do in preproduction," continues Halfon. "From the very beginning we wanted to have Jennifer Garner to play the role of Vanessa, so she was one of those names that satisfied what we wanted for the film and also satisfied the studio. Ellen Page had done a taped reading of the script that had been sent to us, and it was her ability to handle Diablo Cody's language that really made her stand out. And of course she is a fantastic actor. Certainly you can't see *Hard Candy* and not be dazzled by the performance, and Ellen was able to shift from that drama to the lightness of *Juno* with enormous ease. Some financiers might not have been able to understand her potential for that shift, but Ellen read for the role and it was one of those readings where, when you see it, the search is over the minute she starts. It's a revelation: 'Oh, there she is . . . there's Juno.' It was clear to everybody at Mandate Pictures, who had optioned and developed the script for the previous year, that [director] Jason Reitman's choice for the role was Ellen. So when we saw her in August of 2006, following auditions by more than 300 other actresses, that was it and she was cast before we went to Fox for production financing."

Halfon warns, however, that casting is more often than not predicated on numerous variables, including actors' availability and the constraints of the budget, and that aspiring indie filmmakers should neither count on nor expect a transformative or magical moment where everything falls into place after a long search for exactly the right actors. And clearly actors are not chosen in isolation; their relationship to one another and the chemistry between them is a key factor. "A classic example is trying to cast two actors as husband and wife, both perfect for their respective roles, but imperfect as a couple," continues Halfon. "A red flag immediately goes up for the audience: those two would never be married. No matter how good they are independent from each other, you are already behind the eight ball. Often producers and directors will find themselves in a situation where they are thinking, 'This person brings these two things and this other person brings these two things and we have to choose between this interpretation of the role versus another interpretation.' When you have someone who is just an absolute bull's-eye like Ellen was in *Juno*, then you don't have that situation where you are forced to choose between somebody who is close to what you're looking for and another person who is maybe 2.5 percent closer to the mark." Fortunately for audiences, Halfon and her production company, Mr. Mudd, founded with John Malkovich and Russell Smith in 1998, had the flexibility to cast *Juno* with actors who were exactly right for each part rather than what a higher budget or the need to secure a sale in a specific territory might demand.

"We knew who we wanted for the stepparents and we could have cast up on those without having found anybody better than Allison Janney and J. K. Simmons," recalls Halfon, who also produced Terry Zwigoff's *Art School Confidential*. "We opened up the casting a bit on Mark and Vanessa, but we knew that we didn't want Hilary Duff to play Leah or Juno. We knew several roles were going to be filled by actors who were lesser known.

"We were always thinking about the film rather than the budget, which was around $7 million. At one point there was an opportunity to make the film at nearly twice that budget, but the concessions that demanded of the casting ruled it out for us. We knew it would undermine any feeling of authenticity in the final film. When Jason came on, he started to discuss the actors that he wanted to work with and who seemed right for the tone of the film," Halfon continues. "There's a budget level that is dictated by the cast we wanted to pursue and we were okay with that budget level. It is a kind of Darwinian economy. It wasn't the other way around where you get a certain actor and then raise the budget to accommodate that casting decision. If you're going to make a film for a lower budget, the director has to feel like he or she can actually make the film at that budget and the producers have to feel that they can deliver the film for that, and on *Juno* we all felt that we could do so without compromise. In fact, it served as a safeguard. It was not so expensive that the studio felt it had to offset risk by making any of the decisions which so often conflict with the filmmaker's intent and muddy the creative integrity of the film."

Of course, from the distributor's perspective, the thinking is often the bigger name, the better, since recognizable cast members provide a semblance of security in a business where specialized films have to fight or quietly call in favors to stay in theaters if they don't connect right away. Critics historically have a tremendous amount of influence on film audiences—especially when it comes to specialized films—and having a recognizable actor in the cast makes it easier to overcome a bad review. Even though the number of film critics working at newspapers in the United States has been dwindling, a recognizable face can still go a long way toward casting the tie-breaking vote when it comes to deciding which film to see on Friday or Saturday night.

Independent films that don't necessarily need stars include comedies such as *Napoleon Dynamite* or *Hamlet 2*, since they trade on the humor and universal pain of high school. Films likely to premiere online are also less reliant on star casting. Audiences in the online sphere want something that resonates regardless of who is in it, whether it's an unknown such as Bree (Jessica Rose) in *Lonelygirl15* or someone exploding Coca-Cola bottles with Mentos.

However, casting is critical for gritty low-budget dramas because distributors today often feel they cannot afford to bet millions in marketing dollars on ultra-edgy films unless it contains a star-making performance such as Ellen Page's pre-*Juno* turn in *Hard Candy*.

"Casting is super-super-important. I think it's the most important thing in a film in certain ways because you want actors who you know can do what's in your script and who can do what you want them to do, so it's not a constant battle," says filmmaker Anna Boden. "Ryan [Fleck, *Half Nelson*'s director] always says there's a lot a director can do, but you'd rather not have to try to manipulate a performance out of people if you can help it. Fortunately, the actors in *Half Nelson* knew how to do their role, sometimes do it better than we would have had them do it."

Many filmmakers spend weeks searching for just the right leads but only days or even hours casting the supporting roles that are likely to stand out like a sore thumb if the actors cast in them are less talented. This is an area where a casting director can prove invaluable. "Hiring really strong actors is critically important when it comes to filling supporting roles," says Boden. "We already knew Shareeka Epps before we cast *Half Nelson*, and of course Ryan Gosling had already proven himself. But in terms of finding so many supporting actors who were just super–high quality, we couldn't have done it without our casting director Eyde Belasco. And on *Sugar* we had an amazing casting director, Cindy Tolan, who was really willing to work outside the box and not just put out descriptions of the characters to all the agencies but look for nonactors so we could have that mix of actors and nonactors, something which is always really important to us."

Indeed, what filmmakers often overlook is that if the players in supporting roles cannot match the intensity and quality of the leading actors, the gulf between the lead actors' performance and those of the supporting actors becomes glaringly obvious and can often pull audiences and acquisition executives right out of the movie. Strong performances, even from lesser day players or "under fives"—actors who have less than five lines—also raise the quality of the entire production and make the smaller moments in an independent film searing and memorable.

Filmmakers have only to look to Keith David's bravura performance in a single scene as Lieutenant Dixon in *Crash* to see how an incredibly talented actor can electrify audiences and raise the quality of the entire project. "A lot of times filmmakers think, 'This supporting character has two lines in this scene and they're not important, so we don't need to spend a lot of time searching to cast that person,'" says Boden. "And you can't interview a hundred people for a small role, but at the same time, it's that person, that role that's going to mess you up if you don't have the right actor—somebody who's really good playing it. And in *Half Nelson* we had really strong actors across the board, who were all just such a pleasure to work with.

"It's very rare that we would actually audition anyone without dialogue, even if he or she is featured in a scene," continues Boden. "Occasionally we'll cast somebody as a featured extra who we had the opportunity to audition for a speaking role and who ended up not being right for that role."

This is especially true when a character's moment on-screen calls only for him or her to emote powerfully and convey a world of understanding or a lifetime of painful experiences in a look or a gesture. Anna Boden describes a scene in *Half Nelson* in which Dan Dunne explains his George Bush theory to a woman he's picked up, played by Susan Kerner. "She's just listening to him on the bed and doesn't say a word," says Boden. "She is amazing and she is considered an 'extra.' I mean, a 'featured extra'! And she was just phenomenal. She was a friend of one of the producers, so we got the chance to meet her briefly, but mostly we just got super-lucky. She was so great because that is one of the hardest assignments: being able to express so much without having a single line of dialogue and to carry that kind of intensity over the course of a long scene."

Interestingly, Boden and Fleck originally wrote the part of Dan Dunne for someone in his early thirties, and were not thinking about Ryan Gosling, who was twenty-five at the time. "But our casting director knew Ryan's manager, and when they were casually talking about the project one day, his manager suggested it was something Ryan might be interested in," says Boden. "The next thing we knew, we got a call saying Ryan had read the script and was interested in the role. We went to the video store, rented every movie he had been in, and decided that he had every quality that the role required, even though he was a little younger than we imagined Dan Dunne. Ryan's a special actor and really seeks out the roles that he wants. That said, I'm not sure it would be as easy to get him to read a script today."

Getting challenging material to actors without an accredited casting agent can be difficult. But offered the chance to do it again, *Elvis and Anabelle* director Will Geiger says he would have raised more money to cast up his $380,000 road movie *Ocean Tribe* in 1997. "Unless it's something like *Blair Witch* or *Cloverfield*, where the film itself is the star, then yeah, I would definitely hire name actors," he advises. "*Ocean Tribe* opened at the Los Angeles Independent Film Festival in 1996 and got great reviews from the *Los Angeles Times*, *L.A. Weekly*, *Variety*, and other trade papers, but we still couldn't get a U.S. distribution deal. We changed our music, we reshot the opening sequence, we did all sorts of things, but when we screened it again for acquisitions executives they kept saying, 'Sorry, there's nobody in it.' "

Part of the reason identifiable cast members are so important to indies in 2009 and beyond is because spiraling marketing costs cannot be recouped through ticket sales alone. "Filmmakers need to realize that theatrical distribution is often a loss leader and that it's not until you get into international theatrical and DVD sales that you recoup," says former Picturehouse marketing executive Marian Koltai-Levine. "But art films and foreign-language films generally have a tough time in ancillary exhibition windows such as home video, and if retailers like Wal-Mart and Blockbuster won't carry a film on DVD and you can't make a big network television sale, it obviously makes it even more difficult for a distributor to make its money back."

Snatch producer Matthew Vaughn, who directed the 2005 Sundance favorite *Layer Cake* starring a then-unknown Daniel Craig, knows this only too well. His film—which received uniformly enthusiastic reviews from *Entertainment Weekly, USA Today, Variety, The New York Times,* and just about everyone else—was released by Sony Pictures Classics on May 13, 2005. *Layer Cake* opened in ten theaters and expanded in a typical art-house "platform" release to twenty-eight theaters, and later to ninety-eight theaters, before reaching a peak of two hundred theaters on June 3, 2005. Then the film shed its engagements each week thereafter until July 8, 2005, when it ended its theatrical run . . . with only $2.2 million from the U.S. box office. At the time, Daniel Craig was still largely unknown to American audiences, and although *Layer Cake* was a snappy crime thriller, it underperformed theatrically even with heaps of critical praise.

"When a movie's got stars, everyone is interested and will go to see it, but if it doesn't, you have to work that much harder to attract an audience," says Vaughn, who also produced *Lock, Stock and Two Smoking Barrels.* "With *Layer Cake* we didn't have the money to cast up. We could have paid more to get a big name, but the truth is, a big star probably wouldn't have signed on with me since I was a first-time director. But I liked it that way. I like working with new faces, and there were a lot of new faces in *Layer Cake* who are now very recognizable in the States. I was convinced that Sienna Miller was going to be a big star, and it was after seeing *Layer Cake* that everyone was saying Daniel Craig was going to be the next James Bond."

In today's ultracompetitive market, however, an acquisitions executive might point out that *Layer Cake* made only $2.2 million in the United States, *Lock, Stock and Two Smoking Barrels* earned just $4 million stateside, but *Snatch* grossed $30 million with Brad Pitt and Benicio Del Toro in the cast.

Because stars have quantifiable track records that can be called up in an instant on websites like Rentrak or The-Numbers.com, distributors can create best- and worst-case financial forecasts and Excel-based projections based on international estimates and/or weighted averages of previous U.S. box-office figures.

Pricing is based on what distribution executives think a film can earn from free and pay television, video rentals, DVD sales, and theatrical exhibition, both here and abroad. Executives walk through the value in each medium, piece it together in a spreadsheet, and then build it into a price. Unless the company is handling worldwide distribution, acquisitions executives then typically project how much international risk can be shifted to the overseas marketplace by virtue of international presales. Every actor and actress has a value—as do directors—and internal financial models based on overseas territory projections help create a valuation for every movie under consideration.

For this reason, having an actor's name attached makes the film an easier sell because there is value a distributor can achieve around the world that they can't necessarily unlock from the same movie without a known actor (or star) in the cast. Distributors can also determine a project's expected value by the quality of the script and where it's being made—if it hasn't yet been shot—and whether the filmmakers can receive tax credits or incentives, bring in European cast members or shoot part of the film in Europe.

"Today there are more independent films than ever before," says Lionsgate president Tom Ortenberg. "You open up *The New York Times* on any given Friday and there could be a dozen or more reviews," he says. "And it's tough for a lot of them to break out, so if you're looking to justify a production budget of several million dollars and you're hoping to attract a distributor to plunk millions more into marketing the picture, then there are going to be increased pressures to cast it up, to give the marketing team of a distributor something to hang their hats on."

HOW TO ATTRACT NAMES

Surprisingly, the challenge of getting name actors to appear in difficult films may not be the subject matter or having to work for scale as much as the lack of experience of the film's director. "It's often very hard to get actors committed to a first-time director," explains *Monster's Ball* and *The Woodsman* producer Lee Daniels. "Actors need to know that the director can handle a film and actors need to feel safe, especially with edgy subject matter. A lot of them will ask, 'What has he or she directed previously?' "

In *Scarface*, the movie and now the Nintendo Wii version, Tony Montana spells out his theory about how money leads to power and power leads to romantic opportunities. Financing indie films often requires a similar process: the material attracts the talent and the talent attracts the money.

Still, finding a cast that satisfies potential financiers and makes a lead role come alive is no easy task. Some actors will stall and delay discussing a role or reading a script, even when they are interested in the project. According to *The New York Times*, John Travolta reportedly took six months to sign on to *Pulp Fiction*, the film credited with resurrecting his career in 1994. Many actors' agents immediately return unsolicited material unopened, and name actors approached on the street usually don't want to lug a screenplay around all day or put themselves at legal risk by accepting a script from an adoring filmmaker who "loves their work."

However, when it comes to casting independent films, just

like Tony says, cash is king. "There was an actress I approached on the street who was very polite, but who said, 'I really get in trouble if I accept unsolicited material; send it to my agent,' " recalls *Roger Dodger* director Dylan Kidd. "And I sent it to her agent and they said, 'She's offer-only so we're not going to read it unless you have the money,' so we were in that typical bind of 'no money, no talent—no talent, no money.' And what do you do? It's a real issue. I know the industry is set up that way to prevent stars from being besieged with material, but I don't understand why every movie star doesn't have a person whose sole job it is to read every single script that comes in over the transom. If it sucks, they can throw it away after ten pages, but I'm sure they don't want to miss that one good one. If I were an actor I'd want to maximize my opportunities and see as much material as possible, because I wouldn't want to be like Elizabeth McGovern, who Steven Soderbergh wanted for the Andie MacDowell role in *Sex, Lies, and Videotape*, but McGovern's agent was like, 'Who the fuck is this guy?' and didn't send her the script. That's a classic case that probably happens every day."

According to producer Christine Vachon, however, this type of rejection happens to established directors and producers as well. "What inevitably happens is that some director will be chasing an actor or trying to get an actor to read something for months before finally moving on," she explains. "Then eventually director and actor will meet and actor will say, 'God, I loved that movie you made!' Then the director will say, 'Yeah, I was dying for you to be in it!' and the actor will claim that he or she never got the script. And I never know if that's true or if it's the actor seeing the movie and saying, 'Oh, what an idiot I was!' "

Filmmakers who want to reach out to big name actors should not palm them scripts in the street and need to go through legitimate channels, agents who are contractually representing the screenwriter or, although risky, through personal connections to the actor in question. "If you can somehow get a script to an actor through a real, legitimate personal connection, you have a reasonable chance that that star will actually assess your project," says Kim Bangash, whose Orchid Ventures invested in *You Can Count on Me* and *Sling Blade*, among others.

While most struggling screenwriters and directors can't get invited to Gym Jones or the other ultra-exclusive fitness centers where movie stars of today and tomorrow do their crunches and lat-pulls, a dedicated, stop-at-nothing filmmaker should be able to spring for a few nights on the town, even if it takes several months to become the seventh degree of Kevin Bacon. Filmmakers only need to watch the second scene of *Schindler's List* to see how Oskar Schindler was able to ingratiate himself among a certain population simply by frequenting bars and restaurants.

"Every star from Scarlett Johansson to Brigitte Nielsen can be given a script through someone they know," says Bangash, who also invested in *New Jersey Drive*. "It's as simple as going to parties or the Villa or Chateau Marmont every night of the week until you finally meet that someone who knows someone who knows someone."

Recognizable actors will read unsolicited material from unrepresented writers and directors but only if it is delivered by a trusted source, Bangash notes. "It's a lot like the venture-capital business. Venture capitalists won't look at business plans unless they come from someone they know through work or from a friend, and actors who get scripts handed to them obviously have reasons for keeping their guard up."

John Leguizamo, who alternates between independently financed films such as *The Ministers* and studio projects such as *The Happening*, explains: "Everybody is always handing you scripts to the point where you're kind of wary about it," he says. "The big line is always: 'I wrote this with *you* in mind,' and you know they've used that line a hundred times because they're saying that to *me* even though the lead character is some guy in his fifties. So they come up with all these excuses: 'Well, I wrote it with you in mind, but I had to make him a fifty-year-old version of you.' That's a big one. The other one is: 'Oh, this story is so amazing, man. I've got such big stars attached to it. If you became a part of it we could *really* take it to the next level.' And it's like: 'Oh, thanks. What are you, like, some wannabe agent with that kind of yabber?' I see right through that."

When it comes to getting scripts submitted to those who adamantly do not accept unsolicited material, *Donnie Darko* producer Adam Fields suggests going under the radar. "You've got a town full of assistants to agents, producers, and executives who all want to move up the food chain," he says, "and the way they're going to do that is to discover new talent or new projects. I have interns in my office who are reading voraciously to find something special so they can say, 'Look what I found for you.' "

THE RISK OF CASTING UP

Casting big-name actors greatly improves the chances an indie film has of getting picked up at a major festival, but filmmakers need to know it also raises the risk of kiboshing the entire project before a single frame is shot. While trying to attract major names, the producer, director, and screenwriter of any low-budget film are likely to talk up a project—especially its Michael Tolkin "beauty hook," the twist or innovative story point that makes a script intriguing and worth making. Filmmakers will also hand off copies of the screenplay to friends of friends who may be able to pass it to Joe or Jane Actor. In transit, good scripts often get passed along to actors, CEs, agents, or working screenwriters who may want to create their own version, especially if the script was sent as a Word file rather than a locked PDF. Aspiring screenwriters, directors, and producers should never ever send an unproduced screenplay to anyone via e-mail, regardless of the format. Further, screenwriters and producers need to keep a careful inventory of everyone and every third party who has received the script, including the date it was sent. It may seem like overkill, but independent-film producers must keep track of who has seen and received a copy of the script.

If copies of the script have already been e-mailed, a delicately worded follow-up should be sent inquiring when coverage—or a definite "pass" from the actor or actress in question—can be expected.

THE ONE AND ONLY DYLAN KIDD

Because so many aspiring filmmakers have heard the story about how Kidd got his screenplay of *Roger Dodger* produced after handing it to Campbell Scott in a Manhattan coffee shop, most wrongly think this is a legitimate avenue for casting and financing. But for those who haven't heard it, the story went like this: Kidd carried his script around New York City for months before running into Scott, who loved it, signed on, and helped set up the film's financing with Holedigger Films. "Dylan saw me in a restaurant and he handed me the script. Once I read it, I have to say it was a selfish decision," says Scott, also a writer-director. "Three weeks later I called him to say I loved the part and that nobody would give me parts like that. At the time, I was looking for a script that was inexpensive and that could be made for $1 million, so *Roger Dodger* seemed perfect."

For a time, Scott was inundated with screenplays practically every time he left the house. "Even now when I meet screenwriters in the street or aspiring directors I have to make an immediate assessment, like, 'Am I dealing with someone who is for real or do they perhaps have a warped perspective of what's going on?'" says Scott. "But I'm always honest with them and I say, 'I may not get to your script, but if I do, I'll tell you what I think.'"

What aspiring filmmakers should realize is that the odds of this happening to them are incalculably remote. Still, everyone with a script under one arm thinks *they* will be the one exception. Even when a fortuitous meeeting does occur, the most legit aspiring filmmakers can come off sounding like wannabes or total stalker-maniacs. The truth is, when famous actors are standing on line for an iced-blended at the Coffee Bean or buying Odwalla carrot juice at Vons, the last thing they want is to be handed a script that's "going to resurrect their careers" or make somebody's Sundance dream come true. Even so, famous actors are handed stacks of screenplays every day, but there's still only one Dylan Kidd.

While there are unorthodox ways to get material into the hands of name actors, screenplays should be sent to actors only through legitimate agents who officially contractually represent the screenwriter. (See Appendix 2.)

HIRING CASTING DIRECTORS

The trusted and softer sell of using a casting agent is often the best way to go. Filmmakers who don't have the time or the ability to schmooze can instead put between $20,000 and $80,000 of their production budget toward hiring a casting director with solid credentials.

"Paying a casting director's fee is absolutely money well spent," says Cassian Elwes of William Morris Independent.

"I would recommend going to a well-known casting director who has cast films the filmmaker admires and who has been able to reach out and get well-known talent. Casting directors have fantastic relationships not just with agents but also a lot of times with the talent themselves, with whom they've worked over and over. So I think it's really about looking at films that you think are similar or films you think were really well cast and seeing who the casting directors were and trying to reach out to one of those people to work on your movie."

While many top casting directors are hired to work on Hollywood films only after the A-list talent has been secured by the studio or by well-known producers, casting directors often play a vital role in securing leading talent for indie films, sometimes in exchange for a producer credit or a fee proportionate to the film's total budget.

"Casting directors try to get an actor to read a script either with or without an offer on the table," says Ferne Cassel, the casting director on *Monster*, *Boxing Helena*, and *Ace Ventura: When Nature Calls*, among others. "Ideally, a good casting director can get an actor to read the script without an offer because sometimes the script is going out before the production has any money. That's where casting directors are very helpful to filmmakers—they have relationships with agents who can get scripts to actors."

Indeed, while an aspiring director may still be unknown, casting directors are connected and can act as a bridge between talent and a film that could be an indie hit with the right actor. "Getting a script from a terrific casting director like Avy Kaufman or the late Mili Finn can be very important," says *Choke* star Sam Rockwell. "It depends, certainly, but there are casting directors like Mary Vernieu, who cast *Choke* and *Bad Santa*, who can really draw important people to a project."

The problem for aspiring filmmakers with no casting directors is that well-known actors will often "express interest" or even try to plant a flag on, without actually committing to, as many projects as they can so as not to miss out on the next *Little Miss Sunshine*. However, the upshot for many first- and second-time directors is that they have only a list of interested actors, with no firm offers or deals with which to move forward—something that makes the directors sound like wannabes. Some actors can be elusive in the way they pledge themselves to projects by first-timers; until they or their agents get a clearer sense of who else is involved, they may not want to be first in and risk having to carry a film on their backs by themselves.

Even though an actor's agent may know and trust the casting director, that doesn't mean he or she trusts a first-time director or producer with his or her valuable actor client. "A lot of agents today will ask to see that the production funds are in escrow, especially on a small movie where they don't know the people involved," says Cassel. "They are just trying to protect themselves: if you're going to take an actor off the market by having him or her commit to your film or if you're going to go out with his or her name attached to raise funding, the project has to be real. Furthermore, casting directors can't keep going to the well with agents saying, 'Please read this script, I love it.' These days, a project has to be further along."

First- and second-time filmmakers may have the best intentions, but if an actor passes up a big-studio payday to do an indie film, the actor can take a major economic hit if the indie project falls apart, which is often the case. Increasingly, agents at William Morris, Endeavor, CAA, ICM, and other powerful agencies want to know that an independent film is indeed prepped and ready to go should their client decide to come aboard. However, when talent is being used to secure production financing, this penchant by agents to close actor deals at the last minute creates the classic chicken-or-the-egg scenario that first-time filmmakers find so frustrating. Substantial capital is needed to go into preproduction and producers must generally risk investors' equity or spend borrowed capital before a deal with name talent can be agreed upon and signed.

INTERNATIONAL PRESALES

"I don't always agree with how it impacts the storytelling, but with the 'right' cast member an independent film can still get an international television deal and make some money in the ancillary market," says Sony Pictures Classics copresident Tom Bernard. "Independent film and DVD sales have now penetrated the world market—a big ancillary market with international video deals and international television deals."

Exactly how this is done remains a mystery to many aspiring filmmakers who have visions of getting an inexpensive room at the Pierre et Vacances or Hotel Climat in Cannes and then wandering the halls of the Palais des Festivals with a script or an HD-CAM SR trailer under one arm. Unfortunately, that's not how it works. Indie filmmakers looking for presales typically go out to the overseas market via international sales agents.

Producer Pascal Borno, who assembled financing for literally hundreds of films for Dino De Laurentiis, says having to cast up should not be seen as the huge concession many filmmakers often make it out to be. "Casting decisions are not made as carelessly by financiers as all the anecdotes you hear would have you believe," he says. "They're not going to make you put Steven Seagal into a Shakespearean role just because he's big in Japan. International distributors do read the scripts and they advise filmmakers based on the cast they believe can help protect their investment, money which is often allowing the movie to be made. Given those suggestions, you agree on price, you agree on back end, you enter into a distribution agreement, and the movie gets financed."

It's not just Jean-Claude Van Damme, Michael Madsen, Jason Statham, and Christopher Lambert who can attract production funding from international presales. Even indie-cool actors such as Steve Zahn, Peter Dinklage, and Zooey Deschanel have a cash value for international distributors. Their international value is based on television rights, so if an actor has been in other independent movies that appeared on pay or free television in these countries, then he or she is a known entity. Indie filmmakers won't get studio-level pricing, but they may be able to sell overseas television rights with the help of an international sales agent or connected producer rep. How much to pay the actor and how much to spend on the film is always a big question for new filmmakers.

"It's important to think about how much you are going to pay talent and whether that talent is worth what you're paying for them. Do they bring you enough added value to justify the cost?" says Adam Fields. "For example, if you're paying a star $700,000 but you're only able to raise an additional $700,000 from their presence in the film, then you did something wrong. You either overpaid or the star wasn't worth what you paid. If you're paying an actor $700,000 but they're only bringing in a million in guarantees, then it may also be a mistake. You should be able to leverage it much further."

When making deals with top talent, producers must be clear—in writing—what the production will receive in return for the actor's salary. Is it just his or her acting services, or does the producer have the right to raise money overseas from the actor's participation or to include the actor's name and likeness in paid advertising around the world? Can the actor's face be used in the poster once the film is sold? Can the actor's two or three small scenes be included in the trailer to make it seem as if they are starring in the film? Can the acquiring distributor use the actor's likeness in co-branded marketing campaigns with consumer products such as Dewar's (which promoted *The Blair Witch Project*) or Qantas Airways (which had a promotional tie-in with *Whale Rider*).

Fields, who has worked with several first- and second-time directors, advocates a thrifty approach, regardless. "You should always keep the costs down no matter what you're doing: whether you're building a house or making a movie. There's no reason to be profligate," he says. "Whenever you pay for something or pay someone, you have to analyze what service they are providing and ask, 'What value do they bring? What is it costing me?'" These are questions film-makers should also ask themselves when considering expensive name actors for roles in otherwise low-budget movies.

Some actors may reserve the right to allow their likeness to be used for publicity until after they see the finished film, a stipulation that financiers or completion-fund financiers may not be aware of or agree to. "You get an actor who agrees to come onto a film for scale plus 10 percent and he says, 'Okay, guys, I'm going to help you make this movie,' attorney Wilder Knight explains. "But he may not want his face on a poster all over the world or even just in the United States unless he really loves the movie. Unless the movie goes to Sundance and wins prizes, his trademark is being watered down. That's the way the agents see it. That's the way the managers see it. And that's real, that's legitimate. What they'll do is, they'll say, 'I'll do it,' because they have a relationship with somebody. They might get some real money, like $500,000 or something, but that's like a gift if the actor's rate is $3 million or $4 million or $5 million. If you do your deal and you forget to include marketing and publicity, you're going to think, 'We're paying this guy a million dollars and we can use his face in absolutely everything.' And then you finish the movie and you haven't done your homework. You haven't gotten a long-form agreement from this actor and you haven't fleshed out this very important contractual issue."

ACTORS WANT TO WORK

While A-list actors typically accept offers only from well-heeled agents, studio bigwigs, or world-class directors, many actors in the B+ category are amenable to reading and even joining projects that come in over the transom. "One of the dirty little secrets of Hollywood is that everybody below the A-list has a lot of trouble finding work," says Ira Deutchman, president of Emerging Pictures. "Actors in the second or third tier can make a decent payday by playing the second lead or maybe the sidekick to the villain in a Hollywood film, but the fact is these roles are not all that rewarding artistically. Agents and managers are savvy about that and they would much rather have their non-A-list clients working than not working."

Many actors are looking for parts that will allow them to break out of being typecast or to court Academy Awards with edgy material the way Charlize Theron did with *Monster* or Javier Bardem did with *No Country for Old Men*. "Name actors are attracted to independent film because it gives them an opportunity to stretch their artistic legs and to take risks," explains Sundance festival director Geoff Gilmore. "And it ends up serving both independent film and those actors because it enables them to become better actors—to grow in their profession—which they don't get to do by performing

in the same stereotypical roles that they might do or on a television show week after week. I think taking those risks
becomes incredibly important for many of them because so
much of the studio system hasn't enabled them to do that."

Few independent-film projects garner *Juno*-level back
end or as many merchandising opportunities as *Napoleon
Dynamite*, but many become cult favorites that boost an
actor's standing or street cred. "What was great about *Donnie
Darko* was that everyone agreed to do it for scale," recalls
Fields. "No amount of money *we* could have paid them—
considering what they make for a movie—was going to make
a difference. They did it because they wanted to be in the
film. Drew Barrymore is paid eight figures to be in a film. If
she was doing a week's work for a check, there wouldn't have
been enough money we could have ever paid her. She's not
doing a movie like that for the payday.

"When you're going after really big stars I don't think
there's any amount of money you can pay them that's going
to make a difference when they can get $10 million to
$15 million per picture," says Fields. "They're not going to
do your little picture—or not do it—because you can afford
to give them $500,000 or even $1 million."

Righteous Kill star Al Pacino, who appeared in *People I
Know* and who directed the Fox Searchlight–distributed
Looking for Richard, has his own theory. "It used to be that a
film actor would want to take a break from movies by performing in theater, but these days more and more actors are
appearing in small independent films instead," he says.
"Actors used to go back to the theater because that's where
they got to do the 'great roles,' but now you find that many
of those roles are showing up in smaller movies. Today an
actor does a big picture and then he or she does what we
call a 'little picture,' but they're not little pictures, really.
They're just different, but they're perceived to be smaller

because they don't draw the larger audiences, but that's okay.

"Acting in the best scripts—the ones that afford you an opportunity to play roles that are challenging on many levels—is tantamount to playing an instrument," Pacino continues. "It's very similar to the way certain music can inspire a pianist to move his or her fingers faster or to become engaged in certain rhythms. The best scripts allow you to delve deep into a character and find out who they are, and the opportunity to do that on-screen is very infrequent. It's related to the quality of scripts that come to you. You start to realize that the worse the script, the more money a studio will give you. It's almost a given. I think that in independent film you get the great writers and the great filmmakers who come along and have an idea because it's coming from them. Unfortunately, you sometimes have to go through a lot when you agree to do them because you're working under less-than-ideal conditions."

Although aspiring filmmakers think they can fool all of the people some of the time and some of the people all of the time, name actors cannot be conned or bamboozled. In fact, most older thesps can smell a BS artist a mile away and tell straight off when a project is still just a pipe dream, unless *they* participate. "You only really know that something you're being offered is going to be a real film when the airline ticket to the location comes through," explains screen legend Malcolm McDowell, who plays Terrence McQuewick on HBO's *Entourage*. "And I'll tell you one thing I've learned: Never get to an airport and buy your own ticket. Because you know damn well they haven't got their financing. If it's not there, as an electronic ticket waiting for you at the counter, turn around and go home. In other cases, you can be a week before principal photography and you're packing your suitcase to go, and your agent will call and say, 'I've heard nothing from them,' and you just know the money's not there.

You never get too fussed about it. You say, 'Oh well, that's a pity, but on to the next.'"

Despite the occasional indignities, *Vicky Cristina Barcelona* costar Patricia Clarkson says she appreciates the immediacy and intimacy of nonstudio projects. "What pulls you into an independent film is that they're usually made by one person or two: one writer-director, or one writer and one director," she says. "And what makes independent film great is the intimacy, the immediacy, and the fact that it is not filtered or distilled. It is pure, speaking with a certain voice for better or for worse. I'd rather see a flawed pure film any day of the week. I would never ever stop doing independent films. I have to do them. I always will because it feeds me in a way that a big film never can. And that's not to say I don't want to do big films, but I'd rather do one big film a year and three little ones than the opposite."

Clarkson also relishes the chance to occasionally do something different. "Before *The Station Agent*, I'd never been the 'chick' in a film in my life," she says. "But I got to be the chick in that film, which was probably a departure in that it was actually the closest to me. It was the least character part I'd done in a while in a really beautiful story."

Choke, *Moon*, and *Gentlemen Broncos* star Sam Rockwell says name actors are actually looking for several elements in concert. "You're always looking for a good script, a smart director—someone who wants to collaborate—and great actors in the cast," he says. "The participation of someone you know is always nice. Clark Gregg, who directed *Choke* and adapted the screenplay, and I worked together years ago in a play, so it does help to know people. It helps you remember how smart they are. You want to hear their passion and intelligence so you can appreciate their vision of the script and the role and believe in their potential for executing that vision."

Independently financed films are also rewarding in other, more subtle ways. "If it's low-budget enough, you know you're not going to sit around for hours while they tweak the light for the next shot," explains Leguizamo, star of indie films such as *Spun* and *Crónicas*. "That's the thing about independent films: you always feel that energy in them because there is an energy. You're not going back to your trailer to make some calls and play a little Xbox 360. You're on the stint twenty-four/seven."

Hope Davis, who has appeared in several iconic indie films, including *About Schmidt*, *American Splendor*, and *Synecdoche, New York*, points out that decent roles don't fall into an actor's lap every day and that quality is often in limited supply. "It doesn't matter what level you're at, actors are always struggling for good parts," she says. "It doesn't matter if you're at the top of the heap, or the middle of the heap, or the indie heap, or whatever. It's always hard to find something that you really want to work on."

Emphasizing certain themes or issues in a script can be a way to attract name talent to a project. "For *Ocean Tribe* we tried to get Gene Wilder, since the story dealt with cancer," says Geiger. "We were going to give a large amount of our proceeds to Gilda's Club—the charity named after Wilder's late wife, Gilda Radner—and cancer research. We made that offer and Gene liked the script, but ultimately he didn't want to go all the way to Baja, California, to shoot it. But if you can find an angle to bring an actor on board or something that will inspire them to read the project, it's an approach that may work."

Fields, whose credits also include *Brokedown Palace*, says that low-budget producers will have a better chance of landing top talent if they keep their demands reasonable and carefully plan their shooting schedule. "What was great about *Donnie Darko* was that we were able to limit several parts to a week and shoot in a way that was as actor-friendly as possible. We were able to say, 'Come on, do this. We'll shoot you out in four or five days. It'll be fun.' And once you get one actor, there's a snowball effect that happens: 'Look, so-and-so is doing it and they're working for scale. Oh, okay. If *they're* in it, now it's validated.' " Indeed, when it comes to casting big names, a positive disposition and an anchor tenant *who is legitimately signed on* can go a long way. "The participation of someone you know is always nice. It's always good to have some friendly faces onboard, such as Patricia Clarkson or Bill Macy or countless other actors whom I've known and admired," says Rockwell. "It is really bad form, though, when aspiring directors go around saying they have this actor or that actor attached when they don't. It's not illegal but it's something aspiring directors should certainly stop doing. It's just desperation on the part of the filmmaker—it's ambitious desperation—and it's very unattractive. You can't beat truth and commitment."

REHEARSALS ARE KEY

Even with a tight shooting schedule, Pacino advises low-budget indie filmmakers to schedule time for rehearsals and table readings. "I think when you're shooting on a low budget with limited resources, it's a good idea to have a long rehearsal period," Pacino says. "You want to get people together and then go in and really go for it when you're shooting the film. But that's very difficult to do when you haven't really rehearsed. Then it's a hindrance. Weekends help. On big-budget films sometimes you don't have rehearsal at all, and they spend a lot of the shooting day rehearsing, so a big scene that requires three days would be done in two if you had the rehearsal time."

Faced with the need for name actors, some producers

slash crew, locations, and equipment, offering the savings in a lump sum to a well-known actor. However, these sort of unbalanced productions often present their own special challenges. "Huge pay disparities can make for a very unhappy crew," says Deutchman. "What you try to do instead is to convince your big-name actors that your film is going to be an artistic experience worth participating in for less money. I try to frame the film as their 'lift ticket to Sundance.'"

Still another problem filmmakers can face once a name actor enters the equation is maintaining control of the film and the set. "Most big actors are more powerful than the filmmaker or producer, on set and in a lot of other areas," says No Budget Film School founder Mark Stolaroff. "If they're big enough, actors often have a huge amount of control over the film they're working on since they are literally the star of the show. If a director really knows what they're doing they'll be fine, but if it's a first-timer dealing with a decent-size crew and a big-name actor, it can be a little overwhelming."

Indeed, indie-film directors may not be prepared to handle temperamental actors who somehow can't connect to the material on the day. It doesn't matter how well prepared a filmmaker may be if actors decide to hide in their trailers, throw a tantrum, or not show up to set. Some big stars may have hushed-up alcohol or drug problems, personal issues, or odd superstitions that prevent them from performing, causing delays that will instantly throw an indie film's compressed schedule into chaos. Directors should ask around and find out about the person they're considering for a role before writing a check or at least recognize that they may not have any control over a headstrong star or well-known diva trolling for street cred. Indie directors should also be frank with actors about what to expect.

Even the most accommodating actors may not be ready

for the shock of ultra-low-budget, no-frills, no-trailer, run-and-gun guerrilla filmmaking. "The expense of landing a known actor often goes beyond that person's salary or fee," says Deutchman. "DV filmmakers have to take a certain level of care with these actors to give them an experience that they're used to on better-funded productions. As much as many actors say they're open to appearing in independent films, they often have no idea what that really means: having to share a dressing room, being in the same car with another actor each morning on the way to set, minimal craft service, and other potential indignities, like providing their character's wardrobe."

Confessions of a Dangerous Mind star Sam Rockwell suggests being blunt with actors about what they can expect on a low-budget shoot. "Performing in an indie film is like entering a war zone," he says. "There's no money, so you have to rush, rush, rush, and it's often totally guerrilla filmmaking. You get three takes, if that. I've done shoots where I've only gotten *one* take, and that was on a special effects shot. I did a movie about cloning and I only had one shot at it. So, it's intense."

Speaking specifically of movies shot in digital video, Deutchman notes that an actor could be enticed by the economics of DV production, in which the chances of actually making a significant profit are better than on more costly independent films shooting on 16 mm or 35 mm. "When you're taking about net profits on a DV feature, the term actually means something," he says.

THE DANGERS OF PAY OR PLAY

If an actor won't work for scale in a project that is clearly a labor of love, how much should filmmakers offer? Actors' salaries are based on their "quote," usually the amount they got for their last performance. Sometimes agents will make a distinction between studio and independent-film quotes, but other times a producer may have to battle an agent who cites the studio-level quote as an immutable figure. After all, if an actor's value is damaged as a result of a poorly realized or just plain bad indie film, it could very well siphon off thousands or even millions of dollars from that actor's next studio payday.

Like the cardplayers in David Mamet's *House of Games*, some filmmakers think they can bluff their way in or "buy the pot" by offering name actors pay-or-play agreements. In such a deal, a star must be paid a substantial fee whether or not the film begins production on a specific day, a risky maneuver that can sink the entire project.

"You can always push the start date back by a week, but if you're dealing with a huge actor who has a very short window, then everybody has to struggle to make it happen," says *The Whole Wide World* and *Jolene* director Dan Ireland. "But before you get to that point, you should do the math and see if you can really make the start date. You have to remember: the project could go to hell and then you're stuck for the $500,000 you offered a particular actor."

Many filmmakers believe rolling the pay-or-play dice before their production is fully financed is a good idea since an actor's commitment can open purse strings and possibly trigger international presales, but those expecting an avalanche of investment dollars are often disappointed.

Attorney and consultant John Sloss points out that a lot of producers and directors wrongly shoot themselves in the foot or mortgage their projects' upside just to land a name. "You shouldn't go off willy-nilly and think, 'Oh my God, this is a movie star! This actor is worth a million bucks' or 'This actor is worth a million bucks and they're working for scale, so of course the bank will understand that I've given the actor an aggressive back end,' " he says.

Still, many filmmakers think that throwing around pay-or-play offers makes them seem more real or on the level. Many find out too late, however, that the actor they coveted may not have been worth it.

"Here's a typical example. A client came to me and said, 'We negotiated a pay-or-play deal all by ourselves, we're paying this actor $1 million because he's really famous,' " recalls Knight. "This actor was well known in parts of Europe where people would jump up and down and ask for his autograph, but in New York or Los Angeles he could walk down the street and nobody would recognize him. He had done a couple of television spots and had a minor role in a film that was very successful, but nobody would recognize him here. So this filmmaker makes a pay-or-play deal with the actor and then they started to try to put their film together. They wanted to put up a third of the financing but they couldn't get anyone else to come in because they had attached someone with a deal that didn't work in the independent world. They went around to other territories for financing and everyone they spoke to said, 'Why are you paying this guy $1 million?'

"If they had called me first I would have said, 'Let's find out what his going rate is,' " Knight continues. "Actors' agents don't always tell you what the going rate is. They tell you what they'd like the going rate to be. So by not calling me and getting the financial information, they wasted a lot of time and locked themselves in with this actor. I went to two litigators and asked, 'Can I get my client out of this contract?' and they said, 'No.' That's pay or play, everybody knows what it means. Even the little deal memos, the one-pager, is absolutely clear. It's unambiguous: if you don't make

the movie, you gotta pay this guy $1 million. If you make the
movie and you're paying him $1 million, you're overpaying
him. But what happened in this case was they couldn't even
get the additional financing, so they were in a situation
where they were still going to have to pay this guy $1 million
to do nothing. The economic information is an area where
lawyers are very valuable. And if you get it wrong, you very
often come up with a terrible deal or kill your project
entirely."

With no money and all their investors' cash down the
drain, once-bitten filmmakers who find themselves back at
square one might consider producing their films on a mi-
crobudget level, with borrowed DV cameras and minimal
lighting. "At Fine Line we picked up tons of movies that
didn't have any stars in them," recalls former Warner Independent Pictures distribution executive Steven Friedlander.
"We picked up *Trick*, we picked up *The Cup*—about Buddhist
soccer-playing monks, that had nobody anyone had ever
heard of in it—*Cherish* really had nobody in it, and we picked
up *Shine*, when Geoffrey Rush was totally unknown to
American audiences. So it's really about the quality of the
film. I think I speak for everyone who acquires films when I
say that I'd rather acquire a film that I know is going to get
great reviews and has no one in it, than one that has ten or
twelve stars in an ensemble."

Stolaroff has an even more persuasive pitch. "Look at the
history of successful low-budget films: *She's Gotta Have It*,
Laws of Gravity, *El Mariachi*, *Pi*, and *Slacker*. Look at *Blair
Witch*, *Greek Wedding*, *Napoleon Dynamite*, *Once*, *City of God*,
Clerks, or *Open Water*. None of them had name actors. In
some cases they didn't even have *good* actors. But they were
all unique in their own way, and even if they failed in some
areas, they were still able to connect with audiences and be
memorable."

6. The Nightmare of Story and Screenplay Theft

Nowhere is there more apprehension and less understanding about the serious risks faced by indie filmmakers than in the area of story and screenplay theft. In this chapter, as in the others, my purpose is to alert readers to potential problems and pitfalls in the indie-filmmaking process. I bring to bear my own experiences and understandings in a general sense and also those of other knowledgeable figures in the industry. For this chapter, which deals centrally with legal issues related to screenplays and story ideas, I rely primarily on the views and opinions of attorneys who have had experience counseling and litigating on issues of idea and/or script submissions, copyright protection, copyright infringement, and implied contract formation. To alleviate any confusion, and because I did recently unsuccessfully pursue my own claim of copyright infringement and breach of implied contract, I want to make clear that it is not my purpose in this chapter to write autobiographically, and nothing stated here should be understood as commenting on, or as making or renewing allegations regarding, any specific person or claim. Moreover, when I speak of script theft, I am not making new allegations or stating a legal conclusion that any particular person or persons were involved in or guilty of such activity. Finally, I should also like to make clear that none of the attorneys quoted here were directly involved in my case or the subsequent federal court jury trial, and none of their comments here are intended to comment specifically on that case.

Getting ripped off—during the financing interval, the casting process, or even on the eve of production—is common enough to warrant serious consideration and a discussion with the entire cast and crew. While many screenwriters, directors, and producers worry about story theft from time to time, most equate the risk with the chance that they will be struck by lightning. The truth is, most aspiring filmmakers don't realize how terribly vulnerable their projects are at numerous points in the coverage, financing, and casting process. Still others don't realize that some of the things they are doing are actually opening the door for screenplay thieves to prey on them with impunity. The tragedy is that many aspiring filmmakers with the talent and ability to get into Sundance, Cannes, Toronto, or Berlin and become the superstar filmmakers of tomorrow are this very minute sprinting into the arms of people who could hurt them and prevent them from achieving their dreams. There are at least two dozen ways aspiring filmmakers actually help screenplays get stolen in spite of taking steps they think are precautionary, a fact that is especially heartbreaking given the extreme sacrifices most screenwriters, directors, and producers are willing to make to get their films made. For this reason the misunderstandings and terrible myths surrounding story and screenplay theft are real-world dangerous, since the price many filmmakers will ultimately pay can be measured in years of poverty, missed opportunities, long nights spent rewriting scripts or crafting compelling business plans, courting and pitching potential investors, huge sums borrowed to attend film festivals and production seminars, school loans nearing default, broken relationships, and being forever cut off from a life they might have had. As a result, it is critical that screenwriters recognize that script theft can happen at

*any time and avoid mortgaging their home lives and important per-
sonal relationships to chase the dream of becoming the next Tarantino. Of course, it is not just the screenwriter who is hurt whenever an
indie-film script is stolen. The director, producer, and crew lose the
recognition and career boost they would have garnered from being
associated with a compelling or successful project. The viewing public
is robbed of new voices that might have provided profoundly moving
entertainments for years to come. As a result, it is not just aspiring
screenwriters or producers who must be extra careful when it comes
to handling, discussing, mailing, or passing along a terrific screenplay.
Every crew member associated with an indie film can unknowingly
help screenplay thieves derail the project. Fortunately, there are many
ways screenwriters and filmmakers working with them can protect
their most valuable asset if they know what to look out for.*

There are six basic things filmmakers need to know about
screenplay theft. The first and most important is that screenwriters or filmmakers who are sending scripts over the transom to *anyone* without official agency representation are
asking for their screenplays to be stolen. The second is that
simply handing over a screenplay to an actor, producer, or
director on the street, in a coffee shop, in a parking lot, or in
a restaurant is tantamount to giving the script away for free,
since there is no way to prove the script was passed along or
that it was actually received. This is especially true for waiters, bartenders, and baristas in Los Angeles who think that
waiting on their favorite actor is going to give them a chance
to palm someone a script and lead to their big break. A credit
card signature for a coffee or a restaurant receipt is not proof
that a screenplay changed hands or was accepted by anyone.
Third, screenwriters must keep careful records of everyone
who has received copies of the script and exactly which version was sent. Copies of every cover letter and of each specific script sent out should be kept for at least ten years, even

after the indie version of the project is completed. Fourth, every draft or revised version of the screenplay that is ever to be circulated must be officially registered with the Library of Congress for $45 or the current going rate, with an official registration, available at www.copyright.gov. Unregistered revised drafts should never be assumed to be protected or covered by a previous registration, since only the earlier registered draft will count in a legal proceeding. The fifth point is that to bring a case federal court for copyright infringement, the infringing script must achieve a very high threshold of "strict similarity" to avoid having the case dismissed by a judge on pretrial summary judgment. This means that even if all the best scenes or sequences from an unproduced screenplay are stolen, it may not be enough to bring a successful lawsuit.

"It's only a copyright violation if you can show that one work is so similar to the other that [a judge] can find clear evidence of infringement [and rule that the case should go forward and be heard by a jury]," explains attorney Gary Gorham of Leader Gorham. "What surprises people is that the threshold for being able to bring a case is based on the conglomeration of the work and that this totality is the essence of copyright protection in this area. And in the courtroom it often comes down to expert testimony. Juries tend to do one of three things: they like one expert and not the other, they believe one expert and not the other, or they make fundamental, practical decisions that guide their ruling. I've had juries say, 'That guy lied . . . and he's done.' Or 'That [plaintiff's] expert is whiny, we don't really like him.' Or they just don't see the similarities. It's hard to say how juries come up with their results, but it's always surprising."

Finally, the last thing screenwriters and filmmakers need to know about screenplay theft is that while they may be discouraged by negative or even eviscerating script coverage, their projects may still be good enough to steal. No one should ever assume that their low-budget indie script is too out-there or too edgy to be ripped off.

A NEW, SECOND AVENUE

Since the Ninth Circuit Court of Appeals ruling in *Grosso v. Miramax* in 2004, screenwriters can now bring lawsuits in California state court under a "breach of implied contract" claim if enough identifiable elements of their screenplays were used in the infringing script and if the aggrieved screenwriter can prove—ideally in writing—that he or she clearly and in no uncertain terms told the recipient of the script that the script was for sale and that the screenwriter's intent was to sell it. These cases are also difficult to win for a couple of reasons: screenplay-theft lawsuits can be tossed out by a motion for dismissal on the grounds that the stolen script was not original; and because the screenwriter must have enunciated his or her desire to sell the screenplay to the person who received it and not simply that the screenwriter wanted it read and covered, as is traditionally the case. Further, the screenwriter must be able to prove, via e-mail or some other means, that the recipient actually received and accepted the screenplay knowing that the writer expected to be compensated if the screenplay was produced in its entirety or if its premise and best sequences showed up in another film. While screenwriters imagine that a jury would see multiple similarities as a clear sign of copying, an implied contract is not formed unless the writer is able to produce an e-mail or paper trail or some other proof that deal terms were discussed and agreed upon. If a script has floated its way to a would-be screenplay thief via a second, third, or fourth party it can be impossible to prove "access," which means that even if a case does make its way into a courtroom after years of motions and depositions, a jury may be hard pressed to side with the screenwriter plaintiff who cannot prove "based on a preponderance of the evidence" that the alleged thief received or had an opportunity to see the screenplay in question. And since independent or parallel generation is an absolute defense, the aggrieved screenwriter has a difficult hurdle to overcome to prove that similar or identical elements in both screenplays are not coincidental.

Of course, if a filmmaker were to include published songs in his or her film without clearing them or paying the songwriter and copyright holder, the film can be enjoined from release until the songs are removed. If the movie were released with the songs intact, the songwriter could sue for significant damages and most likely win, since permission was not granted and a copyright was clearly violated. But if the best elements are cherry-picked from an unproduced script, or even if the entire screenplay is lifted with minor alterations, the cherry picker can likely avoid civil prosecution because most aspiring screenwriters have not taken the appropriate steps to protect their work and because copyright law in the screenplay arena is stacked against unaffiliated or unpresented screenwriters. Most screenwriters don't know just how tipped the scales are until it's too late and they are in a consultation with a knowledgeable intellectual-property attorney after their screenplay has been stolen or appropriated.

One respected journalist who covers the film industry has described screenplay theft as such a regular occurrence—almost as rampant as file sharing—that it has become a sad rite of passage for aspiring screenwriters, "proof that they can write screenplays worth producing." For this reason, everyone associated with an indie-film production must be extremely careful and make sure that they safeguard what is the most valuable resource in any industry: a great idea.

RECORD-KEEPING IS KEY

For these reasons and others, lawsuits related to screenplay theft are actually *not* clogging U.S. courts due to the fact that most cases are dismissed before trial for lack of triable evidence, simply because the screenwriter didn't keep careful records. Struggling filmmakers are typically not the most organized people in the world, but when it comes to proving a case of screenplay theft that can sometimes take place years after a script was sent out, this sloppiness and carelessness can be fatal. "One of the most important things screenwriters and filmmakers need to do is pay closer attention to record-keeping," advises Toby Butterfield, a partner in the New York law firm of Cowan, DeBaets, Abrahams & Sheppard. "In other words, filmmakers need to keep track of who they've given the script to in an Excel spreadsheet or a similar file. If you want to keep numbered copies of the script using a stamp pad or a $60 Bates stamp [available at any office supply shop], that's a good idea, too."

Asking a film executive, a working director, or a film producer to read a script with the unstated implication that it is for sale or available for financing means, for legal purposes, that the filmmaker is only seeking "advice and critique." An implied contract is created only if the screenwriter or producer delivering the script clearly enunciates to the recipient that the script is for sale and that it is the hope and wish of the screenwriter or producer that the recipient consider the screenplay for sale. Otherwise, it can be argued in court during a breach-of-implied-contract lawsuit that the filmmaker was not selling the screenplay but hoping to receive critique or judgment as to its quality. To overcome this they will need a copy of the cover letter.

"Filmmakers should never just send a script to people without a cover letter, and that cover letter should say something like: 'Thank you for agreeing to review my screenplay in confidence with a view toward optioning, purchasing, or producing it,' " says Butterfield. "Filmmakers should not be bashful about stating what they want—to sell the script or have it produced—rather than letting it be ambiguous. They should state that they would like the recipient to review it and provide any feedback and hopefully option it or purchase it. You should let them know that's what you want since it's no surprise. It is what you want, so say what you want. But overall, you've got to make sure you've got a record of who you've sent the script to and, frankly, why you've sent it, by including cover letters that are respectful and courteous but that make plain your desires. You don't have to be unpleasant about it. You don't have to be difficult. You don't have to ask people to sign a nondisclosure agreement before sending it, since that's a quick way to ensure that someone does not read your screenplay. Filmmakers should be clear in the communication that there is attached material enclosed and that that material is a screenplay. They also need to enunciate why they are sending it, and what they're hoping the recipient is going to do with it, which is purchase it or produce it."

THE DREAMER'S REALITY CHECK

Anyone working on or investing in an independent film needs to come to terms with several facts: (1) The independent-film world is not a lagoon of integrity where vulnerable, over-eager, and unrepresented filmmakers can swim safely. (2) Unrepresented filmmakers are actually *more* likely to have their screenplays stolen in the indie-film sphere than in "regular" Hollywood because indie filmmakers frequently rely on huge favors, handshake deals, "hip-pocket" arrangements, big promises, total hookups, last-minute miracles, big talkers, friends of friends, and terrible advice, rather than on healthy skepticism, qualified lawyers, official agency representation, and formal contracts in the course of everyday business. (3) Independent filmmakers are far too trusting of those who seem like they might be able to give them a leg up or the big break they've been waiting for. (4) As filmmakers get closer to realizing their dream of making their film, they often get complacent or let their guard down, like Indiana Jones's assistant Satipo, who famously remarked, "There is nothing to fear here!" (5) By asking a heavy hitter or executive in the film business to read or take a look at a script without clearly enunciating that it is for sale *to them* and not simply for review, a writer or director creates a situation where that executive can legally make use of the terrific dialogue, great scenes, or even the entire screenplay because of well-established but little-known legal loopholes discussed later that are heavily weighted *against* unrepresented screenwriters. (6) Almost all of the standard release forms that struggling screenwriters are asked to sign leave them open to word-for-word and scene-for-scene screenplay theft, since release forms purposely disembowel the ability to bring legal action afforded by official copyright registration; otherwise they wouldn't be release forms. (7) Registration with the Writers Guild of America is *not* the same as U.S. copyright registration since WGA registration does not provide any statutory protection and only copyright registration allows for the recovery of legal fees, a basic element of being able to secure an attorney on a contingency basis. (8) Any waiter, hairstylist, parking-lot attendant, video store clerk, lawn worker, nurse, landscape architect, bartender, studio executive's assistant, or barista who hands his or her screenplay to a well-known actor, producer, or director has most likely just lost any legal case he or she could ever hope to bring should the script be ripped off in some fashion because the screenwriter will never be able to legally prove access, the most important pillar of any copyright infringement case. (9) Unrepresented screenwriters must send screenplays out only via the higher-priced, signature-required FedEx and must always print out the proof of receipt and the proof of signature pages from FedEx.com on the day of receipt before FedEx recycles its delivery numbers and deletes the Web pages related to the delivery, which FedEx does sooner than most people realize. (10) There is no such thing as an actionable "poor man's copyright" or "common-law copyright" that is somehow created by a film-maker mailing a copy of a finished screenplay to himself or to his parents and then keeping the package sealed; for the purposes of bringing a lawsuit and recovering damages, common-law copyright does not exist—believe it—and is not an actionable legal concept.

"There may be a common-law copyright but there is no common law or anything to sue on," explains Boston-based attorney Howard Susser. "The fact of the matter is that an official registration with the Library of Congress, before the infringement takes place, before the use, is critical because it's going to maximize your rights, maximize the chances that you'll be able to get an attorney to help you, and maximize your ability to be able to recover attorney's fees as part of the suit."

Despite what most filmmakers believe, and despite the contest-related websites that actually encourage screenwriters to mail a sealed copy of the script to themselves, common-law copyright does not afford any real protection to screenwriters or authors or anyone else and as such is utterly useless when it comes to establishing a screenplay's date of creation or completion, or when it comes to convincing attorneys to bring a cause of action in court. As such, it should never stand in the place of registering each new draft with a Form PA (performing arts works, including motion pictures) registration with the Library of Congress. "You have a copyright, a common-law copyright, in your work of authorship once you create it and publish it, but that is separate from having an official copyright registration. The key is understanding when your right exists," continues Susser. "When do you create what is the copyright? You create that when you create the work of authorship and publish it in some way. You don't need to publish it in terms of writing a book. It usually means you just have to put it into some kind of a fixed form. It can't just be an idea in your head. It has to be fixed into some kind of material form. It doesn't have to be published in a magazine or newspaper, but it just has to be fixed, which means that it is published in some way or sent to people. You can sell it, you can mortgage it, you can license it to others, or your copyright could just sit there forever and never be used or enforced. But if you want to sue somebody in federal court for copyright infringement, you have to have registered the document with the Library of Congress first. The registration of the copyright is what is needed to invoke the jurisdiction of the court. Official registration gives you the benefits of copyright, including the ability to recover attorney's fees if your screenplay or novel is stolen from you after your registration. But you'd still need to be able to prove access and that they had received what you sent them and everything else."

As a result of this and other hurdles, frivolous screenplay lawsuits are by no means brought all the time. Indeed, anyone who has actually tried to find an attorney to bring a contingency intellectual-property case will quickly discover that there are only a handful of major law firms in Los Angeles and New York that will even attempt it, and even then only under the best of circumstances. "There are several reasons lawyers turn down these cases," explains attorney Gorham. "It's copyright law, which is tough. It's an expensive proposition to go all the way through with one of these cases and the outcome can be tenuous. It's federal court and lawyers don't want to be there. And then of course you have to deal with artists, who are mercurial and unpredictable at best. I'm always looking for that great case that pisses me off and is worth a ton of money, where someone is getting ripped off. But some important part of the case is always lacking. It's either not going to be worth enough, or the case isn't strong enough, or the access isn't direct enough, or it's just sour grapes on somebody's part. So there's always something missing and you always have to factor that in. Between liability and damages, you always have one weakness and the trick is to identify that weakness before you file the case."

BEWARE OF HIP-POCKET DEALS

While it is often difficult for an aspiring screenwriter to land official agency representation, it is extremely dangerous to allow anyone who works as a manager or agent to send out a screenplay *to anyone* as a favor without a written agreement that explicitly creates an agent-client relationship. Otherwise, in a contract-less "hip-pocket" deal, an agent or manager agrees to shop a screenplay to working actors or established directors simply as a favor to the writer with the unspoken understanding that if the script attracts interest, everyone will benefit, with the details to be worked out later. The problem is that without a formal written contract in place, the agent or manager does not have to take on certain legal obligations or use any measure of care to make sure the screenplay isn't appropriated. Neither does he or she need to make all best efforts to sell the screenplay, to act in the client's best interests, or to maintain a fiduciary responsibility toward the client, since he or she is not representing the screenwriter in an official capacity.

The risks to screenwriters in a hip-pocket deal are significant especially because the person sending out the script is not obligated to keep official records of who the script was sent to, making it impossible to establish a paper trail or prove access should the script be stolen or subsumed into someone else's screenplay. The benefits of a hip-pocket deal to agents or managers are obvious: if the script is worth producing and a name actor or studio expresses interest, he or she can quickly sign the writer and reap the benefit of a 10 percent manager's fee or a 15 percent agent's fee without any work or hassle. And if the screenplay is stolen or stripped of its best elements, the agent or manager may have no legal responsibility or liability if there is no written contract in place. (See Appendix II for a sample contract to use.)

Typically, in a copyright-infringement complaint or federal court trial, a writer's official agent or manager would provide the necessary corroborating "eyewitness" at trial to establish access. In a hip-pocket deal, however, the agent or manager is likely to testify that no contract was in place, and no connection or obligation existed to the aggrieved screenwriter because he or she was not ever an official client.

WGA REGISTRATION VS. COPYRIGHT REGISTRATION

It is critical that screenwriters know the difference between copyright registration and Writers Guild of America registration. One of the biggest myths related to story and screenplay theft is that a WGA registration or an official Library of Congress registration somehow "protects" or inoculates a screenwriter from having his or her story, treatment, or screenplay from being stolen or cherry-picked. The truth is only a copyright registration gives the writer legal standing to sue—the only real remedy writers have—but only where several specific conditions that will be discussed allow an intellectual-property attorney to take the case. The second biggest myth among aspiring screenwriters is that WGA registration and copyright registration are similar or "pretty much the same" in terms of the level of protection they bestow. This is an extremely dangerous assumption because although most aspiring screenwriters want to believe it, a WGA registration does not bestow statutory protection and does not, by itself, give an aggrieved screenwriter the standing to sue. "Can you say filing a copyright registration will always protect a person, in every case, from being ripped off? The answer is no," explains Susser. "On the other hand, it's like chicken soup—it couldn't hurt—and because it's so cheap, it should be done."

A registration with the WGA allows an aggrieved writer to pursue binding arbitration, but this type of dispute mediation is conducted behind closed doors, does not involve a jury or an impaneled judge, is resolved under seal, and requires the aggrieved writer to agree to abide by the decision of the arbitrator before the decision is handed down, and to forfeit the ability to bring a copyright or implied contract lawsuit. For this reason, WGA registration should never be considered almost the same as a copyright registration. Because copyright claims can easily run $400,000 to $500,000 per year for two years, an intellectual-property attorney's ability to recover legal fees is a critical hurdle that *only* an official copyright registration with the Library of Congress bestows. As a result, any screenwriter who only has a WGA registration is unlikely to find an attorney willing to take his or her case even if the script were stolen word for word.

Another myth surrounding what a registration affords is that the WGA maintains a team of attorneys eager to offer legal advice and representation. In fact, the WGA website clearly states that the WGA "does not make comparisons of registration deposits, bestow any statutory protections, or give legal advice." Although this is not a secret, many aspiring screenwriters who have not read the Registration Details section believe that a WGA registration means they will be able to call on WGA-funded attorneys should they need to. Indeed, contrary to popular belief, there is no such thing as GEICO "screenplay insurance" that is provided by a WGA registration. Screenwriters should also know that the WGA is unlikely to reach out to them to offer attorneys, recommendations, moral support, or legal advice, even if their screenplay appropriation claim receives national news coverage or withstands motions for summary judgment or dismissal by studio attorneys.

Aspiring screenwriters currently face a very serious threat from organizations not affiliated with the U.S. Library of Congress who nonetheless claim to offer copyright protection for a fee. Screenwriters should be very wary of sending money or their screenplays to any organization other than the Library of Congress. One of these organizations, calling itself the Writers Copyright Association (WCA), allows screenwriters to upload electronic copies of screenplays through its website and pay $99 for what it claims is a ten-year interval of worldwide copyright protection or $18 for a five-year interval of U.S. copyright protection. *The truth is, the WCA is not in any way affiliated with the Library of Congress and furthermore its mailing address is actually a film studio in Ealing, London.* The WCA states on its website that its registrations do not provide any statutory protections—such as the ability to bring a case—nor does the WCA give legal advice. As such, the WCA and other organizations like it purporting to offer copyright registration actually provide no legal protection whatsoever to screenwriters in the United States. The WCA or its $99 registrations cannot be used to confer the requisite U.S. copyright registration needed to secure an intellectual-property attorney and bring a lawsuit in federal court.

DON'T SIGN RELEASE FORMS

Screenwriters are frequently asked to sign releases to enter online script contests, to participate in pitch-fest seminars, or even to receive coverage from leading talent agencies or studio-affiliated producers. Even well-meaning advisers who work in the industry may tell screenwriters that there is no way around the gauntlet of release forms. However, any screenwriter who signs a release is almost certain to be waiving several or all of the protections afforded by their official U.S. copyright registration, which leaves writers vulnerable to giving away their stories, and possibly even their entire screenplays word for word, for free. Regardless of the best intentions, promises made by a producer's assistant or by whoever is manning the registration table at a pitch-fest seminar, *a screenwriter's voluntary signature on a release form allows the recipient of the screenplay and possibly his or her circle of business associates to avoid legal liability or to push any dispute into closed-door, binding arbitration, which is often a dead end for aggrieved screenwriters.*

"Signing away any of your rights is asking for trouble," advises Susser. "But signing any kind of release at any of these pitch fests or anywhere else before talking to a lawyer is silly, especially when everyone knows at least *one* lawyer. Ten or fifteen years ago, people might not have known what a release does or what a nondisclosure agreement is. Today, there's really no excuse for not knowing what a release form is. Screenwriters can also go to any law school and work with law students or legal aid. There are countless places that will help authors or filmmakers or even mom-and-pop inventors who come up with a great new idea. It's really 'shame on them' if they don't register their intellectual property. If a writer files for copyright registration with the Library of Congress, and has a lawyer review anything they are asked to sign before they sign it, and also doing so before they send their script to someone, then they are at least maximizing their chances of protecting their intellectual property. Anything other than that depends on the specific circumstances. People who are creating intellectual property can easily go on the Web and learn a lot about copyright law and what protections are afforded from copyright registration."

Screenwriters can also go online and quickly familiarize themselves with the language that appears in many of the waivers and release forms that are specifically designed to undercut the protections granted by official copyright registration. For example, in its policies section, the website IndieShares, whose stated goal is to "give people the opportunity to make low dollar investments in films and participate throughout the film production process," posts a limitation of liability: "Under no circumstances shall IS [IndieShares], its licensees, successors, assigns, related or affiliated entities, advertisers, sponsors, providers, contractors, consultants or professional advisors or the parent, subsidiary or affiliated companies of each of them and any of its or their employees, officers, directors, members, shareholders, representatives or agents (the 'IS Parties') be liable for any direct, indirect, punitive, incidental, special, or consequential damages that result from the use of, or inability to use, the site or the services. This limitation applies whether the alleged liability is based on contract, tort, negligence, strict liability, or any other basis, even if IS has been advised of the possibility of such damage. To the extent some jurisdictions do not allow the exclusion or limitation of incidental or consequential damages, the parties' liability in such jurisdictions shall be limited to the extent required by law." Screenwriters trying to make heads or tails of this jargon fixate on the phrase "inability to use," but the waiver's strength is derived from waiving all liability related to *the use* of the site or the services.

And while many aspiring screenwriters have reservations whenever they see such legalese, most go ahead and click on the acceptance box or sign the release form laid out before them because they believe they don't have a choice. Others believe the possibility their screenplay will be stolen or appropriated is remote, or that their scripts are too "out there" or uncommercial to be stolen. Those attending pitch-fest seminars are often comforted by assurances at the registration desk that signing the release is simply a formality to help scare off the people who "bring lawsuits against the studios all the time." The truth is, litigation against major studios or their specialized art-house subsidiaries is not easy or cheap to mount and the means for getting spurious and legitimate claims dismissed are numerous. "There's a sort of big wide area of infringement where it's very hard for an aggrieved party to get a lawyer to enforce intellectual-property rights," explains Susser. "If it's small-time copying and not huge damages or if there are potential [lack of] originality defenses, and potential scènes à faire defenses, a screenwriter might not be able to get to a courtroom."

Since there are no halfway release forms, filmmakers need to recognize that all release forms are inherently designed to block any claim should a case of theft or infringement occur—this year, next year, or even ten years from now. Many screenplay releases "allow" a filmmaker to "retain" his or her copyright and ownership in the work but render that copyright toothless by blocking any legal action if the copyright is ever violated.

What is most troubling about screenplay releases, however, is that writers are asked to sign them as a condition of taking a step forward, often in high-pressure situations where it appears that a big break hangs in the balance. These pressure situations include not being able to participate in a magazine's pitch-fest event even *after* having paid several hundred dollars to register, not being able to have a script read by a major talent agency poised to get the screenplay into the hands of a favorite actor, or as a condition of just getting script coverage from a leading producer's assistant. The truth is, screenwriters and filmmakers should never apply the reckless and idiotic "nothing ventured, nothing gained" ideal to signing a screenplay release. It is not an accident that most screenplay pitch-fest seminars refuse to show their comprehensive release forms to interested registrants until after they have paid $200 to $600 to attend.

Even so, a screenwriter who dreams of making it often thinks, "My script isn't going to get produced if it's sitting in a drawer at home. I might as well take my chances," not realizing that one alternative is to quickly port it to a novel and attract a publisher who can then officially broker its sale to Hollywood.

They must also remember that by signing a release, screenwriters are essentially acting as their own attorney and making legal decisions they aren't qualified to make. "People regularly enter into contracts without lawyers, but you have to remember that any time you do a lot of things these days you're getting into an elaborate contract," explains Susser. "When you sign an agreement for cell-phone service, or rent or lease a car, you're getting into an elaborate contract.

"If you do a contract for home improvements you don't typically get a lawyer. But if you buy a house, you usually get a lawyer," continues Susser. "If you sign a car lease for a year or lease an apartment, you don't typically get a lawyer. Most people, when they take a new job, don't have a lawyer review their employment contracts. But you should *never* sign an agreement relating to your intellectual property without talking to an attorney. I think people will find they can get an attorney to help without spending a lot of money."

HOW TO SPOT RED FLAGS

Any release form, especially one loaded with legal terms such as "foregoing," "hereunder," "herein," and "hereof," is a red flag. Contracts that offer a reassuring line about the writer "retaining all rights to submit this work to other parties," which makes writers assume they are retaining ownership, are another danger sign. Other releases contain comforting language assuring screenwriters that their scripts will somehow remain "protectable literary property," even though the act of signing the document itself tosses all such protections out the window. Language that asks the screenwriter to indemnify the recipient and all parties that the recipient company, firm, or individual does business with from any and all liabilities, losses, claims, demands, costs (including reasonable attorney's fees), or expenses arising in connection with any breach or alleged breach of the other paragraphs in the release should be cause for alarm, even if the screenwriter's mother is the one requesting the indemnification. Paragraphs extending indemnification to others, which often appear between two otherwise innocuous paragraphs, completely disembowel a screenwriter's ability to sue third parties on copyright grounds because the screenplay thief—even one several degrees of separation from the official recipient—is also indemnified from all liabilities. This section also guarantees that any screenwriter-friendly lawyer who might have taken the case on contingency cannot recover attorney's fees.

A later paragraph in most release forms prevents screenwriters from bringing any breach-of-implied-contract claims by stating that the only contract that exists between the recipient and the writer is the written one before them and that all oral representations, promises, comments, assurances, as well as all implied or expressed oral contracts are legally void by their signature on the dotted line. While verbal and implied contracts can have the same force as written contracts, paragraphs limiting the application or scope of any implied contract between the parties effectively prevent a screenwriter-friendly attorney from bringing a breach-of-implied-contract case.

Not accidentally, release forms often also ask screenwriters to acknowledge that the recipient of the screenplay has historically created and may in the future create screenplays, treatments, literary materials, or ideas that may be "similar or identical to" elements in their screenplay. Such paragraphs deliberately require the writer to acknowledge that he or she will not be entitled to any compensation arising from the use of "similar or identical" material or even the entire screenplay, which the release asserts may have been "independently created" by an existing client or provided by any independent source. Despite the fact that it is extremely difficult to prove that material in a putative screenplay thief's script was not in fact "independently created," it is a moot point since the language within this paragraph ensures that anyone who signs this release will not be entitled to any compensation arising from the use of "similar or identical" material. This language also prevents a writer from being able to bring an implied-contract case, because one of the critical elements that must be present to trigger the formation of an implied contract is a writer's expectation of compensation and the recipient's acceptance of those clearly enunciated terms. By signing such a release the writer has acknowledged in writing and by his or her own volition that there is no expectation of compensation.

The un-enunciated expectation-of-compensation question also puts aspiring screenwriters and filmmakers in a spot in other ways when it comes to attending magazine-sponsored pitch-fest events and in terms of sending cover letters to studio executives that disclose the central premise in terms of other films or describe it in terms of a Hollywood "story-cross," in which a writer might describe his or her script along the lines of "*Bridget Jones's Diary* meets *Krull*." Attorneys for any putative screenplay thief can successfully argue at trial that by disclosing or pitching a screenplay to a ballroom full of Hollywood producers and development executives, an aspiring screenwriter was freely and willingly communicating his or her ideas to the world and could not have expected compensation. Further, since the goal was to hone a pitch or to receive a critique *of the pitch* and not of the script itself, no implied contract was created despite the writer's "obvious" intent in attending such an event to possibly attract interest and sell the script.

Each year, *Fade In* magazine is proud to sponsor what it describes as "the year's networking event"—the Annual Hollywood Pitch Festival featuring more than two hundred of the motion picture and television industry's most prominent studio, development, and creative executives, as well as producers, literary agents, managers, and entertainment lawyers to meet with. The *Fade In* ad e-mailed to possible attendees goes on to exclaim: "This is your chance to present your story ideas directly to those in the Business who can actually do something for your career! The Annual Hollywood Pitch Festival is a unique opportunity to pitch your projects to these professionals and even . . . sell your material. Don't be left out!" The problem is that the *Fade In* festival requires all screenwriters attending to sign a release that for all intents and purposes separates them from their ideas and their screenplays for free, since ideas are not copyrightable and the right to sue even in a case of word-for-word copying is waived. This goes for aspiring screenwriters who see a famous actor, director, producer, or movie executive in a public place and ask them if they could listen to a quick pitch or "read the script and get back to them." From a legal perspective, the breathless screenwriter is asking for an opinion, judgment, or a critique and not expecting compensation; therefore no implied contract is formed. Further, since the screenplay is not being presented or tendered with the goal of selling it and is not necessarily accepted by the recipient on those terms, no implied contract is being formed. Thus, strict similarity, the challenges of proving access, and the defense of scènes à faire can disembowel any copyright claim while implied contract claims can be negated by the polite manners of the screenwriter who is hard-pressed to ask a startled director or name actor to buy their script on the spot, sight unseen. Most aspiring screenwriters believe such a request would make them appear impolite, aggressive, or even crazy, even though legally it is exactly what is required.

It may astound aspiring screenwriters to learn (usually from a disappointed lawyer who would otherwise love to help) that they may not have any legal recourse, either because (1) the screenwriter at some point early on voluntarily signed a release; (2) copyright claims can be dismissed before trial unless the script achieves an extremely high threshold of "strict similarity"; (3) non-copyright, breach-of-contract claims can be undercut if the screenwriter only asked for the screenplay to be read and did not enunciate his or her expectation of payment or compensation; (4) the screenwriter did not keep adequate records or FedEx receipts; (5) the screenwriter registered the script with the WGA and not the Library of Congress; and (6) because "access," the single most important pillar of any infringement claim, is extremely difficult to prove if the script was passed along during any fortuitous meeting in a restaurant, a handoff while standing in line for coffee, while walking the dog, getting the car washed, sitting in a doctor's office, shopping at the Promenade, or doing anything else in a public place. Handing over an unproduced screenplay to an actor or to anyone in the film industry is asking for trouble.

Finally, aspiring filmmakers should know that sending short films or spec advertisements to major conglomerates can lead to them being appropriated and made into ad campaigns without any compensation to the writer, director, or producer of the short. While many young directors and screenwriters think creating an innovative "spec ad" for a major corporation is a terrific way to get recognized and start their careers in advertising or filmmaking, this is yet another fairy tale, typically derived from writer-director Charles Stone III's participation in the Budweiser Whassup? campaign. What aspiring short film directors don't know is that in 1999 at the time the Whassup? campaign ad was developed by BBDO Chicago from Stone's short film *True*, Stone was already a working film director (*Paid in Full*) and music-video director with an attorney and official agency representation from United Talent Agency.

The idea that the chief executive officer of a national or international brand might receive a copy of a short on DVD and then hire the writer-director to remake it with a significant budget into a national ad campaign is a myth. What most aspiring filmmakers don't realize or acknowledge is that major corporations have contracts with Fortune 500 ad agencies and cannot violate those agreements by buying spec ad campaign ideas or storyboards from unrepresented writer-directors. However, many companies fuel the spec-ad fantasy by sending intrepid filmmakers release forms, which the filmmakers mistake for interest. The dead giveaway that the filmmakers are being conned are the paragraphs in the releases that obliterate any copyright protection and allow the conglomerate to make its own version of the spot through their official ad agency without paying the writer and certainly without incurring any liability.

One internationally known beverage conglomerate sends all filmmakers who send in their DVD shorts a liability release that actually states that "anyone submitting an idea agrees to limit any claim to $2,000 to cover all damages alleged to have been sustained based on use." Considering that many well-made spec advertisements and short films can cost $30,000 or more to produce and that having an attorney write up an easily ignored demand letter could easily cost $3,000, the beverage conglomerate can rest assured that it won't receive too many claims from aggrieved filmmakers. The release actually goes on to say that if the submitter believes the company has unfairly adopted his or her idea or suggestion, the submitter agrees that the only remedy will be an action under applicable patent, trademark, and copyright laws.

The catch here is that ideas are not protected by copyright law, which means this section of the release deftly prevents anyone from bringing a cause of action based on implied contract, since such a claim is outside the scope of copyright protection; and the concept of scènes à faire means that most discrete scenes in a thirty-second or sixty-second advertisement will not qualify under copyright protection because these sequences would likely occur in any venue where the ad is set. Thus the release for great ad ideas prevents filmmakers from bringing cases based on implied contract on one side and the copyright-gutting concept of scènes à faire effectively limits a filmmaker's ability to bring a claim on the copyright side. An extra layer of protection for the company comes from the fact that most aspiring filmmakers do not take the time to register their completed

DVD or Blu-ray disc with the Library of Congress once they have created their master copy or professional glass master, meaning that the completed film itself is actually not copyrighted, even though the short-film script underlying it may have been.

ACHIEVING STRICT SIMILARITY

One of the things screenwriters don't understand about copyright is that, while a script may indeed be "copyrightable," for legal purposes or for any practical or realistic application of copyright protection, individual scenes or sequences are not safe from being stolen. As a result, a screenwriter may be hard pressed to bring a case simply because the best sequences have been lifted or given a quarter turn, while the rest was left behind.

"That's the problem. If they simply cherry-pick your best stuff, they win," explains Gorham. "What a screenplay thief will often do is to take the [premise and] two or three best gags or scenes but they won't duplicate them exactly. So they may take a comment from a woman's perspective and make it into a guy joke. Basically what they're doing is taking *Sex and the City* and making it *Entourage*."

In fact, for a copyright claim not to be dismissed in the weeks after a suit is filed or in the months before a case goes to court, the script must approach a threshold of "strict similarity" alongside the stolen script, a level that is often extremely difficult to achieve. "The risk of handing over a screenplay to a well-known actor or director is that the screenplay may prompt the famous person to think, 'This is a great idea but I want to do it differently,' " explains Butterfield. "And they decide to hire somebody else—someone they know—to write a script along similar lines with similar themes or ideas. And that may be perfectly legal from a copyright perspective. The risk is not just that someone will take your copyrighted work and use it illegally, but that they will take your copyrighted work and use it *legally*, leaving you with no possibility for a claim. If [the disputed element is] an original concept that nobody has put into a film before, but it's only a concept, then copyright laws don't protect concepts."

So what is the point of copyright law? As it is applied today, copyright law protects published material that exists in the public sphere and ostensibly punishes the wholesale duplication of DVDs, but it does not protect screenwriters the way many filmmakers believe.

Indeed, federal judges are inclined to throw out claims because of a lack of strict similarity or on a motion by the studio distributor related to "a lack of originality" within the story itself. And given that most stories have been told in one form or another since the Bible, it is often very easy to support the lack of originality defense needed to get an aggrieved screenwriter's claim tossed. Screenwriters are often shocked to learn they may not have a copyright case even though the premise and several of the best gags from a script have been lifted. A second shock is that there are not a dozen attorneys clamoring to take the case since it seems— to the aggrieved screenwriter at least—to be a cut-and-dried, eminently winnable case. Copyright cases are expensive and notoriously difficult to win, which is why it is also a myth that the courts are clogged with spurious claims. The truth is that only 1 percent of cases of any stripe ever make it into a federal courtroom. Attorneys are actually wary of taking cases related to screenplay theft because (1) they are easily dismissed before trial; (2) the studios will spend millions of dollars to fight even legitimate claims, which scares off attorneys whose clients do not have extremely deep pockets; (3) screenwriters do not typically have the resources to pay for attorneys' time and services; (4) "demand letters" or "general notice letters" are almost always ignored or responded to with memos from the studio's legal department citing lack of originality and scènes à faire; and (5) federal court is not typically a plaintiff-friendly venue for procedural reasons.

WATERMARKING THE SCREENPLAY

It is incumbent upon every aspiring screenwriter to infuse his or her screenplay with elements that may serve as clear signposts and help him or her achieve a threshold of strict similarity needed to go to trial on a copyright claim. If a screenwriter includes an over-the-top or clearly memorable sequence, such as a high school student who diddles his mother's apple pie or a brilliant but twisted serial killer who sends his last victim's head to the police via local courier, a screenplay thief can easily avoid that stand-out element and keep things generic. However, screenwriters can actually create specific and encoded watermarks in their screenplays to help convince copyright attorneys that their case would be a winner in front of a jury. One way to do this is to intentionally include throughout each act subtle but extremely specific factual errors that few laypeople would spot. For example, if the script is about an American exchange student's trip to China, the young female (or male) protagonist could meet an attractive Frenchman traveling down the Li River through the outskirts of Guilin, and fall in love with him as they pass through Yangzhuo. The screenwriter could have their first kiss occur while looking off at the breathtaking spine of the Kunlun Mountains while listening to the catchy music of Orange Range.

What a would-be screenplay thief might not know is that

if the student and the Frenchman were looking at the Kunlun Mountains they would actually have to be hiking along the Tibet-Xinjiang highway or walking along the Karakax River *in the western Kunlun Shan* and not passing through Yangzhuo, since the Kunlun Mountains are actually thousands of miles away. Furthermore, Yangzhuo is surrounded by smaller karst peaks, and Orange Range is a Japanese alternative rock band, not a Chinese one. Deliberate mistakes like these can easily be woven throughout a script and can provide a sort of LoJack tracking system for proving infringement and helping to authenticate the origin of the central premise. A jury hearing a case with irrefutable signposts is more likely to be persuaded that such specific errors could not be coincidental and that the alleged script thief could not have arrived at them through accidental, independent, or "parallel" generation.

The LoJack tracking system analogy is apt, since the metaphor of a stolen car is the most appropriate comparison that intellectual-property attorneys should use to convey how even a dramatically altered script can still be identified as having been stolen. Stolen cars often turn up wildly altered with new paint jobs and other improvements such as GPS, Alpine stereos, racing stripes, iPod docking stations, new rims, Pirelli tires, and xenon headlights, all of which can make identification difficult. Certainly from sight alone, a car's rightful owner would have a hard time proving that the car was originally his. But if its engine and steel frame match a serial number the writer has embedded in the vehicle, he may have a better chance of recovering his property. The argument juries need to hear is that, like a car, a copyright-registered script is still the rightful property of its owner, even if it has been through a chop shop.

DEATH BY SCÈNES À FAIRE

The foremost hurdle to bringing a legal case is a legal concept that few filmmakers have ever heard of called scènes à faire, or "scenes to be made," which allows all screenwriters to create the basic scenes that films in a certain genre share and even require. Story elements, story beats, and sequences judged to be scènes à faire are those in which characters might perform a common action in a film about that particular topic. For example, a movie about a struggling American high school football team often has a rallying speech delivered by one of the star players during a moment when all seems lost, an incident of racial tension that is later resolved with the bigoted player or parent realizing the error of his ways, a player with a bullying alcoholic dad showing up clean and sober just in time for the championship, and scenes of comic relief from a jovial and typically obese goofball linebacker. The goal of scènes à faire seems reasonable since the film industry might shut down if certain common story elements were *patentable* like computer software or other high technology. Indeed, studios would be hard pressed to shoot a high school football movie without violating someone's patent. Similarly, every new screenplay with an indelible psychopathic killer who dispatches his victims in a unique way would owe a royalty to Cormac McCarthy. However, the problem with scènes à faire from a legal perspective is that it potentially allows an unscrupulous party to steal an entire screenplay as long as each copied sequence in their version is vague or general enough to qualify as a scène à faire and prevent an otherwise legitimate copyright-infringement claim from going forward.

Screenplay elements that qualify as scènes à faire ultimately cannot be used at trial, even if they have a novel or innovative twist that makes them seem fresh and reimagined.

The problem for aggrieved screenwriters is that scènes à faire can be applied to just about any sequence in a stolen screenplay as long as the rewritten sequence is something a person might do in a particular circumstance. And the less exact and specific the action or dialogue in the infringing screenplay, the harder it will be for a screenwriter to prove or even bring a case of copyright infringement. The upshot is that scènes à faire can leave a writer, who may have spent ten to twelve years writing and polishing a screenplay, dead in the water with no claim. Indeed, screenwriters who think they have slam-dunk copyright cases are often stunned to hear the sober assessment of attorneys well versed in copyright issues, primarily that scènes à faire exclusions have undercut the bulk of their similarities and made their claim untenable.

So what to do? The best way to combat scènes à faire is to make every scene in the screenplay so specific and innovative that its elements are harder to borrow or disguise just by being vague and general. Thus, screenplay books that tell aspiring screenwriters to leave the style and model of car or the type of laptop the hero uses generic, since these small details should be up to the director, are wrong. Many of these books say that a Bret Easton Ellis–like focus on brand names will be a distraction to Hollywood script readers who may tear the screenplay to shreds on this point alone. However, *specificity in a script is one of the only ways screenwriters can try to protect themselves from scènes à faire assaults.* As such, every beverage the hero drinks or each type of cigarette he or she smokes should in fact be branded or labeled at least once with the type that the character would choose.

TEMPORARY RESTRAINING ORDERS:
AN UNREALISTIC OPTION

Screenwriters who believe they have been ripped off should know that legitimate lawsuits require sober decision-making derived from calm and clear thinking. Before deciding to share their suspicions with anyone, aggrieved screenwriters should recall that loose lips sink ships and know that they must absolutely see the film for themselves. Screenwriters should never fly off the handle after simply reading an early description, a log line, or even a full-on review in *Variety* or *The Hollywood Reporter*.

They should also recognize that there is a huge difference between thinking their script was ripped off and having a strong legal case that could ever hope to win at trial. While a screenwriter may feel it is extremely urgent that they somehow see the film before it opens, the truth is, there is really no hurry. Pursuing a strategy that involves a temporary restraining order to somehow leverage a settlement is an extremely long-shot option for many reasons, and assembling and vetting the evidence required to file a meritorious lawsuit can easily take six months.

Not only that, but federal judges are hard pressed to grant requests for an injunction or restraining order preventing the release of a motion picture, since doing so would subordinate First Amendment freedom of speech issues by preventing the free expression of the film's director, cast, and its distributor. Furthermore, the judges reason, an aggrieved screenwriter can simply sue for compensatory damages and loss of income as long as he or she can prove access and achieve strict similarity with an appropriately registered script. A judge granting a restraining order against a film's release is almost guaranteed to require the aggrieved screenwriter to post a bond of several million dollars to make the releasing studio whole for any and all lost marketing and distribution expenses, should the screenwriter's infringement lawsuit not prevail. Finally, a judge's denial of a temporary restraining order is likely to actually hurt the case a screenwriter hopes to bring, since it will count as an early strike against the perceived merit of the claim.

If a screenplay-theft claim is legitimate, supportable, and has not been undercut by the writer's poor record-keeping or signed release waivers, aggrieved screenwriters must stay quiet and let their qualified intellectual-property attorneys handle any public statements if publicity is deemed appropriate. Among the "very small bar" of intellectual-property attorneys with the resources and willingness to take on infringement cases, most are in L.A. and can be found in online articles about the subject. Such law firms should be the starting place for those with compelling claims, but only after an aggrieved writer has taken the time to digest what has happened and calmed down so he or she can explain in sober tones why his or her case has merit. Angry would-be plaintiffs demanding to speak to someone immediately or "as soon as possible" will probably not be taken seriously.

"The one thing that turns lawyers away from these cases are 'the crazies,' " explains Gorham. "I get calls all the time from people who just don't sound normal."

FIRST THINGS FIRST: CONFLICT CHECK

Anyone looking for an attorney should always have a family member or a colleague they trust call and quietly request a "conflict check" to make sure that the aggrieved screenwriter is not about to plead his or her case to a law firm that works for the entertainment industry or even the studio the screenwriter hopes to sue. Nothing should be discussed and no letters should be sent until the conflict check of a particular firm has been completed. Aggrieved screenwriters must be very careful not to make any rash moves that might blow their case, such as contacting directly or publicly condemning those they believe to be responsible. A moment's satisfaction can result in a preemptive defamation action that aggrieved screenwriters will have to fight at a significant cost—since defamation claims are not covered under contingency agreements—if a screenwriter shoots his or her mouth off prior to the formal filing of a case. For this reason, screenwriters should never try to negotiate some sort of settlement or compensation on their own, nor agree to binding arbitration that inherently waives the right to a jury trial. Secrecy, conflict checks, and caution should be the order of the day while screenwriters weigh their options. Expert second opinions are also a good idea.

Further, an aggrieved screenwriter should know the calculus that informs whether a law firm will find the case appealing before setting up a call to outline the broad strokes of the case. "It's a risk-benefit analysis that can be explained as a very simple math problem," explains Susser. "Attorneys take the total damages we think we could get, multiply it by the likelihood that we'll get those damages, and multiply that by the likelihood that you'll win. And that gives us the net present value of a potential lawsuit. The NPV of what you stand to get for what the screenwriter in effect 'provided' to the studio that produced the film also gets calculated differently. It depends on how much of the material was taken. If this is a major film and they stole your entire screenplay, then on a successful copyright claim the writer might be able to recover all of the revenue.

"If what you created in a short film was used in one tiny part of a soft-drink manufacturer's thirty-second advertisement, you might be eligible for a consulting fee of just a few thousand dollars, which might make it difficult for an attorney to justify taking the case on contingency since there aren't a lot of damages to be recovered. Each case is different and it's a calculus that a lawyer has to do."

By way of example, if an aspiring director sends his or her clever short film to a soft-drink conglomerate that rips off the idea, an attorney may entertain for a moment the idea that they could recover $100 million in damages if the case went to trial and they were able to win. The lawyer may suggest that there is a 50 percent chance the suit will bring $100 million in damages if the case is compelling and a much more likely chance that the filmmaker will get only de minimis damages and simply a consulting fee. To illuminate the thought processes, the attorney suggests that a 50 percent chance of getting the full $100 million in damages, should the case prevail, puts the expected value at $50 million. But because the attorney projects only a 30 percent chance that the filmmaker is going to win at trial, the expected value drops to $15 million. Since the law firm will receive only 30 percent of that amount as a contingency fee, the expected value drops to $4.5 million. Thus, if the law firm projects that taking the case all the way to trial is going to cost $1 million and the expected value on the investment is only $4.5 million, then it is unlikely the law firm will take the case. The break point for most firms today would have to be at least $10 million or an expected value in the $7 to $15 million range. Put another way, a software company that has a strong case against a huge corporation such as Microsoft may have only a 1 percent chance of winning, but this long shot might be worth pursuing, since the damage award could be $250 million. For most screenwriters, the odds of recovery may be extremely long.

If a law firm won't take the case on contingency—and most do not—screenwriters are most likely dead in the water unless they have enormous resources they can afford to lose to finance a claim. The important thing for screenwriters to realize at the very outset is that they should never wreck their personal lives chasing the Sundance dream or big-time celluloid glory, since their screenplays can be stolen at any time and they may not have any recourse at the end of the day. "I tell a lot of my inventor clients who are going to show someone their invention or their patent idea, 'You know, even if you have a signed nondisclosure agreement and somebody breaches it, you're going to have to actually sue them and that costs a lot of money,' " explains Susser. "So if they use your invention but they haven't accumulated a lot of damages yet [from the use of your patented innovation] you might be in a lot of trouble. You might have to mortgage your house just to sue them and it's only in cases of willful, bad-faith misconduct, and intentional conduct that you can prove, [misconduct] that reaches a certain level depending on the statute, that you can recover attorney's fees. Now in copyright cases, if you have a copyright registration with the Library of Congress, you can get attorney's fees. So there is a significant benefit to having an official copyright registration, but not everyone takes that step."

UNCLE JOE, THE DIVORCE LAWYER

Because a high level of care is required, litigation is a formal and deliberate process, and the more legitimate the claim, the more it is likely to unfold at a slow and stately pace. Any lawyer who has been through a legitimate screenplay-infringement claim knows that it can take two years if not longer to process documents, serve papers, conduct depositions, and move for a trial date. Since it can take two to three weeks to receive a return call from an attorney at a leading law firm, aggrieved screenwriters should use this interval to back up their hard drives and print out all relevant e-mail traffic.

Under no circumstances should screenwriters ever have a lawyer-relative or even a powerful attorney at a respected downtown firm write a "general notice letter" or a "demand letter" telling a studio, indie producer, or writer-director that their nonclient screenwriter-acquaintance "wishes to avoid protracted litigation," in the hopes that it will bring the other side to the table. This is a ridiculous and potentially catastrophic move, since it shows that the attorney sending the letter has no idea how things work. Screenplay claims are covered under E&O insurance policies and do not cost the studios money. Further, film studios *welcome* protracted litigation, since it is over the long haul that plaintiffs make mistakes or lose their stomachs for the battle.

"Lawsuits don't faze the studios," explains Gorham. "They see screenplay-theft cases as a cost of doing business. You have to understand who you're going up against: these guys are not afraid, they've got the money, and they don't mind a good fight. They've got insurance to pay for it and they will take you to trial. So the idea that a filmmaker who has been ripped off might spend $2,000 to $5,000 to have an attorney or their uncle the divorce lawyer send a demand letter as a saber-rattling gesture with nothing behind it is really a fool's errand unless that attorney is ready to actually file a lawsuit and go all the way to trial. If you're about to send a demand letter, then you have to be ready to rock and roll with a finished complaint, which means that as a plaintiff you have to either have the wherewithal to bring a lawsuit—which can get very expensive—or have a contingency intellectual-property attorney who is willing to actually go the distance."

Indeed, nothing should ever be done with the goal of "seeing if we can scare the other side to the table" or, worse still, "taking a shot in the dark." Any attorney who suggests this approach does not know the most basic facts about litigation in this realm. The studios' defense fees related to screenplay lawsuits are covered under the errors and omissions policies of each film. Such claims do not raise the studios' insurance coverage rates. Such claims do not concern the studios in the slightest. Furthermore, there are specialty law firms in Los Angeles who defend major studios against legitimate and spurious claims with equal tenacity and who welcome the work. Finally, there are studio chiefs who are said to quietly brag about the millions in legal fees that go toward defeating screenplay-related claims each year, figures that are reportedly touted among colleagues or in studio business-affairs offices as a badge of honor.

"The problem is, there are all sorts of potential defenses that a film studio or a TV network can invoke," explains Susser. "You think you're protected by your copyright registrations and your FedEx receipts, but when you're the plaintiff, you have to prove all sorts of things. You have to prove how much they damaged you in terms of what you might have earned from selling the screenplay for a fair value on the market at the time, and what lost wages you may have incurred. You have to prove that it's original—since they can move for a dismissal based on a lack of originality—and that it's yours, that you had officially registered it with the Library of Congress, that you still own the property and never waived the rights. And you have to prove that they had access and an opportunity to see it and copy it. In other words, they have many ways to cut down your claim, and almost any one of them can spell doom for you."

Still, it doesn't mean that screenwriters with legitimate claims who feel they may have a case because they kept careful records shouldn't try. As Martin Luther King, Jr., said, "Those who choose to remain silent in the face of injustice become a party to that injustice."

7. Phones Off!

COMMON PRODUCTION-DAY MISTAKES

*I*t may come as a surprise to many filmmakers, but talent and sheer force of will cannot stave off the blindsiding catastrophes that happen during the confusion and combat conditions that are part of any film shoot. Filmmakers who believe they'll be able to figure it out on the day or just get through it somehow can instead end up feeling like they've been flattened by a Mack truck. Indeed, even the most successful indie filmmakers with enviable careers have had a dark moment, or two or three, where their early films nearly went off the rails as a result of equipment failures, personality conflicts, logistical snafus, do-nothing line producers, bad weather, bad sound, or just bad luck. While shooting Jaws, Steven Spielberg was plagued by a malfunctioning shark that no amount of money could fix. Long before Avatar, James Cameron faced near mutinies on the set of Aliens because his all-British crew resented his hard-driving work ethic; his no-nonsense producer, Gale Anne Hurd; and the fact that Cameron simply wasn't Alien director Ridley Scott. David O. Russell's famous fit of pique on the set of I ♡ Huckabees was a YouTube curiosity that *echoed Werner Herzog's apocryphally pulling a gun on Klaus Kinski to underscore his threat that Kinski would be killed if he walked off the set of* Aguirre: The Wrath of God.

Personality clashes are to be expected during any creative endeavor but there are so many moving parts on a film set and so many people who have to perform at the top of their game that it's easy for first- and second-time filmmakers to lose control. Production is the period where the most things go wrong simultaneously, where those with less of a stake in the project drop the ball, and where hundreds of errors and ill portents defy logic but happen anyway. Neophyte filmmakers often believe the quality of their screenplays or their vision will shine through any missteps and help everyone rise above the inherent chaos, but there are literally hundreds of things that can bring down an indie-film production and most are not taught in cheerleading "You can do it!" books on filmmaking. Indeed, any sober manual attempting to detail all the ways a film shoot can go off the rails would probably be as big as the Manhattan phone directory.

BUT THE SOUND WAS GOOD . . .

Because film is a visual medium and because the leading books on screenwriting—such as Robert McKee's *Story* or Syd Field's *Screenplay*—urge aspiring filmmakers to "show, don't tell," first- and second-timers often don't consider how important sound is to their productions.

Many will spend hours daydreaming with the cinematographer about an incredible shot but not think for two seconds about how the sound should figure into the scene, other than making sure a boom isn't in the frame. But as many filmmakers ultimately find out in the editing bay, ignoring the quality of the sound and skimping on the technicians needed to record clean dialogue and avoid ambient noises is a terrible oversight. "As a line producer, I have to be really straightforward with filmmakers and let them know what they can get for the money they're going to spend, but I always tell them to spend money on good sound, which typically means using a boom operator and a professional sound mixer's recorder," says longtime line producer Brian Bell.

Traditionally, the sound department on an independently financed feature consists of three positions: the production sound mixer, the boom operator, and the "third," or "utility," who wrangles the cables and handles "second boom" when necessary.

While sound is important to every independently financed film, where sound really comes into play is in raising the production value and intensity of modestly budgeted horror movies such as *Open Water* or *Cabin Fever*. "After we made *28 Days Later*, people would come up and ask, 'How do you scare people in a movie? Give me three ways.' And I would tell them, 'Sound, sound, and sound,'" explains *Slumdog Millionaire* director Danny Boyle. "That's the way you do it. Sound is the thing that really 'sells the blow' every time. Sometimes in the edit or in a screening you raise the sound up a bit in the mix and certain scenes are unwatchable. People will turn away because the sound amplifies the reality of the image. But if you watch it with the sound off, it's no problem and they're not fazed by whatever you show them.

"So the two bits of advice I give all aspiring filmmakers are to make sure you work in a team and to save more money than you think you need for sound," says Boyle. "The temptation, especially if you're working with limited budgets like our early films, is to spend your money up front while you're shooting, and solve things later. But [producer] Andrew [Macdonald] has always kept money back to make sure the aural, audio impact of our films is on the same level as the visual impact." Good sound can also make up for technical shortcomings, bad lighting, or poorly composed frames.

"The fact that filmmakers don't spend enough money on sound is one of the big things that lets down independent cinema, certainly British cinema, and it happens for two reasons: one is that sound is mostly invisible, and the second is that most cinematographers are bullies and they always want to kick the sound person out of the way," says Boyle. "It's the same in postproduction as well: filmmakers want to spend the money on getting the picture right, but my advice is to spend the money on the sound because it makes a big, big difference. That's one of the things we've always done."

Filmmakers who ignore their soundman's advice and plow ahead anyway can find themselves facing expensive or even cost-prohibitive postproduction days. " 'Waiting on sound' is a very unpopular thing to hear on any set, but it really shouldn't be," says Los Angeles–based sound mixer Ken Pries. "The gaffers and the grips will spend ten minutes or even up to an hour to light a shot and then the DP [director of photography] will show up and make adjustments or changes 'to make it look beautiful.' But if the sound department has to make any sort of correction or drop fresh batteries into long idle equipment or track down a suddenly suspect cable—or if the sound mixer hears something in his headphones and needs to make an adjustment to a lavalier microphone that is picking up clothing noise, things can get really tense. There is little tolerance for troubleshooting problems or for delays related to getting good sound, and there really shouldn't be, since sound is one of the most important elements of any production.

"A sound mixer might say to the AD [assistant director], 'I need three minutes . . .'—let's say to fix a digital menu item in the camera that may have been reset by the camera department or switched into a wrong setting by the camera operator. Some directors will get really impatient, but if they don't allow it to be fixed it can cause major headaches. If he's not careful, the camera operator can also easily brush a record level 'pot' on the exterior of a camera, changing the level to above or below what had been set by the sound mixer to establish unity gain with his own meters. This type of incident can be prevented by securing those pots and switches beforehand and routinely checking them during the course of the shoot, but a lot of directors don't want to schedule the time for sound to do it.

"What may also happen is the director will give a sound mixer one minute to set up his end of the camera before coming back and saying, 'Okay, we gotta go now! Let's go!' even if things aren't 100 percent right. The problem is that if the camera menus haven't been set correctly there's a possibility that the sound that is recorded onto a memory card or a drive or onto an HD tape that day will be affected. But if the sound mixer is given five minutes to go through the mechanics in the camera or in the deck, any problems can be avoided. It's not only that the newer HD cameras can be really sophisticated, but that there are one hundred DV and HD cameras out there, and the setup of each is often quite different. What many new filmmakers don't realize is that while they may know how to use every Facebook widget and all of the latest applications on their 3G iPhone, it's impossible for them or anyone to know all the menu settings on all of the newest digital cameras. And it's very easy for overlooked settings to be not where they should be."

To ensure that production sound is being recorded by more than one device and that filmmakers have a high-quality backup just in case, Pries recommends recording through a mixer to a separate deck such as a Sound Devices 788, an affordable hard drive/flash card–based recorder used on many leading features and television shows. "A lot of new filmmakers these days want to record solely to the camera because they want to save money," he explains. "They tell themselves they don't need redundant systems. But first- and second-time filmmakers should know that good images and lousy sound equals lots of expensive post, which they may not have budgeted for or can't afford. It can be an expense that sinks an indie film that may already be underbudgeted for postproduction."

Although filmmakers chuckle about recording room tone with everyone in place—due to comedic associations with Tom DiCillo's *Living in Oblivion*—the importance of recording natural ambient sound in the room *with everyone still in position* should not be overlooked.

"I always try to record the room sound, and that's more to use to fill in gaps when editing dialogue together," says Pries. "If they're going from one clip to another clip they can use a piece of room tone to create ambient continuity and tie them together. If you have something like an electrical hum and you can record that, the editor can often find that frequency in the EQ [equalization] and negate it if it's constant. But to do that, you'll have to have recorded clear room tone. An editor in post can play noise as an isolated track and sometimes get it out of the recording. But that's not to say that people should go ahead and just record when there's noise in a room."

Buzz, which is different from hum, cannot be negated. An example of buzz is the noise from an electrical shaver, while a hum is more like the quiet noise of a refrigerator. "You can sometimes get rid of hum, which is more of a constant sound source with a little fluctuation, but buzz is harder to get rid of because it typically has a couple of frequencies running through it," says Pries. "But the worst thing of all is radio frequency noise from a cell phone or BlackBerry. The cell phone signal that is picked up through the audio cables and imprinted on the recording is indelible, so you have to keep your phones *off* on set, always. You can often hear it on television, particularly on live news events or interviews or with the pundits. This is because the cell phone receives tracking and e-mail delivery signals. Putting the phone on Silent isn't enough. It should be the rule on set that cell phones are turned off. Good luck getting everyone to comply with it. The iPhone actually has an Airplane Mode option, which resolves this on set, in which case silencing the ringer could be enough if that setting is turned on.

"I recommend more than a minute of room tone, but sometimes it's hard to do because of people's phones; if you get there early, people are setting up, and if you wait to record it after the shooting, people are tearing down and it's hard to keep everybody quiet. But you should schedule a sound person out with his list to record room tone and 'wild track' at any of the given locations."

If you take a microphone and a deck into a diner you can sit there for thirty minutes and get tons of ambient sound, or you can also go out to a street corner and record traffic noise, or go into town and just get the hustle and bustle of daily life. You should record any background noise, any sound that's going to be a part of the environment you might need from a location, like birdsong or wind, or the sea, nightfall, and crickets, or anything else that plays into the audio image of the space where the action is going to take place.

For any low-budget film shooting in a real, working diner, directors need to be sure they have as much control as possible over the quality of the recorded dialogue. The extras have to always pantomime all their actions and conversation, minimizing extraneous noise, which must be recorded later as "wild track" and added in afterward.

Line producers are especially important when it comes to

saving the director from himself or herself by preparing the location sound with the appropriate gear needed to clearly capture the dialogue, and in allowing a sound mixer to override the call for action when ambient noise or some other distraction threatens to ruin the sound in a scene. The sign of a good line producer is one who thinks to include the sound mixer on the scout to make sure each location will work from a sonic perspective.

"I know a lot of line producers who don't listen when the sound mixer says, 'This location's not going to work.' " says Bell. "He'll say, 'It's too loud here, you're not going to be able to hear anything,' but nobody listens. And then of course he turns out to be right after all and the production winds up spending an arm and a leg on ADR [additional dialogue recording] in post that sounds terrible and doesn't match up with the actors. People think ADR is easy but there's always something weird or artificial about how it looks on-screen. I used to do sound, so I always lend an ear to the technicians when they have something to say, but not everybody does."

"You don't want to show up at a location that has been scouted and find it's totally unusable, but it can happen if the line producer isn't on top of it," says Jenny Schweitzer, who, along with Bell, produced the powerfully moving Lodge Kerrigan film *Keane*. "Sometimes it's a perfect location in each and every way, but you have some sound issues that can be tricky to solve in postproduction. Maybe it has eighteen-wheeler trucks whizzing by every few seconds or there's some other sound issue that's barely discernible, like the low buzz from nearby power lines that's impossible to eliminate in postproduction. That's something a good line producer should be pointing out ahead of time. You don't want to show up at a location and find out that sound issues have been overlooked, although when you work low budget, that's always very tricky. It's a sore spot among sound mixers I've worked with in the past."

Just as Robert Crumb taught himself how to draw urban sprawl and telephone towers in order to make his backgrounds more naturalistic, filmmakers need to experiment with how recording ambient sound from their locations on a separate track can make certain sequences more vibrant and real. To see how powerful ambient sound can be in affecting the mood of a sequence, filmmakers only need to walk around town listening to Matt Coneybeare's iPhone app "Ambiance." Producers and directors would also do themselves a huge favor by asking their sound engineers to look at the script before the shoot commences to see if they can visualize where unforeseen stretches of silences might need some sweetening. Toward that end, sound effects CDs or professional samples of wind and faint birdsong can go a long way toward building a sonic landscape and making a location sound even more natural than it actually was. If filmmakers only spent a few days test-driving software such as Pro Tools or the latest version of GarageBand, they would have a much better idea about how to add additional sound effects or manipulate sound elements, be it car horns or layers of Altman-esque dialogue.

To achieve this, high-quality microphones are a must, since running skimpy microphones into a DAT deck or hard-drive recorder is akin to piping ESPN HD or a Blu-ray disc of *Iron Man* into an old black-and-white set. However, most first- and second-time filmmakers try to save money by skimping on expensive, good-quality mics when sound is often the most important though frequently overlooked aspect of a production. "Most people know not to use the onboard camera mic to record sound, but some filmmakers still do it," says Ken Pries. "The onboard mic can pick up transport noise and the sound of your hands touching the camera, but more than that, it's an omnidirectional mic that will pick up things that are happening on the sides and behind you and will probably pick up the sound of the tape running through the camera and whatever the camera operator is doing, rather than what is happening in front of the camera."

Many of the sound problems that cannot be fixed in postproduction require only a little forward thinking before the shoot commences or on the day to avoid hours of heartache and expensive postproduction. For example, while the sound being recorded on the audio track of a MiniDV cassette may in fact be digital, it does not mean that it is CD quality or that it will sound pristine or in stereo. As a result, filmmakers should always test their cameras and their workflows—the path that their video or film footage and its accompanying sound will take from the set, to postproduction, to final master, to exhibition in theaters or on DVD—before they start shooting the actual film. "I only have a few major Write It Down Rules in my class, but one of them is that good sound is more important than good picture, since sound is either good or bad—it's on or off—and it *has* to be good," advises Stolaroff. "It's actually a lot harder than people think to get good production sound, and you have to take it seriously, realize just how important it is, and figure out how you're going to deal with it. If you're going to shoot on digital video, you'll want to test the way you're going to run the sound on the set and marry it to picture. Say you're recording using a boom mic and that sound is going into your sound operator's mixing console. He's going to set the levels and then he's going to send it over to the camera to be recorded onto the videotape. That's fine, but you have to make sure you test it, make sure it actually works, and then have a crew member or your editor actually watch the tapes once you're in production to make sure your sound levels are good. It's also a good idea to have the sound mixer recording sound onto a DAT or hard-drive-based recorder as a backup so if the levels are too low or blown out on the videotape you can go back and replace the sound when you're in postproduction. To do this you'll need to have synched up the recording equipment with what you shot using a slate, preferably a Smart Slate, which is an electronic version of the traditional chalk clapper board."

Filmmakers who are sending their sound wirelessly to the camera may find that none of the sound is usable because the levels are too low, one of the actor's wireless mics was in the off position, or some other unforeseen problem has prevented decent sound from getting to the camera.

Generally, the best-quality production sound will come from using a good directional microphone on a boom that can get as close to the actors as possible without entering the frame. The directional mic Stolaroff recommends to filmmakers on a budget is the two-piece Sennheiser K6 modular with an ME66 short shotgun mic, which costs around $450 to $500. Filmmakers able to spend more should use the Sennheiser MKH60 microphone for around $1,400. Both of these mics have a hypercardioid pickup pattern, which means that they are most sensitive at the front and sides, and reject sounds entering 120 degrees to the rear.

Of course, there are times when using a boom mic is impossible and when wireless may be the only option. "If you are running and gunning outside, if you're shooting a documentary where you need to follow your subject, if you're in a situation where you need to be inconspicuous because you don't have a permit, or if the ambient noise level is really high, you will need to go with a wireless lavalier mic," advises Stolaroff. However, wireless mics vary in recording characteristics, interference resistance, overall quality, and durability. Filmmakers looking for the best sound equipment should also know that they can easily spend thousands of dollars on a good wireless system. "While I can't speak on all the many under-$1,000 wireless systems out there, I personally own the Sennheiser Evolution G2 system, which in-cludes a bodypack EK100 G2 receiver, a bodypack SK100 G2 transmitter, and an ME2 omnidirectional mic," says Stolaroff. "The units are small, durable, easy to use and for about $500, the quality is great."

THE CRITICAL LINE PRODUCER

On lower-budget productions, directors or producers will often hire one experienced outsider to handle logistics and assign them the catchall title of "line producer." What they really want is someone who knows their way around a film set to pull everything together and make the shoot go smoothly. Many first- and second-time filmmakers, however, confuse the role of a line producer with that of the assistant director (AD) and the unit production manager (UPM), and, as a result, end up taking on those roles themselves, something that is nearly impossible for one person to do effectively. It is important for aspiring filmmakers to know the correct terms for on-set jobs and their responsibilities so they can know what needs to be done and can hopefully delegate these tasks to others.

According to guild definitions, an AD organizes preproduction, organizes the crew, and secures equipment. During production, the AD assists the director with the shoot by directing background action and preparing call sheets for cast and crew. He or she also supervises the crew and the overall smooth functioning of the set. According to guild definitions, a UPM coordinates and oversees the preparation of the production, handles all off-set logistics, and typically prepares the shooting schedule and budget, when he or she is not coordinating housing and transportation for cast and crew, securing releases for locations, and ensuring the production's smooth sailing.

Line producers do everything else, inhabiting an intermediate space at the intersection of the project's creative considerations and financial limitations. In general, the line producer's job is to ensure that all the elements needed to shoot a scene properly are there on a given day, and to wrangle everything that was written into the script, agreed upon, and that will be key to making each scene compelling and believable.

"Essentially, a line producer will take the script, break it down, and create a realistic schedule, generate a doable budget for the amount of money that they have, and create a production scenario and a postproduction scenario that works," explains Schweitzer. "Then the filmmaker can assemble a crew and go from there." The critical nature of this position cannot be overlooked, since it is often the line producer who makes sure that minor and major catastrophes are identified early and avoided. For example, it would be the line producer's responsibility when working with a first-timer to raise a red flag that the creaky "mirror-door" G4 the director plans to edit the film on cannot handle HD video from a borrowed Sony EX1. He or she would also be expected to tap someone on the shoulder about the lack of backup hard drives. Filmmakers who think that one backup is enough should recall that Will Smith's character in *I Am Legend* backed up his medical data to six redundant hard drives every night. Hiring a line producer who doesn't think about the project's workflow and who doesn't raise questions early on can often put a director in the position of having to think of everything, a level of responsibility few people can handle and a situation that invites catastrophe.

"No one can simultaneously be the director and the line

producer, so if there is a weak line producer, the most likely scenario would be that the producer would take over that role," says Bell. "But it is a very specific skill set and it would be difficult for anyone to have to become the line producer if they have never done it before."

Of course, the job description of a line producer often changes with any given project because that line producer will be working under producers who may be more hands-on, which will change the dynamic and the authority the line producer has on set. "On our films Danny [Boyle] and I really act as line producers as well, because if you let the line producer dictate everything, you can lose control and that's a mistake," says *28 Days Later* producer Andrew Macdonald. "Letting the line producer take charge is also how things often end up being really expensive, because line producers always want do things exactly the way they've done it before. Many of them don't think even a little bit outside the box about how you would go about, say, doing a London scene with no people. This type of line producer might say, 'They did it like this on *Spider-Man 3* so that's how we're going to do it on this project as well.' And that's how line producers are, they want to play it as much by the book as possible. But the thing is, the direction has to come from the director and producer."

On lower-budget shoots, directors should hire line producers who are willing to improvise and innovate their way out of seemingly intractable situations. "I think you need a line producer who has really risen from the bottom to the top and who can multitask," advises Schweitzer. "Because if you're going to have a smaller crew, the line producer or the person in charge should know how and be able to do the jobs of the people beneath them. You may not have the budget to hire some of those crew members, so you'll need a jack-of-all trades with real experience. On a smaller budget, if you're trying to make a $100,000 movie, the line producer is the person who is going to be taking up all those little tasks that on a larger production you'd have other people taking care of."

A good line producer is also ideally an unflappable, level-headed peacemaker who steps in when tempers are about to flare between the director and the cinematographer. It is the producer's job to make sure cast members are getting along, but a poor line producer can often be the cause of actors' tension or flaring tempers, rather than prima donna attitudes or unrealistic expectations the actors may have. For that reason, any line producer who is introducing tension to the set by stepping into the AD's role of supervising the crew and forcing them to conform to his own misguided concept of military precision is someone who should be quietly reconsidered or even replaced, since it is unlikely that this person will change his method even after a discussion in private.

Having an uptight line producer can be especially problematic if the film is a love story or a light comedy. If actors need to be comfortable and relaxed in order to perform a love scene or really sell an emotional reconciliation, an uptight line producer may undo all of the gentle coaxing the director and first AD have used to achieve a delicate performance. When hiring a line producer, or when filling any on-set position, filmmakers should never take on anyone sight unseen and should recognize that there is a huge difference between a person with a commanding presence who jumps in to solve problems and someone who talks a good game and has all the camera lingo down, but is at heart just a bully or a jerk. The way to avoid a line producer who oversteps the nice-guy AD's role and exasperates the extras and insists on barking "Background action!" or one who strays into the territory of the production supervisor because he wants to make sure the craft service is decent, and to get a solid line producer who helps the filmmakers realize their vision and produce a festival-worthy film is to ask for several impartial references and to ask if he or she has thought through all aspects of the production—including post—and how the choice of camera equipment and post houses will impact the shoot even before a single frame is shot.

HIRING A PRODUCTION CREW

While first-time directors may have a vision of assembling a camera team that resembles the highly specialized members of a U.K. heist flick, such as *Sexy Beast* or *RocknRolla*, more often than not they will run into cinematographers who have their own lineup whom they "always work with." This all-or-nothing, my-way-or-the-highway team typically includes the DP's gaffer, assorted grips, electrics, a camera operator, and camera assistants.

The problem with approving everyone sight unseen is that it sometimes hands the DP control, since the entire crew is made up of his or her people. It can also create a situation where most-favored-nations fee structures work *against* the director or producer, since the DP is able to offer his crew a rich payday or a hookup for previous low-paying gigs on the current producer's dime. In this scenario, a director or producer who agrees to pay the DP $250 per day for ten days but doesn't ask about what other crew members the DP hopes to bring on board for the shoot may end up with a $12,500 bill rather than the DP's fee of $2,500. "No one is obligated to pay that much to cover a DP's entire team, even if he or she says that's the way it's got to be, since the director can just say, 'I'm sorry, thank you very much.' But you have to ask up front how many crew members the DP expects to have on his team and what they each expect to be paid, and you have to leave yourself enough time to hire a different DP if the economics don't work for you," explains Stolaroff. "The lesson is to ask the DP about hidden costs and crew fees early so you don't have people showing up who are expecting to be paid, or else they'll walk off the gig and shut down the shoot, which would be much more expensive."

Something that can quickly increase the production budget significantly is the addition of crew who may not be necessary on a low-budget shoot. "One of the things it's really hard for people to give up is crew," explains Stolaroff. "Once you start putting a crew together, people often think, 'If I'm going to have this guy I might as well have *that* guy, too, and *that* guy,' and then pretty soon you've got fifteen to twenty people. But if you keep it small, you also eliminate certain assistant crew positions just because you have a small crew. You don't need a lot of ADs and PAs, and if you don't have a lot of elements or equipment, you don't need a production coordinator. I shot a short with a four-man crew. We had a DP, a sound mixer, the director, and myself acting as the producer and first AD. We all did multiple tasks and the director's wife got us lunch, and it worked out really well. Even with just a handful of people, it felt like we were making a movie!"

Slumdog Millionaire director Danny Boyle, whose 2000 film *The Beach* was a massive Hollywood production, suggests using a smaller crew and an unobtrusive camera whenever possible. "We shot 70 percent of *Slumdog* with a very small team using what was then a prototype camera, the Silicon Imaging 2k, or Si2k," he explains. "It works with a hard drive that the cameraman wears on his back in a rucksack, and the camera part of it can be held in his hand. It has a gyro attached to prevent trembling, and it gives you incredible flexibility of movement. It also disarms people in a way that helps you get extremely naturalistic performances.

There's the desire to act a certain way whenever people see a
giant film camera, but when they can't quite see where it is
and they're not thinking about it, that helps you enormously.
And so it was a huge benefit to be able to shoot unobtru-
sively in India. The cameras they normally use on the street
there are massive—digital hasn't really arrived just yet—and
with those 35mm cameras it's always a huge palaver, it's a
huge setup. With *Slumdog*, I don't think people really knew
what we were doing half the time given the way we shot it.
They didn't really twig that we were making a film and that
helped us get many of the scenes we might not have otherwise been able to get."

When working at a lower budget level, filmmakers have
to be wary of crew members who work on professional commercial shoots during the week and only shoot indie projects
on the side but expect their full day rate. "I think that a lot of
times the best low-budget films are films where the director
is really part of a filmmaking community of people who will
support him or her in making their film," says *Raising Victor
Vargas* producer Scott Macaulay.

Before hiring a DP and his team, moreover, a producer and
a director should not be shy about checking the crew members' credentials and references.

HOW MUCH SHOULD YOU PAY?

One of the things that bewilders a lot of first-time filmmakers is how much to pay crew members. What is astonishing
is that many filmmakers won't pay $500 per month to
COBRA for their health insurance, but will actually consider
paying a crew member they don't know a rate of $500 or
$1,000 per day on a ten-day shoot because they think it's
simply the going rate. The Jedi mind trick crew members
use on first-time directors is that the crew member will be

turning down a commercial gig to do this short film or be passing up several days of working on a TV show to do this shoot, and so the crew member needs to be paid the same amount. The truth is, commercial crew members and even DPs do not work every day of the month, so this argument is not entirely true. Additionally, while a prospective DP may be well paid as a camera tech on *Law & Order* or *CSI*, his or her assignment on set may be as an assistant to the camera operator and not the show's cinematographer.

Invariably, however, one member will demand more money to work on the project, usually on the eve of production. "This person will typically say, 'I've been thinking about it and I've just been around too long. I can't do it for what you're paying everyone under the most-favored-nations agreement,' " explains Stolaroff. "And every time that's happened the person who *had* to have more money turned out to be the worst crew member. They end up being the person that was the least worth the extra money and the one who, if you could do it again, you wouldn't even take for free. I tell my students at the No Budget Film School that there are people who work on low-budget films for the right reasons and those are the people that you want. And for some reason, the people who say they're bigger than that and have more experience so they deserve more money are always useless. The thing to remember is that if they were worth more they'd be working on studio productions, so those big talkers should always be suspect."

The broader lesson is that no one person should make or break a film production. Very often first- or second-time filmmakers lock themselves in to a start date by reserving equipment first and then get it into their heads that without person A or person B the whole project will collapse, or that the shoot won't be possible without their input. The truth is, this is Dumbo "magic feather" thinking that has no basis in reality. If push comes to shove, it is better to simply start over with a new crew search.

Struggling filmmakers may know how much a family-size box of Rice Krispies should cost or what the price break is on a twelve-pack of ramen noodles, but when it comes to paying a professional DP with his own HD camera they think any number sounds about right. Filmmakers often get into a mind-set that this short film or low-budget indie project is their one shot since they may not ever have the time off from work, the resources, or the will to make another film, so they quickly become willing to pay the moon to just about anyone who says they can help. There is also a flawed line of thinking that quality costs money and you get what you pay for, which drives many new filmmakers to pay more than they should for crew members.

Where people usually get trapped and roped into paying huge fees for crew is when they are not part of a filmmaking community. They didn't go to film school and they have very few contacts as far as crew members go. The bottom line is anyone who wants to charge a first-time filmmaker $1,000 per day to work on a low-budget indie is the wrong person to have on the team. On a $1 million or even a $1.5 million film it's not out of line to pay the DP $1,500 per week. There are mitigating factors if it's a film that's going to be entirely shot on a green screen and a filmmaker needs someone who has that particular technical expertise, but otherwise anyone who wants to charge $7,000 per week is gouging the novice director or producer. "When making a low-budget film, it's important that you hire good crew as well as pay them fair rates that are commensurate with your overall budget," says Scott Macaulay. "Sometimes low-budget filmmakers will meet a DP or production designer who wants to make their studio 'quote'—the amount they'd make on a higher budget film. If you've only got $1 million or $2 million to do your film, that's probably not feasible, and it's also not fair to all the crew members you'll have working for much less. You need to find people who are the up-and-coming stars—people who have done great work on other indies—as well as those bigger names who simply fall in love with your project and agree to work for a lower rate, simply in order to be a part of it."

When filmmakers are making a well-financed movie in the $2 million to $8 million range, there are unions involved and production rules that have to be followed. Indeed, if the production is at a high enough level to be bonded, for example, an experienced line producer who is actually approved by the bond company is required to go forward. However, filmmakers shooting a short film or a student film or a small independent project are usually going to be working with an entirely different pool of aspiring talent, in both the above-the-line and below-the-line areas.

SELF-INFLICTED WOUNDS

As tempting as it may be, digital sound and picture should never be checked during the shoot by running MiniDV or HD tape backward in the camera. Even though most tape-based cameras allow this check to be performed safely, running tape backwards risks stretching the tape and introducing a potentially catastrophic time-code break once shooting recommences.

Film editor David Tarleton urges filmmakers to let the camera roll out for longer than they usually do before calling "Action" and "Cut," to pick up extra beats that may be needed in post and to avoid time-code breaks on DV cassettes. "A time-code break on a digital video shot is usually caused by the director wanting to see a playback of the last shot, and it can be a real disaster in post," he says. "Time code is what allows you to conform your edit decision list to your final edit and run your online smoothly. So if your camera operator stops the camera the moment you call 'Cut,' you may lose the last few seconds of the preceding scene. When you get to postproduction your online may be several frames off because of a time-code break and you may need to do something called 'clean printing,' where you have to match up those missing frames by eye. Otherwise the online will be off when you're conforming it to your offline EDL."

Other threats that can scuttle an entire day of footage include GPS and Nextel-like handsets that emit magnetic fields or periodic radio frequency signal noise even when set to Silent or Vibrate, which can be picked up by wireless mics and digital cameras. All sorts of magnetic fields can create dropouts, artifacts, and skipped frames on both MiniDV and HD tape. "All HDV-standard cameras, like the Sony DSC-V1 or the Canon XL H1, record to MiniDV tape, so filmmakers get about an hour of material on a tape. But the bad news is that HDV is a highly compressed, interframe codec [coder-decoder], which can lead to irreparable dropouts," explains Stolaroff. "Because the compression codec used by the camera compresses material in sometimes as many as fifteen-frame chunks or GOPs [groups of pictures], a single-frame dropout in HDV can affect all fifteen frames of material." Aspiring filmmakers need to keep their phones off and recognize that digital does not mean pristine or permanent.

If the feature is being shot on 16mm or 35mm film, dailies should be printed at regular intervals to look for hairs in the camera's shutter gate or scratches on the negative or the camera lens that might have gone unnoticed. "I would say that even when you're not printing film dailies on a regular basis, you should randomly print them just to be safe," explains *Eternal Sunshine of the Spotless Mind* producer Anthony Bregman. "Print something like 10 percent of everything you shoot on a totally random basis throughout the course of the filming and look for focus problems, jitter issues, clouding, and scratches—anything. It's especially important if you're shooting scenes or situations that have funky looks or tricky camera positions or movements, or if you're using a single camera lens for a good portion of your film. There could be a scratch on the entire film that a filmmaker might not be able to digitally correct. But the big reason you want to print randomly is because you don't always know what odd situations you're even looking for."

Additionally, labeling and carefully logging tapes—even hiring someone to keep a written log of every setup and take—is critical, since it will save days if not weeks in the editing room. Some films can't be edited without meticulous production notes related to each take and each magazine of film or HD cassette.

Ryan Fleck and Anna Boden had $1 million for *Half Nelson* but chose Super 16—a film format designed to be blown up to 35mm—as an artistic choice, given the stock's grainy look and their love of the films of Hal Ashby.

"We always knew that we wanted to shoot Super 16 rather than 35mm because you can be so much less obtrusive using a smaller camera," says cowriter and editor Boden. "With the size of the camera we could shoot the film 99 percent handheld and hurt our DP's back a little bit less. And since we had always imagined *Half Nelson* on really grainy film stock with kind of muted colors, Super 16 was perfect for it. We shot with an Arriflex SR3 on Kodak 7229 film stock and went to a digital intermediate in post. The blowup to 35mm from Super 16 would be easier than a blowup from regular 16mm to 35mm because of aspect ratio, but of course shooting on 35mm and just doing an optical print would have been the simplest post process. We ended up doing a 2K digital intermediate rather than an optical blowup."

Today, going with a digital intermediate (DI) does not cost much more than an optical blowup and it gives the filmmaker more flexibility. Filmmakers who aren't doing much in the way of optical effects, visual effects, or fancy color correction, and who can get a better deal on an optical blowup, may want to save money and go with that option.

WHAT CAMERA SHOULD WE USE?

The first thing aspiring filmmakers often ask themselves is what equipment they should use. After all, they may not live in a city that has a professional equipment rental house or be able to borrow a fancy newfangled digital camera from a friend. And while *Collateral* and *Zodiac* were shot on expensive high-definition cameras—such as the $100,000 Viper FilmStream made by Thomson and the $80,000 Sony F23—most aspiring filmmakers think their only option is whatever is available at the local Best Buy or Circuit City. For some, this is because they plan to take advantage of outdated return policies and get their money back less a 15 percent restocking fee after shooting their film, something a lot of filmmakers joke about but which is, without question, ethically problematic.

To make sure there are no surprises on the day, filmmakers need to run through the entire book with new cameras and go through every button and every toggle, every menu item and every possible combination and manipulation. The camera should be hooked up to the mixer several different ways using different output and input settings so that you can go somewhere and be ready for anything; in general, you can't expect to have time in the field to puzzle the thing out.

Of course there are a lot of first- and second-time film-makers who will get their gear and not do their homework. "This is why preproduction is so important, because you can find and decide on the gear you want to use," says Ken Pries. "The manuals for all the best cameras are all online as PDFs, so you can do all your homework beforehand, giving yourself the advantage of understanding the capabilities and shortcomings of the camera you plan to use and then work with any of the other associated departments accordingly."

What many filmmakers do not realize is that they are almost always better off buying the best high-end camera they can afford from the "prosumer camcorders" page of B&H or a similar section of a competitor's website and having it shipped to them.

The issues filmmakers should consider when buying or borrowing a camera include whether it can shoot in a more filmic 24p mode that mirrors the frame rate of traditional film, whether it shoots in high definition or standard definition, and the camera's "form factor," or its size and weight. Without 24p capability, audiences will be looking at an image that screams video, in all its amplified HD glory, which often makes everything look like a soap opera. A smaller form factor allows a small crew to blend in with the environment and not get noticed. Other considerations that are less important for first- and second-time filmmakers include those related to camera technology such as chip size and number of chips, whether the camera has a fixed or interchangeable lens, its pixel count, or whether the camera has an HD-SDI (serial digital interface) out option.

In 2009, 24p HD cameras were becoming more afford-able, which further accelerated the migration of first- and second-time filmmakers from MiniDV to HD. However, some first-time filmmakers still get caught in a quandary as to whether they should hire a friend of a friend cinematographer who knows about lighting for HD and owns his own gear or simply buy their own HD camera for $6,000 and hire an aspiring DP with little or no experience.

Bourne Identity director Doug Liman advocates investing in equipment rather than exorbitant day rates for rentals. "Today you can buy a 24p HD camcorder for two grand or less, and you can buy Avid or Final Cut software and a Mac laptop for a couple of thousand all-in, so for under $5,000 you can have state-of-the-art editing equipment that rivals anything out there and an HD camera that you own," he explains. "And the good news is you can shoot for two years that way. You can edit for eight years if you want to. This may be a better approach for a lot of people because I think not having enough time is sort of the biggest enemy to filmmaking. Theoretically, when you have less money, you have less time, but that isn't always necessarily true."

When it comes to equipment, the number one rule is, always get the best camera you can afford to buy or borrow. "If you're shooting a narrative feature you really want to use any 24p camera, even a standard-definition 24p camera like the Panasonic DVX-100 used to shoot *The King of Kong*. That to me is the line of demarcation," says Stolaroff. "To me high-def versus standard-def doesn't matter as much as always shooting 24p so your project doesn't look like video. You want to try to get a three-chip camera with at least a one-third-inch chip that has a number of professional manual controls, and there is a range of cameras that will work very well for lots of projects."

While filmmakers used to have to go to film school and learn about lenses and film loading and the mechanics of fragile 16mm cameras, today's aspiring filmmakers can purchase professional-grade HD video cameras from online outlets like B&H, Amazon, or even from the local big-box chains, which often carry at least one high-end model.

However, filmmakers should beware of "free" loaner cameras from equipment manufacturers pushing a new digital format. While it may seem like a great deal, there are no free lunches. Problems often arise after the shoot wraps and the director or producer finds out that this exotic camera format is not in standard use *anywhere* and that they will have to go to Philadelphia or Los Angeles or Hong Kong to clone and hopefully convert to DigiBeta everything they've just shot so it can then be imported into Avid or Final Cut Studio 3. The sticker shock of thousands of dollars, which could have enabled them to buy their own Panasonic P2 camera, will not be as significant as the discovery that conforming from original masters may be next to impossible since the "free" camera format they used is simply not compatible with standard editing software. Sure, the image quality may be beautiful, but workflows originating from exotic or newfangled gear may not be feasible on an ultralow budget and in some cases may require a desperate hunt for professional-grade decks just to transfer the tapes on proprietary memory cards to a more standard format.

"It's the whole penny-wise argument," says Bell. "You try to cheap out on the technology up front, because you don't want to spend as much money on the camera or on the deck, or on some other piece of equipment, you can end up in the last leg of the race and realize it's costing ten times as much to fix as it would have to just have done it right the first time. That's why one of the things that I push for immediately is to have a meeting with the post facility that the filmmakers want to use, and to have a video operator on the set or at least on call at all times, someone who knows how it's going to end up and what kind of equipment is needed to make the job run as smoothly as possible."

For filmmakers working on low to no budgets, Stolaroff recommends the Panasonic AG-HVX200. "It's relatively inexpensive at around $5,500; it has a small body shape or 'form factor,' which means you can shoot inconspicuously; it creates a remarkable image; and it has a number of other useful features," he says. "Most important, for narrative film-making, the HVX200 is a true 24-frame progressive—or 24p—camera. And unlike all the other low-cost professional or prosumer HD cameras—such as the Canon series (XL H1, XH A1, or XH G1), the JVCs (GY-HD110U, 200U, or 250U), or the Sony DSC-V1 or even the new EX1—the Panasonic AG-HVX200 utilizes an intra-frame codec (DVCPRO-HD), rather than a inter-frame codec (HDV or XDCAM), which means filmmakers will have far fewer headaches in postproduction. It shoots true slow motion and fast motion—one of the only cameras in its class that does that—it's 4:2:2, the sound is uncompressed, and probably most significant, it doesn't shoot on tape but rather onto flash memory cards called P2 that are similar in concept to the ones in your digital pocket camera."

These cards, which reached 64 gigabytes at the end of 2008 and are expected to hit 128 gigabytes in 2009, stream-line the traditional workflow, saving time and ultimately money. "As far as no-budget features go, it is now possible to make a film for literally nothing if you can borrow an HVX200, copy your digital files to a hard drive rather than having to do a tape-to-hard-drive transfer, and skip the cost that a tape house would typically charge for a transfer," adds Stolaroff.

Among the digitally shot projects that may inspire tomor-row's filmmakers, *A Scanner Darkly* was shot with an earlier Panasonic model, the AG-DVX100, before being roto-scoped. Miles Beckett first filmed *Lonelygirl15* using a Logi-tech QuickCam Orbit MP webcam before later moving to a Canon GL1 and then to a Sony HVR-Z1 on *KateModern*. Aaron Yonda first cut his teeth on a bulky VHS video camera from his local public access station, but shot *Chad Vader* on a Panasonic Pro AG-DVX100A. *28 Days Later* was shot on dozens of Canon XL-1s while the studio-produced, $25 million *Cloverfield* was shot using using a Sony F23. *The Spirit* was shot using Panavision's Genesis, and *Slumdog Millionaire* was shot on an Si2k.

Another option is the RED series of high-end digital cameras. Developed by Jim Jannard, the founder of Oakely sunglasses, the RED camera from RED Digital Cinema is poised to revolutionize independent filmmaking. The company has set its sights on competing against high-end manufacturers such as Sony, Arriflex, and Panavision in the digital space, and has created an innovative camera body allowing for third-party hardware attachments that can improve upon the technology the same way Linux allows open-source software programmers to tailor the operating system to their particular needs. At a price within the reach of independent filmmakers, RED promises to deliver high-resolution images comparable with the most expesive digital cinema cameras approaching the quality of film. One of the advantages of the RED series is that it can accommodate Zeiss, Cooke, or Angenieux lenses. The RED Scarlet due out in 2009 is generating buzz for its small body size and its ability to shoot in 3K, a standard beyond HD, that could make it the go-to camera for all aspiring filmmakers who want ultra-high resolution at relatively affordable rental or purchase prices.

Other cameras Stolaroff recommends to his No Budget Film School students include the Canon XH A1 and G1. All small-format cameras are highly compressed to be able to fit an HD image on lower-bandwidth media. The advantage of the HD-SDI output of the Canon is that the image is uncompressed. Canon also makes an H1 model without the HD-SDI or Jam-Sync capabilities, for a significant reduction in purchase price. Also recommended are the Sony DCS-V1 and EX1, but Stolaroff suggests avoiding the older Sony HVR-Z1, one of the first HDV cameras offered. Even though it has many appealing features, the Z1 is not recommended for narrative feature films because it doesn't have a true 24p mode like the newer Sony HVR-V1, Sony EX1, and EX3, which can accommodate interchangeable lenses. For better-funded indie-video projects, Stolaroff recommends the Sony EX3 or the Panasonic HPX-170. (For more information on cameras, visit DigitalCinemaSociety.org.)

SCHEDULING ENOUGH DAYS

In addition to underbudgeting, overpaying, and hiring too many people for the crew, filmmakers often underestimate the amount of *time* they will need to complete a short film or feature. For that reason, any line producer who says one day is enough to shoot a short or even a two-minute YouTube video is probably setting up an inexperienced director for failure. This is because there are dozens of errors that can cost a filmmaker an entire day straight out of the gate. On a narrative feature a lost day can also spell disaster if the schedule has been unrealistically compressed or abbreviated.

"A lot of line producers will look at a $200,000 budget and say, 'I'll give you eight or nine days of shooting, that's it,' explains Liman. "But the truth is, I can't make a movie in eight or nine days. Spielberg can't make his movies in eight or nine days, Scorsese can't do it. So many young filmmakers, or new filmmakers I should say, box themselves into conditions that their heroes, the directors they respect most in the world, couldn't succeed in. On *Swingers* I had to level the playing field. I said, 'I'm going to throw out the movie lighting and shoot with natural light—just using brighter than normal everyday lightbulbs—and a couple of other things so that I can have closer to twenty days to shoot the movie.' And my twenty days was really more like forty days because from setup to setup I wasn't spending the time to move lights. So I really had essentially a forty-day shooting schedule that I did in eighteen days. And that made sense because the filmmakers I respect have made movies in forty days. You have to figure out how to level the playing field, and with some of the technology that's available today, I think young filmmakers should be able to have shooting schedules that are as long as some of the people they're aspiring to emulate. On *Swingers* I had plenty of time to shoot, but with only $200,000 you'd typically have to shoot the whole movie in nine days."

Since there is an element of Murphy's law and *Jurassic Park* chaos theory involved in film production, producer Eva Kolodner has a few war stories she shares with the first- and second-time directors she works with through her New York–based Salty Features. "Every filmmaker can make a list of the things they would warn someone to look out for, but there are so many they might all be different," says Kolodner. "The things I would tell people to look out for have to do with making sure you have a signed location agreement so you can't get kicked out of where you're shooting, making sure you have someone who is managing craft service or who is going to make sure that there's food for everyone, and making sure that you have secured a place where the cast and crew can park—you don't want everyone getting parking tickets or even having their cars towed every single day of the shoot. And this one sounds silly but it's important to ask: 'Do you have film? Are you sure you have the unexposed film with you and loaded in the camera?' What typically happens on a first film is that someone forgets to load film into the camera. The film will be sitting there back in the production office but that day's location is fifty miles away, so everything will be ready, everyone's ready to go, but you have no film in the camera.

"Also, saving everyone's wardrobe or taking detailed digital photos or Polaroids of what every cast member was wearing if they've brought their own clothes is very important in case you have to go back and reshoot a sequence or a scene," Kolodner adds. "If you haven't planned for bad weather, your cast can end up soaked and hiding under the craft-service table. Or the director or the main actor won't show up on time because he or she has been in a car accident or a fender bender. An important equipment truck, maybe the truck full of set dressing, will be towed or it just won't show up. Another common one to look out for has to do with keys. Someone will either forget to bring the keys to unlock the equipment truck and you'll lose an entire day, or someone will take the keys to the location with them when they leave for the night and there will be no way to lock down the location that has all the gear and equipment that's been set up for the next day's shoot. So someone, probably you, will end up having to try to sleep on the floor of the unlocked location to protect everything and go without sleep the next day."

The lost-key issue is a much bigger deal than most filmmakers realize. "You always need to have multiple copies of keys: the keys to the location, the keys to the grip truck, the keys to the lock on the grip truck. You have to have a plan for where those keys go each night, and there should always be two sets of keys. The production manager gets one, whoever is responsible for the truck gets the other," says Stolaroff. "Otherwise if someone doesn't show up and they have the one key with them, the shoot grinds to a halt or you have to call a locksmith and have the lock cut.

"You also need to safeguard the truck each night. Filmmakers need to park it in a covered, insured parking lot or have someone watch it so it doesn't get stolen. I worked on a film once where we got to the set one morning and every truck had been broken into and everything that we were making our movie with had been stolen. If you don't have someone on the crew to watch the truck you have to hire a security guard for $500. Don't cut off your nose to spite your face by being cheap with security," Stolaroff continues. "There are things like parking, gas, security guards, and insurance that you have to plan and budget for."

PERMITS AND LOCATIONS

Ed Wood made shooting without permits look comedic, but filmmakers can get in a lot of trouble with local authorities if they get caught without one. Police citations that carry steep financial penalties and the shutdown of the production can result from "stealing locations" or trying to film in public on the sly. "One of the things I teach in my class is that it's a myth that you can shoot in certain places and certain situations in the city of Los Angeles without a permit. It's just not true," explains Stolaroff. "A lot of people mistakenly think you can shoot in your own house, on your own private property, or that you can shoot outside anywhere at certain times of day, or that you can shoot on a public sidewalk as long as you don't use a tripod. None of it is true; low- or no-budget filmmakers really have to check their local regulations and restrictions.

"My big rule, especially if you're shooting in L.A. without a permit, is 'Don't disrupt the status quo.' Don't take up all the parking, don't make a lot of noise on your walkies or cell phones, don't block cars or sidewalks, don't trudge through yards and definitely don't litter. If you're shooting inside a building, get your equipment in as fast as possible and don't leave anything out in the street, not even your equipment truck—drive it as far as it takes to park it."

On *Some Body*, an ultra-low-budget feature that was in dramatic competition at Sundance in 2001, the cast and a minimal crew shot in restaurants and bars by telling the waitstaff that it was someone's birthday. "They'd sing 'Happy Birthday' and have a cake and would be videotaping it like it was a birthday and then shoot the scene they needed to get in the restaurant," says Stolaroff. "But they had no crew and were shooting with just three or four actors wearing wireless mics. Any time you're doing exterior daytime shots, go out with a tiny crew, a small camera, and the minimum equipment."

Of course, a boom will instantly give a production away, as will high-powered camera lights. When shooting night exteriors without a permit, filmmakers need to find locations that are well-lit because the minute a cinematographer starts using professional lights the production is likely to be busted and fined. It may work once or twice, but, as Tommy Lee Jones's character, Samuel Gerard, said in *The Fugitive*, everyone's luck runs out eventually.

8. That Music in Your Head . . . Is Too Expensive

*I*n the darkest nights of the soul when everything is falling apart, the soundtrack humming in a filmmaker's head is often what keeps an indie film—or at least the dream of making one—alive. Even wannabe screenwriters who have written only FADE IN at the top of a blank page often have the songs picked out for the opening sequence and final credits. Music has always been a powerful salve and something aspiring screenwriters, directors, and producers have used to get through the years of rejection and loneliness endemic to indie filmmaking. And while most filmmakers don't think to hire a local art student to storyboard an entire draft of the script they hope to make, they almost always use music to help visualize the set pieces or sequences that will make their films memorable. Indeed, music provides a bridge between the mind's-eye version of the film playing in the filmmaker's head and the actual movie they dream of seeing on the big screen someday. The songs blasting from a Zune or iTunes playlist can also bring the emotional beats a producer or director wants to hit into sharper focus. Unfortunately, they often don't *understand how in an age of DRM-free downloads and Pandora.com, they might not be allowed to use the song that inspired the entire project because of costly permission fees required to marry music to picture. Indeed, while editing programs such as Avid, Final Cut Pro 6, WireTap Studio, and iMovie '08 make it effortlessly easy to drop in a song, prying music out of a rough cut is one of the hardest and most common heartaches filmmakers have to face. Even well-financed directors assume they can leave a track they love in an early cut or festival submission, not realizing that the song may already be promised to an ad agency or car commercial. During post, film editors are always more than happy to drop in the director's favorite songs since they know the director will be delighted when all of a sudden a scene or even the entire film works in a way it hadn't before. Ultimately, however, providing this glimpse of what could be does the filmmaker a huge disservice, since more often than not, the soundtrack planned for an indie film is an enormous minefield unto itself.*

While most indie-film scripts can be categorized as dysfunctional family dramas, hip romantic comedies, or meditations on socioeconomic disparity, nearly all indie-film soundtrack budgets can be described as science fiction or fantasy. Novice filmmakers often communicate their own naïveté and lack of business savvy simply by talking about landing soundtrack deals ("Just like *Juno!*") and the emotional wallop that certain well-known tracks will provide during the last scene and end credits. ("Just like *Zodiac!*")

Part of the problem is that very few of the major film schools in the United States include classes on film music or film scores in their curriculum. "This is where the universities have failed to bring filmmakers and composers together and, more important, explain simple music-rights issues to their students," says ASCAP's senior director of film and television music, Mike Todd. Indeed, there's a complete disconnect in terms of educating filmmakers about what the

implications are of putting a Rolling Stones song in a film—
that they have to clear the licenses or that the Rolling Stones
or David Bowie isn't going to clear songs for under $1 mil-
lion.

"The truth is, nobody ever includes a significant line item
in their budgets for music," says *Hurricane Streets* producer
Gill Holland. "Everyone just assumes that they'll get whatever they want for free or close to it. It's crazy."

Indeed, even the most budget-conscious filmmakers, who
skip meals, shoot black-and-white short-ends, and hold their
shooting ratios below 3:1, want to spend like drunken sailors
whether they have a budget or not when it comes to creating
a soundtrack. "Music inspires the most wishful thinking of
any area of production," says indie veteran and film-industry
consultant Peter Broderick. "Filmmakers may not spend a
lot of time trying to get the script to a big-name actor, but
they will spend months trying to get a Beatles song before
realizing it's never going to happen."

This example isn't a dramatic exaggeration. The filmmakers behind the 2001 movie *I Am Sam* starring Sean Penn
reportedly expected to clear original Beatles recordings and
were forced to put out an eleventh-hour call to nearly two
dozen musicians to have the tracks rerecorded so less expensive cover versions (sung by Eddie Vedder, Aimee Mann,
and Ben Harper, among others) could be included in the
film. The producers of *Across the Universe* did not make the
same mistake in 2007 and recorded cover versions from
the get-go.

In some cases the planets align and filmmakers wonder
what all the nay-saying was about. But more often than not,
the special challenges related to securing rights from record
companies, getting music publishing administrators to also
grant rights, getting permission from the artists in many
cases, and then coming up with the money to pay the going

rate makes dealing with soundtracks one of the hardest and most emotionally draining aspects of production.

"Music creates all sorts of headaches," says Sony Pictures Classics copresident Tom Bernard. "For example, many filmmakers secure festival rights for music but then don't or can't get clearances for the trailer, for broadcast television, for overseas theatrical exhibition, or even for domestic home video. So essentially, we're often asked to buy a movie that can't be shown on television or home video as long as the songs are still in the film. Once we find out the music has only been cleared for festivals or only for domestic theatrical, it's a big problem and it can potentially undo a distribution deal."

The most common misconception is that an artist on the order of Jay-Z, Billie Joe Armstrong, José González, or Leslie Feist will fall in love with a home-burned DVD and grant unlimited rights for a nominal fee. A second popular belief is that there is a record company out there that will pay for all the music—even music recorded by artists on other labels—to secure a soundtrack deal. A third misperception, often fueled by seminars in New York that charge hundreds of dollars to attend, is that "music in film is a great way of generating revenue through the movie's soundtrack!" A fourth myth is that music on 78 rpm records does not need to be cleared because the songs are probably old enough to be in the public domain. Finally, there is a fifth commonly held belief that securing festival rights alone will magically ensure that a song makes it all the way to the final release print.

While MP3 cell phones, 3G iPhones, Zunes, Sansas, Shuffles, Nanos, and Zens have allowed an entire generation to view life as if it were a travel montage from *Drugstore Cowboy* or *Little Miss Sunshine*, legally dropping copyrighted songs into a movie or even a short film that will be shown on

YouTube or Veoh requires permission, lawyers, and significant cash to buy the rights to use the song in perpetuity.
YouTube parodies—such as "Darth Maul's Bringing the Sexy
Back" or Xerxes and Leonidas making eyes to "Saving All
My Love for You"—are typically ignored by record-
company lawyers, but including popular music in a narrative
short film that shows up online can get the clip pulled down
and could bring about a lawsuit.

"There are some sites online that are more strongly
policed than others, but you can't upload an independent
film if it has songs in it that are not cleared," says IFP president Michelle Byrd. "This is surprising to some filmmakers
because it's easier than ever these days to line up a track to
picture—far easier than it was even five years ago. I think
people 'get' now that it's not okay to steal music through file
sharing, but you still get situations where people use songs
they haven't cleared and then find out it's a major problem
when they're trying to sell their completed film."

The three hurdles filmmakers specifically face are (1) the
exorbitant costs of clearing each tune in all exhibition venues
and those that may be introduced in the future "throughout
the universe"; (2) securing usage rights from the record label
and the publishing company that controls or "administers"
the song's publishing rights; and (3) getting additional permission from the artist, the artist's estate or family, or subsequent copyright holder, who may hold veto power over the
record company's desire to license the song.

"If it's a preexisting composition—a song that was written
by someone else—you will always, always need a synchronization license no matter what," says Kristi Gamble, an
entertainment attorney at the New York firm of Kaplan &
Gamble, LLP. "The synchronization license requires the
filmmaker to get permission from the administrator or publisher, like EMI, Sony ATV, Universal, or Warner/Chappell

Music. Often, however, the filmmaker also needs to obtain additional permission from the person who wrote the melody, the person who wrote the lyrics, and/or the person who actually holds the copyright. Filmmakers using the original sound recording also need an additional license commonly referred to as a 'master-use' license."

According to Gamble, if a producer engages a local band or well-known artist to do a cover of a song as a work for hire and obtains releases acknowledging this work-for-hire status prior to recording the song, that producer will then need only to secure a synchronization license from the copyright holder or the entity administering the license on the copyright holder's behalf.

"If an actor is singing a song on camera, such as Stanley Herman singing 'I Only Have Eyes for You' to Sean Gullette on the subway in *Pi*, or just humming the melody, you wouldn't have to get a master-use license because you're not using the original sound recording 'in timed synchronization' with the film," Gamble explains. "An actor doing the singing on camera is essentially doing a cover version of the song." This explains why there are so many new versions of classic songs on most film soundtrack, to the frustration of fans who want to hear the original. Even so, the administrator or publisher must still get a written signature from the artist or copyright holder prior to granting a requested license, a final hurdle that can add months to the clearance process. This last requirement prevents a love song by Clay Aiken or Alicia Keys from someday being used to ironic effect in a film like *Saw VII* or Clive Barker's *Midnight Meat Train*.

Sometimes, however, the publisher may simply deny usage because an artist no longer controls his or her own publishing rights or may have sold them off. This means that even if a filmmaker is best friends with Bono, it's not necessarily up to him to decide whether "Vertigo" or "Lemon" can appear in a low-budget movie.

The foremost reason is money. Before a rights discussion even takes place, most publishing companies will send film-makers a quote to kick off negotiations or to deliberately induce sticker shock and make them go away. "A festival license can cost as little as $100, but usually broad rights to lesser songs are quoted at $7,500 per license," says Gamble. "This means it would cost $15,000 to clear both master-use rights and synchronization rights for worldwide use of a sin-gle song. That's the golden number most music publishing companies begin with for a 'broad rights' license. But for a lot of independent filmmakers $15,000 per song is far too expensive, so they have to try to negotiate it down from there if they can."

Typically, though not always, the synchronization rights are negotiated first so a producer or music supervisor can try to get the master-use rights holder to match that quote. But where the song is used and how it is used determine what the quote will be. "They charge you a different rate if it's under thirty seconds, under a minute, in the main title, not in the main title, on-camera usage, or background usage," says *Donnie Darko* producer Adam Fields, who served as executive producer of several hit soundtracks in the 1980s, including *Flashdance*, *Endless Love*, and *An American Werewolf in London*, while working as an executive at Polygram in Los Angeles. "It all makes a difference."

If a song is reprised more than once—the way the Drop-kick Murphys's hard-driving "I'm Shipping Up to Boston" ran through *The Departed*—the quote can skyrocket. "Even if you have a scene in a bar where a jukebox is playing and you cut away for a few seconds to a scene with no music and then back to the bar, publishers may say, 'That's *two* uses so we're going to double the fee,' " says Gwen Bethel, who served as vice president of music at *Blair Witch* distributor Artisan Entertainment, prior to its acquisition by Lionsgate. "Usage is based on a needle-drop concept, and the way they see it, they're getting a cue sheet that says there were two uses."

Margaret writer-director Kenneth Lonergan was vexed by this rule during postproduction of his first film, *You Can Count on Me*. "Every Loretta Lynn song we had in the film cost anywhere from $15,000 to $25,000 per drop of the needle, and if a character changes the station on the radio, then it's *another* $15,000 to $25,000 depending on the song, so it's a little daunting," he explains. "That's one reason why when you see indie movies, you often hear all this music you've never heard before and will never hear again, because very often it's not published music. It's either written for the movie or it's just demo tracks that indie-film directors get from some up-and-coming or unsigned artist."

While critics hailed *You Can Count on Me* as a stunning achievement for its sure-footedness and confidence from a first-time director, behind the scenes, music rights issues gave Lonergan several headaches. "We had $30,000 that was meant to cover the composer the producers were willing to hire and any source music I put in, which was just . . . not enough," Lonergan recalls. "I wanted very much to use certain songs and I had very specific ideas about the music. The problem if you don't know anything, is that you don't know what's normal and what isn't and you don't know what to expect—you don't know what to look out for. Fortunately, the movie was getting a good response and everybody was liking it in the screenings we had—the response was very positive—and I think I came in under budget. So with some arguing I kept getting them to raise the music budget and I think on *You Can Count on Me* it went up to $200,000 or somewhere in that vicinity."

Still, almost every high-profile independent film has had

a behind-the-scenes push to secure rights that were not granted even to well-known and well-regarded directors. Because most struggling filmmakers are not privy to the months of begging and pleading that go on behind closed doors, many of them waste months pushing for well-known songs in their first and second movies. "In *Election*, we were originally going to use Sade's 'Smooth Operator' in a scene with Tracy Flick and Dave Novotny," recalls *Sideways* writer-director Alexander Payne. "That had even been written into the script but it's hard to get Sade songs for films—she doesn't let people use some of her music. So we were going to use Lionel Richie instead, but it was an expensive alternative. And it became one of those things where it was so key to the story that you say, 'I'll do a million sound-alikes of other songs to get to use one Lionel Richie song.' This is the horse trading you have to do when you're making a movie. You say, 'I'll do a sound-alike for this, this, and this, but we *gotta* spend the money on the one Lionel Richie song 'cause it's a huge laugh.' And when you see the movie, Lionel Richie's 'Three Times a Lady' works just as well if not better in the scene. That's how it is in low-budget filmmaking: the obstacles you run into are often the things that lead you to something better."

Of course, rather than focusing on the soundtrack as a whole, many filmmakers become fixated on one long-shot track while the clock is ticking toward a release date or festival deadline. Although the film was ultimately a major success, *Boys Don't Cry* director Kimberly Peirce might have had to push her release date back, risking its Oscar consideration in 1998, to get Boston's "More Than a Feeling" into her film.

"We were fortunate. Even though *Boys* was made on a relatively small budget, Christine [Vachon] and I realized the best way to cut this movie was to screen frequently," she recalls. "We had about eight or nine screenings for anywhere from ten to a hundred people. This allowed us to fine-tune our edit and the music, how music worked with the visuals, and how the movie played. We would pass out questionnaires asking the audience, 'Which songs did you like, which songs didn't you like? Which songs didn't seem to fit?'

"Music is very important to me in general and therefore very important in my films and in how I think about and create characters.

"Boston's rock-radio staple 'More Than a Feeling' worked perfectly in the skating scene—this was Brandon's moment of pure desire and coming alive, of incorporating his male identity into this teenage world," says Peirce, who later directed *Stop-Loss*. "So he was a girl who was playing a boy but could he pull that off in the most common American sweet fantasy, get-the-girl kind of way? 'More Than a Feeling' epitomized the sweetness of Brandon's desire to win this girl over and to be accepted into the straight teen world.

"We used 'More Than a Feeling' as temp in the editing and then through all of those early screenings. Screening your movie can be expensive and time consuming, but I find it to be the *best* way to test out what you've edited and see how it's playing to an audience. And every time we ran the film everyone pretty much agreed, 'That's awesome! That works perfectly!' " continues Peirce. "I'd check in and kept hearing that we'd have no problem getting it [licensing the song]. Then at the very last minute, it became clear that the Boston track would not be forthcoming, even for what was at the time still a humble independent film with no major stars. A car company was offering Boston a million bucks, and if we wanted the song we had to be in that ballpark. That was great they could get that much money, but a million bucks was like half the cost of our whole movie.

"Losing 'More Than a Feeling' was a big deal because of how well it scored Brandon's desire and how centrally it played in the movie. When we found out the song was a no-go, Nathan Larson, my composer, Bradford Simpson, my associate producer, and I started going through everyone's music collections—people still had a lot of vinyl—looking for a replacement; we literally went through hundreds of songs. We tried female vocals and female rock songs but found that really hurt Brandon's male identity, making him more girlish. Then we tried the male stuff, the 'air' kind of bands like REO Speedwagon and Foreigner. They were great, they got the era right, and there was a sweetness to them, but they were too suburban. It didn't work. And anything too hard made the kids, who looked to be about fourteen years old, look silly. And anything too disco-oriented made Brandon seem a bit . . . gay. We needed this to feel like a crowd of straight teenagers skating in a roller rink in Middle America."

The appropriate track proved elusive, even with several members of Peirce's team compiling lists of what they listened to when they went skating and clubbing as teenagers.

"I had originally thought the Cars were going to be too hip," Peirce recalls. "They conjure up that eighties feel, but they're sexy and sophisticated in a certain techno way. But it does have that Middle America feel, so we tried all the Cars songs and finally landed on 'Just What I Needed,' and it worked great—musically it captured Brandon's desire and carried us from Brandon skating, through a montage, and into the title sequence. The only problem was that it ended short of the sequence. We needed to sustain the momentum into the movie proper. I heard this one beat and thought, 'Why don't we just sample that and double it up?' So we doubled up the tail of 'Just What I Needed' to bring people inside Brandon's journey of trying to be a boy and failing, and added lots of reverb, close echo, and then far echo, and put them on two different tracks and then moved from one into the other to create this sense of transition, of Brandon finally giving up on trying to be a boy in his hometown and taking to the road."

Peirce says the experience was stressful but instructive about how important it is to have several workable choices ready to go, in case one falls through. "Oftentimes you think you need something—some actor, some crew member, some location—you think *not* having it will break the movie, but no matter what you do, you can't get it, so you're forced to find something else—and oftentimes you end up with something better.

"Maybe the Cars were less on the nose and that was better for the film but I never would have realized it if 'More Than a Feeling' hadn't been taken away. I mean, 'More Than a Feeling' was a little sweet, and maybe in retrospect it was nicer to have this slightly harder edge with 'Just What I Needed.' The great thing about the Cars song is it's not as recognizable as 'More Than a Feeling.' There's something fundamentally nostalgic about that Boston song, and as much as I love it, maybe the audience brings too much of their own experience and their own memories to it and can't be as involved in Brandon's journey, quite as much as they would with the Cars. I think the lesson is to not get too set on something, like a song over a certain scene, partly because you may not get it for financial or for other reasons, but mostly because you want to stay fresh to the character's journey and how the song is scoring, not necessarily on how much you may love the song, and that's tough because these songs have a huge power over us."

ACTORS SINGING ON-CAMERA

In the karaoke scene in *Boys Don't Cry*, "Bluest Eyes in Texas" was pivotal to the narrative and was a song the production had to clear before the song was recorded. In *Waitress*, the lullaby "Baby Don't You Cry," sung by Keri Russell's character, was written by the film's writer-director Adrienne Shelly and composer Andrew Hollander. But what often happens is that an actor will hum or sing a single line of a copyrighted song on-camera and instantly create an expensive music-rights clearance headache in postproduction. "A lot of directors think it's wonderful that an actor may have started singing or plinking away on a piano during a take," says Bethel Riley, who worked on the soundtrack of *Sling Blade* in her previous incarnation as vice president of business affairs at Shooting Gallery Records. "It doesn't occur to them that they will eventually have to clear the rights to an actor's improvisation or that a song they think is public domain, like 'Happy Birthday,' is actually owned by somebody who wants a lot of money."

A famous near miss involved Nicolas Cage singing an obscure song he had heard in a bar in Europe once during the first act of *Leaving Las Vegas*, an improvisation that almost cost director Mike Figgis the scene since Cage could not recall the song's proper name. When Figgis finally tracked down the copyright holders in Paris, the rights were not immediately available. Figgis was finally able to clear the song, allowing "You Turn Me On," written by Jacques Merali and Alain Bernardin, to be included in the early bar scene with Valeria Golino. Fortunately for the creative team behind *Half Nelson*, the musical notes hummed by Ryan Gosling in various character moments in that film were not taken from the actor's favorite song or from the 1956 Miles Davis number that shares the film's title.

"We had talked in rehearsals about Dan being the kind of guy who might mumble to himself sometimes, and then totally impromptu on the day, Ryan Gosling did this little humming thing that we just loved," recalls editor and cowriter Anna Boden. "And we were like: 'That's it! He doesn't *mumble* to himself. He *hums* to himself!' Ryan assured us that he just made up the song and that we didn't need to clear it, so we ended up using some for the opening and again at the end of the movie too, just to bookend it."

A problem can develop, however, when an actor or director wants to use an obscure song from an old mix tape or an unlabeled CD but may not be 100 percent sure of the origin or provenance. As a result, music supervisors or studio lawyers may have a hard time tracking down the rights holders to pay for the track. Clearing Bobby Vinton's "Mr. Lonely" for Harmony Korine's film of the same name required only a check and several calls to Sony BMG Publishing, while the music in Korine's *Gummo* was obscure—in keeping with that film's bucolic setting—and potentially harder to get cleared. "The song 'My Little Rooster' was an old Appalachian ballad which I think the actual authorship of is unknown," says Korine. "It was probably brought over from Scotland and later became, in some kind of mutated form, 'My Little Rooster.' The version we used was sung in 1962 by an a cappella singer from Arkansas named Almeda Riddle who was one of the more famous Appalachian balladeers. That song was actually in the anthology folk archives, which is a really important collection of music at the Smithsonian, on a CD marked 'children's songs,' and when I heard it, it just struck a chord: 'I love my little rooster and my rooster loves me . . . and I'll cherish that rooster.' I didn't really think about the Buddy Holly song 'Everyday' [also in *Gummo*] too much. I just liked it. I didn't bring any hidden meaning to it."

One of the most universally liked and widely known songs is "Happy Birthday," but what surprises many independent filmmakers is that the rights are owned by Warner/Chappell Music and not granted for free. Filmmakers on the receiving end of letters from Warner/Chappell are often further surprised to learn that there is no legal defense for *not* clearing a song owned by someone else and that they may have to completely recut or lose a critical scene in their film on the eve of an important festival deadline or face liability. "You either have to pay up or take the song out of the movie," says former Miramax senior counsel Rosalind Lawton. "Of course, you can try to negotiate, but if it's after the fact, they have you completely over a barrel."

To avoid this predicament, music-savvy independent filmmakers know to shoot birthday scenes using the slightly cheesy but free "For He's a Jolly Good Fellow," which exists in the public domain. "It sounds like a silly thing," says producer Gill Holland, "but having a character sing 'Happy Birthday' in your film can cost you tens of thousands of dollars."

Leading television director Jamie Babbit, who wrote and directed the Sundance film *But I'm a Cheerleader* in 1999, urges first-time filmmakers to "stem" their music in postproduction and always keep the film's score and source music on separate tracks. "That way it's cheaper and easier to get a song out of the movie if you have to pull it for some reason," she explains. "That can be a lot better than having to remix the whole film."

Of course, most of this last-minute anxiety and worry can be avoided by simply hiring a talented musician friend to write several original songs as work-for-hire compositions and getting a contract in writing that codifies the songs' work-for-hire status. "You're better off using music you can afford from the get-go because if you have to replace any source cues, you'll have to open up the film, swap out the music, mix in the new cue, re-print-master the reel that's affected, and make a new optical track of that reel," says *Revolutionary Road* and *Secretary* postproduction supervisor Jennifer Lane, who was formerly vice president of postproduction at Miramax. "The interpositive/internegative—a film print used to strike duplicate copies of the film itself—is a film element, so that's not affected, but if you have to change the music you will have to make a new answer print and a new check print because the studio distributing your film or thinking of distributing your film will want a delivered answer print and a delivered check print with the proper soundtrack. It's a tremendous hassle financially, emotionally, and timewise."

Lane, who also supervised postproduction on Robert Duvall's *Assassination Tango*, often warns aspiring filmmakers about "temping" with expensive music. "My suggestion to producers is do not let your directors temp with music you know you can't possibly afford," she says. "Otherwise they'll become attached to it and nothing will ever be as good. There are many filmmakers who are more in love with their temp music than anything that's ultimately in the release print." What is even more bizarre is the phenomenon of first-time directors becoming fixated on a big money track they want to include in the *end credits*, a song that if approved would bankrupt the production or eat up its entire distribution advance.

For this reason, *Synecdoche, New York* producer Anthony Bregman is a stickler for clearing all of the music in his films before he sets foot at a festival. "Clearing music is a really tricky stage of the process," he says. "You want to incorporate music because sometimes the emotional resonance of a scene will often come through more effectively with music, and you really want to cut against cleared music so you know where you stand instead of cutting against music that will never appear in the final film," he says. "If you try to clear something after it's premiered at a festival, the record companies totally know they have you, especially if the film has been acquired. They'll say, 'The film has been acquired with this music; if you want to replace it, it's not only the cost of licensing a new track that works, it's also the cost of going back in and opening up the movie again.' That's why I don't advocate getting festival rights. You should have it all locked down and act as if your movie's going to be distributed, as if your film's going to be a success."

Many filmmakers may believe their music has been cleared, but if they read the fine print of the deal, they will see that the music can be used only at festivals and only if the production commits to making significant payments at a future date. Having to pay an additional $180,000 to clear the twelve songs in a film can make a distributor reconsider the deal or cause the filmmaking team to lose whatever leverage it had going into the negotiations. For this reason, filmmakers who leave the deal-making up to untested music supervisors can get into serious trouble.

The easy solution is always going with music that can be cleared inexpensively. Producers can sometimes placate adamant directors by negotiating a "step deal" with artists in order to lower the up-front cost of music clearances. In this scenario, if the film grosses more than $2 million domestically, as reported in *Variety*, a producer will pay the artist a predetermined bump. Still another payment might kick in when the film reaches $5 million in box-office receipts, and yet another disbursement might be owed if the film ultimately ships a certain number of DVDs or hits a certain rental target on Netflix or iTunes. However, these arrangements carry their own complications. "On the surface those deals have some appeal and they can work in certain situations," explains Broderick. "But they can also complicate things for investors because the responsibility for paying the step comes out of the filmmakers' side, and when the steps kick in, it means the musician or rights holder gets in first position, which can be problematic."

As a result, one of the best ways prospective investors can judge the business savvy of a filmmaker asking for money is to simply ask what *songs* he or she plans to use in the movie. This simple question will often reveal whether or not the budget is underfunded or if the project will have a chance of recouping its financing even if it is acquired. Because distributors almost always insist that outstanding music-rights clearance fees be paid out of the filmmaker's minimum guarantee, any filmmaker who claims that a studio will be happy to pick up the unpaid tab for music-rights clearances is either lying, high, or ill-informed. And when the film's advance is used to pay for uncleared music, there is usually little left over for the film's investors.

Many filmmakers lack funds to clear music up front because they've already spent their production contingency on crane shots, a Steadicam day, or a wrap party, mistakenly believing that soundtrack fees will eventually land in the ballpark after an initial negotiation gets under way. Others cut together sequences using songs that should appear only on a wish list written by Martin Scorsese. "It's not realistic for independent filmmakers to try to get rights to the Rolling Stones' 'Gimme Shelter' or David Bowie's 'Heroes,' " says Mike Todd of the American Society of Composers, Authors and Publishers. "They will almost certainly get a quote of $500,000 for the publishing rights and another $500,000 for the actual recording of the song from the label side. Any fast-talking producer or director who tells a financier that a well-known song can be fully cleared if they just give them another $30,000 or even $60,000 doesn't know the going rate for music clearances." Investors also need to know that if a director they are thinking of backing or investing in has been granted festival or final cut, he or she can insist on using a $500,000 song even in the final credits, handing any profits or investor returns the film might have earned to a record company to clear that one song. Similarly, producers should know that music rights are how directors with final cut can hold the project hostage.

The passion that filmmakers often have for certain songs regularly leads to some of the most contentious and heated arguments related to any project, something *The Jimmy Show*'s writer, director, and star Frank Whaley was surprised to learn. "On a lark I had my producer send Bruce Springsteen a VHS copy of the film with a letter I wrote—which was true—saying what a big influence Springsteen was when I was young and how this movie I had just written, directed, and starred in took place in New Jersey," Whaley says. "We knew that he rarely allowed his songs be used on soundtracks, particularly the portion of his catalog I was interested in, which was from the 1978 album *Darkness on the Edge of Town*."

Whaley, who did not have final cut, says he was stunned to hear that the Boss had actually received the tape and had responded to his request. "I wanted to use 'Badlands' and 'Candy's Room' and he said we could use both for an extremely reasonable rate," says Whaley, who today still gets kudos from fans for his memorable performance as Brad in *Pulp Fiction*. "If you know anything about how tough it is to get music rights, it was an incredible deal."

The problem was that Whaley's entire music budget for his composer, soundtrack, and score was only $15,000, and the usage quote Whaley received for both songs was well above that. "I went to the film's financier, but he said, 'No, it's too much money,' " Whaley recalls. "So we talked to a music consultant to see what she could do in terms of lowering the price, knowing that the quote we had already received was a gift from Bruce Springsteen's camp."

While the music supervisor was ultimately successful in getting the price reduced, the financier still kept his wallet shut. "It was absolutely heartbreaking not to be able to use those songs," says Whaley. "Number one, because Springsteen was my idol growing up, and number two, because they really worked in the film."

Filmmakers are often not allowed to mention the going rate for a particular song to anyone as one of the deal points in a "no quote" deal, since revealing a figure would provide other filmmakers with leverage to keep the usage price locked in at similar levels. However, it is known that guitar legend Chuck Berry demanded and received $100,000 for the rights to use the title song in the 1998 film *Johnny Be Good*. "Chuck wanted it in a briefcase," says Fields, who was working as the film's producer at the time. "We could never get in touch with him, and we were down to the wire on the movie. So when I saw that he was going to be on *The Tonight Show* with Johnny Carson, I found out what flight from St. Louis he was on and went to meet him at LAX with a briefcase full of cash and a contract."

Still, Berry was not swayed. "He said, 'I can't sign that,' and I said, 'Why not? It's the contract your lawyer approved,' " recalls Fields. "And he said, 'How do I know that?' So we had to go back to the office, get Chuck Berry's lawyer to sign a faxed contract, and then fax that copy to the hotel for Chuck to sign. Then I had to deliver the briefcase full of cash to the greenroom at the Carson show."

Because filmmakers may never know going in how much a song may cost for full clearance, director Alexander Payne advises allocating more money to the music budget before a single frame is shot. "It's better to have extra money in the music budget and not need it than to need it and not have it," he says. "And then later if you don't use it, all the money you set aside for your music budget can be used for other postproduction costs. But it's actually very hard to take money from any other element of the production or post-production budget and use it for music. Every penny counts on a low-budget film. When you're at the budget stage if you have in mind that you're going to use known music, you have to make sure there's money for it from the beginning."

HOW MUCH IS ENOUGH?

First- and second-time filmmakers often don't know how much they should budget for music, especially since their initial DV or HD budgets may be under $50,000. Others wrongly think they don't need to budget for tunes because a record company will defer the costs of the music and recoup whatever they need when the soundtrack (of course there has to be a soundtrack) makes a ton of money. Still others explain to investors that music clearances will be free after their film resurrects a classic rock act in the way the studio-produced *Reality Bites* brought back interest in the Knack and made the band's 1979 single "My Sharona" a camp hit in the mid-'90s.

Unfortunately, this is one of the biggest myths going. From January to August 2008, *Juno* reached still less than a third of *Pulp Fiction*'s total. Soundtrack sales have suffered with the overall downturn in the economy and the recording industry, which has seen its year-end tally of albums sold in the United States drop from 785.1 million units in 2000 to 588.2 million units in 2006, 500.5 million units in 2007, and 428.4 million units in 2008. *Juno* aside, most consumers no longer shell out sixteen or seventeen dollars for a soundtrack on CD, preferring instead to buy songs à la carte from iTunes or Amazon. Those who do buy the full disc often purchase it used off Amazon, which cuts the record company and the recording artists out of any additional revenue.

This downward trend has led specialized-film distributors to be far more cautious when it comes to releasing a soundtrack in conjunction with a theatrical release. The days when a hip soundtrack was simply part of the marketing push for a specialized film—if there ever really was such a time—are certainly over, partially as a result of rampant CD and file sharing, LAN MP3 Manager 1.0, the sale of used CDs on Craigslist and Amazon, and illicit downloading from darknets that has led to the closing of an estimated 2,700 record stores nationwide between 2003 and 2009 alone.

The soundtracks that are out there aren't necessarily selling like hotcakes. In the first five months after its release in May 2007, the Academy Award–winning soundtrack of *Once* sold just 169,332 units, whereas years earlier it might have sold three to five times as many copies. In another measure of the downturn, the soundtrack to *Pulp Fiction*, which has sold 3.5 million units since its release in September 1994, sold only 6,725 units in the first eight months of 2008. The *Run Lola Run* soundtrack sold 219,003 units since its release in June 1999 but only 450 units in the first eight months of 2008. The dark and brooding soundtrack to Darren Aronofsky's *Pi* sold 66,550 units since its release in July 1998, but *zero* units in the first eight months of 2008. After *Juno* received four Oscar nominations, the film's soundtrack became the first since *Dreamgirls* in 2007 to reach the top of the *Billboard* charts, pushing its total sales past the 250,000 mark.

In this environment, most specialized or independently financed films cannot count on a soundtrack album deal. But knowing this, how much money should filmmakers allocate for music? Many industry veterans suggest music should represent at least 5 to 7 percent of the overall budget. "On a film that's music-oriented the music budget should be 10 percent or more," explains film producer and music supervisor Alex Steyermark, who served as music supervisor on *The Ice Storm* and *The Boxer*, among others. "Certainly if someone is anticipating doing a musical like *Hedwig and the Angry Inch* they should know up front that they're looking at far more than 10 percent of the budget."

Of course, allocating 10 percent of an already tight budget is a high hurdle for a typical independent film, especially one shooting on 16mm short-ends or non-24p HD that hasn't even budgeted for da Vinci color correcting during post. Without soundtrack funds, filmmakers regularly find themselves screening an impoverished-sounding movie because they didn't think to court local artists. Others load up on festival-licensed tunes in the hopes that a distributor will cover the outstanding clearance tab. "A lot of times we would ask, 'Is the music cleared?' and the filmmaker would do a lot of dancing," says former Paramount Classics co-president David Dinerstein, now president of marketing at Lakeshore Entertainment (*Million Dollar Baby*). "They'd say how emotionally connected they were to a particular cue or they'd say, 'We're hoping for an album advance,' but you knew at the end of the day there was no way those songs were going to end up in the final print of the movie."

Ironically, much of the hand-wringing, legal hassle, and disappointment related to clearing expensive music is self-inflicted and totally avoidable. "I don't tend to use a lot of music, so it's not something I've ever really had to worry about," says *Memento* and *The Dark Knight* director Christopher Nolan, whose noir debut, *Following*, was made for $12,000 on 16mm black-and-white film. "I remember people advising me to 'use lots of great music' so that someone would pick up the movie and then pay the rights, but I doubt that happens much anymore. You get all kinds of terrible advice when you're starting out as a filmmaker."

Bernard, whose company has released several independent films with popular soundtracks—such as *Run Lola Run*; *Groove* and *Crouching Tiger, Hidden Dragon*—asserts that the single biggest misperception filmmakers have is that interested distributors will step in and make their music problems go away. "There was a rumor going around Sundance years ago about an independent film with $700,000 in uncleared music rights," Bernard says. "That's $700,000 on top of what they wanted distributors to pay for the movie. Then when we went to the screening and heard all the songs, we realized that the rumors had to be true. But if we hadn't heard about it, we might not have discovered the extent of the music-rights issue until we were deep into the negotiation process to buy the film, which could have derailed our interest."

Films with huge levels of unpaid (and often undisclosed) liability in their music budgets create mini-subprime-mortgage meltdowns at film festivals every year, as filmmakers who have borrowed against the future sale price of their films realize they have no way of paying for the music that they couldn't afford in the first place. From a film investor's perspective these music-heavy projects eventually become the Enrons or WorldComs of the art-house world: even if the project is sold for a huge multiple, the film's "shareholders" will ultimately get nothing when the advance is eaten up by music-rights fees that the director knowingly chose to include. He or she who caused the implosion with pricey song choices will enjoy the benefit of having the film screen at a major festival with awesome tunes and will get a "golden parachute" in the form of recognition and future directing assignments. Everyone else, including the producer, will get nothing even as the trades report the film sold for $500,000 or $1 million. Worse still, everyone will assume that the still-struggling indie producer is rich, since everyone always wrongly assumes that the acquisitions price in the trade is paid to the filmmakers in a briefcase out of *No Country for Old Men*.

Kim Bangash, who cofinanced *You Can Count on Me* with Hart-Sharp Entertainment as well as *Sling Blade*, explains, "The producers don't want less money to be recouped for themselves or the film's investors, so their incentive is always to try to pare down big, expensive soundtracks. But producers often side with the directors out of some misplaced loyalty to their 'vision,' and fight for these ridiculously expensive songs. Then what happens is the distributor might say, 'You can't swap the music out now, just because it's too expensive to keep in. Part of the reason we're interested in the first place is because of the emotional heft of the film with the music that's in it. Pay for it and then call us back when it's cleared, and we'll talk.'"

Again, one of the easiest ways that someone thinking of investing in an independent film can find out if he or she is being conned is to simply ask the director or producer to provide a list of the songs they plan to have in the soundtrack, and then wait to see either a ridiculous wish list of recognizable (read: unaffordable) tracks and/or perhaps be lied to and told that "a soundtrack deal or a specialized distributor at Sundance will cover the cost of music rights, after the director or producer gets a festival clearance, which is relatively cheap, even for well-known music."

What many first- and second-time filmmakers don't understand is that they are ultimately responsible for delivering the finished picture the way studio acquisition executives saw it at a festival. Far too many directors and producers get into a messy situation simply because they have ignored things that people who know the industry never have to worry about.

STUCK WITH THE TAB

While distributors complain on panels about indie films loaded with uncleared music, there is frequently an eleventh-hour crisis related to music rights that most independent filmmakers who get distribution have no idea is coming. This pernicious late hit is actually the biggest reason to license cheaper songs from local artists such as the Douglas Fir or Antje Duvekot. "Usually, it's a separate negotiation and a significantly larger fee to be able to use a song that appears in the film as the backing track to an entire trailer," explains Bregman. "This is normal and appropriate since it's a very different kind of usage: you're no longer using a song to sell a particular scene, you're using it to sell the entire film—like a television commercial. But for several years now distributors have been arguing that *every* song in the movie needs to be cleared for what is known as 'out-of-context trailer rights.' Essentially, the distributors have shifted the cost of the trailer to the filmmaker."

Having to meet this requirement—which by 2009 was well established—instantly quintuples a filmmaker's music-rights obligation because out-of-context rights are considered a marketing expense rather than a usage fee based on the artistic merits of a film. "It's created a music-licensing crisis because a film distributor will only ever use one or two songs in the trailer—if that. And so for 90 percent of the songs the filmmaker has to pay the moon to clear this way, it's just wasted money," says Bregman.

As a result, a filmmaker who might have been able to spend $60,000 to license two songs must now spend $300,000 unless they use music specifically written for the film.

Long before a film gets distributed, however, filmmakers cut to picture on the assumption that some kind of iTunes soundtrack deal will cover the cost of their music and maybe even bring in some additional funds. "Unfortunately, record companies don't seem to believe in movie soundtracks the way they did years ago," says Bregman. "They're not making bold moves as they once did, and they're also requiring a certain level of theatrical release—like two hundred screens or more—just to take on the album."

This is a problem for many independent films since it presents yet another chicken-or-egg situation for aspiring filmmakers. "The traditional independent release doesn't contemplate going over two hundred screens initially because they're only ever guaranteed fifteen to fifty markets at the start," Bregman explains. "Record companies don't have the entrepreneurial foresight that distribution companies have when they acquire a film. The record company shouldn't be thinking 'Is this film guaranteed to go over two hundred screens but *could* this film go over two hundred screens?'"

This reticence on the record companies' part creates a catch-22 for filmmakers whose projects might have benefited financially and promotionally from a soundtrack deal. "If you have a platform release that gets embraced by critics and audiences and is considered for awards—like *In the Bedroom*—it may be too late to get your soundtrack signed up and on store shelves by the time the film widens out to the two hundred screens the record company required," Bregman concludes. "Soundtracks take several months to get distributed."

ELUSIVE CLEARANCE RIGHTS

Because granting soundtrack rights is considered a "permissive use," the rights holder does not have to grant the license. As a result, filmmakers should definitely start the process months ahead of time and have alternatives ready because without a doubt, there are going to be four or five songs that will just come back denied.

Swingtown and *The L Word* director Jamie Babbit and her music supervisor, Stephen E. Smith, faced a hydra-headed approval challenge trying to clear the music in her $1 million Sundance film *But I'm a Cheerleader*. "We had to get permission from six different family members representing the Serge Gainsbourg estate in order to use 'Chick Habit' during the opening credits," she says. "Our entire music budget was only $25,000, so I used the version sung in English by L.A. singer April March, but the Gainsbourg estate still controlled the publishing rights. We had to make a lot of phone calls to France and it took four months because they all had to agree."

While publishers are often empowered to make licensing decisions on behalf of an artist, the copyright holder or the artist's estate often retains veto power. "If you think about how indelible cinematic connections can be, it's understandable why some musicians might be concerned about what a film is going to do their image," explains former Fine Line Features president Ira Deutchman, now president of Emerging Pictures. "I mean, can you listen to 'Singin' in the Rain' anymore without thinking of *A Clockwork Orange*, or 'Stuck in the Middle with You' without thinking of *Reservoir Dogs*?"

Deutchman also says that musicians' rights holders are often concerned that a song may become undesirable to major studios if it shows up in too many films. "It's not that being in an independently financed film will diminish the value, but rather that if the song appears in a lot of places for very little money each time, it may blow the chances of a bigger payday on a more expensive film."

Frequently, however, the headaches created by music clearances cannot be solved in time even in cases where money is less of an issue. "It actually took about nine months to get the rights to the Indian dance number that opens *Ghost World*," said director Terry Zwigoff. "The only way we even got to the two sons of the original producer of *Gumnaan* was because John Malkovich, who was one of our producers, had put his name on an Indian film called *The Terrorist* in 1998 to help it get seen. And because that film said 'John Malkovich Presents,' most people in the film industry in India have a lot of respect for him."

The track "Jaan Pechehaan Ho," which by some accounts translates to "We should get to know each other" in Hindi, appears in its full glory as a DVD extra, but its inclusion in the opening sequence helps set the tone for the entire film and puts the audience into the mind of Thora Birch's character without a single line of dialogue. The sons of *Gumnaam* producer, the late N. N. Sippy, brought the original negative from India to Zwigoff's postproduction facility and granted him use of the material for reasonable fee. However, Zwigoff was unable to obtain permission to use several American ragtime classics dating back to the 1920s. "Music-clearance lawyers can be very conservative, and they don't want to take any chances that someone may turn up and claim they own [a particular song]," he says ruefully. "So the music-clearance lawyers said I couldn't use a thing in *Ghost World* unless we could prove somebody owned it and then pay them for it."

Zwigoff said he had similar music problems with his first film, the critically acclaimed documentary *Crumb*, winner of the Grand Jury Prize at Sundance in 1994. "Most of the stuff that I was interested in using in *Crumb* was music from the '20s, '30s, and '40s that had fallen through the cracks and never been bought by bigger corporations like MCA, Sony, or Columbia," he says. "For example, I wanted to use a recording of Jelly Roll Morton playing the piano, but because we couldn't prove that these rare Paramount sessions that he played on are not owned by anybody today—the publication rights are owned but the performance rights are essentially owned by nobody—we couldn't use it," he said. "I had to get a musician friend of mine who had studied Jelly Roll Morton since he was six years old to re-create the performance note for note. Then we added [78 rpm] surface noise to it afterward, so it would sound like an old record."

Waitress executive producer Danielle Renfrew—who produced director Greg Harrison's 2000 narrative film *Groove*, which focused on one night in San Francisco's underground rave scene—may have had the toughest time of all simply because Harrison's film featured trance and hip-hop. "It was a nightmare because when we started looking into it, we realized we didn't have all the rights we thought we did," she remembers. "Since many of the tracks were remixes of remixes of remixes, we had to find all the original artists as well. This meant searching for specific deejays all over the United States and the United Kingdom, some of whom didn't have permanent addresses and were crashing on other people's couches."

Of the forty-plus music cues used in *Groove*, which was acquired by Sony Pictures Classics, most required layers of completely separate rights approvals. "We probably had ten times the amount of work most filmmakers face in terms of getting permission from everyone," says Renfrew. "The period before Sundance was a really tense and stressful time because we were still clearing tracks late into our sound mix. Greg had to cut in alternate choices for the songs we weren't sure we could get and then call our music supervisor, Wade Hampton, to ask if he should bring up fader one or fader two. That's how down to the wire it was."

When playing detective becomes too much of a hassle, many indie filmmakers simply skip the clearance step entirely and pray they won't be sued for damages or enjoined from showing their film at a festival. "People try to get away with it because they think, 'Well, the songs I'm using are not very high profile,' " says Lawton. "They put the film in a festival and just hope for the best, but it's a very risky way to go. If the film gets picked up, it can be very tough to clear the rights after the fact because the publishing companies know you really need them."

WHERE TO LOOK FOR MUSIC

Coven director Mark Borchardt, star of the Sundance documentary *American Movie*, urges filmmakers—especially those adept at Rock Band 2 or Guitar Hero III—to consider taking matters into their own hands. "To tell you the truth, I think I'm going to have to learn how to play an instrument, man, and do it all myself so I can end up owning the music rather than having to license it," he says. "The music in the original *Dawn of the Dead* was mind-blowing, dude, and it really inspired me."

Scream producer Cary Woods, an early champion of actor and *Iron Man* director, Jon Favreau, advises filmmakers to reach out to musicians—famous or not—whom they may know personally to create new music for their projects. "More experienced producers encourage directors to utilize the music of their contemporaries, especially friends who will be excited about creating something for a movie," he says. "For example, Harmony Korine was friends with Lou Barlow of the underground band Sebadoh, and asked him to collaborate from the very beginning on *Kids*. Lou read the script, looked at the film early on, and came up with original material for the soundtrack, which ended up being released on the label Lou was on at the time, London Records."

Of course, not all filmmakers have these kinds of relationships. In a pinch, however, producers and directors can check out a few of the archived live sets at kexp.org, the MP3s available at thedouglasfir.com, or the bevy of new artists featured on podcasts of Nic Harcourt's *Morning Becomes Eclectic* at KCRW.com.

Another option is to reach out to rock labels known for breaking new bands such as Seattle's Kill Rock Stars or Austin's Baldillo Records. Filmmakers can also discover lesser-known but indie-film-friendly acts such as the Weepies, Laura Veirs, and the Douglas Fir on MySpace or Pandora.com. Indie artists' websites such as pitchfork media.com, largeheartedboy.com, or cdbaby.com may also provide alternatives to the usual suspects that seem to show up in every indie film.

Bregman urges filmmakers to act as their own artist-and-repertory executives—the way writer-director Zach Braff introduced audiences to the Shins in *Garden State*, or how *Once* writer-director John Carney introduced American audiences to his former bandmate Glen Hansard, paving the way for Hansard and Markéta Irglová's Academy Award for their song "Falling Slowly."

"A lot of filmmakers who finally get their chance can't wait to use someone iconic like Van Morrison, but we've already heard that a million times and it doesn't really make an impact," says Bregman. "Ultimately the thing that a lot of people are already familiar with is often the most boring choice. It's a piece of music that everybody's heard before and it doesn't bring the audience anywhere new. By having to go out and discover new acts or songs that sound like the track you originally had to have, you end up churning the talent pool a little more effectively. You can discover the next up-and-coming act, the way *Juno* introduced a lot of people to the Moldy Peaches."

No Budget Film School founder Mark Stolaroff suggests chatting up the members of local acts after shows in midsize venues such as Boston's Middle East, New York's Mercury Lounge, or Seattle's Triple Door. "Filmmakers just need to do the work," he says. "There are plenty of young bands looking to license their music for free and tons of bands out there who are looking for a break. Plus, every city has one mom-and-pop record store where the cool guy behind the counter knows what's up. Ask him."

Obscure bands such as Godspeed You Black Emperor! or older alternative rock musicians who may not have found an audience with the iTunes generation can also be a good bet. "I love movies," says former Nova Mob frontman Grant Hart, who contributed the soaring and elegiac "Evergreen Memorial Drive" to W. T. Morgan's film *A Matter of Degrees*. "I'm a huge, huge film fan, and in a lot of ways, that was my original kick when I was young."

Previously of Hüsker Dü—a band regularly cited as one of Kurt Cobain's and director Kimberly Peirce's favorite acts—Hart now tours the country as a José González–like troubadour. However, Hart is also interested in composing quiet film scores and opening his back catalog of Hüsker Dü songs such as "Green Eyes" and "Books About UFOs" for independent films. "People got the idea that my early material was un-available because of something [former bandmate] Bob [Mould] once said about Hüsker songs never appearing in movies. People assumed he was speaking for both of us."

However, Hart owns the rights to all of his Hüsker-era and more recent acoustic repertoire, and has the songs administered through Los Angeles–based Bug Music. "To be appreciated by fans is a great honor," says Hart. "And when a filmmaker—or any kind of artist really—wishes to incorporate my work into theirs, the emphasis and focus of metaphor can evolve to a really interesting place."

Working with a single singer-songwriter to write music for the entire film has become something of a trend over the past years, a throwback to such films as *The Graduate*, *Harold and Maude*, or *Good Will Hunting*. As such, discovering the next Simon and Garfunkel, Cat Stevens, or Elliott Smith should be the goal of all aspiring independent filmmakers.

"I think it's really insulting to everyone who helped the movie get made when filmmakers spend huge sums clearing big, commercial tracks," says Los Angeles–based composer and music supervisor Tor Hyams. "Especially when the above- and below-the-line talent probably worked for scale or earned the lowest of below-market salaries. With so many talented bands out there, why would anyone kill themselves to land a track from Radiohead or Alicia Keys or whoever it is they have their heart set on getting? Why not create a soundtrack that is as hip and innovative as the independent film you just made?"

9. Guess What . . . It *Can't* Be Fixed in Post

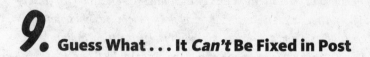

*P*ostproduction can be the single most exciting phase of making an independent film, since it is where the writer, director, and producer can see the fruits of their labor finally coming together on-screen. The writer gets to see her words come alive in ways she could only dream about, the director gets to revel in the happy accidents and the producer gets to heave a huge sigh of relief that the long and often terrifying interval of production is finally over. The biggest irony, however, is that most first-time independent filmmakers cannot afford this joyous occasion because they didn't adequately budget for post and are regularly left scrambling for completion funds or left for dead. This incredibly common delay results in fast-approaching festival deadlines that cannot be met, actors who are no longer available for looping or reshoots, and a loss of momentum that often kills the entire project. Other filmmakers fail to recognize that postproduction is just as big a part of the filmmaking process as production and try to save a few bucks by booking substandard editing facilities, hiring first-time film editors, using unreliable hard drives bought off

Craigslist rather than brand-new 1TB drives, and failing to clone multiple copies of their master tapes or their latest edit decision list (EDL). In short, they act as if making it through the shoot was enough to get into Sundance and simply do not plan for getting their film finished. As a result, what could be an exciting, pleasant interval of discovery is instead an interval of despair. And while the thought of someday winning an award or getting a million-dollar distribution deal keeps many aspiring filmmakers warm through the long, dark years of screenwriting, fund-raising, and dead-end jobs required to keep their projects alive, filmmakers who didn't plan for postproduction often encounter an equal and opposite nightmare reality that is in stark contrast to their dreams of Sundance glory.

Damaged film, location noise, incorrect eye lines, bad performances, missing coverage, digital dropouts, focus problems, lost or demagnetized HD cassettes, color timing shifts, off-tilt tripods, exposed negative, legal clearances, misbehaving extras, dropped P2 cards, time-code breaks—any of these can destroy a scene or even derail an entire project, tossing years of struggle, sacrifice, and heartache out the window. Indeed, hundreds of things can silently go wrong on a film set, but where most of them become apparent and insurmountable is during poorly financed or badly timed intervals of postproduction. Postproduction is also a critical interval since it feeds directly into every indie film's delivery schedule, which in turn determines when a filmmaker and his or her investors can expect to get paid should a distributor buy the film at a festival. While most first-time directors imagine getting a Publishers Clearing House–size check, filmmakers will typically receive 20 percent of the minimum guarantee when they sign a contract and give the distributor the chain of title, and the remainder only when the film and dozens of critical elements assembled during postproduction are finally delivered.

"Everyone always says, 'Don't worry, we'll fix it in post.' But independent filmmakers need to know that some things actually *can't* be fixed in post, and what can be fixed often costs much more than many filmmakers can afford," says Jennifer Lane. "Those who can afford postproduction fixes like visual effects need to know it can cost a small fortune to have a van or a sign digitally removed when it would have cost next to nothing to have someone move the van or sign out of the way during production."

Many filmmakers end up stuck because they pillage their postproduction reserve during the shoot, rationalizing that they'll just deal with it later or magically raise more funds. "There's always that moment where you realize that all the expenses that seemed so important during production—you just *had* to have an extra hour and you just *had* to have that crane day—mean you don't have any money left for post," says *Boys Don't Cry* producer Eva Kolodner. "All of a sudden, you say, 'Whoops! Where's all the money that was supposed to be left over?' "

Distributors hear the sob stories and special cases every day, but there are enough finished films that look great and are ready to be bought that distributors don't need to rescue the filmmakers who didn't save enough for post. "Filmmakers ask for postproduction funds all the time and most distributors say no," says Sony Pictures Classics copresident Tom Bernard, distributor of *Sugar*; *Synecdoche, New York*; and *Persepolis*. "Sony put a million dollars into *El Mariachi* to complete it, but filmmakers today shouldn't use Robert Rodriguez as a business model. They should budget appropriately to get their projects finished, and that includes postproduction and music clearances."

Regardless, *Donnie Darko* producer Adam Fields says a lot of directors still cling to the pie-in-the-sky fantasy that if they can just finish principal photography, someone else will swoop in to cover their postproduction costs. "I always hear filmmakers say, 'Once they see a screener they're going to be so in love with it they'll give us the money,' " Fields says. "But the reality is closer to asking your dad for money as a kid and having him say: 'Twenty dollars? What do you need ten dollars for? Here's five dollars . . . you can have it tomorrow.' "

The truth is, even though *El Mariachi* is the stuff of legend, and accepted as a successful approach, only naïve filmmakers think that as long as they finish a rough cut the indie division or the major studio will step in and take care of everything. As anyone who has actually talked to a studio acquisitions executive for five seconds knows, it is the filmmaker who is ultimately responsible for paying for post and delivering a finished film.

A PHRASE TO STOP USING

Even when a producer comes up with the money to pay for a last-minute "solve," the results can still be far from ideal. "People should really say, 'We'll cheat it in post,' because I don't think anything's ever necessarily *fixed* in post," says Matthew Libatique, cinematographer of *Iron Man*, *Requiem for a Dream*, and *Pi*, among others. "Sometimes you can cut corners with things most audiences won't perceive, like changes in color temperature, light quality, or whether the sun is in or out on a day. And, yes, if it's a moderately budgeted film you can probably afford to put in new skies or digitally remove a truck, but it's a dangerous concept for independent filmmakers to think they can 'fix it in post.' Independent filmmakers succeed on the power of what they can do in production and on camera."

Of course, certain shots that fall under the category of "wire removal" can be cheaper and easier to handle in post—

even for an independent film—than renting a crane and hundreds of feet of drape to cover something that needs to be obscured. "On *Lovely & Amazing* we shot the exterior of a hospital that had the hospital's name on a big sign that we couldn't avoid from any angle," says producer Anthony Bregman. "We could have covered up the sign but it would have been really expensive. And since we were shooting digitally on Sony 24p HD video, we were able to make a decision that it would be an easy fix in postproduction to digitally block something out on a locked-off shot, and it was. But that wasn't really a fix in postproduction, it was a decision we made on the day to deal with it in post."

While films like *300* and *Avatar* have raised the bar on the incredible vistas that can be created on a computer, even the best effects artists using massively parallel 8-core Mac Pro workstations and the fastest video cards available can find it frustrating to have to remove something in the foreground—especially something moving—that wouldn't be there if the director had just asked for another take without it. In this digital age, however, many first-time directors instead think of post and post houses as magic wands that can change water into wine and overcome their carelessness. "The reasons to be as careful and fastidious as filmmakers had to be in the past have somewhat gone away," says Scott Ross, former president of Digital Domain, the effects house for *Transformers 2: Revenge of the Fallen* and *Titanic*. "Nowadays if you have a great take that you love and for some reason nobody noticed that the camera car was re-flected in the shot, you can just remove it if you have the budget. But the flip side—and there's a flip side to everything—is that some filmmakers have gotten sloppy."

The filmmakers who run into the most trouble are those who have not bothered to storyboard by either paying an aspiring graphic artist or using PowerProduction Software's

StoryBoard Quick. Those who haven't storyboarded their scripts early on may not realize what they are missing until they get to the editing room and an editor asks for a reverse angle or an establishing shot. Even though digital tape is cheap enough to keep the film and sound rolling between takes to capture natural moments among the actors, many filmmakers find themselves in the lurch when an editor needs a transition or a reaction shot to buy some time between lines of dialogue and help a scene breathe.

"When you get into the editing room the key thing is having enough reaction shots of people," says *Half Nelson* editor and cowriter Anna Boden. "Sometimes when you're shooting loosely like we shot *Half Nelson*—and a lot of indie filmmakers shoot really loose now—there's a tendency to cover only the person who's talking in a dialogue scene. This is especially true if you have four or five people in a dinner scene. A filmmaker will pan to the person who's talking and then pan to the next person talking, and then the next and the next, but what they forget is that it's really key to hold on shots of the people next to them or the people seated across from them who are just listening."

Having the DP continue to roll a bit after the director calls "Cut" or starting each take as much as a minute or two before the director calls "Action" could be a godsend later. On this, there are two schools of thought. "As far as keeping the camera rolling," says Boden, "it's not so much that we would start a take several minutes before calling 'Action'— which could waste a lot of film—but that we would steal moments on film while we were setting up for the next shot, which helped us a lot in the editing room. Sometimes, especially with nonactors or with the kids in the classroom, we would roll when they didn't know we were filming or shoot while we were getting set up and catch natural behavior of someone just chatting with another person or spacing out, looking in one direction. And you can actually cut those little moments you get when people aren't acting into a scene. It's important to have scenes where people aren't trying to do something, where they're just being themselves or just thinking quietly. Then, when you need an extra beat somewhere, when you don't have really great coverage on a certain line or maybe somebody didn't say the line exactly how you wanted them to, it's really nice to be able to cut away to those reaction shots."

Most aspiring filmmakers, however, can't bear to shoot thirty to sixty seconds of room tone with everyone in place at the end of every setup, let alone shoot quiet reaction shots. Others think that taking time to shoot quiet moments of reflection on a set is anathema to "moving on" or "making the day." Very few take the time to shoot actors musing or reacting silently to what was just said. Still others forget to shoot at least two PG-rated alternate takes of any scene that might be deemed objectionable by network television executives or airlines concerned about showing the original version. If scenes aren't covered, they may have to be deleted or fixed in postproduction by a pricey effects house.

Fields knows the forehead-slapping frustration many filmmakers feel when they find out that a simple fix is going to cost close to $100,000. "Claire Danes's character in *Brokedown Palace* smokes a joint during an important scene and after we wrapped it became a really big ratings issue for the Motion Picture Association," he says. "They were going to give us an R for it but changing the joint to a cigarette digitally would have been prohibitively expensive. We couldn't lose the scene, so we had to carefully cut around it so we never see Claire inhale. It became a really big deal, but it would have been so easy to just shoot an alternate take with her smoking a Marlboro or not smoking at all."

When in doubt, filmmakers should always shoot one

alternate PG or at least a PG-13 rated take with just dialogue and waving arms for emphasis, with no drugs, no nudity, no cursing, and no violence. "Today, showing underage people smoking tobacco automatically bumps you into an R rating," says Michelle Byrd, president of IFP. "Independent filmmakers need to make sure they are super-aware of everything that will be taken into consideration when it comes to getting distribution for their films."

DON'T WORRY, IT'S DIGITAL

With the advent of increasingly automated prosumer cameras that shoot in HD and in some cases 3K, many directors and budding cinematographers believe that everything they shoot—regardless of the lighting conditions—will somehow be usable. However, as an earlier generation of filmmakers discovered, this is not always the case. "There are actually huge problems with that mind-set," says *Charlotte's Web* director Gary Winick, whose $500,000 Sundance entry *Tadpole* was distributed by Miramax in 2002. "The hardest job on many first DV features is for the cinematographer because the cameras want to work without you. Every time you turn on the camera you have to make sure that you have checked every switch and put every automated function into manual mode: the gain, the shutter speed, the exposure, focus—all of it. If you forget one of those things, when it gets blown up to 35mm you're going to notice the result and be very unhappy."

Winick recalls that because *Tadpole's* DP did not abide by this doctrine, there were major problems with much of the raw footage. "You have to really pay attention because you don't want to end up with a contrasty DV film," Winick explains. "The backgrounds tend to blow out really quickly, so you have to make sure that you don't light the backgrounds if you're shooting in MiniDV."

Unfortunately, this was only the first painful lesson. "After our shoot I called Industrial Light & Magic in California and said, 'You can have any amount of money—I'll give you any amount of money to make this look really good. Can you make this film look beautiful?' " Winick recalls. "And they said, 'If the information's not on the cassette, we can't do anything for you,' which I was shocked to hear because not only do people always say 'Don't worry, we'll fix it in post,' but there's this assumption that since it's digital they'll be able to anything with it."

Ultimately, Miramax spent more to enhance the look of *Tadpole* than the film cost to produce, Winick says. "DuArt did a really good job with what we had and I'm very grateful to Miramax, but now I tell film students: 'When the information is not on the tape—when it's not on that little HD or MiniDV or DV-CAM cassette—no matter what you do, you can't fix it.' "

CHRONIC LACK OF FOCUS

What also cannot be fixed for any amount of money is an out-of-focus shot or a character who comes up soft because the assistant cinematographer pulled against narrative. "All focus-pulling issues should be brought up, discussed, and worked out when you're blocking the shots," says Libatique, cinematographer on Spike Lee's *Miracle at St. Anna* and Darren Aronofsky's *The Wrestler*. "If you want to keep two characters in focus at the same time, you should increase the depth of field by shooting a different f-stop on the lens and then you work the focal length. If your lens is wider, you're more likely to hold it all in focus at a certain f-stop. If your lens is longer, you're prone not to be able to hold it at a certain f-stop."

This is important to remember because focus problems cannot be undone without reshoots, an important bit of news that should inspire directors to keep their eyes glued to the video-assist monitor. "Focus is something you really can't fix," says Lane. "You can fix a shot that has a light stand or a flag in the corner of the frame with an optical or digital zoom-in, but that can lead to focus issues as well, especially if the project was shot on video."

Having to push in creates other problems as well, since the image integrity of MiniDV does not allow for digital enhancement or digital push-ins of more than 10 percent. "MiniDV footage doesn't hold up well at all," says Miller. "Anything captured on MiniDV is going to start showing pixelation or distortion the minute you push in, and you're going to have to effect the shot in some way to compensate, like with a digital soft blur or something to pull the 'jaggies' out."

Those shooting on film or professional-grade HD may be able to push in as far as 20 to 30 percent on stable, locked-off shots. "Or if you capture something on film and transfer it to Digital Betacam or HD in a telecine, you can push in quite a bit," says Miller.

Of course, a filmmaker might not even *know* they need to zoom in to crop out a boom, a light stand, or an obnoxious extra drawing attention to himelf unless they used a professional-grade camera monitor during production. "Professional monitors all have a button called 'underscan,' which allows you to see what the camera is recording. Cheaper cameras will crop their viewfinder image closer to the area known as 'picture safe,' " Tarleton says. "On a normal television set or low-rent camera monitor, you won't see what's being recorded beyond 'picture safe' because that 10 percent area at the edges of the frame is cropped out, but nonlinear editors, computer screens, digital projectors, and professional monitors show you everything."

This means a filmmaker could theoretically sail through production and postproduction only to find—when screening the locked cut on a studio executive's laptop screen, a high-end HD television, or worst of all, a major festival's video projector—that light stands and booms are appearing liberally throughout the film, making the production look like amateur hour. "I used to work for an Internet company that did a lot of streaming video," Tarleton says, "and we always cropped the image down to 'picture safe' in post so we could trust that we weren't going to have anything wacky showing up in the corners of the frame. You can avoid that by just checking underscan." Because it can still happen even in this modern era of digital TVs, filmmakers need to screen an early DVD cut on all sorts of devices, including Macs, Windows Vista PCs, DLP projectors, Archos-like devices, iPhones, and iPods.

BEWARE AUTEUR HYPOXIA

In addition to "temp love," something all aspiring filmmakers need to look out for during postproduction is a syndrome that could be termed "auteur hypoxia." This condition often strikes first-time filmmakers as they get in sight of the finish line when getting into Sundance begins to look like a real possibility. It starts when a director falls in love with their rough cut, which to them flows and looks great on an edit suite monitor. Even though they may still be crashing on couches, the hypoxic director thinks he has, with a single film, ascended into the pantheon of great names like Truffaut, Godard, Bergman, Altman, Ford, Allen, Ashby, and the rest.

During the shoot, most new directors and producers are so stressed out that they are often just concerned about making the day. They are likely to make mistakes constantly and go over budget by forcing their crews to work overtime to cover up their oversights and bad luck. However, once these new directors and producers get into postproduction, and they realize they have survived the shoot unscathed, many will stop thinking of themselves as Nick Rev in *Living in Oblivion* but more as Francis Ford Coppola in *Hearts of Darkness*. As auteur hypoxia sets in—usually as the film continues to cut together beautifully—many new filmmakers will suddenly forget about everyone who helped them get to this glorious moment. They will forget about the grip who ran down the stairs because they were missing a Kino light, they will forget about the DP who trained for years at his or her craft to capture an impossible shot or camera move, and they will forget about the producer who made it all possible by putting up the money and giving them their big chance.

In the final stages of auteur hypoxia, a tunnel vision sets in so that it appears that the only two people left in the world are the director and the film editor, since they are the only ones who have the vision and talent to be true auteurs. Well, the director anyway. With so much to edit and so little time, the hypoxic filmmaker forgets about his friends, family, girlfriend or boyfriend or significant other, parents, siblings, and everyone else who isn't helping him fulfill his dreams right then and there. The problem, however, is when it all falls apart—as it very often does—there is no one left to help many of these hypoxic directors pick up the pieces. Certainly there is often no one left who wants to sit and watch the film that inspired them to torch every relationship to complete.

WHAT'S THE WORST THAT CAN HAPPEN?

In *Body Heat*, petty thief Teddy Lewis tells his pal, struggling attorney Ned Racine, "There are a hundred ways to screw up a job, and if you can think of ten, you're a genius." With low-budget filmmaking it often seems as if there are a *thousand* ways to court disaster and no way to foresee even a fraction of them. In some instances the methods used to overcome these catastrophes are rarely disseminated, since few directors and producers want to admit that their project was almost ruined or that it needed rescuing. Avid editors are regularly sworn to secrecy and the anecdotes that might help others someday avoid a similar fate are lost to the ages like ghost stories never told.

A crestfallen filmmaker may be relieved to find out that, in fact, unintentionally cockeyed camera angles can be fixed in post. "There is a digital effect called 'clocking' where you can rotate the frame a few degrees left or right just like you would rotate an image in Photoshop," explains Lane. "This often happens in documentaries or in narrative features where they're doing a lot of handheld camera work. Basically, you load the whole shot into a digital composition program and reposition it, frame by frame. If the camera was locked down on a tripod or a dolly during production, and the whole shot is permanently set at a wrong angle, you can actually fix it optically rather than digitally, which is much more cost-effective."

The problem is that filmmakers with cockeyed footage may not divine the best way to go about repairing it until costly fixes have been applied and their festival edits have been shipped. "Every post house you go to has their own bag of tricks—some of them have more than others and some of them don't have a clue what they're doing, they're just mak-

ing it up as they go along," says Los Angeles–based postproduction supervisor and DVD authoring technician Philip
Miller. "It's like surgery, there's an artistry to it that you get
from a particular doctor. You hear stories about someone
going in for a five-hour operation and not coming out for
twelve hours. That's because very often you have a situation
where one 'solve' causes other problems or leads to the
entire film needing to be 'fixed' a certain way."

Miller advises filmmakers to talk to a post supervisor
before they start shooting and to make sure the project's line
producer knows a thing or two about postproduction. "It's
the best way to go in the digital age," he says. "Because post
is at the end of the process, any problem you have there can
be potentially devastating in terms of breaking the budget or
just leaving you dead in the water."

Keane coproducer Brian Bell points out that part of the
problem is that most line producers don't understand postproduction at all and as a result don't push the production
team to test their workflow before the shoot commences.
"Producers and directors need to take it upon themselves to
get a postproduction supervisor or someone who knows
about post to step in early on," he says. "One good way of
avoiding a big mess is to have the post supervisor and the
editor on just before production begins so you can have a
powwow with everybody involved, and start working backward from postproduction. In other words, if you designate
your path beforehand—especially with digital—and you
know where you're starting from and where you're going to
end up, then it can save you a lot of time and headaches."

Garrard Whatley, copresident of Santa Monica–based
audio post house RocketWerks, says filmmakers need to
agree on technical standards during preproduction to avoid
added delays and expense during post. "If there's a little
more communication between everybody up front, a lot of

bad situations could be avoided," he says. "We worked on a film where the sound on the set was recorded on DAT at 16 bit, 48 kilohertz, but the composer's score arrived at 44.1 kilohertz, which meant that in the editing, the music played back at the wrong speed throughout the entire film. We had to convert all the 44.1 kilohertz material to 48 kilohertz for the entire feature, which cost the production a lot of money."

WHEN DISASTER STRIKES

Few filmmakers realize that if FedEx loses an important reel of film negative or a digital master, the most the company will pay is $500 "for the replacement of one-of-a-kind items." Even if a filmmaker insures a FedEx shipment for $50,000—which can be done for an additional $250—the overnight delivery service will reimburse a shipper only for the replacement cost of the film stock or the actual digital cassette, and only after FedEx determines the extent of its own liability following a review of the filmmaker's written complaint that must be received within fifteen days of the allegedly botched delivery.

"You always want to make multiple clones of your production masters, on tape and hard drive, before beginning post-production; you never ship your original masters unless absolutely necessary; and always read the fine print before handing over your original negative to a lab," says Los Angeles–based film director and editor David Tarleton. "Labs all have pretty much the same policy: if they screw up your negative, they'll buy you some new film stock and that's it. Most labs won't pay for what it cost to capture your movie on a piece of film, and that's one good reason to have production insurance. Production insurance is critical."

Cross-country transport of masters should be avoided, but

important tapes and reels of original negatives can be insured by the Transglobal Insurance Corporation for up to $50,000 per FedEx container. The cost is $500, but filmmakers should know that a claim will be considered only if the damage or loss is directly caused by fire, flood, earthquake, explosion, or by the collision, derailment, or overturning of the shipping company's conveyance, vehicle, or aircraft.

Certainly many well-known directors working today have gotten away with not insuring the digital tapes and film reels of their first projects, but there are thousands of talented, would-be filmmakers whose projects never got to Sundance or anywhere else because of perforated film negative and lost HD or MiniDV cassettes that kiboshed their projects and broke their spirits.

No Place Like Home—the second film of *Harder They Come* director Perry Henzell—was derailed for several decades when the lab that was developing his footage lost the film stock. "The company we were developing the negative with actually went out of business and they shifted our materials to a warehouse in New Jersey," recalled Henzell in 2003. "Somehow half the film was lost. It was completely devastating, as you can imagine. The lesson is, don't run out of money while you are shooting your feature. It happens a lot to filmmakers even to this day. In my case the financing kept coming and going and coming and going and it was very difficult. And then finally, when I did raise the final money to finish the film, it was too late, the lab had lost the negative."

While Henzell's tragedy represents a catastrophic worst-case scenario that decent production insurance would have covered, other problems are more common and not always included in lesser-risk premiums unless filmmakers check the fine print.

"Scratched original negative is probably the worst thing

that could possibly happen," says Lane. "An original negative can get scratched when loaded into the camera, when it's unloaded from the camera, when it's developed at the lab, printed at the lab, or handled by the negative cutter. It can also get scratched when the film is run through the Ranks, when it gets run through a cleaner, at a digital house when they're scanning the negative or at an optical house when they're handling your film. Labs all have a million and one safety systems, but occasionally things happen."

Lane, who post-supervised *Doubt*, *Revolutionary Road*, *Secretary*, and Michael Almereyda's *Hamlet*, among others, says that in some situations digital sutures can be applied to the original negative, depending on the extent of the damage. "But this is not really something the average filmmaker can afford," she adds. "If there's a scratch on an entire camera roll or reel of negative it could cost hundreds of thousands of dollars to fix."

FAULTY SUSPENSION BRIDGES

Experienced filmmakers know that a script is effectively rewritten during the shoot by the actors and the conditions related to production and then rewritten yet again in post, but what many filmmakers don't realize is that during post-production, the key pillars of the story's structure can collapse.

"If you move a line or a shot from here to there, you may suddenly need a new transition between scenes because now your lead character already knows what she's supposed to learn in the next act," says Andrew Williams, now vice president of International Creative at Paramount Pictures. "The problem is, there may not be any additional footage or transitional scenes that were shot to pull you out of this story hole you've suddenly created. Postproduction can easily turn into a big jigsaw puzzle and filmmakers often find they're missing a few important pieces."

One of the easiest ways out of this pickle is to cobble together a new expository scene from long tail ends before a director calls "Cut," which then can be repurposed into reaction shots and additional dialogue recording (ADR). Many film schools famously advise students to always grab medium shots of a few lead characters casually walking away from camera—as in the opening sequence of *In the Company of Men*—which can be used if needed as the foundation for a long ADR exposition.

Far more elegant, however, is a happy accident that happened during the production of *Half Nelson*, when filmmakers Ryan Fleck and Anna Boden were able to add story points and dialogue in a way that filmmakers should remember to emulate. "We ended up changing one of the answering-machine messages in post and it was really nice to have the flexibility to be able to do that," says Boden. "We didn't know we were going to do that and it's not why we shot the answering machine, but I know that I once heard Coppola say, 'Shoot somebody on the telephone from behind,' so you can add it in later or explain something that may not be clear."

Indeed, filmmakers should shoot a wide shot and an extreme close-up of lead characters listening to an answering machine so that messages can be added later on, as expository elements are needed. Another approach is to shoot an improvisatory take, where the actors, in character, describe their hopes and needs and what is going on in their lives as the character, in what might be termed on-set ADR. The director can prompt each of them by asking "How does your character feel?" and then "What does your character think is going to happen next?"

"The answering-machine message [in *Half Nelson*] was written as a message from the teacher that Dan Dunne had attacked a couple nights before. But we changed it to a message from his mom in post," said Boden. "We didn't change it for exposition, but thought it would be more meaningful at that point in the movie to get a call from his somewhat absent mother."

Of course, sometimes ADR is necessary simply because the production sound is not usable. Unfortunately, during preproduction, the director and cinematographer may decide that a particular location is perfect but forget to bring their soundman to the scout, only to find in the middle of the shoot that the location they love so much is unusable or problematic. "Sound problems are just endless," says Eva Kolodner. "Sometimes you're just too much in a rush, or it's just not anyone's concern, or the sound guy is going, 'There's a hum from the air conditioner . . . There's a hum from some kind of interference being picked up by the wireless microphones.' And the line producer or someone may say, 'We can't hear it, just shoot, just shoot!' And you shoot and then later you're in the editing room and the editor will say, 'There's a hum from the air conditioner and this entire day is unusable. It's so loud! Didn't any of you hear it?' "

The repercussions of not taking the sound engineer along to scout locations ahead of time were made painfully clear in the 2002 documentary *Lost in La Mancha*, which followed the dissolution of Terry Gilliam's European-financed narrative feature *The Man Who Killed Don Quixote*. Gilliam, who had previously directed Johnny Depp in *Fear and Loathing in Las Vegas*, is shown dragging Depp and an increasingly skeptical film crew to a muddy and remote location that happened to be in the flight path of a NATO bombing range. Try as they might, recording dialogue in between the roar of F-18 fighter jets was impossible.

And while audiences will put up with the static composition, poor lighting, or poor-quality video featured in *Tarnation* or *The Blair Witch Project*, the sound has to be pristine. First-rate or even stellar sound and clear, crisp dialogue recording levels can often compensate for poor blocking and make any film, even one streaming on YouTube or Snag-Films.com, seem far better than it is.

"We had to have nine million ADR sessions for *Spin the Bottle* because none of us realized how loud everyone's shoes sounded clomping around on the wood floors of the old house in Vermont where we were shooting," remembers producer Gill Holland. "It would have been so easy to put a blanket down where people were walking and just not show their feet or to have the actors take off their shoes. How hard is that?"

A lot of times, technology doesn't work. Filmmakers will try to record ADR on a USB-enabled dictation recorder so they can port the resulting audio interchange file format or MP3 file to a hard drive, but forget that their microphone quality is mono and flat. The Belkin TuneTalk for iPod can theoretically record wild dialogue lines in stereo AIFF, but these recorders often pick up audible transport noise from the iPod and radio-frequency noise from nearby cell phones. More important, the devices' preset recording level may differ wildly from the microphones that were used to record production sound. Additionally, phantom reverb can often show up if a large empty space such as a rehearsal stage or an empty theater is used to record wild lines, a problem which cannot be ironed out or equalized. This often surprises filmmakers who don't completely understand the complexities of sound waves traveling through empty rooms. The best bet is to record rehearsals with high-end recording gear and the best lavalier mics available and to record one last take at the end of every setup directly into the boom, with the actors standing still and clearly enunciating their lines.

Today many of the sound recorders used by professional production sound mixers record to hard drives rather than to tape. The Fostex MR8-HD ($349) is an eight-track recorder that records sound to a 40 gigabyte internal hard drive. The Fostex FR-2 is a more expensive ($599) two-track recorder that records to either a CompactFlash memory card or a PCMCIA Minidrive. The Marantz CDR-420 is a higher-end unit ($1,199) designed for location recording. PDFs for each of these devices and others are available online.

Another postproduction sound headache that is easy to prevent has to do with actors stepping on each other's lines, either accidentally or in the directors' pursuit of realism. While Robert Altman never seemed to mind overlaps, most filmmakers should make sure every line of dialogue is isolated. "If the actors are talking at the same time during a take, there really isn't a way to separate them in post—they're married together," says Whatley. "Sometimes it can work and seem verité, but it's much better to have the individual lines recorded clean and then *create* that overlap in post if you want it rather than being stuck with it. It gives you more choices in the editing room and it's a much safer way to go."

Where this overlap becomes a dire problem is when it spills over during a close-up. "Say you have two actors screaming back and forth in an argument but they're cutting each other off," explains Whatley. "You're in a tight single and the other actor starts talking before the actor on-camera stops speaking. The offscreen actor is in the room only for performance, to enhance the performance of actor A, but they're messing up the close-up because they may be delivering a line you already heard actor B deliver in the medium shot over the on-screen actor's close-up."

The "solve" in this case, says Whatley, is to shoot the argument at the same emotional level as the wide shots but make sure the actors give each other a beat or two before delivering their lines. "It can be a difficult thing for actors to do, but if they're good they can pull it off," Whatley says. "One of the biggest problems and one of the biggest reasons to have to ADR the whole scene is because actors have stepped on each other's lines during one or the other's close-up."

THE SOUND MIX

Many new filmmakers make the mistake of mixing for a the-atrical presentation when 99.9 percent of the people who screen their film will be watching it on DVD or Blu-ray. "If the final exhibition medium of your project is video and peo-ple are going to be screening it on a television, make sure the sound engineer at your 'sweetening' session is mixing to a clunky old television speaker and not to perfectly imaged cinema speakers or the latest ultra-fancy TV," exhorts Tarle-ton. "You have to at least listen to a final playback on a crappy little television before you leave."

Skeptical filmmakers will recall the "car test" that the recording engineer played by Geoff Minogue did in *Once* after the band's demo CD was completed. In the film, the engineer explains that since record executives listen to music on the long ride home, albums mixed to sound best on a car stereo are in many ways more compelling than those mixed on perfectly imaged Krell speakers.

"Your film will never sound as good in any theater on the face of the Earth as it does in the mixing room during post-

production, and that's just because the acoustics of the mixing room are carefully balanced and perfectly calibrated,"
explains Bregman, who produces films through his New
York–based Likely Story production shingle. "You also don't
have a bunch of moviegoers absorbing the sound, opening
bags of M&M's, crunching popcorn, slurping drinks,
crunching tortillas, coughing, talking, or having their cell
phones go off."

American Teen director Nanette Burstein, who was
awarded a directing prize at Sundance in 2008, says a sound
mix can turn into an endless aural tug-of-war as one change
begets another and another. "It was really hard getting the
levels right in *The Kid Stays in the Picture* [2002] because
there's music throughout the entire film and Bob [Robert
Evans] doesn't have the clearest voice in the world," Burstein
recalls. "It was a total nightmare and we were constantly
fighting music and sound effects and voice-over leading up
to Sundance, and then when we screened at the Eccles Theater we were dying. Bob's voice was too separated from the
music and we kept getting nervous and telling the projec-
tionist to turn it up, which just made it worse. After Sundance we totally remixed the sound for our theatrical
release."

To take advantage of a theater space the size of the Eccles
or the Ziegfeld, some film editors may want to include wide
sweeps in volume to establish the distance of a far-off character speaking from the back of a room, when in reality all this
does is cause acquisitions executives screening the film on a
television or a laptop to miss lines of dialogue as they adjust
the volume.

"Don't be afraid to make changes if your film doesn't
sound the way you want it when it's played on a television,"
adds Tarleton. "Even though it may be against a sound en-

gineer's religion, you may want to mix right to an old television from the get-go and set all the dialogue at the same level."

COVERAGE IS NOT ENOUGH

Generally, the biggest problem less experienced directors run into during post results from not understanding the kind of coverage they needed during the shoot. A scene may have been covered six ways to Sunday, but if the director forgot to shoot inserts of the lead actors sitting in repose, turning their heads from left to right and back again, and indicating with their eyes that something is happening in each corner of the frame, an editor may not have a transition he or she needs and may not be able to cut to a close-up on an action that feels organic.

"A lot of times I'll have people come in with miles and miles of coverage that's unusable because what they really needed was a specific reverse angle, or an over-the-shoulder point of view to establish eye lines, or a simple pan to show the audience the geometry of the characters in the room and where they are *in relation to each other*," says Tarleton. "It's a simple thing that would have taken five seconds to shoot and there's absolutely no way to create it in post."

The perverse irony is that many filmmakers think they're saving time and money by not shooting these seemingly insignificant elements. "Very often people will say, 'You don't need to shoot someone entering or exiting frame—you're just going to cut that out anyway,' but sometimes that's exactly where you need the cut to go," says *Sweet Land* producer Gill Holland. "In one instance we had a scene with two people sitting on a stoop talking, and in retrospect, we really needed one of them to get up and walk away—it would have been the perfect transition—but we didn't have it and so the cut always felt like an awkward edit."

The director can also have a headache in post if the DP didn't insist on shooting the entire action during each setup. "I always tell people to shoot the entire move and make sure you've got some overlap in the coverage, especially when it has to do with an action like opening a car door," explains New York–based film editor David Frankel. "When you're cutting, you want to move in and through a cut based upon that action. Instead, you get directors who are stuck in a shot during editing because they started the coverage late into the action *after* the guy has already gotten out of the car. Everyone's always so concerned with line readings and dialogue, but directors limit their options even more by not shooting overlaps."

The best way to remember to shoot transitions is to write them into the shooting script, storyboard them before production, and make sure they are actually scheduled into each shooting day. "It's important to think about the transitions and what's going to connect your scenes so that visually or emotionally there's some kind of thread that makes it feel more like a sequence than just two separate scenes," says Boden. "When you're shot listing, there's a tendency to shot list scene-for-scene and only think about how you're going to cover the scene and not about the transitions so much. But if you're in the shot-listing stage and you take the time to think about how you're getting from one scene to the other, it makes your life so much easier in the editing room. You don't always have to do it. Not every scene needs a great transition from one to the other, but if you're occasionally thinking about some interesting transitions between scenes, it makes your movie feel like more of a full thing once you get into the editing room, instead of just a collection of pieces."

Similarly, many filmmakers forget to shoot coverage that establishes where the characters are in the world and how they got from Point A to Point B. "If you're shooting in Chicago, why not shoot twenty minutes of outdoor b-roll on one day," says Paramount Pictures vice president of International Creative Andrew Williams. "You've got the crew, you've got the camera, and the actors are in character. What does it take to shoot one of the stars walking down the street with the Sears Tower in the background? Nothing. But people forget to do it."

Still, other filmmakers overlook the possibility of leveraging the city they are in as a character. For example, a film about an aspiring Latina dancer in Spanish Harlem screams for exterior shots of the star walking around her neighborhood to give the film a sense of place, or along Fifth Avenue to establish a "fish out of water" feel, or outside Juilliard from Lincoln Center Plaza to telegraph her hopes and dreams. But too often filmmakers fail to schedule a day to capture the local sights and sounds such as old men playing dominoes or the real-life music blaring from cars or a nearby upstairs window.

WE'LL CLEAR IT IN POST

Filmmakers who wait until post to start addressing rights-clearance issues can often see their projects delayed by several months. Indeed, more than a few directors and producers realize only in postproduction that the faded eagle T-shirt the lead character wears throughout the picture is actually a copyrighted Harley-Davidson trademark that may not be used for free, if at all, especially if drugs or alcohol factor into the story.

Even documentaries, which could claim journalistic protections of capturing life as it happens, are not always immune from expensive rights-clearance challenges related to logos. "Documentary is more of a gray area because if you're in a public place and somebody walks by with a boom box, it's a whole different set of rules," says _Art School Confidential_ director Terry Zwigoff. "If that was a feature and somebody walked by you'd have to clear the music. But when I made _Crumb_, we ended up licensing some music for a sequence in which that happened and substituting it in so we wouldn't run the risk of being sued. It's hard to capture anything truthful sometimes because of all the rights and clearance problems."

Burstein was lucky to learn about the clearance issues related to _The Kid Stays in the Picture_. "The first thing we did before we started was to have our associate producer scan all these photos in at low res, which took about six weeks," she remembers. "We had an archivist who was helping us find the stills and footage that we needed, so whenever we would run out of something we would give him a call and say, 'Do you have this image anywhere?' Then our archivist told us, 'You know you need to get permission from every actor that appears in the film either from their estates or, if they're still alive, from their agents.' "

Other filmmakers aren't so lucky. Indeed, those who wait until post to begin clearing rights are likely to find their own hopes and dreams relegated to a shoebox under the bed along with the HD cassettes and photos that could have told a great story.

10. Your New Best Friend
THE PRODUCER REP!

*P*roducer reps—who broker the sale of completed indepen-dently financed films to distributors—are an absolutely critical part of the process, but the term has become outdated. By some time in 2000 or 2001, "producer rep" had taken on a pejorative whiff of ambulance chaser or vacuum-cleaner salesman, even though every-one en route to a festival with a finished film still needed one. While the original meaning of the term was someone who represented the film's producer, in the early years of the new millennium it came to signify someone who pounced on filmmakers after a festival accept-ance or early screening, spinning a yarn about being able to sell the film to "Harvey" for more than Happy, Texas or Tadpole, even though they had nothing to do with those sales. Today the most com-petitive indie films going to festivals already have sales representation in place from Creative Artists Agency; Cinetic Media; William Morris Independent; United Talent Agency; Lichter, Grossman, Nichols, Adler & Goodman; the Film Sales Company; Schreck Rose Dapello Adams & Hurwitz; and Submarine Entertainment, among others—reps who *never have to hustle, wheedle, or even raise their voices to sell a film. Elegance and panache are now part of the sales package—even under an ARC' TERYX Sidewinder jacket from REI or trudging up an embankment to a toasty condo. These days, maintaining a classy negotiating style is just as important as the sale price in the trades. These salesmen of the indie-film festival circuit do not wear snazzy Century 21 sport coats or travel by RE/MAX hot-air balloons, but they represent the producers of most independently financed films the way a real-estate broker would, usually for 5 to 15 percent of the sale price and in many cases for a stake in any net points the production team might share over the life of the deal. For uninitiated first- and second-time filmmakers, producer reps, sales consultants, or whatever term of art they may be referred to in the future are the people who make the magic happen, the mythic figures who can convince a skeptical distributor to cut a seven- or eight-figure check for the rights to release a well-received film. And just as homeowners usually hire Realtors to help sell a house rather than twist arms, beg, or play hard-ball with buyers, indie filmmakers hoping to broker the sale of a fin-ished motion picture often turn to experienced professionals who know the business and the players, and can give the production team guidance where they need it. It is important to know what producer reps do and how to make sure the filmmakers relying on them are being appropriately represented and not being sold a bill of goods. And whether filmmakers are hoping to cover a Saab 9-3 Aero Sport or finally afford health insurance, when faced with the prospect of gen-erating real bids for an unsold film, most will end up in the hands of well-connected rough-and-tumble intermediaries who love movies but live to seal the most competitive deal.*

Emerging Pictures' Ira Deutchman, who has worked on both sides of the negotiating table—first as a producer rep for *Metropolitan* and *Sex, Lies, and Videotape*; and later as founder and president of Fine Line Features—suggests hir-ing a rep early in the process, possibly even at the production phase. "Inexperienced producers need help on several fronts, and that means hiring someone who is going to pre-market the movie, position it for festivals, work with the festivals for the best slotting possible, work with the press, come up with a strategy for launching the film, deal with the buyers, and ultimately, negotiate whatever deals come along."

What filmmakers need to realize is that just because they may have talked a big-name star into appearing in their tiny indie film for a song, taking the same approach when it comes to negotiating the sale of the film at a festival is reckless, irresponsible, and just plain dumb. The right rep can maximize the project's sale price and help filmmakers launch their careers. The wrong rep can leave the same film high and dry and send the production team home with nothing but a suitcase full of regret. For this reason, the right rep can be one of the most important additions to the project, since he or she is a direct conduit to landing the deal.

According to John Sloss—whose Cinetic Media represented indie milestones such as *Little Miss Sunshine*, *Napoleon Dynamite*, *Boys Don't Cry*, and *Bowling for Columbine*, among others—the best producer reps are dynamic, charismatic, and tough when they need to be. "The ideal producer's rep would actually be two people: the ingratiating good cop who beats the drum for a movie and is every distributor's best friend, and the bad cop, strategizing behind the scenes, manipulating interest, and ultimately, negotiating aggressively all to obtain the most beneficial deal for the filmmakers."

Hiring a bad cop who has seen it all and isn't afraid to play hardball allows producers and directors to distance themselves from tense negotiations or the political fallout of a bidding war. Filmmakers also hire reps to show their investors that an experienced hand is driving the sales process and that their investment is being safeguarded to the best extent possible. Finally, the bad-cop rep keeps the filmmakers from being beaten up by executives who are famous for being tough street fighters.

"For the films that I think have huge sales potential, I would not dream of sitting in a room and negotiating with Harvey Weinstein, I would absolutely have a rep," says *Loggerheads* and *Beautiful Darling* producer Gill Holland, who has used producer reps in the past and acted as one himself. "I would assume the rep's participation would be worth more than the percentage you pay them because just like a star actor, a star negotiator can enhance the value of a movie. On the little films, I can do it myself and not give away the producer rep's percentage, which on the smaller projects you may actually need to get investors their return."

While the biggest festival sales will always grab headlines and inspire legions of aspiring filmmakers to "follow their bliss," as Joseph Campbell suggested, indie-film purchase prices have been falling to the low-six-figure range and many films are getting acquired with no upfront advance at all. There is still a widespread misperception that many independent films sell in the mid-six-figure range or the low-seven-figure range, a price point that is actually quite rare. Filmmakers who base their business models on the seven- or eight-figure advances quoted in *Variety*, such as the $4 million Fox Searchlight paid for *The Wrestler* in late 2008, should know that defrayed postproduction costs or future production commitments may be included in those numbers and that, regardless, they are on the high side of most acquisitions levels. For example, headlines surrounding the sale of *Hustle and Flow* in 2005 pegged the deal at $16 million, but the text explained that the film sold for $9.3 million and the remaining $6.7 million was to be put toward two additional projects by its producer John Singleton.

But unknown filmmakers should not expect specialized distributors to extend such largesse for their first or second films. For the smaller films, it's no longer about driving the price up; a producer rep's goal may be just to sell the movie and get some kind of distribution, since so many festival films are not sold these days.

THE REP'S ECONOMICS

Distributors and producer reps go back and forth on whether high-seven- and low-eight-figure minimum guarantees are still achievable. Sony Pictures Classics copresident Tom Bernard says filmmakers shouldn't think that they are ever going to land such massive deals, even though many secretly pine for them. "The fact of the matter is that the big sale is an aberration," he says. "In many cases—actually, in all the cases—it's overpayment, and the likelihood of it happening is like winning the lottery."

The $7 to $11 million purchase prices paid in recent years for North American rights have driven some distributors such as Sony Pictures Classics toward financing films like *The Jane Austen Book Club* and *Sleuth* to avoid having to aggressively pursue completed films at a festival. Bidding wars and aggressive preemptive purchases do still occur (such as *Hamlet 2*, which Focus Features bought for $10 million in 2008), but specialized divisions are not forced to make outsize bids. On the contrary, the companies are typically run by savvy executives prepared to pay large sums for films they feel passionately about or believe in.

For example, when Summit Entertainment bought the $20 million independently financed *The Brothers Bloom* in 2007, the goal was to make a statement and launch itself as a studio with a dramatic splash and an iconic debut. "A film like *The Brothers Bloom* builds their brand, builds their relationships with exhibitors, and builds their relationships with filmmakers," explains Micah Green of CAA, who helped broker the deal. "A film purchase like that brings much more reward to the studio than just the upside of a particular film's revenue. Similarly, the *Hustle and Flow* deal some people still point to came about as a result of Viacom wanting to relaunch Paramount Classics and make a statement about synergy. They didn't overpay, since they were prepared to potentially lose money on that film in order to have a movie that was a unique fit for their brands: MTV and Paramount. So they may have overpaid on some level but not because they were 'taken' by a seller. They arrived at Sundance in 2005 prepared to pay a huge sum because they weren't going to lose *Hustle and Flow* over a couple of million dollars. And from a branding perspective it had a lot of value for MTV and for Paramount. No one wants to pay more than they need to for a film, but there are independently financed films that are in fact worth $5 to $7 million or more up front for a minimum guarantee."

If producer reps are usually talented negotiators skilled at securing a film's highest price, it's for good reason—most work on commission with no up-front fee. Cassian Elwes, who along with Rena Ronson reps films for William Morris Independent, charges 10 percent of the film's net proceeds to its producer, more if the agency was involved in the film's packaging. The actual fee depends on the size of the film, the amount of work involved in setting up the film's financing or simply brokering the sale, and whether the agency was involved at the film's inception or became attached after it wrapped.

Cinetic Media—a consulting firm specializing in project financing, sales representation, and corporate advisory services—reportedly charges between 7.5 and 15 percent, since it is not a talent agency and therefore not bound by agency rules. Although some filmmakers believe that a leading sales operation such as Cinetic Media can broker the sale of their film with very little work, it often takes leading consultants a lot of effort to effect a sale, and sales consultants and reps are known to spend up to a year or more working on smaller or more challenging films to secure the best deals.

"The sales game has definitely changed since its heyday in 2000 and 2001, and a lot of people have left the space," explains Green. "The agencies have put more energy into their independent departments, but they are not really focused on small, independent movies. They're really focused on bigger movies and trying to get a bigger piece of those films for themselves and their clients, rather than just setting them up as studio projects. Creative Artists eliminated its indie group and launched a film-finance group that deals in the full spectrum of films with independent financing, so we work on $500,000 documentaries and on $100 million movies. If they are controlled by an entity other than a studio, then we can and do get involved in arranging the financing and the distribution, but that could be a Tom Hanks action movie, a foreign-language film, or a small documentary.

"The budget levels they are able to assemble are pretty high, in some cases $20 to $25 million that they can do or at least co-finance," Green continues. "I don't know that there's really a ceiling to it but I think what it reflects is certainly a change. The focus in 2001 was on these smaller indie films that were sold at festivals, but I think the agencies decided they don't need to fight over smaller titles like *Napoleon Dynamite*. Their thinking is: 'We represent huge stars and so we can package and sell—or not sell—and just package and take participation in a film like *The Matador* or *Crash*.' So that's what they've been doing. Over the last couple of years the agencies have been migrating away from small movies because they feel it's not worth their time to go to Sundance, have a small film not sell for a lot of money, and then have to deal with a disgruntled client. So the attitude is that they should be focused on bigger movies with bigger stars, and whether they're independent and sold at a festival, or they're just structured as independent projects and have distribution up front is of little consequence to them."

The upshot is that there is an inflation of sorts taking place, where independent films are expected to be cast with mainstream actors rather than up-and-coming actors or unknowns, and that the production value is expected to mirror the biggest Hollywood productions, regardless of the budget or limited resources.

To improve the quality, producer reps have been getting involved far earlier and taking fees and in some cases executive-producer credits for assembling the financing. This serves two purposes: it makes sure the reps have films to sell when they are completed, and it helps take films off the table at an early stage to avoid fierce competition the minute a hot new talent is identified.

It used to be that the first contact a filmmaker had with a producer rep was when he or she got accepted to Sundance. Today, the top-tier sales companies do far less running around chasing films and courting new filmmakers following the release of the annual Sundance lineup, thanks to referrals, leads, and tip-offs by festival personnel. "On the better movies, the bigger movies, filmmakers are usually referred to reps and sales agents," says Green. "Either the film was put together by an agency and so they're already attached to the film in some way, or they tend to be referred through relationships to people who sell movies before a filmmaker knows they've been accepted to a major festival."

AVOIDING BOTTOM-FEEDERS

In a controversial move, some unaffiliated reps have begun to charge retainer fees to filmmakers who have not been able to secure traditional representation. "There are self-described reps out there who prey upon the dreams of aspiring filmmakers who have made films that are marginal at best," says Deutchman. "A few reps will even charge filmmakers just to screen their movies, and to me that's a complete sham. If a rep truly believed in a film and its potential, he or she wouldn't think about charging for anything."

Green believes legitimate sales reps don't charge consulting fees or ask for retainers. "If someone believes in the sales potential of a film, they're not going to require anything up front, and if they *are* requiring money up front, filmmakers should be nervous about that person's belief in the film's potential," he says. "This is work that is generally done on spec and if it's not, then I wouldn't hand the film over to that person. If you can't find anyone to rep the film on a percentage, I would advise filmmakers to rep the film themselves."

Some argue that independent reps not affiliated with a well-known agency or established company sometimes charge filmmakers a retainer fee to try to sell small films that don't have major cast elements attached since they are difficult for stand-alone reps to take on speculation. The thinking is that as non-24p MiniDV films become less of a money-making option in the marketplace, working purely on a percentage of sale basis becomes an increasingly dicey proposition. In the mid-'90s it may have been easy for a filmmaker going to Sundance to engage a rep for a percentage of the sale, but some would argue that micro-budget filmmakers should consider paying retainer fees if they cannot get representation for their films by leading sales agents. Although the bigger reps do not charge fees, they also won't consider films that lack significant upside potential. Their justification is that distribution deals for smaller films often do not include minimum guarantees from which they draw a percentage. The exception is when taking on a smaller project allows a rep to introduce a hot new talent to the world.

Still, Holland, who has sold numerous small indies, won't rep a film unless he thinks it can sell for more than $100,000. "It's just not worth my time," he says unapologetically. "To do it right you have to massage the festivals, and there are 80,000 festivals. You have to organize the screenings, and even if you know all the distribution people, that doesn't mean they will necessarily show up. You have to get the press to attend, and then you have to make sure all the distributors hear what the press thought of the film."

WORKING THE FESTIVAL

In today's depressed acquisitions climate, it may be a fool's errand to look for a rep without knowing whether a movie be marketed in a way that will make critics want to recommend it, moviegoers want to see it, and indie-distribution executives want to buy it? For some lucky filmmakers, the first contact they'll have with producer reps is when their film gets selected for Sundance. Once the lists are published in the trades, the most aggressive reps will contact filmmakers to offer their ser-vices. As Willie Sutton said, he robbed banks because "that's where the money is," and producer reps attach themselves to films en route to festivals for the very same reason.

"Deals tend to happen very quickly at Sundance, Toronto, and Cannes because the process of evaluating and assessing a film's value is accelerated in that environment," explains Green. "It's being screened for everyone simultaneously: buyers, critics, exhibitors as well as general audiences who are probably closer to an art-house film audience than any distribution screening would ever be. And because there are so many reactions distributors can gauge, there's a lot of information to measure against their instinct about a film. Literally, a distributor can know—sometimes within an hour—which critics are going to support a film when it's released, what theaters would be interested in booking it, whether an audience generally responds to the film or not, and the level of interest of other buyers. And all of that combines to create an impression among individual buyers that is far more powerful than if they had seen it in a screening room on the lot in Los Angeles. At a festival things can happen quickly because there's no reason to wait; distributors just *know*."

"Festivals, especially Sundance and Toronto, allow you to create the 'Great Moment' for your film that impresses potential buyers," says producer Mark Stolaroff, founder of L.A.'s No Budget Film School. "I was at the Eccles Theater—yes, the Eccles—when *Pi* premiered in competition in 1998. Everybody went to that screening—it was sold out, it was totally packed, there was the incredible energy of 1,100 people. It was such a thrilling moment when the audience went crazy, that the buyers said, 'Wow, this is *that* kind of movie: it's unique, it's intelligent, and it's got audience appeal.' And that's when the offers flew in." Ten years later, this is still largely how indie films are sold, in the electrified air of Park City, Utah. In 2008, *Ballast* and *Frozen River* were well received at Sundance and subsequently sold to IFC Films and Sony Pictures Classics, respectively.

Any good film will play better at an oversold festival premiere than it will on DVD or Blu-ray in a Deer Valley bungalow (in between an executive's rolling calls) or during lunch in a studio executive's office that could double as a Pacific Design Center showroom. Producer reps generally prefer selling their wares at a major festival where the buzz can lead to a bidding war for a promising movie. But despite the hothouse atmosphere, Cassian Elwes, who has sold films such as *Sling Blade* and *Happy, Texas*, does his best to discourage filmmakers' unrealistic expectations. "A lot of filmmakers come in with stars in their eyes about how they're going to get $10 million for their movie," he says. "They think, 'You've done that before, so you're going to do that for me.' I think those kinds of deals are the exceptions rather than the rule."

Neither does a huge Sundance sale guarantee a long career. "What I tell filmmakers is do the research," says Bernard. "It's really simple to go back to the headlines for any number of years in *Variety*'s website, take a look at all the movies that played at Sundance, see what movie was 'hot' or got lots of money like *Introducing the Dwights*, and then see the results. It failed. Or see the movie that didn't get the hot money and see the results."

While a significant minimum guarantee and poor box-office performance are not always or even frequently related, Elwes encourages filmmakers to simply revel in the fact that they have been invited to a major festival and not to think of their film as a bridge to future financial stability. "I tell them the main thing is to enjoy themselves, because it's not every day you have a film that's going to be spotlighted in competition at Sundance," he says.

While humility and graciousness were once hallmarks of struggling independent filmmakers, many first- and second-timers these days seek fame and fortune and act as if they are God's gift to Sundance, even though it may be their first time there. Still others act as if they are doing distributors a massive favor by even allowing them to bid on their films after a screening. While many of these indie filmmakers profess that they would never sell out or make a superficial Hollywood film, they still act like the prima donnas lampooned and held up for scorn in the educational and entertaining *Living in Oblivion*, the cringe-filled documentary *Overnight*, or the dated but still chillingly accurate *The Big Picture*.

Bernard says he often sees a Powerball Lotto mentality in today's would-be auteurs. "We'll meet with filmmakers and we'll ask, 'What do you want for your movie?'—thinking they want it handled a certain way or that they think a certain audience should be reached. Instead, they say, 'A million dollars!' They literally think it's going to be like selling a Matisse or a Picasso at Christie's or that an auctioneer will be there to take bids: 'One million dollars, there! Two million, over there!' The film schools and these other programs are not preparing their students for what happens after a movie is completed. There isn't anyone out there telling them that this media myth that they'll go to Sundance and become famous is just that—a myth. And as a result, a lot of young filmmakers carry on like they're about to be the next big thing."

Another misperception filmmakers have is that distributors are actually interested in buying their film before having seen it. In fact, what most studio acquisitions departments are doing when they reach out to filmmakers is simply creating a database of projects in production that may or may not show up at major festivals over the next two to three years and trying to decide early whether they should keep each film on their radar.

"Filmmakers should be aware that the fact that studios are calling reflects nothing: it's just a sales pitch like you'd get from a telemarketer and nothing more," explains Green. "It's not a bad thing that someone from an agency or one of the studios' acquisitions departments is calling you, but you shouldn't read anything into it because until someone has seen your film, they have no idea if they want it or not, if it's appropriate for their slate. They may not even know what the film is about, so a filmmaker should never say, 'Oh my God, we've made it! Someone from Fox Searchlight just called and asked about our movie!' And filmmakers should also never adopt an attitude when they talk about their film or say something like: 'We're really confident Fox is going to buy our movie' because of X, Y, Z reason."

Additionally, filmmakers should never make the mistake of sending a screener to a studio executive in the weeks or months before a festival, even if it sounds like a good idea at the time. Acquisitions executives would always rather see a film alone before a festival and not have to evaluate it and compete for it during the feeding frenzy of Sundance. Very often the levels of offers filmmakers may get for their films before a festival are under $100,000, whereas the right positioning and audience response at a festival could easily drive up the purchase price of the very same film to $2 million. Showing a studio acquisitions executive a copy of a rough cut or first pass can have disastrous consequences because they may never want to see the final version and it can undercut a producer rep's ability to position the film or generate excitement for it among the acquisitions community especially if someone has already seen it and yawned.

Studio executives want to buy the best movies they can for as little money as possible, and not help the filmmaker to make as much money as possible. Their job, therefore, when approaching a major festival is to see as many films as early as possible so they won't feel like they might be missing the next big movie or arrive late to the bidding war should an undiscovered gem turn up. The filmmaker's job is to help the sales representative maximize the value of the movie by keeping it under wraps and generating interest and excitement that will in turn build a market.

PRODUCER REPS VS. SALES AGENTS

Producer reps who sell completed films to distributors are not to be confused with sales agents typically hired to sell international territory rights before (or after) a film is completed. Filmmakers can and should hire producer reps early in the process, but a sales agent should be hired based on the production team's financing strategy.

Lower budget films typically should not have international sales agents attached until the project is completed, while higher budget films may need to sell off international territory rights to generate the funds needed to make the film. Similarly, projects requiring gap financing will have to sell at least two international territories (at or above projected sales levels) before a bank will release the funds. Still other filmmakers may want to lower their investors' financial exposure by selling a few international territories before the film is completed and will hire a sales agent to put rights on the market.

Producer reps and consultants often act as the caretaker of worldwide rights and negotiate with international sales agents on behalf of a producer, treating the decision to broker an international sales deal as part of the strategy to clinch the U.S. distribution deal. Some producer reps will tell filmmakers that lower budget films without bankable stars are unlikely to secure strong international presales, making the hiring of an international sales agent prior to the film's completion a premature goal.

INKING THE DEAL

Once a film screens, the audience reaction, press response, and impressions of the acquisitions community will spell its destiny. A producer rep and his or her team will quickly collect the reactions of distributors and press and communicate them to the filmmakers. Cinetic Media even maintains a secure website where its clients can read synopses of acquisition executives' comments. Then the rep will try to seal the deal that very day, build on good buzz, or spin-doctor a low-energy screening or poor reception. In the rare case of a standing ovation and mass adulation, terms can be negotiated immediately, before news of a major distributor passing or a negative review can hit the trades.

The rep will speed-dial between competing bidders or lock himself in a hotel room with the filmmakers' first choice of distributors until a deal is sealed. An aspiring director may have a preexisting relationship with a particular mini-major or specialized distributor, but filmmakers typically decide who would be best suited to distribute their film by simply seeing what types of projects a distributor releases, what the campaigns look like, and how aggressively the films are promoted. And while most filmmakers don't have access to the specific economics of the films they hope to emulate other than what's available from Rentrak or The-Numbers.com, producer reps maintain a wealth of information about purchase prices, distributor performance with certain genres, and each company's record for paying filmmakers.

Bernard believes filmmakers should ask hard questions and not always accept everything their rep has to say as gospel. "They really need to ask, 'What's the information about the various companies? How are they different? Are they stable? Who has television deals and who doesn't? What's the best time of year for them to open my movie? Does the distributor we're considering have too many movies already in the pipeline?' " he says. "Most filmmakers are just looking for confidence. They're confused or overwhelmed about what to do next. They don't know what to do, so they're hiring a rep to steer them through the waters, but too many filmmakers give away control and far too much of the upside in their films to the rep. There are filmmakers who pay $10,000 or $15,000 just to get representation for their movie, and then give away 10 to 15 percent of the profits for the life of the film, which is a sin. They should only be giving away 5 percent of the sale and that's it, but instead you have a situation where one of three sellers controls the movies that go to Sundance, and whatever they say goes."

Although festival press and filmmakers often focus on a film's advance—which is frequently reported with future production-budget commitments baked into the number, inflating the true acquisitions figure—there are several other critical deal points and monetary commitments reps must address which are usually not reported in the trades as part of the headline-grabbing sale price.

"I think the actual release commitment is just as important, if not more important, than the financial commitment up front," says Elwes. "There have been situations where films were bought for large amounts of money and then dumped by distributors because the right people didn't see the movie until after the film was bought. In a Sundance situation, the acquisitions people sometimes have nothing to do with the sales or marketing. So a film is acquired and all of a sudden the sales-and-marketing guys get this movie—they've had no say in it, they've had no time to see it or think about it or give any feedback—and they think, 'We don't see a market for it. We don't get it, and we're not behind it.' "

According to Green, prints and advertising (P&A) commitments are less of a concern than the inclusion of "key market" clauses in the distribution contract. "I would say contractual protection against them bailing on the movie or spending halfheartedly is not such a big concern anymore. Generally when someone is paying a significant advance, they'll spend the requisite amount to release it. Specialized distributors aren't buying as many films as they used to, so if you do sell your film you pretty much know what you're going to get in terms of P&A. They're going to give it a real shot. But you don't want the P&A number to be a 'give' in your deal and you do want to safeguard against them getting cold feet about a certain market or level of release. That's why the release commitment is important, especially when you're dealing with smaller distributors. When you're talking about selling a film to a smaller company, you want to make sure they're releasing it in key markets, including the most important cities for specialized films: New York and Los Angeles."

Typically, the more a distributor pays for an independently financed film, the more it will need the film to succeed and be profitable in order to get their money back, which is why many reps say the best insurance toward a good release is an aggressive minimum guarantee.

Former Paramount Classics co-president David Dinerstein says it is more important for producer reps to demand a cohesive marketing strategy than a big up-front payday. "It's wonderful to say you have a deal with a studio, but if you're a first-timer and your film doesn't do well in theaters or on video because a distributor didn't know how to position it, you're going to be hard pressed to get a second film made," he warns. "It doesn't mean the film has to gross a huge amount of money, but it does have to be handled in a certain way so it can be seen by a large group of people."

CRITICALLY IMPORTANT DEAL POINTS

In addition to guarantees that a film will open in at least ten of the top twenty-five markets, reps will also attempt to waive the studio overhead fees and expenses that are assigned to each film that often delay recoupment and try to strike favorable deals with regard to how revenues are defined and disbursed. In almost all independent-film sales the minumum guarantee (MG), or what people think of as a film's "sale price" at a festival, is actually just an advance on net profits that will be paid as part of the filmmaker's deal.

The widespread misperception is that an independent film sells for a certain amount that covers its production cost (plus a little extra to help the filmmaker move out of her studio apartment), and that when all the marketing, P&A, and overhead costs are recouped, the filmmaker, producers, and investors will start to see funds from the film's release. In truth, the MG is an advance against a filmmaker's back end once a film is making a profit, a date that may be accelerated or delayed based on negotiable deal points. What also surprises many filmmakers is that the MG is seen as a nonrecourse loan against the back end that also has to be recouped *with interest*, as if it were a typical bank or car loan. Thus the price paid for the film at a festival is *not* free money and cause for celebration but an interest-bearing loan, paid back with the net revenue of the film. The filmmaker must remember too that the millions of dollars in marketing costs required to get the word out about their films must also be recouped along with the studio overhead fee that is applied to back-end revenue, further delaying the film's break-even.

With a risky or challenging film that has no advance, the rep might propose a profit-sharing component to the deal whereby at least some percentage of net revenues accrue to the filmmaker after the distributor breaks even. However, profit-sharing deal points should never be considered "either/or," since a deal that does not include at least some back-end and/or profit participation could lead the filmmaker to miss out on a significant payday if her film turns into a hit. In summary, deal points filmmakers need to be aware of include fee and royalty numbers; studio overhead fees, which can sometimes be knocked down or negotiated out; interest charges on the MG; and the cross-collateralization of revenue streams—all of which can affect the film's profitability even if it is a runaway success.

The studio's wish to cross-collateralize the revenue of an independent film between domestic and overseas revenue and between theatrical release and home video can further delay an indie film's ability to reach its break-even point. In a deal in which the revenues are cross-collateralized, the losses or deficits in one area, such as domestic theatrical release, must be offset by profits in others, such as overseas theatrical release, before any overages can be paid to the filmmakers. As a result, in a deal involving a distributor buying world-wide rights, a producer rep may try to ensure that international profits are not cross-collateralized against domestic losses. "It's very rare to sell a film for more than $5 million and have an uncrossed worldwide deal between domestic to international," says Green, "but it is possible. And at lower purchase levels, it's very possible. Often a domestic distributor won't value the foreign rights on smaller dramas or Americana material as much as they value the domestic component. They also may not value them as much as some independent foreign sales agents would, so filmmakers can make more money by selling domestic distribution rights to a studio and then doing a separate foreign sales deal."

In the late '90s, Miramax made a point of aggressively pursuing worldwide rights. Today, producer reps are frequently able to make more money for the production team by selling off territory rights directly to international buyers, since this allows them to uncross revenues that might otherwise be pooled together with losses in the United States. "This is where a leading agency can help not just in getting a domestic deal," says Rena Ronson of William Morris Independent. "On *Hard Candy*, I did three individual international foreign territory sales that helped us get the best possible deal for the film and earn significantly more money for the filmmakers." Finessing these deals is an art that requires salesmanship and expertise in a specialized area of deal negotiation against rough-and-tumble film executives who like to think of themselves as tough negotiators.

On *Super Size Me*, Cinetic Media set up the most aggressive deal it could for director-star Morgan Spurlock, while retaining the best possible back-end participation deal, which included uncrossing all the revenue streams from home video and theatrical release. This meant the film could be a hit in one venue and theoretically fail in another and still provide some cash to the filmmaker. Cinetic Media did a direct-television deal, separate theatrical and video deals, five international deals directly, and then a foreign sales deal of remaining territories all of which were uncrossed so when there were overages, money went directly from the individual distributors to the filmmaker.

As a documentary filmmaker who had struggled for many years, Spurlock might have easily been tempted to accept the biggest headline-grabbing advance from a single distributor looking to buy worldwide rights for the film. "But because Morgan spent very little money making the movie he had the flexibility to sell the film for less money up front in order to maximize his back-end potential on the film," explains Green, who was working at Cinetic Media at the time the deal was negotiated. "And that's what Morgan did. He left some money on the table up front, he took a lower aggregate MG from all these individual deals so he could take a bigger piece of the profit. He believed in *Super Size Me* and was absolutely sure it was going to work and be profitable. And when the film in fact became very profitable, he looked like the smartest guy in the room, and he had much more money coming to him than if he had just gotten an extra million dollars in his advance."

WHEN TO LOOK FOR REPS

Because there are so many pitfalls to navigate, filmmakers are advised to find producer reps as early as possible. "I generally recommend that filmmakers do their homework about potential reps even before their film is accepted to festivals and make a list of who they want so they can start showing the film to them in the order of preference," Green says. "There are festivals that are more appropriate for certain films, and the sooner they start working with a rep, the sooner he or she can help guide them through the process."

Sloss advises filmmakers to meet with potential reps and politely ask what may be considered hard questions. "Filmmakers should ask: 'How are you going to sell my movie? Do you think it will sell? In what medium? Who do you think are the potential buyers? And what is your strategy?'" he says. "And a question that people really need to ask is: 'If my film doesn't fly off the shelves right away, are you going to maintain your commitment to getting it sold?'"

Indeed, the difference between a committed rep and someone who takes on a huge number of films to see what sticks may decide if a film gets a distribution deal or not. Some argue that it is impossible to provide professional attention let alone a personal touch when a rep has fifteen to twenty films. Still, what else is a filmmaker to do? Those who don't hand over their completed projects to well-known agencies, sales companies, or individuals with established track records may risk their shot at selling their film at all.

Going with a new name or someone who only dabbles in repping feels to many like a potentially dicey proposition.

"My attitude is that unless you're working with a major player with a really great track record and obvious relationships and experience, I think you're better off on your own," says Green. "I'm not talking about the 'Big Film' with huge potential that could be the hit at Sundance and incite a bidding war like *Son of Rambow*. But if you have a tiny film that's going to require a grassroots effort or handholding, then I just think it's unlikely that an inexperienced rep will be bringing much to your project and you might as well retain as much control as you can over the sales process. That way at least you know who saw it, and if people from a certain distributor don't get back to you, then you know what happened there."

Indeed, a filmmaker may not ever know what really transpired because an inexperienced or new rep may not have kept detailed records or even a phone log. The filmmakers won't know who the rep spoke to, for how long, and exactly what was said. Another risk is that an unknown or novice rep may talk a good game but have very little "live fire" experience in the trenches, a combination that can be disastrous. What filmmakers don't realize is that, ultimately, good representation isn't as much about making introductions as it is about marketing and knowing how to position a film for specific buyers.

"There are a lot of people who know how to negotiate a deal when there's already interest, but few people who know how to truly market a film to distributors," Green continues. "That's why I say a filmmaker is better off doing it themselves if the alternative is signing on with someone who doesn't have very much experience. You need a lawyer once you get to the negotiations phase, but to get people turned on to your film, you are probably more likely to wind up with a better level of interest if you take responsibility for it and do the legwork yourself."

Either way, filmmakers are encouraged not to simply let go of their film just because someone is brokering the sale. "We want the filmmaker to be involved in the process with us—it's their movie, not ours," says Elwes. "We think they are entitled to be part of the process, especially meeting the distributors and taking part in negotiations. It's very much a part of the learning curve for them, and we think they should participate."

Another job for the producer rep may be mediating among a director, a producer, and the film's financiers. Howard Cohen, Roadside Attractions cofounder and a former agent with United Talent Agency, says that in his previous incarnation as a rep for films such as *Billy's Hollywood Screen Kiss*, *Trick*, and the modern *Othello* adaptation *O*, he often found himself walking a tightrope between investors who wanted their money and filmmakers who in some cases wanted to hold out for a theatrical distribution deal rather than jump at a straight-to-video offer. "It's a significant problem, and I faced it all the time," he says. "I think the misperception a lot of filmmakers have is that just because they've made a good movie, someone's going to want to buy it and release it theatrically."

Sometimes a smaller company may offer less of an advance but more careful handling than a bigger company less adept at releasing a film in a certain genre. Similarly, a prestigious small distributor that is sure to boost a filmmaker's reputation may be bidding against an executive at a new distribution company with foreign backing who is hoping to make a dramatic statement by throwing around more cash. Or, as occurred with Henry Bean's *The Believer*, Allison Anders's *Things Behind the Sun*, and Tommy O'Haver's *An American Crime*, filmmakers may have to decide between a

cable deal with a network like Showtime and a meager theatrical offer that makes a breakout success unlikely.

When it comes to playing referee between filmmakers and
financiers, Elwes says, "In the long run, I think we're able to
make both sides happy because we always help them pick the
distributor who is going to do the best job with the movie.
As for the financiers, as long as they make their money back,
making a huge profit is not as important as being put on the
map as serious financier-producers so they can get their next
movie off the ground."

However, there are several schools of thought on this
issue. "If you get a bigger advance from one company but
they plan to release it straight to video, versus another company that might be offering less money but is committed to
releasing it theatrically, you have to decide what is more
important," says producer Adam Fields. "Is it the money or
the desire for people to see your film in a theater, which pre-
sumably was the reason you spent a year or two of your life
making it in the first place?"

This question presents a quandary since it strikes at the
hearts of idealistic filmmakers who draw from a well of
lunatic optimism to stay in the fight for as long as they feel
they need to. That's often the biggest crisis facing filmmakers today. "How is making a small independent film a
profitable venture? How can I sell this business model to
investors, and what is it that I'm promising them?"

WHAT TO DO IF YOU'RE REJECTED

More often than not, first and second independent films,
even many of those shot on 35mm, do not get accepted to
major festivals. Although some producer reps may pass on a
film not deemed to have solid launch possibilities, others will
devise alternative strategies for rejected films or those that

missed festival deadlines such as holding individual or group screenings for distributors or screening excerpts of scenes at a festival, even though the film is actually not an official entrant. The former strategy worked for *Sling Blade*, which was bought by Miramax just after its producers learned the film was rejected from Cannes, and the latter approach worked for *Boys Don't Cry*, which Cinetic Media sold to Fox Searchlight in 1999 on the basis of a twenty-minute clip reel.

There is a widespread misunderstanding about how *Boys Don't Cry* was sold, since many filmmakers think that they can simply show a mishmash of sequences of an uncompleted film to a studio executive by handing them a pre-loaded iPhone or by running an HDMI cable from a high-end Dell or Sony laptop into the HD-ready TV in a busy hotel lobby and magically sell their film, as long as they can keep the executive watching for the full twenty minutes.

"The reason *Boys Don't Cry* was able to be sold with only twenty minutes of footage is that all of the buyers, including Fox Searchlight, were really interested in the movie and loved the script but were concerned that no actor was going to be able to pull off the lead role and no audience was going to buy a female actor convincingly passing as a boy," explains Green, who was a senior executive with Cinetic Media at the time the film was sold and who screened the clip reel in his condo. "And so when we showed the footage it was mostly just Hilary Swank's performance. The film had the right mood and great cinematography but Swank's performance was incredible and so the lingering question everybody had just went away, which is why suddenly everyone started bidding for the film. But it's not like anyone can show up at a festival and screen their film for people on a handheld DVD player or video iPod and get it sold off of that. In the case of *Boys Don't Cry*, it was a film coming from a well-known production entity, Killer Films, and it was repped by Cinetic, so interested distributors would have pre-bought the movie blind or would have financed it from the get-go if they had they been able to see Swank's performance, and once they saw some of it there was no reason to wait for the rest of the film."

THINGS TO WATCH OUT FOR

While producer reps are beloved by filmmakers whose films have sold, they are often despised and cursed by those whose films were rejected by distributors or who received less-than-ideal deal terms. With the wrong clauses in a distribution contract, for instance, a popular niche documentary can sell 100,000 copies on DVD and still never reach profitability. So while a rep's ability to successfully secure distribution depends largely on the "heat" produced by the film itself, deal savvy is still a critical component, since investors can be left holding the bag even on a film that gets picked up.

"A filmmaker can get into a situation where he or she lands a deal but it's going to cost them an additional $50,000 to satisfy the [distributor's] delivery requirements which weren't discussed during the negotiations," says producer and consultant Peter Broderick, who repped Chris Nolan's first film, *Following*, which played at Toronto and later at Slamdance in 1999. "It's a really complex and difficult world—and filmmakers need to have folks on their team who can help them avoid making mistakes, which in some cases can have serious repurcussions."

When a festival ends with only nibbles but no sale, a common complaint is that a rep may have had too many films on his or her plate and didn't push a particular film hard enough because another project had more obvious salability. "I don't want to trash people specifically, but a lot of producer reps approach their business like playing with lottery tickets," says Green. "They sign up small movies in the hopes that something will happen quickly. They will make a few phone calls, and if nothing happens, there's nothing to prevent them from just sitting on their ass and going about their day, doing other work while the filmmaker thinks that this person is diligently working to find other distributors."

Another realization filmmakers have in hindsight is that their rep asked for too much of a cut if the film sells for a very high multiple. "When you pick a producer rep, you have to be really careful about what you're giving away," explains *Open Water* producer Laura Lau. "The tendency is to want to say things like: 'Thank you so much for working on my film! Whatever you want, *you can have it!*' But you really shouldn't do that. I know filmmakers who have given their producer reps bumps when they totally didn't need to. It's their *job* to sell the film."

Lau initially had very low expectations for *Open Water*, her second shot at producing, since it was made for only $150,000 and shot on a MiniDV Sony PD150. However, the film sold at Sundance in 2004 for $2.5 million and went on to gross nearly $59 million worldwide.

Filmmakers often forget that producer reps take 10 to 15 percent of the film's net overages for the life of the deal, a figure which can add up to a significant number over as long as fifteen years. "For instance, a rep might come to you and say, 'I'll take 5 percent now, and then if it makes a certain amount, it jumps to 7 percent,' but you don't have to agree to that," explains Lau. "You need to be thinking about your best-case scenario instead of your worst-case scenario. But instead a lot of filmmakers think, 'It'll never make that much, that'll never happen, but it will incentivize the producer rep to do a better job if I offer him a bigger cut.' Again you need to be really careful and think about your best-case scenario and negotiate your deal as such. I think a lot of times filmmakers are so excited to get *anywhere* that they don't really think about what is the best deal for themselves in the long-long term."

What many low-budget filmmakers don't realize is that bigger-budget independently financed films with stars in the cast often sell immediately after their first festival screenings, which is why the producer rep's rate is often a far lower 5 percent rather than the typical 10 percent, since there is much lower risk on the producer rep's part for a film that's almost guaranteed to sell for a significant multiple. As a result, filmmakers should not shrug and agree to standard deal points if their film has stars or is more commercial or mainstream than the typical, offbeat specialized film.

"That's also true when it comes to signing a distribution deal," Lau continues. "You're so excited and as an independent filmmaker—getting any kind of distribution—you're just grateful to get any kind of deal, so you leave it in the hands of the professionals. But Chris [Kentis] and I really tried to be on top of every detail of our film, including the more business-related aspects such as accounting, distribution, and legal."

In the current acquisitions market, managing expectations and keeping a sober perspective on what is possible is key. Reps can end up overselling a film to the film's own production team, raising expectations beyond what the rep could ever hope to deliver. Says Dinerstein, "Sometimes a producer rep will tell a filmmaker there's interest in his or her film so he or she will think the rep is doing their job. But the reality is there's interest in *seeing* the film, not in buying it."

And despite protestations to the contrary, there are those who doubt the producer rep's ability to walk away from a bigger advance in favor of an offer from a smaller company with a stronger or smarter release strategy. Bernard—whose company is known for its modest advances and careful handling of films such as *Synecdoche, New York* and foreign-language hits such as *Black Book*; *Persepolis*; *Crouching Tiger, Hidden Dragon*; and *The Lives of Others*—is skeptical. "There is one drawback with a lot of these producer reps, especially the ones who are handling large amounts of people, and that is that they are working on their percentage and not trying to match the film with the right distributor," he says. "They take their 10 percent and put the film with a big-money distributor that doesn't have the sensitivity for releasing the movie, and you end up with a disaster."

On the other side is Green, who says, "Distribution companies want the filmmaker to take all of the risk. But filmmakers should find a distribution company that's going to share in that risk, someone who is going to make the filmmaker whole, recoup them on their investment in making the film, and make some sort of assurances. That way, you know the distribution company is committed to putting significant resources into the film's release.

"What IFC or any of the other low-paying distributors want to say is: 'We want to pay as little as possible and we refuse to pay more than a couple of hundred grand for this movie because we're not sure how much money *we'll* make on it. But let us release it and trust in our ability to make the film work,'" Green continues. "And when you hold that up against another distributor who is offering a sizable minimum guarantee to make the filmmaker whole and is basically making the same pitch—'We believe in the movie, we're not sure how much it'll make, but we want to put all of our resources behind it and really give it a shot'—then there's just no argument left for going with somebody who isn't willing to do that. It's irresponsible to your investors not to let them take the financial risk off the film-maker's shoulders."

SINGLE IN A REPPED WORLD

So what if a repped film doesn't sell? The number of film-makers who leave festivals crestfallen is higher than most people realize, especially after the theatrical failures of recent festival acquisitions such as *Son of Rambow*, *The Signal*, *My Kid Could Paint That*, *The Ten*, *Joshua*, *La Misma Luna*, *The Wackness*, and *Brick*, among others. "Everybody goes into Sundance thinking they're going to walk away with a distri-bution deal, but the reality is it doesn't matter who's repping your project—only a certain number of films have that potential," Green says.

Although all producer reps say they continue to work dili-gently on selling films that don't catch fire at a first festival, the sad truth is that the more time that goes by, the harder it may be to make the sale. "People are going to have the per-ception later on that your film screened at X festival and nobody bought it, so it's probably not any good," Broderick says.

Indeed, if a film doesn't nab that big festival pickup, the producer should be prepared to stay on top of his or her rep and, if necessary, develop his or her own grassroots strategy to get the film seen by the right people. "A lot of times, nobody knows better than the filmmaker how to position a picture," Bernard says. "A filmmaker should never just stand back and let the producer rep work his or her magic."

Holland advises filmmakers to be psychologically and financially prepared to go it alone at some point and not to wait until the last minute to come up with some sort of Plan B. "Sometimes the producer of an independent film has to be ready to act as the film's producer rep and possibly even as its distributor," he says. "They say, 'Anyone who represents himself in court has an idiot for a client,' and that may make me an idiot sometimes, but the job of the producer is a little more multifaceted these days and so you have to be thinking with a producer rep's hat on.

"On *Sweet Land* we were winning every festival we played and getting low-ball offers from distributors, so we raised some more money to distribute it ourselves," recalls Holland. "We were able to go out with it theatrically by hiring Jeff Lipsky [formerly of Lot 47 Films] to do the theater bookings and grossed $1.7 million. It just took some legwork. Now I consider putting a line item in every budget for self-distribution, something between $100,000 and $500,000, especially for films that have niche markets that the bigger distribution companies are not going to think it's worth their time to exploit." As daunting as this may seem, Holland says it can be done with a $60.00 copy of *The Hollywood Creative Directory*. "You have to put together a database of every distribution company in the United States, every home-video distributor, every possible television outlet," he adds. "There are a hundred little distributors. And then you have to find out what their tastes are and try to guess—from asking a lot of questions—what they pay, what you can expect in terms of creative input, and what you can expect in terms of release. We released *Spin the Bottle* for a week at the Pioneer Theater in New York and sold video rights to TLA Video. It came out on DVD and did really well. You just have to be prepared to do all the work yourself."

The problem with this approach is that today's DIY filmmakers often have little by which to judge the strength of their deal because baseline comparisons are hard to come by, especially when distributors are offering token advances of $200,000 or less for many acquisitions in 2009. "Nobody wants to have to tell anybody that they didn't make any money, so a lot of times deal points are kept secret between producers and distributors," Holland says. "Producers acting as their own reps can hire entertainment attorneys to assist in the actual negotiations or they can gather information on bidders' deals by calling up the producers of other films in its catalog, but they might not get an answer."

At the end of the day, obtaining a good producer rep is just one more step among the many that are taken to get an independently financed film into the marketplace. But just as filmmakers should not lose heart if they are rejected from Sundance, they also should not despair if they are passed on by the top reps. Difficult or unproducible scripts like *Being John Malkovich* can suddenly become hot once elements are attached. Similarly, a film that everyone passes on distributing can turn into *Memento*, *Greek Wedding*, or the highest-grossing independent film ever made, *The Passion of the Christ*. Just ask Bob Berney.

11. All or Nothing
DISTRIBUTION DEAL BREAKERS

or those who dream of seeing their films unspool in glorious 35mm, securing distribution can be particularly challenging since it often seems as if the only thing separating a good movie that earns a respectable sum from a bad film that nobody ever sees is a single distributor giving the project a chance. Indeed, some of the biggest theatrical windfalls might have been missed if surprise hits such as The Passion of the Christ, My Big Fat Greek Wedding, The Blair Witch Project, Memento, *and* Open Water *had debuted on cable or through Netflix, which has been a buyer since its 2006 post-Sundance acquisition of SherryBaby. The problem is, there are several filters on the way to theatrical distribution, the foremost of which is a festival acceptance committee, and they are tough. Filmmakers should recall that even Chris Nolan's debut,* Following, *was rejected by Sundance and Slamdance in 1999.* Following *premiered at the San Francisco International Film Festival and then went to Toronto, and only then was it invited to Slamdance. The competition for festival slots has only intensified. In 2009, 3,661 finished feature films were submitted for 120 slots at Sundance—up from 3,624 in 2008 for the same 120 slots. To put these numbers in perspective, Sundance's current 3.3 percent acceptance rate makes it harder to get into than Harvard (7.1 percent), Princeton (7.8 percent), Yale (8.3 percent), Columbia (8.7 percent), or Stanford (9.5 percent). Out of the nearly 200 or so features that screen at Sundance, only 12 will get theatrical distribution, or around 5 percent. Compounding the difficulty is the fact that indie films that might once have been seen as possible singles or doubles such as* The Tao of Steve *are rarely given a chance at the box office now that each year seems to bring a runaway specialized hit such as* Juno, Little Miss Sunshine, *or* Sideways. *The fear among distributors is that the typical acquisition will perform more like Miramax's* The Station Agent, *a $1.5 million production that won the Audience Award at Sundance in 2003 but eked out only $5.8 million theatrically, or* Son of Rambow, *purchased for $7 million at Sundance but which grossed only $1.7 million in 2008, hardly enough to even cover its marketing budget. This winner-take-all paradigm is then echoed when films reach video stores, since more copies of hit titles are stocked than of those that didn't catch fire theatrically. This explains why even well-shot, lovingly crafted dramas like Doug Sadler's* Swimmers *or Chris Eyre's* A Thousand Roads *regularly wind up stuck in festival-circuit limbo: just as Ivy League schools often reject thousands of applicants with perfect 4.0 averages in favor of those with a specific talent or extracurricular interest, specialized distributors put a premium on acquisitions that plug a hole in their release slate or that are part of a genre they believe will be the next big thing. Distribution is also about finding an appropriate release corridor that is free of competing specialized films in the same genre and also free of mainstream blockbusters such as* The Dark Knight, Iron Man 2, *or whatever franchise captures the public's imagination and wipes out the competition during its opening weekend. Fortunately there are several new self-distribution opportunities coming into focus, and more theaters with* *digital projectors, which should make it easier for independently financed films to reach a wide audience.*

While many aspiring filmmakers believe they have a killer pitch that would make a terrific indie film, the threshold for what is actually salable and releasable has been raised so high that dozens of well-shot films with recognizable stars are rejected by Sundance each year. Still others that make the cut often leave the festival without distribution. For this reason Miramax president Daniel Battsek encourages aspiring filmmakers to make sure their scripts are as good as they can be before going out to talent because compelling, sophisticated stories are often the deciding factor. "Increasingly, a great idea is not enough," he explains. "The rigors of the filmmaking process are as important as the idea itself, so you need a great screenplay and you need a director who really knows what he or she is trying to get up there, and yeah, if you can get some stars or some aspiring stars, that puts you ahead of the game. But your script should always be in the best shape it can possibly be in. You should always have the writer do one more rewrite."

The ability to actually make a good-looking independent film with affordable HD equipment and commonly available editing software and computing power has created a glut of films that often cannot find distribution in theaters or on video.

"I think these are kind of the best and the worst of times for independent film," says explains Lionsgate Films president Tom Ortenberg. "On the plus side there are all kinds of new avenues for distribution and exhibition and financing of motion pictures. And thanks to digital innovations, films can be produced for cheaper than they ever could be before. On the other hand, given the number of films that are released and given the number of entertainment choices that the public has, breaking through the clutter to get an independent film seen is harder than ever. So it's a weird dynamic that it's perhaps the best time ever to get an independent film made, and it's perhaps the hardest time ever to get an independent film seen. And as a distributor, the economic models for independent film have always been difficult and now are as hard as ever. There are new revenue streams, but again, breaking through the clutter is becoming increasingly difficult and often, but not always, costly."

The problem is for every box-office success such as *Juno* that ends up for sale on DVD at Starbucks, there are many independent movies that do only a fraction of that business. "In 2002 films like *The Good Girl*, which grossed $14 million, was a reasonable best case, and *In the Bedroom*, which grossed $36 million, and *Monster's Ball*, which grossed $31 million, were considered breakouts," continues Ortenberg. "Today, for every one of those there are a hundred independent films that end up grossing somewhere between zero and $1 million, which is something a lot of aspiring independent filmmakers overlook."

Bob Berney agrees: "A lot of films can be very good and do very well but gross only $700,000 or $800,000 at the box office because they're a small foreign film or just an indie that plays only at specific art houses."

The make-or-break opening-weekend is partially to blame since films that "open" get to stay on screens and make money, while those that don't immediately click with audiences have their marketing budgets cut and are often pulled from theaters before word of mouth can build. This in turn means that specialized distributors who buy independent films have become far more selective about what they pick up, significantly lowering the odds for aspiring filmmakers shooting non-24p projects in their backyard or local diner with no stars.

"Although there are several potential homes for independent films now, the road to market is an incredibly expensive one and the number of independent films that don't make their money back far outweighs the number that do," explains Battsek. "And therefore even those of us who are desperate to find new filmmakers, to find new voices, to find new films are cautious. I lead with my heart whenever I can, but my head is not far behind and my finance director is always by my side. It is a business, and however much you allow your passion to come into play, you still have to keep a very firm handle on the business prospects for movies, which is why many don't get picked up. Even among films we have chosen to produce, there are many that are, on some level, very difficult to make."

Of course, what astonishes many first- and second-time filmmakers with less complicated projects is the fact that a completed film does not mean they are on their way to a red-carpet premiere. "What's amazing is how many filmmakers every year get accepted to a major festival only to discover afterward that it's not at all a guarantee of success," says producer Mark Stolaroff, founder of L.A.'s No Budget Film School. "Everyone thinks they're going leave Sundance as the next Jared Hess or Miranda July, but that's really the exception rather than the rule. So many filmmakers go home with only the cans of film they came with, some business cards, a week's worth of laundry, blurry digital photos, free T-shirts, expired ski-lift tickets, and a suitcase full of disappointment."

Since this is the harsh reality no one wants to acknowledge, filmmakers need to think about their film's distribution, the competitive landscape distributors are facing, and the economics of distribution long before production begins, rather than waiting until their films have wrapped. In short, distribution considerations should not be "a bridge we'll cross when we come to it." Distribution and exhibition alternatives such as BitTorrent.com and Amazon's CreateSpace are as much of a consideration as casting, and something aspiring screenwriters, producers, and directors need to have thought through even as they start to put elements together.

"Independent filmmakers can now offer their films to Amazon customers in DVD and digital formats through CreateSpace," says Roy Price, director of Amazon Digital Video. "This is a great opportunity for independent filmmakers to reach a large group of customers who enjoy independent film. And, as time goes by, there will be more opportunities to monetize content just as it continues to get cheaper to produce content. The number of people creating films and making some kind of living by it should increase exponentially." Indeed, according to the research consultancy In-Stat, total worldwide user-generated video revenue is expected to reach $1.2 billion by 2012, with more than 160 billion user-generated videos forecasted.

RAISING YOUR DISTRIBUTION IQ

Understanding the customer and his or her needs is the first step toward selling anything, be it a movie, a new car, or a new brand of detergent. In this case the "customer" is the specialized film distributor or her assistant on the lookout for compelling indie acquisitions.

"In a buyer's market filmmakers need to recognize what motivates distribution executives," says longtime entertainment attorney Steven Beer, of the New York firm Greenberg Traurig. "One is content, meaning something fresh and distinct; two is pedigree: A-list actors, a recognizable director, or a producer with a track record; three is competition, or concern that another distribution company will get an inside track or acquire something before they can; and four is fear, in the sense that they will want to minimize their risk and exposure."

Filmmakers also need to get a sense of the checklist distributors go through when considering a potential acquisition. For example, if the project is a star-laden ensemble drama, executives will want to review the performance of similar films or comparables such as *Crash*, *Magnolia*, *Happy Endings*, *Grand Canyon*, *Short Cuts*, *Syriana*, and *Traffic*. The films *For Your Consideration* or *Waiting for Guffman* would not be considered good comparables in this case because although they have large casts and are improvisational, Christopher Guest films lean more toward comedy and irony. Then they will discuss among their teams what factors drove those films' successes or failures theatrically.

Too often, however, filmmakers fail to do a simple analysis by making a list of similar films and looking up their box-office performance on Rentrak or The-Numbers.com, and then taking the necessary step of asking themselves if they are about to make a film that anyone might actually want to see.

"I think filmmakers absolutely have to think of the broader audience and make films that everybody—not just themselves—wants to see," explains former Picturehouse senior marketing executive Marian Koltai-Levine. "They need to look at the broader audience for specialized films and get a sense of what people are actually spending money to see, and making a list of comparables that would support actually going forward with a project is a critical step."

Among the questions filmmakers need to ask themselves are: Was it the release date? Was it Oscar consideration?

Had certain topics such as the War in Iraq fallen out of favor? But most important of all: Has a studio's distribution and marketing staff had experience with this type of film before? Do they know how to distribute it and in what theaters? Does the film need a slower platform release where they add additional cities each week, or would it earn more in wide release similar to a typical Holllywood film?

Even within a slower platform release, there are variables that can make the difference between a modest hit and a breakout success. Because seasonality and competition in the marketplace also play an important role, filmmakers should create a thumbnail sketch of possible corridors of distribution by looking ahead eight to twelve months from the day they expect to wrap production in order to to pick out the best time of year to release their movie. A competitive landscape of upcoming films can be created by looking at release-date schedules on Rentrak or from forward-looking release dates regularly posted on MovieWeb.com. Some distributors speak internally about "building a corridor" of at least two weeks when there won't be films in the same genre that could confuse or siphon off moviegoers.

Filmmakers can increase their distribution savvy by generating lists of at least six films that are similar in tone and cast level to the one they are working on and then calculating a range of outcomes that represent best-case, middle-case, worst-case, and Hurricane Katrina total-wipeout scenarios. Although it may seem counterintuitive or discouraging, the wipeout example should be just that: a previous example of a film that failed to connect with audiences. This exercise will show distributors that filmmakers have thought through every possible outcome and that they are thinking realistically about their films' theatrical prospects, which are tougher than most filmmakers realize.

"You never really know if something is going to succeed

because the nature of independent film is that it's execution-dependent, and often lacking on quantifiable commercial elements," says producer Ted Hope. "You can't put down the quantifiable elements of success because so much depends on talent, execution, and serendipity. So there's no guarantee of success. But you can say, 'I'm not an idiot. I'm not going to make something that's completely off the wall, and so I'm within these bounds from here to here.' You can say, 'If we get these sorts of stars and that sort of budget, here are the financial numbers of previous films and how they performed.' In business plans, all people reference are the success stories, and those are rare. If you want to write a sound business plan, look at the median. Look at the films that basically sucked but still somehow found a way to make their money back. Even with the best planning and conservative action, timing can change things significantly. As great as *In the Bedroom* is, something more than the writing, directing, and acting contributed to its $32 million domestic box office. The distributor, Harvey Weinstein, was going after his eleventh consecutive Best Picture Oscar nomination. His marketing spend was as much about that as it was about the picture. And let's face it, it's rare that such a dark picture finds such a large audience—I've always thought the film connected with audiences more than usual because after 9/11 crowds were looking for some way to understand their grief and what they were feeling at the time."

Given that theaters keep half—or often slightly more than half—of an indie film's box-office gross, what a film "made" theatrically should never be considered the "breakeven," even though it almost always is thought of in those terms. All movies released theatrically must earn at least double their production and marketing budgets to break even without the help of international and ancillary revenues.

"So many films that cost $5 million to make end up at a

festival where they sell for only $200,000 or less for the U.S. advance or are glad to be sold at all," explains former Picturehouse president Bob Berney. "That's probably the most common thing. But think about it, the initial marketing budget is a couple of million dollars, which may not be a lot compared to studio films but the risk adds up by the time all the money to acquire and market the film is tallied."

Specialized-film executives agree that theatrical exhibition requires an increasingly complex analysis and a definable audience that can be counted on to support a film. "Distribution is the toughest part of the business because no matter how much theaters say, 'We're going to keep your film in' or 'We'll give you a two-week window,' if there's somebody right behind you or you're not grossing, you're out," explains Koltai-Levine.

"It's not that theaters are giving up on specialized films and replacing them with commercial films like *Spider-Man 3* when they don't perform," explains Fox Searchlight chief operating officer Steven Gilula. "It's that there's always another specialized film waiting to take their place. So unless you get a good response in that opening week, there are other independent films waiting in the wings to move you out of the way."

"It's not like it once was when independent theaters couldn't get movies so something you were releasing would be able to stay on a screen," says Sony Pictures Classics co-president Tom Bernard. "Theaters today—even the Lincoln Plaza or the Angelika in New York City—will take the lowest grossing film that weekend and throw it off and put another one up because there are so many movies out there vying for screens. The stakes are also much higher because *The New York Times* doesn't offer low-budget films any advertising discounts, and because distributors are forced to spend an exorbitant amount to open each film since theaters can keep trying new movies if yours doesn't cut it."

Better-financed or better-connected filmmakers can create sophisticated release corridors and look up film comparables data on Rentrak, an invaluable online service studios use to analyze performance data with a level of detail second to none. Rentrak compiles information about specific theaters where box-office grosses for a particular film were strongest. Adding attributed Rentrak data to an indie film's business plan will certainly make it seem more professional and show investors that the filmmakers have carefully thought through their project's viability beyond the outsize promises and Tarantino references in most fund-raising documents.

SMALL CAN BE BEAUTIFUL

Smaller distributors are usually looking for personal stories that deliver a powerful emotional charge. Accordingly, filmmakers should emphasize the most dramatic beats in their projects or the overall effect the story has on festival or test audiences when courting boutique theatrical distributors.

"Really, for us the question is how do we feel about a film," says Zeitgeist Films cofounder and copresident Emily Russo. "It has to be something that we really love and respond to. We want to know if there's something of interest about the film, something worthwhile, something that will leave a lasting impact after you've seen it or that you might want to see again, something that will be memorable. That's what we're really looking for. Often we're just responding to the work and what it does to us because we figure if it elicits a powerful response in us, it will certainly do that to others."

Of course, each specialized distributor has a personality and style that defines its imprint. Lionsgate Films has done

well with urban and genre fare, while Sony Pictures Classics
has had a run of success with foreign-language films such as
The Counterfeiters, *The Lives of Others*, and *Persepolis*, as well as
with stranger-than-fiction documentaries.

Some distributors, such as Strand Releasing and Zeitgeist,
however, actively seek out new filmmakers with a unique sensibility. In 2003 Zeitgeist distributed *Nowhere in Africa*, a
German film which grossed $6.2 million theatrically in the
United States and won the Academy Award for Best Foreign-
Language Film. Unfortunately, giving smaller distributors
short shrift—even though they may have the ideal sensibility
and passion to release a feature—is a tragic and frequent
blunder of many first-timers, who would rather their producer reps land them a big splashy minimum guarantee that
will put their film on the cover of *Variety*. "It's been our mandate to try to discover new talent at the very beginning of
their careers," says Russo, who gave directors Christopher
Nolan and Atom Egoyan their breaks by distributing *Following* and *Speaking Parts*, respectively. "Our focus has always
been and continues to be discovering new talent. *Following*
was a great first film, and although it didn't do very well at
the box office, it became an important link in the chain of
Christopher Nolan's career, who three films later directed
Batman Begins and then of course *The Dark Knight*."

Nolan had applied to the 1998 Sundance and Slamdance
festivals, but *Following* actually premiered at the 1998 San
Francisco International Film Festival before playing at
Toronto and then at Slamdance—not Sundance—in 1998.
The film was later included in New York's New Directors/
New Films in 1999.

"Where there is a challenge, we are not afraid to take it, as
we have done with Todd Haynes, whose first film, *Poison*, was
released to great critical and financial success and who went
on to direct *I'm Not There*. François Ozon, who entered the

mainstream with *Under the Sand, 8 Women,* and *Swimming Pool,* was also introduced by Zeitgeist with *See the Sea* and later with *Water Drops on Burning Rocks,* so our catalog is really filled with these kinds of 'discovery filmmakers' whose early work we championed," says Russo. "We obviously don't have the bucks to compete with the major studios, but we can make a small film a success, something that a studio cannot always do."

When considering multiple distribution offers, enthusiasm for the project should count for a lot. "We have found a number of filmmakers who are willing to take less money up front from us in return for our passion and commitment to do the film justice, and that's something we find very gratifying," says Ortenberg. "We have found generally that when we get into a bidding situation at a festival, in the pictures that we have been competing against other distributors for, we are not usually the high bid. I think that our track record and our ability to produce, market, and distribute challenging material is very attractive to filmmakers."

What many filmmakers overlook because they do not regularly read the trades is that smaller distributors often have superstar distribution executives among their ranks, such as the Bob Berney–era Newmarket Films, who are willing to take an innovative approach to marketing films that may need special handling. Additionally, a smaller distributor may be on the verge of becoming a mini-major in its own right following an influx of new capital. Similarly, Showtime was once looked at as a second- or even third-tier option before it became the home of such groundbreaking, risk-taking, and exceptionally well-crafted series as *Dexter* and *Weeds,* among others.

"It's always sad when filmmakers forfeit a relationship with someone who understands them in favor of someone who promises a commercial breakthrough," says *Adoration* and *Felicia's Journey* director Atom Egoyan. "I don't think anyone can actually engineer that—I think it happens when you least expect it—even though a lot of people pretend that they can. No distributor can really guarantee that. But there is this cliché now, about the film that gets the million-dollar advance and rockets the filmmaker into their studio deal, and every year there is the film that goes that route. But if you're more artistically driven, the relationship you have with the distributor who shares your vision and your passion is going to be the most cherished and important bond you can have because they're the ones who are going to contextualize your work in the right way. If you're artistically driven you have to always think about your long-term career and the body of work you are creating as opposed to being a one-hit wonder or taking your payday. You need to feel that you are being represented in a way that accommodates your own vision of yourself. So filmmakers who are motivated by money and hoping for that breakthrough are usually doing themselves a real disservice."

The allure of cash on the barrelhead is hard to resist. However, according to Koltai-Levine, "Many new filmmakers have these altruistic ideas that they're going to go with the best distributor for their film. But guess what? If one distributor is offering $10 million and that makes them whole by two and a half times, a lot of them will take the money. At the end of the day, it often comes down to who is going to pay the most. People getting back-end deals don't see the cash for a very long time, so when there's cash on the table, a lot of them take it."

By going for the big-money deal, filmmakers may pass up the chance to be the *next* Atom Egoyan by not considering lower bids from passionate executives who would give their projects special care and handling rather than a cookie-cutter release strategy that may not work with their film.

"Pairing a movie with a distributor that is not the right one so you can get the big-money deal is really certain death for a film," says Bernard. "Often the producer rep puts the film with a big-money distributor which may not have the sensitivity for releasing the movie and you end up with a disaster either way: the film tanks or if it somehow becomes a success, there are no overage checks to be sent back to the filmmakers because the studio spent it all to 'gross the film up.' In other words, they may spend $10 million in prints and advertising to get to $10 million at the box office. Then you're actually $5 million in the hole," since marketing costs have to be recouped and because exhibitors keep half.

If an independent or specialized film has seen some early success at the box office, distributors are often incentivized to spend more on marketing to push the grosses past at least $10 million, since that has been the benchmark where the ancillary value of a film on DVD, Blu-ray, and in other windows typically becomes significant. "The filmmakers end up calling the producer rep and saying, 'We just did $10 million at the box office! Where's all the money!'" Bernard continues. "But had that film been in the hands of another company, it probably would have been very profitable because another company would have spent less on prints and advertising and been more watchful and sensitive to the theaters it was booked in, more sensitive to the marketing, and they also wouldn't have had to recoup the hefty purchase price of the film.

"Films die on the vine because distributors don't put them in the right theaters, because they don't design television ads that connect to the audience the film was actually made for, or because they have relationships with ad agencies and theater chains that aren't right for that particular movie," Bernard concludes. "It may be they have obligations related to commercial product that they have to play in commercial theaters instead of art theaters, or they may have people working for them who are just not familiar with a specialized type of release."

STARLESS COMEDY'S TOUGH ROAD

Typically any film that has high playability in front of audiences has a good shot at attracting interest. Oddly, however, the indie films that have the toughest time landing distribution are not low-budget homages to *Saw V* or *30 Days of Night* but light romantic comedies without recognizable stars. "Independent comedies are often very difficult to sell because comedies by nature are often not the best-reviewed films of the year," explains Ortenberg. "And indie comedies sometimes fall into a 'tweener' category of not really arthouse pictures but also not big or broad enough to play in the big commercial multiplexes. That makes independent comedies among some of the toughest sells in the business."

Berney has a similar theory. "I think romantic comedies are really tough because people tend to think of independent films as edgy or really outrageous, and when you have something that's sort of beautifully sweet, critics often dismiss it or simply don't care," he says. "Even if they like actually like it, they won't want to admit it, since it's into the 'nice' film territory. I think *Greek Wedding* changed the landscape a bit and distributors started to say to themselves: 'Wait a minute, maybe there *is* an audience for nice,' but generally when you have a first-time director and no stars, it's a really tough sell. Independent films have to have either four-star reviews or solid word of mouth to perform, and if these films don't work, you don't have any ancillary because you don't have a star, a hook, or anything. So it can be a risky business to try to release a comedy without any stars. If you are going to try it you just put everything forward and sometimes it works, sometimes it doesn't."

While studio-produced R-rated comedies such as *Superbad* or *Forgetting Sarah Marshall* do not necessarily need stars to succeed, Cinetic Media founder John Sloss says that starless romantic comedies produced independently often fall into that dreaded "tweener" category. "The classic example is a film that is for all intents and purposes a mainstream movie with a no-name cast, which if it were made by a studio with Cameron Diaz would gross $60 million," he explains. "These light romantic comedies get made all the time but nobody's going to release them. Nobody's going to buy them because specialized distributors don't have enough money to pledge $20 to $30 million to buy awareness, and *Greek Wedding* notwithstanding, few distributors are going to take the risk to buy awareness for a romantic comedy with no stars in it, no matter how good it is."

Distributors would rather see a darker, tougher movie that has real awards potential like *Half Nelson* than something that's more mainstream, explains Micah Green of Creative Artists Agency. "*Kissing Jessica Stein* was a tough sell to distributors. Cinetic Media tried to position it as the female Matt-and-Ben story and interest distributors based on that. And they eked it out, and the film sold for a little less than $1 million. Today very few specialized distributors are looking for the next *Kissing Jessica Stein*. They are looking for horror films because they feel like they can pretend those are bigger movies and release them as big broad genre projects, like *Cabin Fever*, but for the most part, the rest of the indie sector is focused on awards and really high-profile auteur films. No one wants the rest of the stuff."

HOW A WEDDING WORKED

While the release strategies of specialized distributors may seem like alchemy to uninitiated filmmakers, there are some simple tenets of launching a film that all distributors adhere to. Foremost in that decision-making process is choosing the right opening weekend to find an interval of at least a week without direct competition in the same genre and clear of any tent-pole films such as *Transformers 2: Revenge of the Fallen* that appeal to a wide audience. Obviously opening a low-budget love story on the same day that a major studio is kicking off a date movie with Cameron Diaz or Katherine Heigl is probably risky. Similarly, opening a tiny indie drama on the same weekend that a highly anticipated blockbuster hits theaters may also be problematic since Hollywood "popcorn releases" can suck up every ticket sold on their opening weekends. The challenge is that there may only be one or two weekends per quarter that are truly free of competition.

"Getting a foothold in a crowded marketplace is really a challenge," explains Berney. "For example, when we opened *Whale Rider* we were careful to be one of the only independent films opening that day. But that rarely happens. On Friday, July 25, 2003, there were something like eighteen films opening in Manhattan, including some really big ones like *Seabiscuit* that had upscale audience appeal. That's hard to compete against, so it's really important for distributors to pick the right date where they may be able to own the market—if only for a brief moment—to get the film established. In early summer 2008, we opened *Mongol* in a relatively uncrowded indie marketplace, and it performed quite well, even though the studio tent-pole titles were making the general schedule very busy. The specialized audience and theaters were starved for interesting films. Sometimes you just can't do it because it's kind of crazy nowadays to find a free weekend."

Although his strategy is no secret, Berney has had a golden touch when it comes to releasing Spanish-language films such as *Pan's Labyrinth* and *Y tu mamá también*, and challenging pictures such as *Memento*, *Monster*, and *My Big Fat Greek Wedding*, which prior to release was considered by many to be a theatrically unreleasable made-for-television movie.

"In a typical independent platform release, we monitor the initial reviews and adjust the marketing spend and expansion after the first weekend or possibly the first two weeks," explains Berney. "If reviews are strong and business is good, we may add a few more theaters but try to wait at least two weeks." We've found that if we really let it sit for a while and continue to let the word of mouth spread, that's better than expanding wider the very next week. And the same thing applies as we go into other cities. We may add more cities or pull the film from certain theaters depending on the grosses. We feel like word of mouth has to be really strong because that's what's going to sell your film. If you read a brief description but then somebody tells you, 'You have to see this performance, you have to see this film,' that is what it's going to take to make a film successful. Critics and marketing will get people in the first weekend, but ultimately audiences have to really love the film and talk about it."

While filmmakers are out raising money, they will repeatedly cite *My Big Fat Greek Wedding* as a shorthand for indie films that make their investors fabulously wealthy, but very few know how the 2002 hit achieved its $354 million worldwide gross, other than the fact that it somehow connected with an underserved segment of older adults who rarely went to the movies. The truth is the film's distribution strategy played a critical role in its huge grosses, much of which might have been left on the table had a different approach been taken.

"One of the most important keys to the success of *Greek Wedding* was restraint," Berney says. "We moved slowly and selectively to increase the number of theaters, even as the film's receipts kept climbing, which ensured that the initial theaters were always packed. Comedy plays best in a full house, so having consistent sold-out shows made the film an event rather than just another movie, and it made certain theaters a destination for this event. This was true in all the cities where it was playing and was very important because people started going again and again with friends early on and they always knew the theater where the film was playing."

The takeaway for impatient filmmakers who don't understand the dynamics of specialized "platform" releases is that slow and steady wins the race.

"The producers at Playtone really understood this on *Greek Wedding* and it was tremendously helpful having marketing partners of their level work with us on this very unique plan. We moved very selectively to increase the number of theaters, even as the film's receipts kept climbing and even as everybody wanted us to go bigger and wider—fast," explains Berney. "It's counterintuitive because the temptation would be to say, 'Great! Let's blast it out, now that it's working!' And everybody, including the theater owners, wanted us to do that. But we kept that go-slow philosophy even as we went wide. We didn't go super-wide, and always kept it selective in terms of the theaters we chose even as we hit $200 million. By having it stay in the theaters where it was playing as long as we could, people could say, 'Hey, let's go see *Greek Wedding*,' without having to look in the paper.

"But it was also really selective in terms of the theaters we booked it in. The other thing was our ability to be very flexible. In other words, even when we opened in eight markets, we took a hiatus for a couple of weeks because during Greek Easter, the Greek community really just goes to church. So we stopped and waited and added theaters two weeks later. This restraint was not easy to pull off with everyone, including theater owners in other cities wanting to play the film right away," Berney continues. "So to be able to say, 'Okay, we'll wait. We'll take *this* market, but wherever there's a big Greek community, we'll wait two weeks and do whatever it takes to accommodate audiences,' is a strategy that major studios have historically not been able to execute because their stakes are much higher and their plans are often inflexible."

Many of Berney's biggest indie success stories have employed a wait-and-see approach that doesn't always stick to a set expansion schedule. "*Memento* was another really great film that ended up making $25 million with the same type of restraint," Berney continues. "With *Memento* we had a long-lead planning campaign that we worked on for a year, with a big Internet component to the marketing."

The producers and financiers of the film, Newmarket Capital Group's Will Tyrer and Chris Ball, truly had made a bold move in financing and producing *Memento*. They were correct in judging the audience's sophistication but ran into issues with the distributors and gatekeepers at the time. No acceptable offers were made, and they decided to put their money where their convictions were and finance the domestic release of the film as well.

Weekly per-screen averages are another metric that distributors use to judge the initial success of any film. If an independent film is earning $20,000 per screen or more, it tends to be in good shape, while $15,000 per screen is considered passable, and anything less than $10,000 per screen spells trouble. "There's no hard-and-fast rule. It really depends on the competition that weekend in the specialized marketplace," explains Bob Berney. "For example, in most of 2008, the grosses were mediocre, so a $15,000 weekend really stood out." The problem for smaller independent pictures is that they need several weeks to catch on or connect with their audiences, while high-profile specialized films with recognizable cast members—such as *Good Night, and Good Luck*; *Crash*; and *Little Miss Sunshine*—have raised per-screen average expectations for the entire sector. "When you see an independent film doing $20,000 per screen on 160 screens, I think that kind of sets the benchmark," says Cassian Elwes of William Morris Independent. "So if your movie opens and you only do $3,000 per screen, then your movie is never going to work. Theaters will move on to the next one since there's a plethora of independent films to choose from. The more successful independent films these days set the bar for the level of business one has to do to have some kind of staying power, and every year there are more and more releases waiting in the wings. You go to Toronto and there are forty movies looking for distribution."

The costs associated with marketing and the number of competitive, often exceedingly well-made films still looking for distribution after any major festival has created a "speed-dating effect" where any number of hiccups or blemishes can get a film cut from a distributor's short list. After all, acquisitions executives have to take a much harder look at which independent films are actually worth not only the purchase price but the required marketing expenditure, which is where distributors are forced to take the biggest risk. Meanwhile, studio spending to "buy the grosses" during a film's opening week have driven up what specialized distributors need to spend just to "break out of the clutter" and get on moviegoers' radar screens.

"The costs are still going way up for us, and it becomes very risky for specialized distributors because one misstep can wipe you out," explains Berney. "Just going out with your film too big, too strong, picking the wrong release date, or getting clobbered by the competition on a particular weekend can be very costly. It's getting to the point where people can get nervous about even releasing a film at all since you've got to be able to pick your release date exactly right."

HAVING TO GO IT ALONE

One of life's baffling mysteries is why so many well-made indie films that could be breakout hits if given the chance are so frequently passed over for distribution. Every year there are hundreds of completed films that look great and work artistically but simply don't make the cut for one reason or another. *Variety* and *Vanity Fair* often celebrate daring specialized distributors such as Lionsgate when they take big risks with films like *Diary of a Mad Black Woman*, *Secretary*, or *The Grey Zone*, but the truth is that hundreds of seemingly commercial independent films are forced to consider a range of nontheatrical options when it comes to reaching paying audiences.

"Everyone says the multiplexes are driving out the independent films, and filmmakers think the big, bad multiplexes don't care about art films and are somehow keeping their films from audiences who want something new, but that's really a misperception," explains Weinstein Company distribution chief Steve Bunnell. "I would say it's often the other way around. A lot of times distributors don't want a multiplex booking—they don't even ask for them—because it's not in the distribution plan. For an independent film to play in multiplexes, it needs to achieve a certain level of awareness in the marketplace, and that's usually a function of how much a distributor is spending on advertising."

So what happens when the phone stops ringing and all that's left is a stack of festival applications and piles of shut-off notices and Roxio Toast 9 Titanium–burned DVDs? The good news is that digital projection in Emerging Pictures–affiliated theaters—like New York's Thalia and the larger 800-seat Symphony Space, and competing venues in Los Angeles such as the American Cinematheque, Landmark, Laemmle's Sunset 5, and Aero theaters—and Amazon's DVD publishing initiative with its subsidiary CreateSpace are opening up new avenues for independent films that do not attract offers from leading specialized distributors.

With the development of ever-more sophisticated digital projectors—such as Sony's advanced CineAlta projection systems installed in AMC movie theaters in Dallas, Indianapolis, and both Riverside and San Diego, California—studio-grade, high-quality digital exhibition is becoming more of a real option. Additionally, new advances in Texas Instruments DLP projectors are being announced every day. This is an important development not to be overlooked, since many indie filmmakers are certain they need to spend $50,000 to $100,000 for a 35mm blowup before they've even been accepted to a festival in order to put their best foot forward. These filmmakers may also be overlooking the fact that several theaters at Sundance and hundreds of theaters around the country are now equipped to show movies shot in standard definition or HD that have been transferred to HDCAM, a high-definition version of Sony's Digital Betacam standard.

"It is not necessary to spend big money to transfer to 35mm film before you get accepted into Sundance," explains Stolaroff. "A Fox Searchlight film with a $15 million budget slated for a June release would screen on 35mm. But if you have a small Latino film without a producer rep or agency representation made for less than $1 million, with no certainty that it is going to get picked up, then you are making a big, expensive mistake transferring to 35mm for Sundance, especially if you think potential distributors won't take you seriously unless you screen on film. That is just old-school thinking that will cost your investors and the film's producers a lot of money."

While independent filmmakers may be able to show their digital films using the lower-quality digital projection systems many theaters use to screen preshow advertisements, the obstacle is that most multiplexes in the heartland need to be convinced that giving up a house to a nonrepresented low-budget indie without a studio distributor will be more profitable than simply putting up another showing of the fourth or fifth *Bourne*, which will almost certainly bring in more foot traffic to the concession stand, where theaters make the bulk of their profit margins. Audience disinterest during the slam-bang action-filled summer season can limit the box-office upside of upscale studio dramas and indie films alike.

Ira Deutchman, who, with partners Giovanni Cozzi and Barry Rebo, formed Emerging Pictures in 2003, and one-time president of the IFP's New York chapter, believes that a film-less digital revolution will transform the theatrical exhibition sector just as it has the online video arena. "Emerging Pictures' business model is to take advantage of the fact that there is an enormous amount of quality filmmaking going on worldwide that the current economic structure cannot support," he says. "With the stakes being as high as they are, even the mini-majors can't afford to make, produce, or acquire low-budget movies that don't have built-in hooks like stars, special effects, a high concept—something to pull in audiences—which means the so-called little independent films of today now mirror big studio films. The opportunity that exists in this arena is for someone to strip it down to square one, start all over again, and figure out how you can make a profit with genuinely small movies and not do it the same way everybody else is doing it. So if you can create a new economic structure that can in turn create value for these copyrights, then you're in a position to build a library and build an independent film company with very little investment."

Emerging Pictures installs digital projection equipment in museums and performing-arts centers across the country, and presents independent films at a lower ticket price point to encourage "sampling" among today's finicky art-house audience—given the multitude of distractions from the latest iPhone widgets to Wii Fit and Facebook friend updates. "The institutions that house the Emerging Cinemas (as the theaters are known) already have constituencies that are compatible with our audience," says Deutchman. "They have e-mail addresses and direct connections with their audience, which means we don't have to spend tons of money promoting the programs."

Another option is to look for distribution opportunities with any number of niche cable or pay-television networks that are increasingly gaining in stature and prestige. "Premieres on HBO are seen by more people than maybe 5 percent of all independent films released theatrically," says Sloss. "I think filmmakers are becoming open to new media to showcase their work and I think it's going to be good for everyone. We've certainly worked on films that were sold directly to Blockbuster, that were sold to HBO, or that were sold to premiere on Showtime, but there's this obsession that a lot of filmmakers have with premiering on the big screen." In 2008 Cinetic Media created Cinetic Rights Management

(CRM), to broker the sale, digital encoding, and online distribution of independent films that leave major festivals without traditional theatrical distribution and classic independent films that deserve new appreciation. The division, run by Matt Dentler of South by Southwest and Janet Brown, was set up to supply emerging, well-capitalized VOD outlets and the proliferating online distributors such as iTunes, Netflix, and Amazon.

With independent films like Edward Burns's *Purple Violets* debuting exclusively on iTunes for $14.99 in November 2007 and with direct-to-Netflix titles such as *SherryBaby* having been streamed and rented more than 700,000 times through that service, many indie filmmakers are beginning to look beyond traditional exhibition platforms. "A lot of times a director will say, 'But I want to see my film up on the big screen,' or 'But I want to have a film premiere at Sundance,'" he says. "Well, tell me where your family lives and we'll rent out a theater in your hometown for a night and hold a mini-premiere there."

I'm Not There producer Christine Vachon, author of the bestselling memoirs *Shooting to Kill* and *A Killer Life*, says the most innovative aspiring filmmakers are beginning to think outside of the box about getting their films seen by the widest possible audience. "I think a lot of filmmakers are starting to realize that theatrical distribution is not the be-all and end-all or the Holy Grail," she says. "There are a lot of other ways to get your movies out to the general public that are perhaps more effective, and I think that's the way that independent film is moving."

Yet another myth among independent filmmakers is that if no distributor expresses interest, filmmakers can just self-distribute by getting the closest eighteen-plex to give them a screen for half the proceeds. In truth, traditional movie theaters are not like bowling alleys, where anyone with the right shoes—or an $1,800 35mm print of their first feature—can eventually get a lane. There are often economic factors and long-standing business relationships that prevent unknown directors and producers from securing even the poorest-performing house in the biggest mall-plex in town. Even so, many filmmakers wrongly assume that the local multiplex will free up the screen for half the proceeds or a flat fee, in what is known as a "four-wall" situation.

"Essentially you're renting theater space," explains former Landmark Theatres executive Bert Manzari, now president of film and marketing at Sundance Cinemas. "You pay an exhibitor X amount of dollars to guarantee his 'house nut' for the right to show your film there and then you get to keep the excess above that, so it's essentially renting a theater. A lot of four-walling goes on during Academy Awards season in Los Angeles, when you'll see a lot of pictures staying on screens because they're being four-walled and distributors are doing it to guarantee that their films have theater space."

It is important for aspiring filmmakers to understand the economics of exhibition before they start talking to distributors. The exhibitor's house allowance, also known as the "house nut," is a weekly figure that represents an amount of money agreed upon between the theater and the distributor that is the cost of business for that week. The "film rental" is divided after that allowance has been achieved.

However, while major studios can easily swing such deals in New York and Los Angeles, filmmakers in these and other cities usually find this arrangement prohibitively expensive, even in the few circuits where four-wall deals may be available.

"In Manhattan you could probably find a theater for $10,000 per week but it may be as high as $40,000 or $50,000 per week," says Manzari. "But there has been and still is such a glut of film trying to force its way into the marketplace that I'd say four-walling is becoming a decreasingly viable form of distribution for individual independent filmmakers. At Landmark we didn't do it very much because we were under such tremendous pressure all the time and sometimes the politics became overwhelming. It was really tough to tell distributors we did business with, 'We're going to take your film off a screen to play an unknown film from some guy who just walked in.' The reality is, we never had a shortage of films that needed screens. We had a shortage of *good* films. But we never had any shortage of films to put on those screens."

Even still, filmmakers will point to the local marquee and ask baffled friends and family how is it that independently financed films they feel are subpar managed to secure a screen. "Just because you see specialized product in a multiplex doesn't mean someone is four-walling," says indie veteran Connie White, who started programming independent films at the Brattle Theatre in Harvard Square in 1986 and went on to do theater bookings for several leading art houses, including the Coolidge Corner Theatre in Brookline, Massachusetts, and the Broadway Centre Cinemas in Salt Lake City, Utah. "It more likely means that the big commercial theaters are trying to capture the art-cinema audience in the market that Landmark is in, in addition to playing all the major studio films. They want a piece of every pie, so they may have one or two screens allocated for specialized fare, but the vendors they're dealing with to place them are distributors, not independent filmmakers."

Ironically, specialized theaters that typically play films such as *The Visitor* or *The Diving Bell and the Butterfly* often have fewer screens to spare for the intrepid soul with an HDCAM of their film or a 35mm film reel under one arm. This is especially true now that some art houses are occasionally dipping into mainstream fare to increase foot traffic. "The theaters I book are not multiplexes—one has six screens but many of them have only two or three screens—so they don't have the room to four-wall," White continues. "Somebody could have $100,000 to promote their film and four-wall it, but the theater may not have the ability to say, 'I can free up the screen,' and make that space available."

There are exceptions that keep the four-walling myth alive, but even when it is possible, the cost can be prohibitive. "A press screening in most American cities can cost $600 to $800, but in Manhattan it can be triple or quadruple that number, per screening," explains Steve Bunnell of the Weinstein Company. "In a smaller situation—a smaller theater or a smaller community—it can be half of that number. It's just raw economics. Theaters get as much as they can and typically whoever's paying tries to pay as little as possible. If you're talking about daytime screenings where they are just opening the door, that's one thing, but a full-on four-wall situation would usually cost much more than that."

"The truth is, though, they can't free up the screen because there are just too many films lined up on the runway waiting, and it's not an economic issue, oddly enough," says White, who founded Balcony Releasing in 2002 to help plan theatrical distribution strategies for independently produced documentary features such as *Daughter from Danang*, *The Same River Twice*, and *Sir! No Sir!* "So a filmmaker who just shows up with a 35mm print of their film in New York, L.A., Boston, Chicago, or a top ten or top twenty market and expects it to get a proper theatrical opening run is going to have a tough time finding a screen even if they have money. If a filmmaker wants to rent a theater for a onetime showing on a weeknight or weekend matinee there would be lots of opportunities for that—but to occupy a screen for a one-week run is a different matter."

With no distributor-backed offers in sight and four-walling increasingly limited, it often makes more sense for filmmakers to quietly pay a distributor to get a scrappy indie film up on screens in what is referred to as a "service deal" or rent-a-studio arrangement. These deals can work to attract audience interest but they have had an uneven track record, as evidenced by the dismal box-office performance in 2005 of *Harsh Times*, an intense crime thriller that writer-director David Ayer reportedly financed by taking out a $2 million mortgage on his house. The release of *Harsh Times* was repeatedly delayed in mid-2006, and grossed only $3.3 million theatrically after playing for just thirty-one days in November and December of that year. More recently, the *failure* of *Bottle Shock* called into question the efficacy of service deals.

This may have been a result of that film's shortcomings or it may have been a result of broader pressures facing the specialized sector that led Paramount to absorb Paramount Vantage and Warner Bros. to shutter Warner Independent Pictures and Picturehouse after absorbing New Line Cinema in 2008. However, the reason service deals don't work is simply because the distributors releasing the movie may not be as invested or vested in the movie's success as the filmmakers, and with less on the line they may not try as hard. Additionally, independent films released through service deals are often movies that have failed to get distribution through traditional acquisitions, so they may be inherently less marketable and more difficult to sell to audiences. Of course, there have been a number of historic and headline-grabbing service deal successes, many distributed by Bob Berney, who at various companies raised the bar on the definition of success for independently financed films. Berney, who started his career in exhibition and worked at the Inwood Theatre in Dallas for four years before running

Newmarket, was able to increase the scope of the projects and the size of the releases from the outset at Picturehouse because of the backing of HBO and New Line Cinema. But he will always be renowned for challenging the conventional wisdom and making hits out of *Memento*, *Greek Wedding*, and *The Passion*, among others, films that were thought to be uncommercial if not unreleasable by distribution executives who had refused to take them on.

However, BitTorrent, Netflix, Amazon Video on Demand, and other websites continue to open up opportunities for aspiring independent filmmakers to exhibit their films beyond their immediate circle of friends. And as broadband speeds in U.S. homes migrate from 8 to 10 megabits to Fios, the 100 megabits available via fiber-optics in Japan and South Korea, Internet content will be able to be downloaded with the speed of HBO On Demand heralding a new era of indie feature-film content distribution via the Web.

"Historically there were only a few doors to get content to a large number of people, and those doors were typically slammed shut. Today there are numerous outlets to really satisfy some needs that people have to be heard, either by like-minded individuals or by a large number of individuals looking for user-generated content," says BitTorrent CEO Ashwin Navin. "So the ability to create, the ability to edit, and the ability to distribute content has been democratized and the last piece comes as a result of BitTorrent most prominently, and some other mechanisms having surfaced as well. The environment where marketing is likely to take off first is MySpace, Facebook, YouTube, where there are huge numbers of people associating with each other around similar interests, and they can build a community around their product and market themselves more effectively. The community aspects of MySpace or Facebook make them more powerful than any other community on the Web."

Navin suggests that independent filmmakers will soon be able to attract significant global audiences, much in the same way that bloggers have acquired significant followings today, especially if filmmakers can make inroads into communities such as Playstation 3 Home, LinkedIn, Twitter, Plaxo, and Xbox LIVE. For example, a Facebook-sponsored online film festival underwritten by HP, Cisco Systems, or Microsoft could be "attended" by literally millions of users, rather than the tens of thousands who attend traditional festivals such as Sundance.

The technology is already in place. BitTorrent started offering filmmakers the ability to post full-length motion pictures on its site in February 2007. Content creators do not require a home server, and need only to have their films already posted on a public-facing website to be mirrored on BitTorrent alongside content from leading Hollywood studios. "We've now come very close to basically opening the door to any filmmaker to publish right off their desktop with a taxonomy by category, by genre, and then by 'tags' as well, so there's a way for short films and feature films to be organized and browsable from our site," Navin says. "And the other cool thing is that it's not just about movies or television shows or MP3s. If someone produces video in a series, we have a template that allows them to self-publish episodic video. If someone wants to self-publish a music album, we'll allow them to publish multiple tracks within one compilation. So we're trying to be flexible on the templates and then the taxonomy will be something that average people can get their arms around. It won't be too 'techie' or too sophisticated in the way that it's organized."

For aspiring filmmakers, this means that the day may not be too far off when a future entry-level 24p HD camera from Best Buy or Fry's Electronics allows someone to make his or her own *Napoleon Dynamite* or *Cabin Fever* without having to worry about getting into festivals or securing distribution through traditional channels.

"People still underestimate the amount of video that's watched on the PC, whether it's a rented DVD, a video podcast of the nightly news, or short YouTube content," says Navin. "There's a lot of hours spent in front of the PC as a media-consumption environment, driven by the fact that a lot of people multitask when they're watching video now: they've got a Facebook page open, they've got a downloaded video from BitTorrent in another window, and they're chatting with their friends in a third window."

However things eventually shake out, whether moviegoers end up renting indie films on a next-generation Kindle or projecting them on blank walls using pocket-size UltraBrite LED projectors, the filmmakers who are thinking about distribution before they shoot a single frame are more likely to get their movies seen than those who let fortune or fate carry the day.

12. Getting Your Film Seen
SMARTER MARKETING

Although many aspiring indie-film mavericks who claim to know the industry better than anyone maintain that commercial considerations should be secondary or even disregarded completely, the truth is that even the most edgy, novel, and challenging films need marketing hooks to help distributors create movie posters, Internet banner ads, YouTube extras, slide-show podcasts, and teaser trailers. After all, what good is a groundbreaking independent film if nobody ever sees it and appreciates its brilliance? Even films such as Happiness, Requiem for a Dream, Keane, The Living End, and Kids needed marketing campaigns to let people know they were "coming soon to a theater near you." As a result, any filmmaker who fails to consider this important factor before starting out is likely to face an ocean of regret after the harried marketing executive seizes on a less-than-compelling sales pitch or tells the distribution team to pass altogether because the marketing department can't really visualize an effective campaign that will help the film open. Indeed, if anyone beyond the filmmaker's immediate family is ever going to see the film, it needs to *be advertised and pitched to increasingly fragmented audiences with more entertainment choices than ever before. Filmmakers also need to have some idea of how they plan to market their film effectively at festivals so audiences will actually attend frequently inconvenient screenings and help generate that all-important festival buzz. Simply putting up lime-green* Lost Dog *flyers or handing out postcards is no longer a viable approach, now that PR-savvy filmmakers are pulling out the stops. As a result, even the edgiest would-be auteurs need to come up with poster ideas, an ad campaign, and a smart approach to marketing long before they start shooting or casting. Coming up with a hip campaign or a clever gimmick, such as Lionsgate's partnership with the American Red Cross and Yahoo! to encourage* Saw V *audiences to give blood, should not be considered crass commercialism but an integral part of the process filmmakers need to embrace.*

There are three additional questions all filmmakers will ultimately have to answer: What is the film offering or selling to the audience? (Is it romance, redemption, catharsis, a night in a haunted house, or a gritty examination of the human condition?) Who are the primary and secondary audiences for this film? (Is it single women eighteen to twenty-four, thirtysomethings on their second date, African American couples, underserved adults, gore-mongering teen boys who would rather be playing Dark Space *or* Resident Evil 5, *or some other readily identifiable demographic?) And, finally, does the film have high marketability (such as name stars that will attract a fan base) or high playability? (Is it rousingly entertaining, once people get over their skepticism about seeing it?)*

Even though the affordability of 24p HD cameras and ultra-fast computers have put the tools of production within easy reach of just about everyone, many first-time directors and producers are in for an unpleasant surprise at the end of the indie-film rainbow. The cost of marketing and distributing independent films in theaters has risen so high that each year a smaller percentage of completed indie films ever reach movie houses. Independently financed films will increasingly debut on Netflix, Movielink, Amazon Video On Demand, or various pay-for-download services, but without theatrical distribution, the paydays from network television and DVD are diminished, as are the chances that a filmmaker will be able to recoup his or her investors' money.

"The threshold for what makes a film theatrical these days has definitely changed," says Fox Searchlight distribution chief Stephen Gilula. "The frustration that so many directors and producers feel as a result of not getting their films released is a result of the distributors—who have to risk a significant investment to put the film out—not being convinced they will be able to get audiences into theaters."

Therefore, it is both the best and worst of times for independent-film directors and producers. Making a glossy-looking debut has never been easier, with cameras such as the Red Scarlet, Sony EX1, or Panasonic HPX-170, but getting films out to the public remains a puzzle. "The business of independent cinema has been difficult these last few years because the cost of marketing has skyrocketed to such a degree that it costs a lot of money to put out even the smallest movies," says *Pulp Fiction* producer Lawrence Bender, who went through a period of financing low-budget Sundance entries such as *The Chumscrubber* and *An Inconvenient Truth*, following his successes with *Good Will Hunting* and *Kill Bill 1 and 2*. "In some ways it's harder to get distributors to pick up the smaller movies, but on the other hand almost every distributor is looking for that small movie that can turn into a huge hit, so it's something of a paradox."

Of course this wasn't always the case. Indie-film acquisitions executives used to make their bones by taking a huge risk with dicey choices—movies such as *The Crying Game*, *Welcome to the Dollhouse*, *Twin Falls Idaho*, *Smoke Signals*, *Star Maps*, or *Hard Candy*—that were long shots, marketing be damned. Today, however, with so many advertising dollars riding on each indie release, major distributors won't even consider a film unless their marketing team believes in it.

"A film can absolutely be its own best asset and that's really the best sort of movie to have," explains Miramax president Daniel Battsek. "A film that gets fantastic world of mouth, that you can screen and use the audience seeing it to build on advertising, is really what you're looking for. Of course, if that's all the film has, if there's no other way of positioning that film, then you can screen the hell out of it and you're never going to get enough critical mass to break through. And so I think the ideal is that you've got a film that has something to sell and it plays very, very well. *The Diving Bell and the Butterfly* was certainly a film that fit into that category. We screened *Diving Bell* for French groups, literary groups, and cinema groups, and for the medical community because I think it had such a hopeful message for people treating serious illnesses. And by doing that you're taking the movie out of the core audience and showing it to a different group that maybe doesn't usually see a subtitled movie, and then suddenly you're breaking through a barrier. If you have a movie that can cross over or break through or go beyond the borders that you would normally see, then you should definitely think of that secondary audience."

The catch-22 is that while independent films are by definition "alternative" and in some cases made in defiance of easy positioning and zippy taglines—try distilling the power and elegance of *The Lives of Others* down to a single sentence—filmmakers who don't understand mainstream marketing issues or who thumb their noses at them may never get a chance to make a second or third film. "Some filmmakers say, 'Hey, man, it's not about the box office,'" says Neil LaBute, writer-director of edgy projects such as *In the Com-*

pany of Men and *Your Friends & Neighbors*. "I've even said that, too. But the truth is you're not making films so you can show them in your basement to a few friends. You're putting your films out there as popular entertainment and hoping there's going to be a greater audience for them."

Some first-time filmmakers confront buyers or even their own investors with the keeping-it-real attitude of the Misunderstood Artiste: "This project isn't going to make any money. This film is a prestige project and isn't going to earn any more than *Raising Victor Vargas* or maybe *Half Nelson*, regardless of what we spent on it, and that's the way we want it." But these would-be Andy Warhols are forgetting two rules that apply to indie-film economics even more than they do to major Hollywood releases: that great art won't affect anyone if nobody ever gets to see it, and that the film business is in fact a business, not a charity or a patronage.

Layer Cake director Matthew Vaughn says, "I always wonder about the filmmakers I meet who say it's not about the box office. I wonder: 'Then why are you making a movie?' With *Layer Cake* we had intentions of making a movie that people would go see and that was always the plan."

And while many indie filmmakers secretly dream of sales on the scale of $10 million for *Hamlet 2*, $9 million for *Hustle and Flow*, $7 million for *Son of Rambow*, $5 million for *Choke*, or $4 million for *Waitress*, very few actually understand the financial realities of contemporary movie marketing and how a distribution contract's all-important marketing section can impact an indie film's visibility and profitability.

"We tell every filmmaker we work with: it's not about how much money you get at a festival but what actually happens to your movie once it's released," says Cassian Elwes of William Morris Independent, who has repped indie milestones such as *Sling Blade*. "If you've spent a year or two working on something, you don't want to see it over and done with in a flash. But that is what can happen."

Donnie Darko producer Adam Fields agrees. "The way movies open and close these days, if you miss the strike zone with the marketing you're dead," he says. "You may only have one week to prove yourself, and in some cases you don't even get that." And though it ultimately became a cult film on DVD and BitTorrent for generation Y, in its initial theatrical run *Donnie Darko* grossed only $64,000 during its opening weekend and was quickly pulled from theaters. Marketing executives from competing distributors would likely explain that the film's poor showing meant that its marketing campaign was selling the wrong message, not connecting with its target market.

Even a movie as popular as *Juno* could have been lost in the crush of specialized films released in the fall and winter of 2007 had it not been so well positioned and deftly marketed by Fox Searchlight.

"A film like *Juno* can absolutely be overlooked or disappear before positive word of mouth can build, benefiting DVD sales but missing out on the kind of visibility that happens with a successful theatrical release," explains the film's producer Lianne Halfon. "We did a film like that. *Ghost World* was discovered by most audiences after it was out of the theaters. The critics loved it when it came out and the reviews were overwhelmingly positive, but it didn't do nearly the box office that it could have because it just didn't have the kind of specialized marketing and positioning that it needed."

Ghost World, a film that was tonally similar to *Juno* in many ways, started out with a very strong per-screen average of $19,758 in five theaters in July 2001 but was platformed out to only 128 theaters at its widest point in September 2001 and grossed only $6.2 million theatrically, despite almost universal critical acclaim.

"United Artists didn't have a strong sense of how *Ghost World* was going to play before it was released, and it wasn't really until they did the first test screening that they had a sense of that film," recalls Halfon. "Plus, there was an entire change in the administration of United Artists from the time of that first test screening to the release date and the new team did not have enough time to build a marketing strategy. There is no question that with each success of these break-through indie comedies, there is more astute marketing and more money available for the potential crossover release that Fox Searchlight has mastered."

The production company Mr. Mudd had a dramatically different experience with *Juno*, which grossed more than $140 million domestically. "With *Juno*, Fox Searchlight had an understanding of the marketplace and they were proac-tive, not just reactive," explains Halfon. "They didn't wait to see what the reviews were and how people responded after the first four weeks. Searchlight already had a sense of how the film would play by the time they opened it, and they secured the theaters needed to take advantage of the fact the film plays not to one specific audience but to several audi-ences. It's an unusual in that it plays very well to teenagers Juno's age but also plays very well to people who are the age of the stepparents and the adoptive parents. Searchlight didn't choose one audience over the other, they went after all of them. And because they correctly identified their audience before they opened, there wasn't the delay in tailoring the marketing that crushes so many independent films—where by the time there's a critical mass of awareness, the film is gone."

What scares independent filmmakers who have been through a theatrical release is just how close blazing failure and meteoric success can be to each other. A wonderful movie that is poorly or modestly marketed, such as *You Can Count on Me*, can underperform or even crash and burn, while a flawed project with a bulldozer campaign or terrific marketability, such as *The Blair Witch Project*, can become a huge box-office hit. "Filmmakers can actually start marketing their movie the moment it goes into production by creating a website, by courting various types of journalistic coverage—since there are a lot of periodicals and publications that cover films in production like *Filmmaker Magazine*—but more often than not in the independent world people spend most of their time drumming up financing and trying to get the film made," says Senator Entertainment's Mark Urman, former president of THINK-Film. "It is really possible to get your film on the radar screen the minute you call 'Action,' but most people just don't think about it that way. Filmmakers often approach marketing and publicity on a catch-as-catch-can basis even though they have the same goal ultimately as the businessmen they want to distribute their film: to attract a significant audience."

WHAT MARKETING COSTS IN REAL DOLLARS

In the studio world, marketing budgets easily run $15 to $25 million regardless of the cost of the film, and can even go as high as $75 to as much as $200 million for tent-pole blockbusters like *The Dark Knight*. In the specialized sector, marketing budgets range from a low of $150,000 at some of the smaller distributors to the low millions for a mini-major committed to a film's release and a subsequent Golden Globes or Oscar campaign. But while these numbers may be a fraction of what a Hollywood studio spends to promote a summer popcorn flick such as *Iron Man*, there is consensus in the independent sector that marketing costs have gone through the roof.

"The competition is fierce and each company feels like it can't afford to be outdone," explains Sony Pictures Classics copresident Tom Bernard. "It's not like the rising tide raises all boats either, it's kind of the opposite. I don't think you're seeing grosses going up across the board, but marketing spending sure is up."

Previous generations of specialized moviegoers have begun to have children and are turning to Netflix, TiVo, on-demand options, and box sets of *Scrubs*, *Family Guy*, and *Weeds*, among others. Younger moviegoers are spending hours each week playing *Braid*, *World of Warcraft*, and *Mass Effect* rather than going to the movies. Others are downloading movies from Xbox LIVE and PlayStation Home rather than heading out to the theaters. People just have so many options fighting for their leisure time and leisure dollars that filmmakers and studio executives have to really be able to *convince* the public to see their movie. And making noise when releases are up against studio films is more difficult than ever.

While a major studio release usually opens on 2,000 and sometimes 3,000 screens, indie films often still receive a more limited platform release to test the waters and build slowly, rather than going for that all-or-nothing opening weekend. For example, the low-budget musical drama *Once* opened on just two screens in May 2007 and expanded week by week to 20, 60, 95, and 120 screens; peaking on 150 screens in August 2007, before dropping down to 81 screens in late September; 65, 57, 25 in October; and finally 9 screens in November of 2007. Most independent films don't enjoy the benefit of a seven-month platform release, but those that do can slowly build word of mouth and become a must-see for discerning audiences.

Depending on the initial numbers, an indie studio will either increase or cut spending planned for additional markets as well as the dollars allocated to sustain the initial run.

To establish how much they are going to spend marketing a film, indie distributors make a list of comparables— similarly themed films that performed well in recent years— and then back up into how much they can afford to spend to achieve those same results. For example, an unreleased independent film about an aspiring ballet dancer living in Spanish Harlem could be benchmarked against a spectrum of ascending financial outcomes of *Girlfight*, *How She Move*, *Dance with Me*, *Honey*, *Step Up*, *Save the Last Dance*, and *Dirty Dancing*. Since it is unlikely that any film on the subject would ever unseat *Dirty Dancing* as the box-office champion or that a low-budget indie made for less than $2 million could match the box-office success of *Save the Last Dance* without the marketing muscle of MTV, realistic comparables analysis would exclude that title. Since *Honey* had a name star in Jessica Alba and *Dance with Me* had Vanessa Williams, the remaining comparable acquisition executives are likely to reference would be *Girlfight*. As a wild card, *Raising Victor Vargas* could be included as a comparable, given the target film's Spanish Harlem setting and likely romantic subplot. When setting up their own lists of comparables, filmmakers should follow the studios' example and be exceedingly conservative about their projections. Including a total wipeout as a possible outcome shows that they are sober and realistic about the projected earnings for their film. In this example, *Girlfight* is probably the comparable that a distributor would weigh most heavily in in any projection.

As part of this exercise, a specialized studio might consider a battery of special screenings to test audience reaction

and get a better handle on where money should go in the
marketing mix to maximize publicity and interest. Audience
testing could prove that the film has struck a nerve or hit the
zeitgeist at just the right time, which could move *Save the
Last Dance* back onto the list of possible comparables. But
because it is statistically unlikely that any new film would
unseat the best-in-class example, it is inaccurate to suggest
that the new film would approach the high side of *Save the
Last Dance*, which grossed $91 million. Conservatism is key
with comparables, and filmmakers should know that audience testing can provide overly optimistic false positives.

"The first problem with audience testing of independent
films is that it costs $22,000 to do a single screening. The
other thing is that specialized audiences tend to self-select
out," says Marian Koltai-Levine, formerly head of marketing
at Picturehouse. "If you recruit for a film like *Vera Drake*,
you're recruiting on an abortion-related paragraph [in
the solicitation flyer or e-mail] with a star named Imelda
Staunton and a director named Mike Leigh. So the only
people who are going to show up are people who have seen
Mike Leigh films, and as a result you're not getting a fair
test. *The Year of the Yao*, a documentary about Yao Ming, is a
film you could consider testing, but you are still getting people who are self-selecting who are basketball fans or part of
Yao's fan base. So instead of audience testing, exit polls can
test the word of mouth." Exit polling takes place with paying
audiences opening weekend, and helps determine the audience composition and quality of word of mouth so the distributor can adjust ad targeting and the media buy.

Even a modest platform release can be pricey, though. A
respectful release in one or two cities can easily cost more
than the production. Before a studio spends $1,000 to $2,000
on a single film print it is likely to have spent something in
the vicinity of $300,000 just to open in one city.

Bob Berney, who planned the marketing and distribution campaign for *My Big Fat Greek Wedding* as a senior vice president at IFC Films, says the amount spent can easily come in at double or triple that bare-bones figure, which filmmakers forget has to be recouped before they will see any overages. "To aggressively open an independent film you think has a real shot, it's very tough to spend under $1 million," he says. "The problem is that a lot of films don't even cost $1 million to make and won't even do $1 million at the box office. A lot of really good films only make $700,000 or $800,000. It's tough out there. You never really know how a film will perform, but by the time we got to the release date on *Pan's Labyrinth*, we knew it would not be seen as or forced into the niche of the typical 'foreign film' category. After its triumphant premiere at Cannes, followed by screenings at Toronto and the closing night of the New York Film Festival, as well as incredible reaction and buzz on various chat rooms and important sites, it was clear it would break out. We just didn't know how far it could go."

These days the marketing costs are so high that even a compelling acquisition can become a financial risk. On a successful film many specialized distributors can end up spending more on marketing than it costs to buy or produce the film. Fox Searchlight spent far more to market *Kissing Jessica Stein*, *The Deep End*, and *The Good Girl* than it cost to actually make the movies.

"First- and second-time filmmakers who are not thrilled with the minimum guarantee that's being offered need to consider that we're also making a sizable, usually seven-figure bet on a marketing commitment," says Lionsgate president Tom Ortenberg. "And so as far as we're concerned, that's part of our investment. The marketing commitment is every bit as important as the minimum guarantee, and we do insist that producers and their sales agents take that into consideration."

Indie filmmakers who receive the luxury of $1 million in prints-and-advertising commitments from their distributors can expect a multi-city push that probably does not include television ads simply because the bulk of any budget under $2 million will get eaten up by fixed costs like posters, film prints, publicity stills and slides, DigiBeta or BetaSP tapes of key scenes for television broadcasters, and 35mm trailers and important newspaper ads in the first two cities.

Internet marketing is becoming increasingly important, especially the inclusion of trailers, desktop wallpaper, and other still photos available on sites such as the Internet Movie Database, Apple, and MovieWeb. And while many studio-created websites are often so complex as to be confusing, the website for *Juno* was a hit with Facebook-focused young adults.

"Searchlight did word-of-mouth screenings and outreach, but they also did the smartest Internet campaign I had ever seen," explains *Juno* producer Lianne Halfon. "They designed a website [the "Junoverse"] that actually seemed designed for the segment of the film's audience that focuses on the Web. And it presented a film that was accessible to many different types of people within that age range and encouraged repeat visits to the site in ways that appeared organic to the tone of the film."

When it comes to generating memorable ad impressions, many marketing executives emphasize traditional media as still the most effective avenue for creating awareness and that all-important "wannasee." "For most people television still plays a very large role, as do print ads in newspapers and magazines, in the movies they go to see," explains Koltai-Levine. "The thing that I worry about, to be honest, in terms of online marketing is that it's so disposable. People may go to *The New York Times* website ten times each day or even have it set up as their home page, and as a result, I'm not sure that those ads resonate, because repeated exposure diminishes the impact. Eventually people say, 'I just went through that,' or they click on the link in the upper right that says 'Skip This Ad.' "

The diminished effectiveness of traditional advertising has only complicated the apocryphal quandary in which a frustrated marketing executive is forced to tell his or her CEO, "I know that 50 percent of our advertising is working, I just don't know which 50 percent." Indeed, as more ad dollars migrate to the Internet, media companies cannot afford to *not* have a significant presence online, especially as the subscriber rolls of daily newspapers continue to decline and given that so many young adults and millennials use TiVo to skip ads and prefer to spend time on Facebook, YouTube, or Xbox LIVE rather than watching traditional TV.

"The problem for the industry is that the ability to measure the effectiveness of online advertising as a driver of theater attendance is still very much in its infancy," explains Fox Searchlight co-COO and marketing president Nancy Utley. "We advertise online because logic tells us that that's where our audience is starting to live and breathe, especially the independent film audience. And we know that people are consuming more and more of their information and news on the Internet as well as engaging in a lot of social networking. But just looking at Internet 'click-through rates' and 'numbers of unique users' isn't really a gauge of effectiveness right now, as far as advertising that drives people to go to the movies.

"For TV advertising, we have decades of information that tells us how different ad campaigns translated into tracking, we have research about which ads translated or didn't translate into box office revenue, and we've been looking at those same advertising reach and frequency numbers and TRPs [targeted rating points] and tracking data for decades. So as an industry we have a handle on what network and cable TV can do in terms of driving audience interest. But we just don't have those kind of tools for the Internet, or they're still developing, so we're often going by our gut and just hoping the steps we're taking are effective, even though we may not yet have a clear understanding of how our advertising is translating—or not translating—into moviegoing behavior."

And while sites such as Google, Amazon, Netflix, and iTunes can track and record a wealth of consumer data whenever an online search query, a banner ad, or an e-mailed marketing message "converts" into an online purchase, the ability to track consumers' buying behavior from their computers to their neighborhood theaters is not yet in place. Even Fandango and AOL Moviefone cannot, in most cases, track what ticket buyers on their sites were thinking or seeing before deciding to make a purchase decision.

"Today we can tell if a consumer visited a website for one of our films, but because people don't self-report their behavior very accurately, when you poll to see why someone decided to go see a movie, they can't really tell you," continues Utley. "So if you poll people and ask, 'Why did you decide to go see *Choke* this weekend?' to measure the effectiveness of your online advertising, our experience is that people can't accurately tell you why they decided to see something. They might say, 'I heard an ad on the radio,' even though there weren't any ads on the radio. What they heard was a local DJ talking about the movie. Or another person might say, 'I saw a trailer,' and you think they mean a trailer in a theater, but when you probe a little deeper you find out that they had actually seen a TV spot rather than a full trailer. Or maybe they saw a TV spot and a NewYork-

Times.com banner, but the problem is they often can't accurately tell you which one of those ad messages pushed them to the theater that day. So as an industry we just have a lot more work to do to try to determine what online activities really do, in terms of translating into box office. I think it's also incumbent upon the people actually selling online advertising to go out and conduct more research and get more information about how online banner ads and streaming video can be effective, under what circumstances and for what movies. Because right now as far as Internet advertising is concerned, we're still flying blind to some degree."

The Internet is also altering many of the dynamics that used to drive a traditional platform release. Indeed, marketing departments' ability to "cheat the trailer," or position a film in a way that will at least get moviegoers' butts into seats for a film they would actually like if they gave it a chance, is much tougher. Young people's penchant for texting "S-U-X" to everyone in their SIM card or venting their disappointment to their Facebook profile directly from the theater via their iPhones, Samsung Instincts, or Blackberry Pearls has raised the stakes and risks for companies that distribute specialized films.

"Today, word-of-mouth travels exponentially faster than it did even five years ago, so there's not too much marketing spin that can be put on a challenging film, because marketers get found out very quickly. And so the speed that word-of-mouth travels now forces marketing departments to be honest," explains Utley. "All the social networking sites out there today definitely make it easier to get the word out, so it's great when you have a terrific movie like *Juno*, and everyone tells everyone about it very, very quickly. But it's also a double-edged sword because people can find out just as quickly that a movie is disappointing, despite what the marketing has tried to put forward."

The glut of information from sites such as Variety, Ain't It Cool News, IMDb, TMZ, Movieweb, and The-Numbers .com has also raised the sophistication of the average film fan to the point where many see themselves as film critics or arbiters of cinema, rather than specialized film lovers, making the task of marketing indie films harder still. "There are so many blogs and so much information about films out there that any news—good or bad—moves across the Web at lightning speed these days," says Bernard. "Ten years ago, I couldn't have gotten the word out about a movie like *Persepolis*. It would have taken months. Now, news from Cannes and everywhere else is part of everybody's blog. There's news, there's photos, there's live interviews from *The Hollywood Reporter*, everyday people are following the grosses, there's webcams on top of the Palais to watch the red carpet—and so your average college kid knows what's going on at festivals. Somebody turns their laptop around and shows everybody what's going on at a festival. But it also lessens the impact of traditional advertising because people are always multitasking now: they're looking up something online, they're reading e-mail, they're IMing, and they're listening to iTunes or Internet radio at the same time. They are processing about four different pieces of information simultaneously from the Web, and somewhere in there is your film's banner ad."

Because the most dedicated specialty-film audiences live in New York and Los Angeles, these towns are considered make-or-break markets for any indie release. Ironically, however, "New York and Los Angeles are two of the most expensive media markets and you need to run ads—for more than one week—in several different newspapers to get the word out," explains Koltai-Levine.

Most indie filmmakers don't realize that the big numbers involved quickly introduce an element of high-stakes gambling into what is supposed to be an artistic endeavor. "If you're taking out just a quarter-page ad in *The New York Times*, it's going to cost you roughly $27,000, and that's just one day in one newspaper," says former Paramount Classics copresident David Dinerstein, now president of marketing at Lakeshore Entertainment (*Million Dollar Baby*). "The Friday half-page ad on the day you open is going to cost about $53,000, and that's before you put ads in *The Village Voice*, the *Los Angeles Times*, *Time Out New York*, *The New York Observer*, *Newsday*, or the *New York Post*."

On a film with crossover potential, trailers and film prints can add up to $350,000 of the prints-and-advertising budget. "Even if you cut a trailer on your home computer, for the moment you still ultimately have to 'finish' to film and that alone can run anywhere from $5,000 to $15,000," Dinerstein continues. "If you go to a trailer house with a solid reputation, that's going to add another $12,000 to $30,000 before your voice-over artist comes in, adding another, say, $2,000 to $3,000." When a distributor creates 100 copies of the trailer on 35mm, that adds another $3,000. Shipping costs are about $200 per move, so if a film print moves to five theaters during its run, the cost of that print including shipping would total roughly $2,500 each. So a five- to twenty-five-market release could easily cost $500,000 worth of newspaper ads and $350,000 in trailers and prints for a grand total of somewhere around $850,000.

And then there are poster (one-sheet) costs. "Professional one-sheet printing costs are roughly $1 per poster, and the average print run requires 2,000 posters for theaters and maybe another 2,500 to put up on construction sites," says Dinerstein. "That $4,500 does not include design costs, which can be as little as $2,000 if the director designs it or creates it, or between $8,000 and $40,000 if he or she uses a vendor with designers on staff, which they usually do." Each city where the film is playing could add another $2,500 worth of "wildposting" costs to the overall budget, bringing the poster-related costs of a five-city platform release to $45,000 and bringing the marketing subtotal to $895,000.

Finally, out-of-house publicists such as MPRM are often hired by distributors. A New York publicist might handle New York and major national print media, a Los Angeles publicist would service L.A. as well as West Coast–based television and radio shows, and sometimes even a third firm is hired to handle the smaller regional markets. These outside publicity costs can add another $20,000 to $40,000 to the marketing budget. This brings the grand total to roughly $935,000, still without a television ad.

"The cost of hiring outside PR agencies on a film can be a big chunk of the marketing budget," says Jeanne Berney, currently public relations and marketing director at the Film Society at Lincoln Center and former executive vice president of Film and Digital Entertainment at the PR firm of Rogers & Cowan. "Hiring outside agencies for New York, Los Angeles, and regional territories in the top twenty markets can range in cost from $40,000 to $150,000 in fees alone. For instance, many specialists—from Oscar-campaign consultants to celebrity publicists—are often hired in addition to the agency doing the national publicity campaign. Ten to fifteen agencies around the country typically are also hired and paid by the distributor to do regional publicity, and all of this is in addition to the regular publicity line items in a marketing budget, including press screenings, press junkets, public-appearance tours by actors, and film festival premieres." Again, all without a television ad.

"Television commercials can cost anywhere from $200 on public-access cable at 3 AM to about $1 million in prime time during the season premiere of a hit sitcom in the *Friends* mold, and that's just one commercial," says independent-film distribution veteran Jeff Lipsky, formerly of Lot 47 Films. "But because you want people to see a television commercial over and over again to achieve a certain frequency and reach, you've got to run it at least forty to a hundred times during a two-week period."

For those indie films where television advertising makes sense, "you have to spend $500,000 or so to get yourself going, and that's just a ballpark figure," says Koltai-Levine, a move which would raise the aforementioned marketing total to close to $1.5 million.

However, even without television ads, the remaining $50,000 of a $1 million marketing budget is easily spent. A premiere party that attracts press coverage and paparazzi can easily cost $50,000, says Dinerstein. "The costs associated with hair, makeup, and transportation to get an actor worth the time of the paparazzi to a premiere and to the party can cost $10,000 these days." Hotel rooms and airfare for actors on junkets and publicity tours can eat up another $40,000. And then there are the costs of special screenings and Web marketing, which are increasingly part of indie-film distributors' marketing strategies. While Web marketing averaged 3 percent of the total ad budget in 2005 and 2006, the Internet portion of a specialized film's ad campaign has increased to 6 to 10 percent of the advertising budget in 2008 and 2009, a line item that can hit $300,000 or more. "Internet advertising has dramatically increased in cost as buyers migrate from newspaper to online ad space," explains Bob Berney. "For an independent-film release, it varies widely, but the cost can be well over $500,000 for an expensive campaign, increasing as the film grows and expands." On the high side, Fox Searchlight reportedly spent $1 million on Web advertisements for *28 Days Later*, and that was in 2002.

To release a film nationally with television ads, a mini-major can spend $22 million in the two weeks prior to and the week of the film's release, regardless of what the project cost to produce. Screening programs designed to build crucial word of mouth can add $300,000 or more to the marketing line of the profit-and-loss statement of a specialized release. Similarly, audience testing can add an additional $200,000 to expenses that have to be recouped before any overages are paid to the filmmakers. For example, Picturehouse's *Pan's Labyrinth* opened with an initial publicity and advertising budget of $8 million, which increased to $35 million as the film garnered acclaim on the way to its Academy Award win in 2007. "The marketing budgets on *Pan's Labyrinth* and *La Vie en Rose* were prepared, as all Picturehouse releases were, specifically for each film," explains Berney. "There really is no template for these types of films. In the case of *Pan's Labyrinth*, we made a calculated bet that the film would cross over to a younger genre audience and a broad Latino audience in planning our opening spend. *La Vie en Rose* was a more traditional art-house-release budget, however being very aware that the early marketing money was also generating an early awards season buzz." Many times a studio can drop close to $26 million during this same interval because that is simply what it costs to release a studio film nationally.

"In the independent world to aggressively release a film that you think has got a shot in the marketplace, it's very tough to spend under $1 million just to get it open, and a lot of these films don't even cost $1 million to buy at a festival and won't even do $1 million at the box office," explains president Bob Berney. "It's rare that an independent film breaks $1 million theatrically. It's just really tough out there."

For small distributors like Strand Releasing (*The Living End*, *Psycho Beach Party*) or Zeitgeist Films that don't have Focus Features' or Fox Searchlight's marketing budgets, free publicity—reviews and feature coverage—is a factor strongly considered when acquiring the film. "When [copresident] Jon Gerrans and I go to a festival, we search out the critics and poll them to find out what they're going to say about the movie," says Strand Releasing copresident Marcus Hu. "We almost have to know their opinion ahead of time. Is this going to be a critically driven film? Is this going to be something that has a lot of feature article material? Or is there a good marketing angle that can be achieved with only a small amount of advertising?"

Strand, who more recently has had theatrical success with *The Edge of Heaven* and Claude Miller's *A Secret*, gained a significant level of awareness for its Sundance acquisition of Fenton Bailey and Randy Barbato's narrative feature *Party Monster* in 2003, when Barbara Walters did a segment about the then recently reinvented Macaulay Culkin on ABC's *20/20*. Terry Gross of National Public Radio also devoted a segment to the project, which also starred *Big Love*'s Chloë Sevigny and *Robot Chicken* cocreator Seth Green. "A four-minute ad on ABC would cost millions and millions of dollars, but that's in effect what you get for free when *20/20* does a segment about your film," says Hu.

Because the ideal marketing mix involves newspaper ads, posters, trailers, publicists, television spots, screenings, publicity tours, and the Internet, escalating marketing costs can put distributors in an untenable financial position even before opening night.

"When international theatrical [revenue] kicks in and home video kicks in, that helps you out, but when you start figuring the numbers, your P&A can leave you with a hefty exposure," explains Koltai-Levine. "That's why distributors have to be very careful about how they market every film."

Now that even a one-week "flight" of sponsorship on

NPR's *Morning Edition* costs $130,000, Bob Berney warns that distributors can quickly find themselves spending more on the initial marketing than an indie film could ever gross. "But then if you underspend you may never give the film a real chance to get out in the world. That's why if you are entering into a service deal or distributing your film DIY, you have to remember to allocate for success. If you need to support the film beyond the initial markets or its first weeks of release, you can't count on any cash flow coming in from the first weeks from the exhibitors."

In many cases, making an indie film financially viable from the distributor's perspective means either loss minimization or box-office optimization. The goal is to spend carefully so the studio and hopefully the filmmaker can make a profit. This can be difficult because the parent studio charges a percentage of its operating costs to each film it distributes. Many filmmakers may not realize that the tone of the campaign also has to match the type of theatrical release the distributor has planned for the film.

Although it is ancient history now, the theatrical release of *Tadpole* bears revisiting since its failure is instructive. *Tadpole* was promoted in trailers as if it were a commercial film rather than a low-budget indie success story like *El Mariachi*.

Tadpole sold for as much as $10 to $11 million and had a name cast, but it was clearly a modest digital movie, which meant it should have been marketed as an art film for the Lincoln Center and Laemmle's Sunset 5 crowd. Indeed, the film's platform release schedule was designed to attract the specialized moviegoer, but because its ad campaign was aimed at a broader audience, neither group showed up to support the film. Reviews, historically critical for specialized films, were mostly three-star instead of four-star, and the specialized-film audience decided to stay home. As a result,

Tadpole died from a contraindicated marketing plan. This is what distribution executives mean when they say that many independent films need special care and handling in order to connect with their respective audiences. In 2008 and 2009, however, the level of cajoling and convincing required to get specialized moviegoers out of the house seemed to hit new levels.

WHADDYA THINK OF THE GROSSES?

Worries that distributors aren't spending enough to aggressively market a film are one of the most common complaints heard by specialized distributors. However, just as underspending on marketing can cripple a film, overspending can devour any potential profits. "You start small and hope that the word of mouth among the audience that likes it best will allow the film to build and maybe catch fire," says former Miramax president of theatrical marketing Dennis Rice, now United Artists' president of worldwide marketing and publicity. "If you can't get this to happen, you cut your losses and move to video so you will lose less than had you committed significant P&A support. There are times when you work to maximize your box office at the expense of profitability; you've essentially 'bought' the box office since you spent almost as much on marketing as you made."

Many factors can contribute to a studio's decision to overspend on a film's marketing. The first is simply a well-intentioned desire to support the film and increase its box office. A studio may also feel it needs big, splashy ads to massage the ego of a valuable director, star, or producer. Or it may be seeking to garner year-end awards and Oscar nominations, enlarge its market share, or make a statement to the industry at large.

While such lavish spending can help position a film's producers, director, and actors for future projects, this money's-no-object approach is often not the best thing for an independent film's investors or crew members still waiting to be paid because of the fees and charges that eat into theatrical film revenue.

For its services in distributing a film, a studio will take a distribution fee (usually 25 to 35 percent) from the box-office "rentals," the funds returned by theaters to the distributor. The distributor will also deduct marketing, publicity, promotions, and P&A costs as well as the entire advance already paid to purchase the film at a festival. The longer a film stays in theaters, the more these charges add up, meaning that the expenses and overhead charges can often stay one step ahead of the rentals or profits that would theoretically go to the filmmaker and investors.

If the film is still in the red—which it almost always is—the losses from theatrical distribution are deducted against income or profits from other ancillary venues such as home video, television, airline showings, Netflix streams, AppleTV, Amazon Video On Demand, and PlayStation Home. And while revenue models differ in these mediums, they return money to the distributor first before the filmmaker is eligible to receive a dime.

Just as Stanley Kubrick was famous for suggesting marketing and positioning ideas to top Warner Bros. executives, new filmmakers can take a more active approach toward their marketing by identifying the primary and secondary audiences their films might appeal to and then making informed suggestions to indie-studio executives when offers are being made to distribute their film.

"From a marketing perspective, it's important to always go after the core audience first," advises Battsek. "Do not 'stretch' until you have satisfied your core audience. We try very hard first and foremost to let the people who we genuinely believe are going to love a certain movie know it's for them and let them know we don't think we have them in our back pocket. With a film like *No Country for Old Men*, we started out with the Coen brothers' fans and let them know that if they loved the Coen brothers, they were going to get a great Coen brothers film. Then, only after we had satisfied them, we expanded the audience for *No Country* from there. You'll see it all the time where the marketers at a distributor have decided that the core audience is coming anyway, so they'll go for the secondary and third- or fourth-tier audience from the start because they're stretching to reach them: 'They're the ones who are going to give us our profit. We don't need to worry about the core audience. They'll show up.' But that's often not the case."

Bernard advises first- and second-time filmmakers to keep a watchful eye out for break points in profitability that might be eaten up by sudden aggressive marketing in the name of increasing box-office grosses toward the end of a film's theatrical run. "[*Pineapple Express* director] David Gordon Green, who directed *All the Real Girls*, had a real sense of the profit and loss on that picture," he says. "He would call all the time to make sure we weren't spending his profits, because he knew where the profit margin lay."

Koltai-Levine, however, says a filmmaker's gut reaction is to feel as if the distributor that bought their film is somehow letting them down. "You can get into arguments like: 'You're not spending enough money,' " she says, "but most of the time the studio is spending enough. And secondly, it's the studio's money. The important thing for filmmakers to understand is that when you sell a film it's the studio that is putting up the money for P&A, and they're not trying to lose it. They're trying to make more. The studio isn't trying to screw anyone by scrimping on marketing."

The age-old Hollywood law of thermodynamics holds

true for indie films as much as it does for major studio releases: no business, no show. "The economics are basically that you spend a certain amount to generate a certain amount of box office, and the question becomes: If you spend more to generate more box office is there going to be a profit on the picture?" explains Bernard. "At the end of the day the bottom line is going to be did the picture make money?" This profitability, however slight, often has a lot to do with whether an aspiring filmmaker gets to make a second movie.

WHY SPEND SO MUCH

Given Bob Berney's point that marketing costs can easily eclipse the box-office potential of specialty films, how then do distributors stay in business? The answer is that domestic theatrical marketing campaigns are increasingly viewed as loss leaders for ancillary venues such as DVD and are intended to create awareness for a film in subsequent windows of exhibition—television, home video, and in some cases even international theatrical. Historically the theatrical box-office grosses directly impacted the grosses in these mediums as well. Breakout successes do happen, but filmmakers need to remember that indie titles on big-box store shelves are usually the exception rather than the rule.

The theatrical box office is used to establish the number of copies purchased by video outlets as well as the amount that a television network will pay to show the film over a given period. And while studios employ sophisticated revenue formulas when determining their marketing spends, the core principle here is simple: the more popular or seemingly popular a film was theatrically, the more people will want to catch it on pay television if they missed it in the theaters or own it on DVD if they liked it the first time. *"Pan's*

Labyrinth had a tremendous home entertainment release, going well beyond our expectations, even with our record-breaking theatrical numbers and Academy Awards," says Berney. "All the major retailers, including Wal-Mart and Target, did big business on the film, and it's a title that will be successful for years to come as well. However, that's not to say that the general specialized market is easy or growing on DVD. In fact, it's a tough market now, and films have to achieve very strong theatrical box office to have a meaningful life on DVD."

However, Koltai-Levine points out that this sort of benchmarking often applies only to studio films and major breakout successes such as *Little Miss Sunshine* or *Pan's Labyrinth*. "Many indie films have no life on home video," she says. "That's because most art films don't get great video exposure. Often companies like Blockbuster don't want to carry what are perceived to be art films, especially foreign-language films. Ancillary rights on foreign-language films are very limited and it's difficult to get television deals. There's typically no merchandising or licensing, so that's a big challenge." The other problem is that independent films get less than the classic 15 percent of whatever they achieved in their theatrical gross for a network television deal.

For smaller independent distributors, pushing an independent film's theatrical gross over the $2 million mark can mean the difference between a powerhouse Columbia Tri-Star Home Video deal, which could ship a minimum of 50,000 units, and a lesser deal from a small specialty distributor that would be lucky to sell or even ship half that amount.

Because the expenditure involved is so large, distributors often have to judiciously select which of their various films should receive an Oscar push. In the process some indie films, however critically acclaimed, can be slighted. For example, a well-received indie that is released in the spring and arrives on video in the fall may have already returned most of its initial revenue to a distributor. Thus, there may be little incentive for that distributor to mount an expensive Oscar campaign.

"Like someone who educates himself to make a film, I think [filmmakers] should learn more about what an independent film's box-office potential really is," Koltai-Levine says. "If you don't know what you're doing and aren't practical about what your film's grossing potential is, that's when you get yourself into trouble."

THE MARKETING COMMITMENT

Filmmakers blessed with multiple bids for their films often choose distributors based on previously successful films or some vaguely expressed preference for a particular distributor's marketing ideas. However, filmmakers heading to a festival to sell their films should educate themselves first about each company's strengths and weaknesses when it comes to marketing.

Attorney Steven Beer, head of the film division of the New York firm Greenberg Traurig, suggests carefully reviewing a list of prior films with similar elements to determine which distribution companies have succeeded with films similar to theirs. "These precedents provide a useful model and show which distribution company will make the best partner and how to maximize the relationship and the opportunity," he says. "Filmmakers need to do their homework, see what model the distributor is presenting, and decide whether or not it's a good fit for their project. Most clients are so focused on getting their film print ready for a festival screening that they sometimes overlook the importance of understanding the distribution landscape going in."

Before signing a distribution deal, a filmmaker should discuss with potential distributors their initial thoughts on the film's marketing campaign. Which of a film's characters or elements will be highlighted? What are some concepts for the one-sheet? Which of the film's cast will be asked to do publicity? What time of year will the film be released and in how many theaters?

Filmmakers should also note that the answers to these questions, however expansive, will not be guaranteed contractually until and unless they are put in writing. "There is an integration clause in every distribution agreement that says if it's outside the scope of this agreement—meaning if it's not included in this final version of the document right here in whatever paragraph—then it's not enforceable," explains Beer. "Every long-form distribution contract includes that phrase, which means that good-faith discussions occur before signing, but if it's not in the agreement, there's no obligation. I'm not saying they promise things in bad faith, but sometimes when the filmmaker goes back to the distributor and says, 'You promised me X, Y, and Z,' it can be very hard to hold them to that." Indeed, oral representations are almost always superseded by written contracts that negate many deal points that may have been promised during the courtship phase.

What will be guaranteed in a distribution contract are the broad strokes of the distributor's marketing commitment. Generally, distributors will pledge a certain amount on marketing to open the film in New York, Los Angeles, and a specific number of the remaining top twenty markets. Distributors will also usually commit to releasing the film by a specific date, but not always.

"In the past, some specialized distribution arms had a reputation for buying films and then not getting them out into the world or shelving them," explains producer Eden

Wurmfeld. "The thought that something you've worked on for years might actually never see the light of day because the studio has a another film just like it coming out and they don't want the competition, or whatever the reason is, can be pretty terrifying. In the case of *Kissing Jessica Stein*, Fox Searchlight didn't guarantee a specified number of screens or a P&A minimum, but they did guarantee that they would release it in twelve markets, so I was really very happy since we knew that it would be on at least one screen in twelve markets. And when the film was released in 2001, they did everything they said they would and more than they had agreed to contractually."

For filmmakers with multiple offers, the terms of the marketing commitment can be negotiated up. However, consultant Peter Broderick cautiously describes one increasingly common scenario confronting filmmakers who have only one interested party. "At Sundance a few years ago a number of distributors started offering filmmakers token advances or no advances with P&A commitments equivalent to the advances they had previously offered. So rather than give a $400,000 advance, the distributor would offer a $400,000 P&A commitment and a token advance.

"Now on the face of it, this new approach had a certain logic and appeal because filmmakers realized that without a major marketing commitment their movie could just vanish without a trace. But then if the movie doesn't perform well the first weekend, the distributor may come back and ask to be let out of the P&A commitment. The distributor may call and say, 'The movie is just not working, so we want you to reconsider the P&A commitment. If you hold us to it, then the additional dollars we put into it from this day forward will be lost and none of us are ever going to make any money. But if you let us out of it, we may be able to make money on the video.' "

As Broderick observes, this scenario offers the filmmaker an unpleasant choice. "If the film isn't an instant success, should the filmmaker let a distributor out of its P&A commitment and give up on the theatrical release, hoping he or she will eventually receive some returns from television and video sales? If he or she holds the distributor to the P&A commitment, the filmmaker may reduce the chances of receiving a return, since marketing costs have to be recouped before a filmmaker can see a payment from the theatrical performance of his or her film, and risk alienating the company that has control of his or her film for years to come."

WHO HAS MARKETING CONTROL?

Beyond the "numbers" issues that can be spelled out in a distribution contract, a filmmaker must often duke it out with a distributor over input in the marketing campaign. "We went around and around with the poster but decided that we needed to choose our battles and we wanted to focus more on the trailer because we felt like the trailer was what was going to get butts in seats, given that we had a romantic comedy with two women leads," recalls *Kissing Jessica Stein* producer Wurmfeld. "And so we thought if we could kind of draw people in with a really funny trailer, that was going to do more than any poster could do since we didn't have anything to put in the poster that would register with audiences. And generally, I don't believe that people go to a movie because of the poster. I mean, they may want to buy the poster after they've seen the movie, but that's about it."

Lakeview Terrace director Neil LaBute argues that when it comes to marketing, every battle is worth fighting. "Marketing is the place where one has to be tenacious," he explains. "You do have a voice and you have to keep that voice active by letting [marketing executives] know that you're either happy or displeased. Although you may not be able to make the final decision, ultimately you can be involved in shaping it."

Margaret writer-director Kenneth Lonergan saw these tensions firsthand during the release of *You Can Count on Me* in 2000. "I had sort of a noodgy, no-power-except-consultation-and-complaining hand in the marketing and was basically totally ineffectual in determining its course," he recalls. "I would say I was 50 percent happy with how they handled it. They did a very good staggered release, releasing it in New York and L.A. and then kind of built it up from there, which everybody agreed was a good idea. It's called 'platforming,' I think. And then there was this incredibly good response, but rather than saying, 'Hey, we might get this incredibly good response! You know, if we quadruple our advertising budget and spend the money we've made, we could make $20 million on the movie,' instead of the ceiling of $10 million that the film ultimately grossed theatrically.

"I don't think they could have spent more than $1 million or $2 million on advertising, really, for the entire theatrical campaign, and if they had spent $5 million on advertising," Lonergan adds philosophically, "if they had taken a small risk—maybe it would have been a large risk—my guess is that they would done twenty times better with the movie. The movie was probably the best-reviewed movie that year. Out of sheer egotism I read dozens and dozens and dozens of reviews, and I think I read two reviews that were bad out of all of them. People just really seemed to like it but the studio absolutely refused to spend money on more advertising and to go wider with it, which is a shame because I think it could have been a much bigger movie if they had not been so shortsighted. I think the most screens the film was on was 150 screens, briefly, but I think *In the Bedroom* was on 2,000 screens the following year in 2001. But for *You Can Count on*

Me, they basically followed right behind the response and never, never did anything to try to push beyond that. So they didn't do anything negative, certainly, but they didn't do anything extra, either. They had a budget and a projected profit and they weren't going to go beyond that no matter what happened."

Sources within Paramount report that the P&A spent on *You Can Count on Me* was actually $6.1 million for North America, and that the next-highest P&A break point that would have made sense would have been at $15 million, which would have required *You Can Count on Me* to be a $30 million grossing, *In the Bedroom*–level hit in order to break even on that expenditure. These sources also point out that Fox Searchlight's *Once*, one of the best-reviewed films of 2007, followed the nearly identical arc of *You Can Count on Me*, with a platform release peaking at 150 screens and a domestic theatrical gross of $9.4 million, as compared to *You Can Count on Me*'s $9.2 million domestic theatrical gross seven years earlier.

In all fairness, this conservative approach was likely a result of the strictures decreed by Paramount's former chief Jonathan Dolgen, who famously imposed a fiscally conservative approach focused on minimizing risk and maximizing return on investment for capital already spent. One of the easiest ways to do this was to put a cap on marketing budgets and let the chips, or in this case the films, fall as they may.

Unfortunately, independent films need marketing dollars to reach beyond the increasingly fickle and wary art-house audience. The argument against increasing the P&A spent as an indie film does well is that for every additional dollar spent on marketing, the studio needs to recover twice, three times, and soon four times as much revenue in return, since theaters typically start out keeping 60 percent of the box office on small independent films, and then a greater percentage as the film stays in theaters week after week. There-fore, an indie-film distributor can very easily spend all of the profits it has made in its theatrical release only to "gross-up the picture," as the film's earning power almost inevitably tapers off. Indeed, the risk to indie-film distributors with a hit on their hands is that they can quickly plow what would have been a healthy $5 to $10 million in profits into addi-tional marketing that increases the theatrical gross by an incremental amount and actually leaves the studio in the hole or barely at break-even theatrically.

Lonergan acknowledges in retrospect that the previous administration at Paramount Classics may have had its hands tied, in a pre–Paramount Vantage era that predated *My Big Fat Greek Wedding*, *Sideways*, *Juno*, and more recent hits that have shown specialized distribution executives what heights are attainable with careful handling and a heavier foot on the gas when warranted. "I think they didn't have the money, or the parent company didn't ever give them the budget to do something more aggressive," he concedes. "It was a small classics division at the time and I think they projected that they were going to make $2 million profit with it. I think the movie grossed $10 million domestically before home video and DVD. They bought it for $3 million or so, and they probably spent a couple of million on publicity, so they probably made a few million on it. Now I have been in situ-ations, particularly stage productions, where I had a similarly enthusiastic response from audiences, and the play's produc-ers did not even measure up to what Paramount Classics did, and these producers basically let the play die because they wouldn't even do the minimum based on the good response. So Paramount Classics did stay completely at pace with the response, they just never outpaced it or tried to make it big-ger than they had projected it would be initially."

When creating business plans or discussing distribution

goals with specialized film-distribution executives, filmmakers can now look up names of projects they feel are similar to theirs in tone, subject matter, cast level, and production value on Rentrak or The-Numbers.com and create spreadsheets that show the highest screen count achieved, the season in which they were released, and the films' corresponding box-office performance. The dates, grosses, and screen-count data on The-Numbers.com are easily transferable via cut and paste to Excel spreadsheets, allowing aspiring filmmakers to support their positions with hard facts and figures, the foundation of all winning arguments in the increasingly bottom-line-oriented specialized-film industry. With this information in hand, filmmakers can make reasonable projections to their potential investors or confidently push back if a distribution executive suggests a limited release on a tiny handful of screens because no film in that genre has ever grossed more than $5 million theatrically. If the filmmaker feels a proposed release schedule is not aggressive enough for a film they think has the goods, the filmmaker will be able to point out that *Super Size Me* reached a theatrical gross of $11.5 million with its highest screen count of 230 screens, that *Whale Rider* had a $20.8 million theatrical gross by platforming out on 556 screens, or that the exhilarating *Brick* underperformed, possibly because of its shocking finale, challenging patois, or dark sensibility but possibly due to a wait-and-see marketing approach, grossing only $2.1 million on a maximum of 45 screens.

Today the marketing budgets for independent films are significantly higher since the marketplace is so fragmented and the cost of newspaper, online, and especially television advertising has skyrocketed in the last few years. "The marketing budgets for *Vera Drake*, *The Sea Inside*, and *Maria Full of Grace* were about $3.5 million without counting the Academy campaigns," says Koltai-Levine. "You can equate that to a Vin Diesel movie at that time that probably had a budget of $45 million or a film in between which probably spent closer to $20 to $22 million on marketing. These are slim pickings, but since you're only going to get forty cents on the dollar from exhibitors you have to spend judiciously and see what you can do with it."

Because decisions such as these obviously can be tense, some distributors choose to involve the production team in the marketing process on a very limited advise-and-consent basis, or sometimes not at all, a scenario that may not become apparent until after the glow of a big festival sale has subsided and the film is about to be released.

"I think some of the bigger studios want to own the marketing and keep filmmakers somewhat out of the loop when it comes to planning the campaign, but I've always been inclusive in that part of the process," explains Bob Berney. "A lot of times what goes through my head is trying to find out organically where the film came from by meeting with the director, the screenwriter, and the producer, and finding out who they were trying to reach and what they were trying to say. And I usually find that the directors have fantastic ideas about marketing, and how not to market the film as well.

"Guillermo [del Toro] was a great supporter and advocate of the multitiered marketing campaign of *Pan's Labyrinth*," continues Berney. "Utilizing the world's top festivals (Cannes, Toronto, and New York) gave the film a tremendous critical response. At the same time, we presented the film to the genre audience at events like Comic Con and at screenings with Ain't It Cool News, C.H.U.D., and other outlets. He is a director and fan completely at home in both worlds. We also talk to exhibitors, we talk to critics, we analyze the release date and how wide we want to go, the availability of the talent, and what festivals were coming up in the interim. We look at opportunities and we look at the obstacles and try to come up with the plan that avoids the obstacles and maximizes all the opportunities, like a chess game."

Simply finding a weekend free of direct competition or a glut of new releases is one of the biggest challenges specialized distributors face. "It's incredibly difficult to find an open release date these days with the calendar as packed as it is," explains Battsek. "Going back to the early days, there was Miramax, Gramercy, October, and Sony Classics, which was one of the first specialty units. Now there are twenty or so specialized distributors and then there are all of these new financing companies that can make movies and in some cases distribute movies as well. So it's very crowded, making competition one of the most important issues. When we look at how to date our movies, we look at what everybody else is doing, who has movies out there. We tend to have the sort of movies that tend to be released between Labor Day and the end of the year, so our calendar is also incredibly packed."

Having a discussion early on with potential suitors can help allay filmmakers' fears that their film's release may be delayed or that the film could be hastily dumped into the marketplace with little fanfare, depending on the competitive landscape.

"One of the most important things you want to look at is the release date," says industry veteran Dennis Rice. "Knowing that you're never going to get an open window, you try and figure what's the best time of year for the type of movie and who are we going to go up against. You try to navigate around that, but it can be difficult when there's always three or four new independent films coming out every week. You can also be compromised by a studio that picks an arbitrary release date because they see it as an open window and don't realize their campaign might not be ready—say, the trailers don't work—and you don't have enough time for your marketing and publicity plan to work effectively in the marketplace."

PUBLICITY STILLS CAN KILL YOU

One of the most obvious marketing pitfalls independent filmmakers fall into again and again is also one of the easiest to avoid in retrospect: a lack of decent on-set photography to use in publicity stills. *Open Water* producer Laura Lau learned this firsthand when it came time to publicize the film with director-husband, Chris Kentis.

"Lionsgate knew right up front that we didn't have a lot of publicity materials because we had made the film with no crew—we told them we didn't have anything—but it's definitely worth the investment to bring on a still photographer and be really specific about the kind of shots that you want," she explains. "There was a shot of me and Chris on a boat—one that was used everywhere—that looked *terrible*, and the reason is because my cousin shot it. He was using a regular still camera but he didn't know anything about film and he was shooting with 400 ASA, which is fast film, on a very bright day, so the shots were way too grainy. Most of the shots were so grainy they were almost unusable."

Budgeting for an on-set still photographer, even on an ultra-low-budget film, is one of the tenets of smart independent filmmaking that Koltai-Levine and others have spent years urging directors and producers to follow, to no avail.

"It's not even that they don't use the right equipment or that they think that the latest 14-megapixel camera from Staples will do the trick," she explains. "It's more that they don't hire professional photographers. That's the problem. Still photography is the place where filmmakers usually think they're saving money but later on they're forced to pull frames from the film or freeze a MiniDV still frame and it never looks good."

Bad still photography can potentially limit the audience for an independent film, since the poster is usually created from a compelling still that tells the story in one image. Additionally, the publicity photo that runs with the local newspaper's review is often the only marketing "touchpoint" to inspire moviegoers to see the film or skip it, a fact usually lost on filmmakers too busy fighting the pitched battles of production to care. A lack of compelling still images makes twenty-minute Sundance Film Festival slide-show podcasts, like the one on iTunes for Fox Searchlight's *Once*, impossible to create. In an effort to save money, however, filmmakers schedule only one day of still photography rather than having someone on set for several weeks.

"If the photographer is a good guy and is spending a lot of time on the set, getting to know the cast, everybody will feel comfortable with him being around," explains Danny Boyle. "People will do extra things for him, like run a scene again for a still photo and stuff like that, whereas if he's a stranger and brought in for only one day of photography, the actors may say, 'Oh no, I'm not doing that again.'" This makes capturing compelling "true" images of the characters for publicity elements such as splash screens, slide-show podcasts, and screensaver wallpaper almost impossible.

"A lot of times independent filmmakers are so busy trying to get their films made, they're not actually thinking that it's going to get picked up and marketed," Lau says. "They're not planning for that and their resources are so limited for the production that having a professional photographer on the set seems like a luxury. But it doesn't cost a whole lot to take care of that aspect of the production, and I would definitely recommend it. We had no crew whatsoever and no unit photographer on *Open Water*, so the shots we had to use for publicity stills, of the actors with the sharks, were 'pulls' from the film, which was a problem since we shot in MiniDV."

Producers and directors should spend a few hours on movieweb.com and also look at the types of images magazines and newspapers like to publish—photos that look like they are "in action" and where actors can be seen clearly—and set about capturing the shots they need. Unfortunately, festival applicants often believe that they will have time to shoot their publicity stills *after* they get accepted or even after the film is sold, something that is often not possible given that the actors have moved on to other roles and the energy or the vibe they had on set isn't the same after the fact.

The most innovative filmmakers are giving their actors such $150 HD cameras as the Flip Mino HD to record on set making-of materials for the DVD. Other times, an indie film may have terrific on-set photography shot using a 16–20 megapixel high-end digital SLR or a traditional 35mm Canon or Nikon, but for whatever reason a perfect poster shot that could sell the story in a single image was never staged.

"It is surprising how often a film we are thinking of acquiring will have two main characters but no usable photograph of those two main characters in character together," says Fox Searchlight's Nancy Utley, who started out in the business as an assistant media planner at Grey Advertising in New York in 1978. "It's a common oversight because aspiring filmmakers don't consider what the marketing department is going to need."

"Our lack of still photography didn't affect the poster, but it might have, since our actors didn't want to suit up again and get back in the water," Lau says with a chuckle. "Even if they had, it would have been too expensive to fly them back to the Caribbean to use the same shark populations."

Lau advises independent filmmakers to be similarly forward-thinking when it comes to archiving still frames and video elements for website extras, and photo-album slide shows for the eventual DVD or Blu-ray release.

"On each production you need to think 'Who are the key players?' And 'What would I like to see on a behind-the-scenes making-of on E! Entertainment Television or a special feature on the DVD?' What materials do you want that will support your film?" Lau says. "The way it goes most of the time is that the movie wraps and you start to look at what you have that's left, which is why a lot of the material you see on DVDs feels like an afterthought. Instead the DVD should be considered part of your movie and you need to make sure you shoot your additional material before production begins and along the way while you're shooting the film. It's almost like shooting a second feature.

"I remember thinking that on my next project I'll be thinking about the special features right alongside as I'm making my feature so I won't just be looking around for deleted scenes or whatever we can cobble together at the end of a shoot," Lau concludes. "DVD is still important these days, so filmmakers need to come up with something that's really strong—something extra that's going to help sell the film on video."

Of course, first-time filmmakers often don't follow this advice since their hands are already full with the logistics of shooting the film itself. With the expansive capacity that Blu-ray DVDs now provide, extra features such as cast and crew interviews, making-of documentaries, multiple camera angles, alternate endings, video game–like guided tours of various film sets, and other still-in-development interactive features will become an increasingly important part of the home video experience. For a primer on what behind-the-scenes material should be budgeted for and shot-listed, filmmakers only have to rent the WETA-produced comedy-horror film *Black Sheep*, which included a wealth of glossy, well-shot special features, or the making-of segments from *Eternal Sunshine of the Spotless Mind* that can be viewed on the website of Buzz Image (buzzimage.com), or any one of the *Lord of the Rings* multidisc special editions from New Line Cinema.

"We always urge filmmakers to shoot usable behind-the-scenes footage, because increasingly, marketing departments and the filmmakers themselves need interesting elements that they can put on a DVD or put up on the Internet," says Utley. "They can either be segments about what was happening while the movie was being shot or interviews with the cast and filmmakers—but it's best to take the time and shoot those segments at the time of production. You don't have to have a lot of fancy equipment. It's really more about just having it on your mind and actually sitting down to think about it before production begins: 'Okay, what are my DVD extras going to be?' and 'What tools are going to be used to market the film?'"

Of course, at the end of the day, there is still one element that can make all the difference when it comes to marketing and pulling in audiences. As many leading specialized distributors will point out, the best marketing tool an independent low-budget film has is often the film itself, whether it's an accessible comedy such as *Juno* or a moving drama such as *Once*. "When it comes to marketing, a really good film can be its own best asset," says Utley. "A film always has to have at least some marketable elements: brilliant reviews, great word-of-mouth, or its cast, but 'playability' can also be a film's strongest marketing element. A film like *Waitress* succeeds because audiences respond to it emotionally and tell their friends how much they enjoyed it." To get to that point, however, first- and second-time filmmakers and aspiring screenwriters need to pretend they are advertising executives and think about what it will take to position and publicize a new product being launched into an increasingly crowded and competitive environment.

"It's hard enough to make a great movie, and it's also hard to start thinking about marketing materials while you're on set, but it does help the cause later on," says Utley. "When you're trying to explain a film to audiences it's important to have usable 'trailer moments,' where a character says something memorable or where a character explains what the movie is about to someone in a coherent way, so that you don't have to use extensive or artificial voiceover when you get to trailering. It's always much better if you can use something organic to the film itself so you don't have to have that Voice of God saying 'In a world where this or that can happen . . .' or a trailer voiceover that says: 'So-and-so didn't know he was going to get into such-and-such . . . but guess what happened.'"

13. What's Next?

CAREER STRATEGIES FOR MAKING IT

*S*cientists measure momentum by multiplying mass times velocity, but calculating career momentum in the independent-film world can be a tricky business. After a festival acceptance, a terrific audience reaction, a solid review in Variety, and a flurry of calls from agents and executives, how should aspiring filmmakers benchmark their progress and plan their next move? It's hard enough to get even a single project financed, cast, produced, and distributed, let alone set out to make a whole slate of films from day one. After all, if the first one doesn't go anywhere, will they be able to keep the dream alive and navigate the ragged edge of disaster while trying to do it all again? It turns out that part of being a successful filmmaker is having a five-year plan (or even a twenty-five-year plan like Dignan in Bottle Rocket) and knowing what the next step will be after that first project is in the can.

Having a career plan is also important because established producers and studio executives looking for new talent will invariably ask "So what's next?" as an invitation to sell them on a terrific idea. And just *as filmmakers may need a business plan to attract big-money investors to invest in their first project, they also need a road map of what they want to do later, not only to convince specialized distribution executives to finance their subsequent projects but also to be able to make smart decisions in the short term and be open to opportunities that may come their way. Some in the business believe that all filmmakers need to have several projects ready to move to the next level at all times, such as a short film and two original screenplays, or a completed feature and three treatments, or five well-thought-out pitches and two finished screenplays—as if the right combination will provide the winning hand in a high-stakes game of indie-film Texas Hold 'Em. These combinations are not set in stone and one terrific script is enough to move a career forward despite what some might say, but filmmakers should have a clear idea of what they want to do next in both an ideal and a not-so-ideal world. Tomorrow's working filmmakers need to get their rap down and not let their momentum slip away, since the second and third film a director makes can often boost or bust a budding career. For example, after dazzling audiences with* Shine, *a film that introduced U.S. audiences to* Pirates of the Caribbean's *Geoffrey Rush and* Eastern Promises's *Armin Mueller-Stahl, director Scott Hicks has had trouble recapturing the level of interest and acclaim his 1996 film generated. Similarly, after winning the Grand Jury Prize at Sundance in 1999 with his debut film* Three Seasons, *writer-director Tony Bui has, as of 2009, yet to direct a second film.*

To some, planning to make a second film in the middle of the first seems too ambitious, while others would rather not tempt fate with too many big dreams. However, the likelihood that a filmmaker will need to make a second or even a third film before the industry will sit up and take notice is almost guaranteed. Charlotte's Web *director Gary Winick didn't get accepted to Sundance until submitting his fourth completed feature,* Tadpole, *in 2002, which was subsequently bought by Miramax for $11 million. Christopher Nolan didn't get into Sundance with* Following *in 2000 but has enjoyed an enviable career* *after Bob Berney's distribution savvy helped* Memento *connect with audiences in 2002 and gross $25.5 million theatrically. Marc Forester directed the dark Sundance feature* Everything Put Together *in 1999 before his breakout success in 2002 with* Monster's Ball *led to jobs directing* The Kite Runner *and* Quantum of Solace. *Each of these directors might have decided to call it a day at some point early in their careers had they not had an idea of how their first projects fit into a larger goal and how they planned to climb the next rung on the ladder even in the face of the constant setbacks that impede all film-makers' forward movement.*

Just as box-office grosses can drop 70 percent or more after a single breakout weekend, studio interest and press buzz surrounding new indie filmmakers can dissipate faster than dry ice in a high school science project. In this era of disposable everything, newly discovered screenwriters, directors, and producers must have additional scripts or at least a few well-thought-out pitches ready to go lest they lose the momentum that may have taken years to generate.

"After *The Tao of Steve* came out in theaters in 2000, my mom told us to make hay while the sun is shining," says Greer Goodman, the film's coscreenwriter and costar. "Today, knowing what I know now, my advice to filmmakers would be to get that second screenplay finished as soon as possible."

Goodman and her sister, director Jenniphr Goodman, and *Tao of Steve* coscreenwriter Duncan North had actually heard this advice long before their debut film became the darling of Sundance in January of 2000. "Our producer Anthony Bregman had told us a million times: 'Get going on another script.' And he was 100 percent right," she remembers.

Bregman, who was just one of several producers and studio executives who were eagerly awaiting the Goodman sisters' next script, often delivers this same advice to filmmakers overwhelmed by the sudden rush of attention they had always hoped for. One big misperception is that they will land a three-picture deal that will cover living expenses, a snazzy Mac Air, and a salary of some sort while they take meetings and develop new scripts. Those whose films do get acquired are often shocked at how much work they still have to do and can only wonder how they will find time to write a new script while completing the arduous task of meeting a specialized studio's schedule of delivery elements. Regardless of what happens, Bregman remains emphatic: "Filmmakers should be thinking ahead even before a first film is finished so the moment it comes out—either at a festival or in movie theaters—they'll be able to answer the question that almost everyone will inevitably ask: 'So what's next?' " he says. "For example, Ed Burns was able to sustain that initial rush of buzz and awareness to get his second project set up. When Ed brought *Brothers McMullen* to Sundance in 1995, he already had the script he wanted to do next, he knew which one he was pushing, and his priority at the festival was to say, 'I want to be in production on *She's the One* by next summer.' Fourteen years later, I wish I had a slew of writers and directors who followed that example. But for the most part, the frenetic scramble to get films finished in time for Sundance usually leaves filmmakers with no time left over to prep a new script for afterward."

The casual query of "What's next?" posed over cocktails at an IFP event, over reporters' notepads at Sundance or Slamdance, or in a studio executive's office in Nakatomi Plaza often inspires dread among fledgling filmmakers, since the pressure to pull a rabbit out of a hat a second time can be intense. A filmmaker who may have spent ten or eleven years writing his or her first film is now expected to have another stellar script or even two or three ready to shoot in just a few months. "The question of 'What's next?' never goes away," says *Memento* writer-director Christopher Nolan. "I still get asked that, usually when I'm in the middle of editing."

Many filmmakers feel similarly exasperated at the thought, since they may have maxed out their credit cards, destroyed relationships, or sold their old CDs and DVDs and countless personal belongings to support themselves while making the previous film. "The very night I finished my first documentary I went to a party and someone said, 'Hey, that's great! What are you doing now that it's done?'" recalls *Roman Polanski: Wanted and Desired* director Marina Zenovich, whose first effort, the 1998 Slamdance doc *Independent's Day*, was a wry look at Sundance and Slamdance and the tribulations aspiring filmmakers face. "It was an important moment for me because I realized, 'Wow, it's over. And now I have to go on to the next thing.'

"I so specifically remember where I was at that moment: at a function at the Academy on Wilshire. And I just remember that it blew me away when someone had the nerve to ask me: 'What's next?' Now that's normal for me. I expect it. Now I know to think about it. And even as I was finishing *Polanski* I was thinking, 'Oh, I better have something up my sleeve.' I spoke to another filmmaker who sold his doc at Sundance in 2007 and he actually told me: 'I wish I had been more ready with my next project, at Sundance.'

"The thing is, these projects are so all-enveloping that you often don't have any free time to focus on anything else," she concludes. "What would be ideal is to have a script you've written that you want to direct, but that takes a lot of time. And the older you get, you have less time to write because you're putting your energy into your family. I used to spend my weekends trying to figure out how to further my career. Now that I have a child I have much more limited time to do that. The flip side is that I am much more focused as the time is so limited."

Another roadblock to future success can be the trappings of the last success: Tribeca Film Festival panel discussions, invitations to coach aspiring writers at the Sundance Screenwriters Lab, parties in the Hollywood Hills, receptions at the Directors Guild of America, studio pitch meetings, quick coffees with old friends, on-the-lot screenings, hours of co-op *Call of Duty 4* on a fifty-two-inch plasma, and premieres at the Sunset 5 or the Ziegfeld can certainly fill a new filmmaker's dance card and prevent him or her from putting in the enormous amount of time and commitment needed to do the actual work of screenwriting, adapting books, or shot-listing.

Successful filmmakers recognize that they cannot afford to ease off the gas until they have made their mark with a second or third project. "Quentin had studied people's careers and he saw that a director's second film was often more important than the first when it came to sustaining a career," says *Pulp Fiction* executive producer Stacey Sher, who would go on to executive-produce Zach Braff's debut, *Garden State*. "Quentin thinks that the first film gets you to be able to make your second film, but that your second film determines whether or not you're going to have a career and how many more movies you get to make after that. If you look at filmmakers who have longevity there are obvious exceptions, but when a second film goes awry, it takes people longer to get back on track."

Given this constant "what's next" refrain, many producers encourage filmmakers to look for obscure novels that may not yet have been optioned and contact the rights holders to set up a low-fee option that includes "elevator" payments if a studio becomes involved in its development. Instead, however, what usually happens is that filmmakers party or kick back until the clock is ticking down on their fifteen minutes of fame. Unable to crank out an entire script in this short interval, even with cases of Red Bull or an IV of venti Americano, they search in vain for well-known books with available rights that match the sensibility of the film that originally got them noticed. Finally, a sense of panic develops as the fear that one wrong move will bring their budding careers to a screeching halt sets in. *Fade out, roll credits.*

"Filmmakers often become paralyzed, obsessing over what their second movie is going to be, and then they don't make a film for three or four years," says *Kids* producer Cary Woods, now an executive at Plum TV. "My advice always is just go back to work. Find a project that you're comfortable with, one that excites you again, and don't worry about it being more important or less important than your previous film. You don't have to top yourself."

Strand Releasing copresident Marcus Hu, who worked with *Jesus' Son* director Alison Maclean, *Keane* director Lodge Kerrigan, and *Get Over It* director Tommy O'Haver when they were all first-timers, says an even less ambitious approach is perfectly acceptable. "If you're waiting in development hell, take a DV or HD camera and make a small, intimate movie," he says. "If you have to, find a music video to direct but just keep working."

Many filmmakers find themselves taking several years off or leaving the business for an extended interval after a huge success or major disappointment. After *Julien Donkey-Boy* failed to connect with audiences in 1999, writer-director Harmony Korine found himself at a career crossroads and didn't make another film until 2007. "I kind of lost interest in things and wasn't really sure I was going to keep making films," he recalls. "I felt like things had just left me and there was a disconnect, so I tried to do other things and experience a different kind of life. It's kind of a long story, but you know, I was out there in the wilderness."

While the independent-film world moved on and found

other *enfant terribles* to celebrate, Korine traveled the world, visited Brazilian rain forests, and took odd jobs for several years before returning to filmmaking. "I needed to get away from that world for a while, so I went to the Amazon. I went to the jungle and I did a lot of strange stuff for jobs and for fun.

"Then I started getting ideas again and I started to feel like I could do it again," he says of his return to directing with *Mister Lonely*. "I really wasn't very good at anything else and movies were always what I loved and they were all I wanted to do. And I started to feel like I could do it again. I became inspired by life stuff, you know, the sun, the breeze, the water, just basic things. I started dreaming again and there was something I wanted to do."

THE ARC OF ALEXANDER PAYNE

After *Sideways* grossed $71.5 million theatrically in the United States and another $99.7 million on DVD domestically in 2005, it was clear that writer-director Alexander Payne had arrived. Critics and audiences had embraced his high school comedy *Election* in 1999, but now Payne was a superstar. *Sideways* was such a huge hit for Fox Searchlight that specialized distributors were given marching orders to analyze the company's strategy and emulate it. The film inspired dozens of articles about wine, the new economics of specialized distribution, and a new era of cinema for grown-ups. Ironically, however, even though he was the man of the hour, Payne had never had an easy road. In fact for years his career was delayed by what he explains were a number of misplaced assumptions.

"When you go to film school and you want to be a director, you usually don't have a plan in mind that you later execute, you just kind of see what your options are at a given moment," explains Payne. "What hooked me into staying in Los Angeles after graduating with an MFA from UCLA was that I had a hit student film. I had one of those dream scenarios where after an end-of-the-year screening of student films, I got calls and offers from agents and producers and studio people. So immediately I thought, 'If there are opportunities to get financing in Hollywood, and that's what these people do for a business, I'll stick around and try that out.' Because of the attention I was getting coming out of film school, I thought, 'I'm going to be making a film within a year. This is wonderful! What a wonderful opportunity I have!' But it was actually five years before I got to make *Citizen Ruth*, and that's really what it is to make films."

Had Payne thought through what might be an acceptable plan B, he might have cut that five-year interval in half or at least mitigated some of the frustration and setbacks that have certainly driven less committed film-school graduates to pursue other lines of work. *Citizen Ruth* producer Cary Woods (*Swingers*, *Scream*) remembers just how tough things were for Payne starting out. "The problem was that Alexander was not attracted to the kinds of, let's say, more commercial material that studios generally reserve for young filmmakers," says Woods. "Studios might take on a young, unproven filmmaker, and to the extent he or she is willing to work on material the studio feels is commercial, they'll take the risk. But Alexander has been and still is interested in material that is somewhat unconventional relative to what we think of as common commercial fare. All of his work attests to that. Even though Paramount financed *Election* and New Line financed *About Schmidt*, you wouldn't say that these films were among their more conventional releases. And *Citizen Ruth*, certainly, was never going to be a studio movie."

While it's easy to summarize that all's well that ends well,

Payne admits he might have avoided at least some of the heartache and years of poverty had he come up with a formal career strategy.

Back in 1990 Payne had landed a coveted writing-directing deal at Universal and was paid to write, as he says, "whatever inspired him." Going against the grain and eschewing the so-called rooting interest most actors look for in a character or the themes of self-actualization typically found in mainstream studio projects, he set about writing an introspective film about a quiet lead character full of regret and self-doubt. "That script, *The Coward*, would eventually become *About Schmidt*, but at that point the studio was completely uninterested in pursuing it," Payne recalls. "I thought, 'Okay, I'm just going to rewrite it and move back to Omaha. I'll take a finance class, raise a million dollars, shoot it on 16mm, and go from there.' But I didn't know how to start."

Ultimately, Payne reconsidered and stayed in Los Angeles. "If you want to make cars you have to live in Detroit," he says. "I never changed my lifestyle from that of a student and lived on the money from that unsuccessful first attempt to get *The Coward* made."

Rather than following what would later become George Clooney's credo of participating in commercial fare such as *Ocean's Eleven* so he could afford to attach himself to deeply personal, low-budget projects such as *Good Night, and Good Luck*, Payne continued on his path of working on scripts that were extremely challenging and in some ways the exact opposite of what Hollywood expected to see from an award-winning film-school graduate.

"In February 1992 Jim Taylor and I happened on the idea of *Citizen Ruth*, so we started pursuing that," Payne recalls. "We spent six months writing it and then worked with some dead-end producers for about eight months before I finally bumped into producer Cary Woods at a Thai restaurant on Venice Boulevard. Cary was one of the few people who remembered me from the film-school screenings two years earlier. He said, 'What are you up to, and why haven't you made a film yet?' And I said, 'Oh, I don't know . . . Just a little abortion comedy. You're not going to want to read it. Everyone hates it.' And he said, 'No, no, no. Let me read it.'

"Some people who had read the description of *Citizen Ruth* would say, 'This is a Lifetime television movie,' " but I would say, 'No, you don't understand, it's a comedy . . . It's gonna be really funny.' "

Of course, any film about reproductive rights starring a still up-and-coming Laura Dern was bound to be a tough sell, even for an edgy, specialized distributor such as Weinstein-era Miramax. The concern was that if the comedy came out too broad, the film could seem insensitive, but if its politics were too strident, the end result would be a civics lesson instead of entertainment. Either way, millions in production and marketing dollars would be riding on a first-time director taking on one of the most divisive, taboo subjects.

Still, Woods remained optimistic. "The thing is, Alexander's script was so original that I stopped in my tracks as he was describing it to me in the parking lot," he remembers. "Political satire is the most difficult thing to do in film, and *Citizen Ruth* was a satirical look at an extremely sensitive subject. He turned one of the most controversial topics in America into a commentary on fanaticism that exists on both sides of the issue."

Hollywood's purse strings would remain pulled shut for three more years. "I had run into Cary in August of 1993 and I didn't shoot *Citizen Ruth* until April of 1995," says Payne. "It took that long to get the financing together. And by that time I was just going nuts. I had moved out of Los Angeles and up to Chico to go into a type of self-imposed exile for about eight months."

A sleepy college town at the north end of the Sacramento Valley with one of the largest municipal parks in the United States, Chico, California, was famous for providing the lush exterior locations for the original *Adventures of Robin Hood* starring Errol Flynn.

"I literally moved to a town where I didn't know anyone, did a lot of yoga, and started work on another script that I thought I could shoot very cheaply on 16mm. By this time I had given up on *Citizen Ruth*—I thought no one was going to make it—but then I got a call from Cary. He said, 'I'm going to put my hand in my own pocket and set you up in a casting office and let's see if we can get some casting going, and then off the casting momentum we can try to get the financing to make it.' "

Woods's strategy worked, and since he had just produced the first *Scream* for Miramax—an enormous runaway hit that would spawn lucrative sequels and the comedic *Scary Movie* franchise—he was able to convince Harvey Weinstein to give Payne a shot. Weinstein agreed *Citizen Ruth* could go forward, provided Woods forgo his own fee on Payne's abortion comedy, a tough deal that Woods nonetheless agreed to. Ultimately, *Citizen Ruth* was heralded as "an American classic" by respected film critic Anthony Lane of *The New Yorker*.

Woods secured his position as a film producer able to identify new talent and get them the chance they need to prove themselves, but the truth is that had Payne decided he wanted Indian food instead of Thai on that August night, he might still be living in Chico, never having had the chance to someday direct *Sideways*, which by some estimates has now grossed an estimated $350 million worldwide in its various theatrical and ancillary avenues. The lesson is that many younger, similarly situated filmmakers may also be leaving their careers to the winds of chance if they don't stop to make a career plan and get advice from producers and unbiased film executives as to whether it is truly viable.

"It's very important for young filmmakers—actually for filmmakers of any age—to know when to capitalize on those small windows of notoriety, on those windows of success, in order to facilitate getting their first project or their next project made," says Payne, who now advises younger filmmakers as part of the Sundance Screenwriters Lab. "Some people have that instinctively, but it's taken me a while to figure that out. It's not about being aggressive—that's such an American concept of how to get ahead—but more about knowing what you're going to do next. I don't always know. I'm slow. I'll finish a film and then think, 'I got that out of my system. Now what?' And while you're thinking, 'Okay, now what do I want to do?'—which to me seems like a natural process—that's when your window of notoriety and your heat comes and goes. Today people say, 'You're doing so well,' and I say, 'Yeah, but look how many years it's taken me.'"

On some level Payne might have had an easier route early on and more opportunities at bat had he used his studio assignment as a launching pad, with the goal of financing *Citizen Ruth* after earning a living as a gun-for-hire, studio-financed writer-director.

Film consultant Peter Broderick believes this may be a risky approach, since even staunchly independent filmmakers can succumb to the allure of Hollywood. "They might say, 'I'm just going to do this for a little while—I'm just making these movies that don't mean anything to me because I'm learning my craft,'" Broderick explains. "But it's hard to go back once you achieve a certain lifestyle and a certain level of production support. You don't just say, 'Okay, now that I've arrived, I'm going to go make a movie like *Schizopolis*.'"

Still, as much as the average filmmaker believes there is legitimacy—indeed, nobility—in resisting the siren song of the major studios and in avoiding any hint of selling out to the Man, the risk is that the dark years of temp jobs and crushing poverty spent trying to get risky material set up as a debut film may ultimately crush a filmmaker's spirit and prevent even the most dedicated filmmaker from actually directing or producing a feature.

In September 2001, *The Woodsman* director Nicole Kassell won the screenplay competition at Slamdance. "That was the first kind of clear seal of approval that I was onto something," Kassell recalls. "But then it took a year before playwright Steven Fechter and I could find a producer." Another full year would click by before Kevin Bacon and his wife, Kyra Sedgwick, signed on to the project, a dark meditation on pedophilia and redemption.

"Kevin signed on January 6, 2003, but Christmas 2002 was one of the lowest points in my life, of just thinking that my movie's not going to happen and I'm not happy and I don't know what's going to happen," Kassell says. "I talk a lot about passion, patience, and perseverance. That you have to have all three or you're not going to get anywhere because it takes a long, long time to get your film made and nobody's going to be your cheerleader to keep you on the project. You have to be so passionate about it that it's contagious to the people around you."

"There's no set pattern and every filmmaker's story is different," Payne says. "Every film's story is different. So it's hard to predict where your own filmmaking chips are going to fall. It's a zen of what roads you discern are open to you and what roads you take. I was at UCLA Film School recently, talking to the MFA students and I told them I would have had no idea that coming out of film school I would be making studio films. You get out in the filmmaking world and you see what offers are coming in, you see what material is striking you, what themes, what movies you already like that you want to emulate. All these things come into play and you just feel it out because you don't always know how you're going to get there. Am I going to need independent sources of financing or am I going to need foreign financing that I put together and later find a U.S. distributor? Am I going to shoot it off credit cards like Robert Townsend or Kevin Smith for $50,000? Am I going to get a studio assignment, and if it is a studio thing, what are the prices there? How much control will I lose? Who am I getting involved with? Today young filmmakers come up to me and say, 'You know, I've been trying to get my film made for eight months . . . or sixteen months . . . can you help me out?' And I tell them I understand their frustration and I know that agony, but I can't give them pity. That's simply the process. As Hyman Roth says in *The Godfather: Part II*, 'This is the business we've chosen.' "

WORKING IN TELEVISION

Another surprise to most aspiring independent filmmakers is that many of their heroes do not make a living simply writing or directing independent films and could not even if they wanted. For example, Miguel Arteta could not have survived since 1997 on the payday or the residuals from *Star Maps*, *Chuck & Buck*, and *The Good Girl*, and has made a living directing episodes of *Six Feet Under*, *The Office*, and *Ugly Betty*, among others. Similarly, indie-film directors such as Allison Anders have supported themselves in between films by directing episodes of *Sex and the City*, *Cold Case*, *The L Word*, and *What About Brian?* Meanwhile *But I'm a Cheerleader* director Jamie Babbit has had a long and successful career directing episodes of *Nip/Tuck*, *Gilmore Girls*, *The*

L Word, *Gossip Girl*, and *Ugly Betty*. Kassell has directed episodes of *Cold Case*. Even Quentin Tarantino has directed episodes of *CSI*. As a result, independent filmmakers are wise not to turn their noses up at television work and to think about how they might even repackage their films and shorts into television pilots.

"That's another dirty little secret of independent film: often the only way to get money to actually live is by working in television," explains Slamdance cofounder Dan Mirvish. "Filmmakers that are just making one-off shorts and playing the festival circuit need to expand their worldview a little and say, 'Hey, wait a minute! This could be turned into a series, and someone might actually pay me to do more of these things.' If they have something with an appealing antihero character and an intriguing premise, then they really need to ask themselves, 'What would it be like if someone were to ask me to make more of these things? What would that entail?' And; 'Should my short film have more of a narrative arc?' "

Of course, most indie filmmakers are so obsessed with getting their dark, edgy short films into festivals that they lose sight of their future opportunities, finances, health-care coverage, significant others, friends, apartments, and possible jobs in the "square" world.

"Until they actually have to start preparing delivery elements, filmmakers don't realize just how expensive it is to show a short in a festival: you historically have to output your film to 35mm film, which can cost $5,000 to $10,000 for a short and anywhere from $50,000 to $100,000 for a feature; you have to fly there with your production team, which can cost $1,000 per person; and then you have to stay somewhere and eat for a few days—all while taking time off from work or quitting your day job," explains Mirvish. "Then, when you do show your short, there are maybe a hundred people in a dark room and *maybe* one of them has some connection to the film industry, and that person may or may not be impressed and may or may not feel like identifying himself in a room full of aspiring filmmakers. I don't know if it's quite happened yet, but I think people will start to ask themselves, 'Why am I bothering to submit to film festivals? Why pay all that money when it's free to put it on YouTube, or any one of a number of other websites, and have 50,000 or 100,000 people see it and maybe twenty of them are in the industry?' I mean, at some point, people are going to do the math and ask themselves, 'What's the point of going to a film festival again?' "

WORKING IN TEAMS

Some talented filmmakers seem to hit the jackpot straight out of the box, but one thing that is consistent in their stories is that they work in teams and do not try to do everything themselves. Filmmakers who do not have collaborators or friends in the business often believe that the only way they can make their film is to spend their own money and call in every favor. As a result, their world gets smaller and smaller as people stop returning their calls. Closest friends and significant others can quickly become alienated as the filmmaker's passion takes on a level of mania and she takes on too many responsibilities. For this reason, working in teams is always a better option, since the work is spread around, the anxieties can be shared, and less of a burden is placed on any one individual.

"One thing I learned after moving to L.A. was how important it is to work with other people," says *Lonelygirl15* cocreator Miles Beckett. "In the spring of 2006, I tried launching a series of comedy videos on my own, hiring actors, writing, directing, and even designing the website.

But I found it overwhelming. At the time, a friend of mine, David Canchola, shot the videos with his JVC high-def camera while I wrote, directed, and produced the videos. Then, when I had the idea for *Lonelygirl15*, I was fortunate to find two fantastic partners: Ramesh Flinders for the creative, and Greg Goodfried for the business. I met Mesh in April at a friend's birthday party at a karaoke bar in L.A. called the Gaslite. I met Greg in February at my birthday party—his wife is friends with a mutual friend. Greg's wife, Amanda, is now the series producer of *Lonelygirl15*. Mesh and I ran the show on our own, writing, filming, and editing *Lonelygirl15* for a couple of months, but I know we would still be sitting in our apartments if not for Greg. Greg set up meetings in August 2006 with various talent agencies and Internet companies. We had a trailer on a DVD for what a *Lonelygirl15* television show or feature film could look like, and we kept all our meetings with people very secretive."

Other filmmakers plan their careers as a series of hastily executed Frogger jumps that put them at risk of being run over or falling into the river. Others have their initial success happen *to* them, in the sense that they have somehow managed to capture lightning in a bottle—such as the directors of *The Blair Witch Project*—and may not know how to do it again. Still others would be able to replicate the style and charm of their first success, if they only had more time to get their ducks in a row before attending their first major festival.

Greer Goodman says she experienced that exact thought shortly after *The Tao of Steve* started to gather festival buzz at Sundance. "There was a feeling of 'Oh my God, here's our tiny window of opportunity. Quick! Do something before it closes!' " she recalls. "But we don't work that fast. Jenniphr lives in Santa Fe and we collaborate by e-mail and occasional flights back and forth. I don't know how these people who write an entire script in two weeks do it."

Legend has it that writer-director Paul Schrader bashed out his first draft of *Taxi Driver* in two weeks while living out of his car following the dissolution of his marriage. Tarantino claimed in a television interview to have written *Reservoir Dogs* in just two weeks. It was later claimed in some Internet circles that *Reservoir Dogs* borrowed elements from Ringo Lam's 1987 film *City on Fire*, available on Netflix, in which an undercover cop played by Chow Yun-Fat infiltrates a gang of thieves who rob a jewelry store and end up in a Mexican standoff.

While it can take years—not weeks—to write an original screenplay or create a compelling story drawing from personal experience, optioning existing books, a newsworthy person's life rights, or magazine articles can be a much faster route to generating a second or third script while the first project heads into the final stretch. "My advice is to take your three favorite books, figure out which one you want to adapt, and get the option rights," advises *Spring Forward* producer Gill Holland. "Too many independent filmmakers feel they absolutely have to write and direct, but some directors should just hook up with a writer who's got a good script."

Directors with one finished film who are looking for a subsequent project can meet aspiring writers at events such as the Sundance Screenwriters Lab or by waiting to see who congregates at the podium (writers!) following a panel discussion on independent film in New York or Los Angeles.

THE MYTH OF THE THREE-PICTURE DEAL

After the Sundance success of *Next Stop Wonderland*, in 1998 writer-director Brad Anderson was sidelined by something he never would have expected: a three-picture deal with the Weinstein-era Miramax. "People who aren't in the business might say, 'Hey, I saw the last movie that guy directed years and years ago—where's he been all this time?' " he remarks. "Meanwhile I'd been working my ass off!"

Anderson, who would later direct an astonishingly gaunt Christian Bale in *The Machinist* in 2002, had several scripts in various stages of development at Miramax after *Next Stop Wonderland* delighted Sundance audiences in 1998, but ultimately, none of them were produced by the company. "If a production deal starts to actually get in the way of making films, it's not much of a deal," warns Anderson. "You're better off building relationships with companies and working producers who are going to move your material through the system quickly. After all, in your lifetime as a director how many movies can you make?"

Anderson wrote and directed *Happy Accidents* and *Session 9* for IFC Films and USA Films (a precursor to Focus Features), respectively, shooting in Manhattan and upstate New York with budgets of under $1.5 million. More recently, Anderson directed *Transsiberian* in 2008 with Woody Harrelson and Emily Mortimer. "What's important is that you actually get to make the films you want to make without having to spend an inordinate amount of time trying to get them made or having to convince people that they're viable," Anderson says. This can be a tightrope, however.

"You can't try to do the Hollywood thing without money in the bank or without a day job," says Mark Stolaroff, founder of L.A.'s No Budget Film School. "Let's say you're at Sundance in 2010 or 2011: by the time your movie gets picked up—if it does at all—it could be well into 2012 before it gets released. During that time you're not suddenly rich, not by a long shot, and you still need money to pay the rent, to dub HDCAM copies of your film, and to pay for addi-

tional 35mm prints of your film. And it's not always instant
coffee as many filmmakers expect it to be. During the Weinstein era, Miramax was criticized by disappointed filmmakers
for buying films at festivals and then delaying their release
for years and in some cases, like *Prozac Nation*, delaying them
indefinitely." *Prozac Nation*, which starred Christina Ricci
and Jason Biggs, screened at Toronto in September 2001,
where it was indeed acquired but never given a theatrical
release, and debuted instead on the Starz cable network in
March 2005 before going to home video.

As far as staying afloat is concerned, jobs in the entertainment industry or in some downstream area of production
can provide good training for being a producer or director,
but many may be a detour that leads filmmakers in the
exact opposite direction. For example, many attorneys and
MBAs with dreams of someday becoming screenwriters will
often pursue jobs at studios in strategic planning, business
development, international distribution, or marketing only
to find that the intense hours leave no time for screenwriting.

Producers and development executives, however, do like
having aspiring screenwriters and filmmakers on staff—if
only as readers and assistants—since the unspoken promise
of someday reading one of their unproduced screenplays is
all it takes to inspire indentured servitude or at least a level
of dedication and commitment usually reserved for the mail-
rooms of CAA or William Morris.

Director Jenniphr Goodman eschewed the Hollywood
gauntlet after her first film hit because she wanted to stay
close to home in New Mexico and have another child.
"There were offers to direct shows and commercials that I
didn't seize," she says unapologetically. "My agent would tell
me that so-and-so wants to meet me or this other one wants
to meet me—there were a lot of opportunities I probably

squandered by living in Santa Fe and by having children. But I look at people like Richard Linklater and Victor Nunez and think, 'They work from Austin, they work from Florida, and they still make the kinds of movies they want to make.' They are my role models."

Some filmmakers move to New York because they feel it is somehow more legit or that it represents the true epicenter of indie-film production. However, many longtime veterans of the New York scene question this theory. "If you're going to work in the film industry, you have to acknowledge that Hollywood is the place where people get the majority of movies made," says Holland, who maintains an office in New York but who moved to Louisville, Kentucky, in 2006 to start a family. "I don't think we should have this perception anymore that indie film is the Holy Grail and everything else is evil. Too many producers and directors struggle for years trying to keep it real and end up going broke and having to leave the business."

Holland recounts that after *Hurricane Streets* won the Audience Award and prizes for Best Cinematographer and Best Director at Sundance in 1997—the first trifecta at the festival—he balked at opportunities to visit Los Angeles, a decision he later came to regret. "In L.A. there are a hundred production entities where you can set something up," he says. "If you win a prize at Sundance, people will take a meeting with you. Our director Morgan J. Freeman went out there, but I didn't capitalize on the success of *Hurricane Streets* like I should have because I thought of Hollywood as antithetical to the kinds of films I wanted to make, not realizing that the methodology of making them out there is the same and that there were tons of folks in Los Angeles who could be helpful."

Holland and Freeman went on to make *Desert Blue* in 1998 with Christina Ricci and a nineteen-year-old Kate

Hudson, but it failed to garner the level of acclaim that *Hurricane Streets* had received. "We kind of rushed *Desert Blue* because we had the money, all sorts of people were excited about it, and we had a great cast lined up," recalls Holland. "The problem was the script wasn't quite ready, so while it did well as a Samuel Goldwyn release theatrically and Sony Home Video DVD, *Desert Blue* was not as strong as it could have been in some respects."

In an industry whose mantra could be "What have you done for me lately?" a disappointing follow-up can diminish or even undo the goodwill and excitement generated by the previous film. For this reason, filmmakers must be careful not to follow advice they know might be ruinous and to be the stewards of their own destinies when it comes to choosing a second or third project. Whatever follows should allow them to hone their craft while not being judged harshly by the industry for turning out a failed feature film.

Since his debut *Star Maps* in 1997, West Coast–based Miguel Arteta has made a living periodically directing episodic television in between feature-film projects, an option that many filmmakers fail to consider. "It's not like I was close-minded to the idea of making a movie with a studio—I would have, but the material was never good enough," says Arteta of his shift to TV. "I read the script for *The Mod Squad* and it was not a hard decision passing on that. *American Beauty* was the only time in the two years in between my films where I came across something that I thought, 'Man, it would be really great to get this.'"

Since directing *Chuck & Buck* in 2000 and *The Good Girl* in 2002, Arteta has directed episodes of *Homicide: Life on the Street*, *The Office*, *Ugly Betty*, the short-lived *Snoops*, *Freaks and Geeks*, and an episode of *Six Feet Under*, among others. He also directed a pilot with Martin Scorsese entitled *Elizabeth Street*, about the clash of cultures in Little Italy. Arteta says working on *Homicide* was key to securing health cover-age and Panavision-rig directing experience for many an independent filmmaker in between projects.

"It's a great way to stay afloat and support my dirty little habit of independent filmmaking," Arteta continues. "I treat my feature films as my priority and the television shows come when I have time, but you can make close to $30,000 per episode, which is only four or five weeks of work. *Homicide* has capitalized on indie filmmakers' ability to handle edgy material and get it done fast. In fact, I think *Homicide* producer Tom Fontana might actually have been the single biggest supporter of independent filmmaking because he took people from the festival circuit and gave them an opportunity to join the Directors Guild of America, make some money, and stay alive until they made their next inde-pendently financed project. Barbara Kopple has directed *Homicide*, Whit Stillman has done it, and Nick Gomez did one. That's my recommendation to try and stay afloat—you've got to get your movie done any which way you can and filmmakers shouldn't dismiss the idea of working in TV."

The truth is, studio rewrite assignments or other paid screenwriting gigs—most of which are based in Los Ange-les—are extremely rare, as are overhead deals or advances on future, as-yet-uncompleted indie-film projects. Very few specialized distributors give filmmakers "walking-around money," and if they did, it would be a one-, two-, or three-picture deal, which are not as common as many aspiring filmmakers think.

Indeed, filmmakers' idea of what will happen to them next is often based on what they have seen on *Entourage*. In the real world, first- and second-timers need to remember that during the interval between when their first film sells at a festival and when the film actually comes out, they will not necessarily be rich or swimming in money and may need to go back to their day jobs or find freelance assignments to keep the power on and a roof over their heads.

THE MYTH OF REWRITE WORK

Screenwriters who have received good notices for a spec script—a screenplay written without a buyer waiting for the final draft—or for having written a well-received feature film that made money may be able to get rewrite work at major studios, as a way to hone their craft while writing a second or third original script. "Kevin Smith made really good money writing on a lot of studio films and was still able to have the freedom and autonomy to make the small films he wrote and directed for himself," says Warner Bros. development executive Matt Bierman. "Fees start at scale, which is around $70,000 or so, and then your quote builds from there. If you do a good job, you get a raise on the next one and the next one and the next one, so you could be making a lot of money very quickly."

Still, Holland tells filmmakers not to quit their day jobs, even if they have a stack of trunk scripts or an invitation to a major festival. "The truth is, it's hard to get a paid writing gig unless you've sold a spec script for a ton of money or you've written a film that got released and became a huge hit," he says. "And there are only so many assignments out there that need rewrite work or book adaptations. Every film that gets made today is either a best-selling novel, a remake, or a giant sequel, and there's no way you're going to get that writing gig. They're going to give it to Kenneth Lonergan, Ronald Bass, or somebody who's already established."

Although the $1 million *The Tao of Steve* had a soundtrack on Milan Records and was considered a bona-fide indie hit in 2000, grossing $4.3 million theatrically and widespread acclaim, its cowriter Greer Goodman was not offered script rewrite work for $200,000 to $300,000 per assignment, nor was she given a bungalow on a film studio lot or presented with the latest fancy laptop. "Certainly no one said, 'We will pay you to write your next film,' " she says, dispelling a notion that most aspiring screenwriters hold dear. "What everyone said was: 'Show us your next script when you're done.' "

This speaks to the need to have a source of income, most likely something non-film-related, to jump to even after a film is picked up at a festival, lest the filmmaker not have a way to make his or her rent after returning from Sundance or Slamdance. Bregman agrees. "You hope that all of the films you make will at some point spawn greater films by the success of the previous one, but it's not a bad idea to protect yourself, just in case."

14. Documentary

**Y**ears ago, the box office performance of Fahrenheit 9/11, March of the Penguins, and An Inconvenient Truth held out the promise of a coming golden era of theatrical documentaries. Finally, it was said, Middle America had learned to appreciate "docs" as an art form after becoming acclimated to years of Survivor and The Real World. It looked as if the public had embraced what used to be known as "The 'D' Word," and were even going to see documentaries on dates in movie theaters. The market for docs at Sundance began to heat up, and for a time there was a glorious idea that documentary filmmakers who focused on topics of interest to the genral public could get well-made films in front of thousands, if not millions, of people, in theaters where people paid cash money rather than simply on PBS or the Discovery Channel. It was time, after all, for documentary filmmakers—who struggle just as mightily and with fewer resources than their narrative counterparts—to get a taste of the respect and dinero that always went to everyone else.

Sadly, that promised era is still a dream, at least for now. In 2007,

My Kid Could Paint That *was purchased at Sundance for $2.5 million and* In the Shadow of the Moon *was bought for $1.5 million. Both projects failed theatrically, chilling the market for theatrical distribution of compelling documentaries. Today, specialized distributors are no longer sampling the merchandise, and when they do it is with more than healthy skepticism. Minimum guarantees have largely gone away, and except for home video distributor Docurama, self-distribution through Breakthrough Distribution and HBO, which is still a leading platform, documentary filmmakers in need of a break may feel like they are out of luck.*

However, there is now a very interesting opporunity for tomorrow's documentarians that may allow those who think about their projects in a certain way to tell compelling stories and potentially make money. This revolutionary approach is simple: to focus on traditional three-act storytelling—which can be gleaned from books like Bob McKee's STORY, *Syd Field's* Screenplay: The Foundations of Screenwriting *(and his paradigm worksheet at SydField.com), and guides such as* 500 Ways to Beat the Hollywood Script Reader—*and to structure their doucmentary films as if they were narrative films with the same type of compelling character and story arcs that make narrative cinema compelling to wider audiences. The reason today's documentary filmmakers should take this approach is not only because their films will be tighter and more focused but a new, emerging opportunity exists to sell off the narrative remake rights to well-made docs following a three-act structure and storytelling paradigm, and to possibly get the chance to direct or produce the remake for pay, rather than having to scrape and struggle to raise funds for their next documentary.*

A recent beneficiary of this business model was The King of Kong *director Seth Gordon, who was hired to remake a narrative feature version of his wildly entertaining 2008 Slamdance doc about Steve Wiebe and Billy Mitchell's competition for the Donkey Kong world record, which still continues to this day. Although the feature version's title is not yet announced, Gordon is slated to direct and will no doubt become a filmmaker whom audiences come to know and seek out in the coming years. To follow in Gordon's footsteps, documentary film-makers will have to think outside the traditional way of shooting and editing, and make sure they follow several tenets of narrative produc-tion: shooting coverage, shooting inserts, telling the story through action and motion (rather than voiceover or straight-to-camera inter-views), and identifying heroes and villains that acquisitions executives can imagine being played by mainstream Hollywood actors.*

Of course, not every documentary can (or even should) emulate the storytelling style on display in The King of Kong. *Certainly a doc-umentary about the trials and tribulations of the singing crocodiles of Madagascar or the mating habits of great whites (who meet up by the dozens alongside the carcasses of rotting dead whales) may not follow a traditional "suspension bridge" storytelling structure. But the sto-ries of hardship and injustice faced by civil rights workers who marched at Selma, the challenges that horribly burned soldiers com-ing home from Iraq and Afghanistan must deal with, the ongoing plight of wrongfully convicted death row inmates and any number of new environmental health hazards, all can be told with an emphasis on traditional narrative storytelling, focusing on people whose stories are interesting, clever (but certainly unscripted) dialogue that is emo-tionally moving and relevant, and, most of all, character development in a crucible of a central goal's achievement or denial. Rather than simply making a documentary about a topic of interest with the idea of informing the viewing public or capturing a slice of life of an inter-esting person who warrants such attention, documentary filmmakers who want to survive need to focus on storytelling and the sales oppor-tunity that exists from brokering the narrative remake rights to the stories that are often, as the saying goes, stranger than fiction. On this same tack, documentary filmmakers will increasingly be able to make deals with video-game publishers as they make better use of the enormous storage capacity of Blu-ray discs. For example, a future ver-sion of* Endless Ocean, *for a second-generation Nintendo Wii with faster chipsets and an internal hard drive, would be able to include* documentary film content about global warming, coastal towns being affected by over-fishing and pollution, or just the life and times of smiling sea otters and their friends. Similarly, a documentary about championship bowlers and their trumphs and tragedies would make a terrific addition to Wii Bowling 3.0, since it could help put the game play in context and provide consumers with what is known in retailing as a value-add. Most important, the new avenues for getting documentaries in front of consumers, such as video games that ship on Blu-ray discs and ultrafast Wi-Fi connections to 3G and 4G iPhones and similar devices, will allow today's documentary filmmakers to get their docs seen by millions of people and monetize their art so they no longer have to starve. "Penury" and "documentary" may rhyme, but aspiring documentary filmmakers who think outside the box can look to a future when those words no longer have to go together.

For traditional documentary filmmakers attending festivals this year, there are more ways than ever to self-distribute, through companies such as Breakthrough Distribution, Amazon.com's CreateSpace, Netflix, and other emerging distributors, and more ways than ever before to aggregate and advertise to enormous populations of consumers who would like to buy a DVD focusing on a particular topic of interest as a gift or keepsake. Two examples of this emerging paradigm are the documentaries Faster, which focused on extreme motorcycle racing, and Brats, which focused on the lives of military families and the children who earn that nickname. With sites like Facebook bringing together huge populations of people focused on topics of interest, it is now possible to market, publicize, and self-distribute documentaries on DVDs with just a laptop and an Internet connection at the local Starbucks or Peet's Coffee. Documentary filmmakers who don't mind traveling can take their show on the road and screen their films with increasingly powerful and portable digital projectors for schools, youth groups, or other organizations that might respond, and then sell professionally packaged DVDs directly to consumers from the podium after a short Q&A or from a merchandise table nearby. The point is, there are ways that documentary filmmakers can make *money, and they should no longer think starvation is somehow part of the bargain. Those who disagree should recall that many respected documentary filmmakers, including Errol Morris, make a lot of money shooting commercials. Still others shoot well-paid "industrials" for major corporations and are subsequently able to pay their rent and utility bills on time.*

Seth Gordon, the director of *The King of Kong: A Fistful of Quarters*, was late in realizing that one of the biggest opportunities arising from his completed documentary, which screened at Slamdance in 2008, was in getting it remade as a narrative feature film with major Hollywood actors reprising the roles of real-life Steve Weibe and Billy Mitchell.

"And as a documentary, prenegotiating life rights with the individuals in the film was a key factor too," says Gordon. "We had all of the usual clearances you get for a documentary related to people's names and likenesses, but it became clear to us as people saw *Kong* that at least as interesting to a potential buyer as the documentary itself would be the remake rights to make a narrative feature. The thing is, selling remake rights to make a narrative feature requires a different kind of release from the individuals in your documentary. You need a life-rights agreement for that, not just a name-and-likeness release. And it actually became an important part of becoming salable, so we had to go back to the favorite 'characters' from the doc and try to negotiate with them. The problem was, some of those characters were also in *Chasing Ghosts*, another video-game documentary that was at Sundance the same time we were at Slamdance in 2008, so that became another battleground."

A life-rights release goes beyond the name-and-likeness release documentarians need to get before they start shooting, and essentially says that people give the rights holder the permission to remake the documentary as a fiction film, and to allow them to be portrayed as characters even while using their names in a subsequent project. Or, words to that effect. "It's just crazy, because most people if presented with a clause like that in a release wouldn't sign it," explains Gordon, who went on to direct *Four Christmases*. "In our case, we didn't even attempt any of that. We just used name-and-likeness releases that said, 'We are allowing you, the filmmaker, to use my name and likeness in the making of *this* documentary,' which is a much more palatable document to sign."

Going forward, documentary filmmakers could potentially make their projects more salable if they follow a traditional three-act structure and if they arrive at a festival with life rights intact and ready to be brokered to an interested distributor who recognizes the dramatic possibilities inherent in their stories and who sees their doc as a ninety-minute trailer for a possible major motion picture "based on a true story." Indie-doc filmmakers who find this idea abhorrent should recall that, good or bad, *A Civil Action*, *Silkwood*, *Erin Brockovich*, *Charlie Wilson's War*, *Schindler's List*, *Good Night and Good Luck*, and *The Pursuit of Happyness* may not have been based on documentaries, but typically they were all based on true stories and real people who had been written about in bestselling books and probably deserved *60 Minutes* episodes or History Channel documentaries. The tough part, of course, is in getting people to sign away a right to be portrayed in a film they haven't seen yet. However, there are ways to make the idea perhaps more palatable.

"Typically a life-rights agreement has a dollar amount attached to it," explains Gordon. "So what usually happens is, you give the subject of your unmade documentary a dollar against a certain option—say, for the sake of argument, $10,000 when the remake rights get purchased—and then the contract would stipulate that he or she gets let's say

$25,000 when the narrative feature remake actually gets made. So there's a stair-step kind of payment structure. They don't get a lot up front but they don't get screwed either when the film gets acquired. It's basically an option agreement that says: 'We'll give you X now and then Y later on when the option is exercised to make the film later.'"

Regardless of the negotiations involved, obtaining life rights during or before the shoot seemed absurd to Gordon and the producer Ed Cunningham at the time he was filming *The King of Kong*, since on some days they questioned whether the doc would ever be completed. "I felt real parallels between the obsessive-compulsive gamers that we were portraying in *Kong* and the degree to which it felt like an obsessive-compulsive act for us as filmmakers in sticking with the completion of *Kong*, even when there was no rational reason for us to keep going," says Gordon. "It's so unlikely that you'll ever sell the film. It's so unlikely even that you'll get most people to even *watch* the film, so why are you even bothering to do it? In our case, we couldn't stop. We couldn't really justify going ahead with it, but we just felt like we couldn't quit."

Originally, the project had been envisioned by Gordon and his small team of two cinematographers, a producer, and a simple light box as *Spellbound* with video games. "The rivalry between Billy and Steve was not something that we had planned," Gordon recalls. "We thought we were going to cover Kong and Pac-Man and Ms. Pac-Man and Q*Bert and all these different rivalries. And we had followed Doris Self, who we thought was among the rivalries we were going to focus on in our original vision of the movie. We kept her in because she was a wonderful character, and also because she and Billy had a very special relationship. But as we got to know Billy and Steve better, their story emerged as the dominant story line because they were so black hat/white hat, at least in how they treated each other."

What also emerged was the perfect underdog story that seemed to track with the three-act structure of classic sports films that feature a crushing defeat, personal trials, a training interval, and finally a bittersweet ending, as found in such films as *Rocky*, *Hoosiers*, *Breaking Away*, *The Karate Kid*, and *Rudy*. The problem was getting acquisitions executives to believe that a "rivalry" between two guys standing in front of a video-game cabinet for ninety minutes could be compelling drama and even the stuff of a major studio remake.

"The smartest thing we did was to cut a trailer for the film even before we cut the film, because it was a great way to get interest out there and also was actually a great way to guide us through the editing of the documentary," recalls Gordon. "Cutting a trailer before we cut the film forced us to tell the story in two minutes, and forcing yourself to tell a story in two minutes is a really good way to know how to tell your story in ninety minutes. It gave us the guideposts of each story beat we had to hit within each part or act of the film.

"We had a three-act structure built right into the trailer and it made it easier for people to understand what the film was before they saw it, which helped in the initial reception of it around town. Because if I tell you I've got this great documentary about these two guys who are going head to head on Donkey Kong, most people will say: 'Not interested . . .' But if I say, 'Hey, check out this trailer,' and I hit all the right beats, that can really help convince the average viewer and also an independent studio executive or a distributor to say: 'Okay. This thing could work!' And that was something that really did help us early on. My goal was to parlay a very tiny project into other work opportunities, so that helped in that way. And then it actually ended up being our theatrical trailer."

Because documentary film budgets are typically far less than those of narrative features, one would think that getting a doc up and running would be relatively easy. After all, renting an HD Panasonic HPX-170 camera, a tripod, and two 64-gigabyte storage cards could cost as little as $500 for the weekend. Still, many would-be documentarians find themselves hamstrung by the question that haunts most independently financed films: How much money should we raise before we start? This question, while prudent in the narrative space, prevents countless indie documentaries from ever getting made and leaves many important stories untold.

Two-time Academy Award–winning documentary filmmaker Barbara Kopple, codirector of the Dixie Chicks' *Shut Up & Sing* and the narrative feature *Havoc*, advocates kicking things off sooner rather than later.

"Making documentaries is about choices," she explains. "It's a personal choice to start or to wait until you have the full budget, but I would always just go ahead and start because if you don't start now you may miss certain points of your story. If it's a good enough story, you'll catch up to things you don't get during subsequent breaks needed for fund-raising, but if you have $200,000 and you want to start, then you're on your way and you're actually doing it—you're dealing with real life and you're making your dream come true. And if you do have to stop midstream and raise more money to complete the film, well, then at least you can show potential investors what you've shot so far and say, 'Hey, look at this! Look at what great characters these people are!' "

According to This Is That Productions cofounder Ted Hope, running out of money early in a documentary production is actually nothing to be ashamed of. "You often come across a lot of interim cuts that require new funding cycles to continue, something that would be almost impossible to do with a narrative feature," he says. "What you'll often see with documentaries is a project that's just a proposal and maybe a three- to five-minute basic foundation, or a film-maker who has raised enough money to get a project from that point up to, say, an hour of material, but who is now raising more money, so you often see projects that are evolv-ing step by step by step. There are organizations such as the IFP that often help find and accommodate that type of incre-mental financing of documentaries."

During this ebb and flow of financing, documentarians will need to maintain a positive outlook and not be con-sumed with anxiety that important elements of their stories are unfolding without them. They will also need to avoid the temptation to call it quits during long stretches of rejection. "There's always a reason for people not to fund your film," says Kopple. "They'll tell you it's too commercial or it's too this . . . it's too that . . . it's too whatever it is. There's always a reason when it comes to money. Money is a tight, hard commodity no matter who you are, and it's always tough for anybody to come by."

Grizzly Man and *Rescue Dawn* director Werner Herzog sets the financial threshold at a reasonable figure that most aspiring documentary filmmakers can achieve. "You can make a documentary in digital video with just $10,000," he says. "There are ways to do it. As long as you are able-bodied you can work the night shift as a welder, as I did in high school, and start saving. I keep telling the film students who ask me for advice: 'Go out and work as a bouncer in a sex club for two and a half years. That's where real life is. You will gain insight into real life *and* you will earn the money you need to make your film.' "

Making up a realistic budget means looking at the funda-mentals of telling each individual story. "Whether the doc is an advocacy piece, a historical piece, or a portrait, filmmakers should determine what is key to telling that story—what access is needed and what are the costs associated with that access," says Kelly DeVine, content consultant with Tribeca Film Institute and former IFC acquisitions supervisor. "Is travel access key? Is third-party material access key? And if so, does your 'pickup' entail a distributor having to pay for those elements or will you have to pay for them out of the advance you get from a distribution deal? Will a distributor walk away from a deal once they discover how much the licensing fees are going to cost? Spending money early for advice from an attorney well versed in intellectual property law, using resources like American University's Center for Social Media's materials regarding fair use issues, consulting with Tribeca Film Institute's joint project with USC Law School IP Clinic and Creative Commons for sample tool kits for licenses, or choosing, for example, to use original music to score your film as a work-for-hire piece so you will own those elements—all can go a long way toward smoothing the way for filmmakers to distribute their film using traditional or nontraditional models."

The filmmaking costs of documentaries usually come at the very end, when filmmakers try to clear rights to third-party footage and other materials. This is good advice given that the huge costs associated with procuring rights clearances can easily run several thousand dollars, if not more, to clear important archival footage and much more to clear well-known film clips owned by major Hollywood studios or music clips from famous artists.

"I think often one has to get going without all the funding in place," says Nick Broomfield, director of the narrative feature *Battle for Haditha* and the documentaries *Kurt & Courtney*, *Biggie and Tupac*, and *Aileen Wuornos: The Selling of a Serial Killer*. "I think especially when you're starting out it's very difficult to get the budget you think you want right up front. I certainly never did when I was starting out, and I think often filmmakers need to take the risk and prove their passion to financiers with footage they've shot and involve them at that stage. Nowadays with DV cameras you can certainly get going and then hopefully get some people interested when you've got something to show. And that way people can see a bit of what you're really excited about. I think you've got to just get going with it and demonstrate your passion, especially at the beginning. It's very important because I know so many people who sit around forever waiting for all the money to fall into place and by that time the subject has moved on or the topic has redefined itself."

THE PERILS OF NO BUDGET

Getting started with a budget that amounts to whatever happens to be in the filmmaker's bank account at the time is a brave approach, but documentarians going this route must steel themselves for hard times. For all her accolades and success with unique documentaries such as *Wild Man Blues* and *Shut Up and Sing* Barbara Kopple has also had her share of shut-off notices from the phone and power companies.

"It happened to me a lot when I was making *Harlan County U.S.A.*," she recalls. "Nobody believed in me and my electricity would get turned off. I would walk home, walk up all the stairs, and take a bath by candlelight. Sometimes I'd feel really sorry for myself and sing that Jimmy Cliff song 'You Can Get It If You Really Want' with tears coming down my face. But no matter what happened, I never wanted to give up . . . never. I felt so lucky just because I was doing it. A lot of people did help me and I got a lot of grants and a lot of family members and camerapeople to help me. But you can always think of the sad stories of people not supporting you and the electricity being turned off."

Kopple points out that almost every documentary film-maker has a tale to tell. "In 1990 I was making a film called *American Dream* that took place in Austin, Minnesota, and the fund-raising for the film was so difficult," recalls Kopple. "I remember one day going into the Union Hall and some-one said, 'Barbara, there's a call from your office!' I picked up the phone and they said, 'Barbara, we only have $200 left in the bank. What are you going to do about it?'

"And I said, 'I don't know, I'll call you back.' The people I was filming had decided to go on strike in a Minnesota win-ter, so we were standing on the picket line when it was 60 degrees below zero with the wind-chill factor. I was pacing up and down this Union Hall thinking: 'I'm freezing. I can't even get my body warm. And I've only had three or four hours of sleep each night for weeks and that's been a lot. What *am* I gonna do?'

"Someone came to find me later that day to say my office had called again and I said: 'No, no, no! I don't need to talk to them. I know what they're going to ask me and I haven't come up with anything.' And they said: 'No. They really have to talk to you. It's an emergency.' We needed money for more film. We had *nothing*. So finally I got on the phone and they said, 'We just got a $25,000 check from Bruce Spring-steen,' and I just burst into tears. It was a donation we had been trying to raise for six months, and it got us from $200 to $25,200 in one day. I was told later that everyone at the office had picked up all the phones to hear me cry. Because they had never heard me cry."

Very often the lives of the documentary filmmakers them-selves are more dramatic than the subjects they are covering. "I remember once it was so cold in my bedroom that ice formed in a glass on the nightstand," recalls Ken Burns, director of *The War* and other iconic documentaries such as *Jazz* and *Baseball*. "It was 1979 or 1980, and I was working on *Brooklyn Bridge* at the time. It was January in New Hampshire and we had an oil burner but we couldn't afford the oil so we used two woodstoves. But every morning around 4 a.m. the stoves would go out and we couldn't keep our house warm. When I was first moved there, I had just assumed that becoming a documentary filmmaker and becoming a historical documentary filmmaker was like becoming a monk and taking a vow of anonymity and poverty.

"It was very tough going, which is why perseverance is key. You actually don't have to have a talent for documentary filmmaking. But you have to be ready to get up at 4 a.m. and work for fifteen hours a day seven days a week because that's what you want to spend your time doing. If you've got that drive, if you feel that sense of purpose, then absolutely go forward with it. But know that your career as a documentary filmmaker is never going to be handed to you."

SELLING INVESTORS ON DOCS

One major misperception first-timers have is that documentaries don't have to be pitched to investors like narrative features. Compounding the problem is the fact that the type of filmmaker who chooses to make a documentary is typically less inclined to give a big, showy pitch to potential investors. Documentary filmmakers may be uncomfortable having to hustle Hollywood-style to raise financing for what they consider a noble idea rather than a commercial endeavor. What they don't realize, however, is that pitching and selling the "sizzle" is just as important for those who make documentaries as it is for screenwriters of blockbuster action films and Ringo Lam–inspired heist pictures.

"The main capital that you need for these projects—and I mean this really seriously—is the capital of your own complete passion," explains documentarian Ric Burns. "The first real money in the bank is your own passion for a project, and if you have that, if you have that deep commitment, then you will definitely find somebody who will say, 'You know what? If this person believes in this so deeply, we'll definitely get someplace.' And if you have that passion, then absolutely let other people see it."

If that means channeling their inner P. T. Barnum to raise funds with a breathless pitch, that's what they may have to do. Documentarians seeking private equity need to overcome any psychological hurdle they may have about appearing impolite and understand that today, in a down economy, they will need to hustle just like their narrative-feature counterparts. "When I pitch a project, what comes across is how far I would go to get this movie made and why I love it, why I want to do this movie more than anything else in my life. Why I would make the biggest sacrifice to get this movie made. And that comes across," says *American Splendor* producer Ted Hope, who also produced the documentary *The Devil and Daniel Johnston* in 2005.

However, many aspiring documentary filmmakers are unsure how to frame their projects for people with money, and cannot enunciate exactly what business model their project should follow. Today documentaries can recoup their production cost from direct DVD sales, pickups on HBO, or sales to special advocacy groups looking to promote a particular topic.

"I end up enthusiastically pitching my films—but not to investors, I pitch to foundations," says Ken Burns. "I pitch to corporations for underwriting dollars, to public television executives, to a variety of different sources. I'm looking for grant funding and so it's a different kind of pitch, it's not a commercial pitch, but I still need to be able to sell the importance of my subject, because there are many more good filmmakers and many more good ideas for films than there are grants or money available to fund them. So even though I'm not pitching to individual investors, I'm still pitching."

PIRACY HURTS INDIES, TOO

One of the things that independent documentary filmmakers may not have counted on is piracy of their films. Most indie filmmakers believe that songs and movies should be free and have no qualms about downloading free music or buying used books on Amazon, rather than buying new ones, but with bandwidth speeds increasing daily piracy can come back to bite them as well.

"The piracy of *King of Kong* was unbelievably extreme," recalls director Seth Gordon. "There were so many people that ripped it and distributed it and showed it to people and copied it and burned it, that it really impacted the way the film got distributed ultimately. It probably helped the word-of-mouth but it was so rampantly pirated in the Hollywood community—I mean there were public screenings happening way before we were in theaters, unsanctioned and without permission. And that's super-exciting if you're the filmmaker who people are just enthusiastic about and if they're enthusiastic about your film, but in terms of . . . organizing and marshaling a theatrical distribution, it got in the way of the film's box-office performance, because everyone saw it without paying for it. The theatrical box-office gross was around $500,000, maybe a little better than that but not much. I mean, why go see it if you've already seen it on DVD? The problem is that documentaries, and independent film in general, appeal to such a select group of people that heavy piracy can actually have an effect on box office. We tried to shut it down, but it was next to impossible. Because Picturehouse was part of Warner Bros., we tried to have their team that deals with piracy get ahead of everything." But no such luck.

For this reason and the depressed acquisitions climate, documentarians need to keep an eye on their budgets. "There's no hard-and-fast rule when it comes to budget since it's not like widgets or plumbing supplies," says Eamonn Bowles, president of Magnolia Pictures, who distributed *No End in Sight*, *Capturing the Friedmans*, and the Al Jazeera documentary *Control Room*, among others. "How much you should spend on your documentary is really about what you think the market will bear and whether you think the money is well spent while you're making the film. If spending to add a certain polish means that it's going to be more salable, then you should spend a little more to get it. It usually goes the other way, though, in that documentary filmmakers have so little money to begin with that they're not going to be able to make it for more than it should cost. That's the reality. The reality is that filmmakers are usually scratching together the money to finish the film. But each documentary is a singular work of art—hopefully—and each one has its own economy for how it's going to get out there."

Magnolia paid no minimum guarantee for *Control Room* or for *Capturing the Friedmans*, which was distributed as a service deal, a distribution arrangement in which a film's producers pay a percentage of revenue or a flat fee to have a narrative feature or documentary distributed theatrically, in which all revenue goes to the producer after expenses and the percentage of revenue or flat fee to distribute the film is paid.

Distributors typically collect 35 to 50 percent of the theatrical gross of documentary films but next to nothing from pay-cable channels, since documentaries have historically been contractually excluded from studios' pay-television output deals. This reality caps the level that specialized distributors are willing to pay in advances to even potentially commercial documentary films. For example, the G-rated *Arctic Tale* looked like a surefire hit and enjoyed a massive in-store marketing blitz from Starbucks but grossed a disappointing $1 million theatrically. *This Film Is Not Yet Rated* has a powerful cult following and is be considered required viewing in many circles, but this documentary about the Motion Picture Association of America and its rating policies barely made $300,000 theatrically.

"The big disadvantage documentaries have had is that there has been very little value from the pay-television window, which means as a distributor there's not nearly as much of a chance to make your money back," explains Mark Gill, chief executive at The Film Department, who as head of Warner Independent Pictures purchased an early version of *March of the Penguins* for $1 million at Sundance in 2004. "If you have a *Penguins* or a *Fahrenheit 9/11*, then of course there will be a high level of interest, but documentary filmmakers are lucky if they can get any money from pay television simply because documentaries have been excluded from pay-television output deals. This lack of revenue from pay television makes it an even greater imperative to keep your costs down during production. Since there's less revenue coming in, every cost—production, distribution, and marketing—just has to be that much lower."

Documentary filmmakers who are accepted into Sundance should also tamp down their expectations since very few are ever bought for dizzying multiples following a rowdy screening that inspires a bidding war, no matter how compelling or well made they may be.

"Historically, there hasn't been the kind of upside—the ultimate upside—available with documentaries," says Fox Searchlight COO Stephen Gilula. "It's something of a catch-22: because there's been a limit to the theatrical revenue you could earn with a documentary, distributors haven't been able to spend the kind of money needed to really market them appropriately. It still doesn't quite flow through to the ancillary markets and so it's a matter of finding the right film that can have that kind of upside on cable and home video as well, since it's still more limited than many filmmakers realize."

SUBJECT MATTERS

Of course investors are more likely to support a documentary if the topic is closer to their hearts than one that might be extremely obscure or potentially upsetting. Audience response tracks similarly, with relevant social or political topics and extreme sports and nature subjects attracting more interest and revenue than those that may be less accessible. For example, *The Bridge*, a riveting and important documentary about people who commit suicide from the Golden Gate Bridge, grossed just $180,000, while the *Buena Vista Social Club* grossed $7 million and *Enron: The Smartest Guys in the Room*, a documentary considered required viewing in every MBA program in the country, grossed $4 million theatrically. This is not to say that documentaries should not tackle tough subjects, but getting a film made and getting a film seen in this economy may warrant a temporary reorientation for a first project.

"Most of the documentaries that have worked theatrically have had something extremely captivating emotionally about them, whether it's the human component or in some cases the ability to identify with wildlife and their predicament, but every one of them has a very strong emotional component," says The Film Department's Mark Gill. "It feels to me like the one thing that will be true, no matter what, is that if you make something emotionally involving that's distinctive, your chances are pretty good that people will show up. A strong concept, one that has the possibility of creating that level of emotional involvement, is what's going to win the day."

Key to that involvement is a lack of cynicism and a level of honesty going into the project that will inform the piece and prevent it from playing like an episode of *Cops*. "My advice to struggling documentary filmmakers would be to be true to yourself, be true to your subject, and don't forget your audience," advises Lionsgate Films president of production Tom Ortenberg. "That last one is true whether you're making a doc or a narrative film: you still always have to keep in mind who is the audience for this. That doesn't change just because you're making a documentary."

"It still comes down to subject matter," agrees copresident and cofounder Tom Bernard. "Errol Morris is a very entertaining filmmaker and sort of a brand name when it comes to documentaries, but his film *Dr. Death* did not do as well as *The Fog of War* because the subject matter was not as appealing to the public. Look at something like *Capturing the Friedmans*, which got a lot of attention from critics but moviegoers didn't really respond at the box office in relation to the positive reviews. *The Fog of War* covered a subject that sounds dry, but its theatrical grosses went up each week because the film was incredibly entertaining and basically covered the lifetime of a lot of people who are alive today, from World War II to the present. And it was done in a way that was very thought-provoking. In many ways it mirrored the second Iraq war, which made it interesting to a lot of people since it was relevant to current times."

Documentary filmmakers hoping for a theatrical release should not be shy or embarrassed about creating projects that are broadly entertaining in addition to being informative and provocative. "It's tough to think of any documentaries that performed well that don't meet the criteria," asserts Ortenberg, whose company partnered with Bob and Harvey Weinstein on the distribution of *Fahrenheit 9/11*.

"Filmmakers need to keep in mind while you're making your film that there's a better-than-average chance that you're not going to make your money back, even if your all-in budget is under $500,000," says Brian Newman, CEO of the Tribeca Film Institute and director of its Reframe project. "Distributors—well-known distributors—will tell you that it's a good success for them if they sell between five and fifteen thousand DVDs of a film, so if you multiply that out and factor in all of the marketing and distribution costs, there's not a lot of money there."

Of course, this reality doesn't stop many aspiring documentary filmmakers from secretly harboring dreams of becoming Michael Moore–level success stories, even though they may not admit it to their parents, spouses, or themselves. "Filmmakers will see a documentary film by a well-known documentary filmmaker like Errol Morris or Morgan Spurlock, and see that something like *Standard Operating Procedure* or *Where in the World Is Osama Bin Laden?* will play at the Angelika or at Film Forum, or maybe even at a Landmark Cinema, and go around the country and play at film festivals," explains Newman. "Then the filmmakers will get this idea: 'Well, the filmmaker must be doing really well from this.' But 99 percent of the time, even the best-known titles have not made their money back theatrically. When they see a documentary film or even any other independent film has made $25 million at the box office, it's still very likely that that film has not seen a single cent of profit, because most of that money was spent on marketing and distribution. Even films that have gotten Academy Awards, such as *Born into Brothels*, likely didn't make much back from theatrical exhibition. And filmmakers have this skewed perception that when you see these big numbers at the box office, it means that that is money coming back to the producer's pocket—when in fact that money has already been spent. These days, theatrical is often a loss-leader for DVD sales."

Newman points out that by selling the DVDs on site from a merchandise table and by handling the distribution duties, or by self-distributing through an array of nonexlusive retailers and e-tailers such as Breakthrough Distribution and Reframe, the filmmaker can realize greater and more immediate returns. Self-distribution, however, requires a great deal of time, dedication, and effort, and may not be for everyone. But today's aspiring documentary filmmakers are inventing new strategies for getting their films into the hands of consumers.

"As the marketplace keeps shaking out, people are starting to question how to sell their films, and smart filmmakers are going to come up with some kind of system that allows them to play these festivals, market to an audience, and sell DVDs when they know they're not going to get any kind of traditional distribution," says Newman. "The game is completely changing and it's ridiculous that six hundred people who see the film are walking out the door without buying a copy. I am sorry to tell the filmmaker, but those people aren't going to remember the film six months from now, whereas if they are primed to buy a copy right after the screening they might buy two and also send one copy to their mother back home. If they have forty dollars in their pocket they might part with it right then and buy two copies."

Unfortunately, most documentary filmmakers today still believe that simply getting into a leading film festival almost assures tham a distribution deal with a major distributor, and a generous minimum guarantee that will put them on easy street. "That's a huge misperception," explains Newman. "Even if you get into one of the better film festivals like Sundance or Toronto, anything like that, it can still be very hard for your documentary. And you can be accepted into literally dozens of film festivals all over the world, tour the world, see a lot of great things and come home, with no more money in your pocket but just a great trip. And your film still may not have sold or done anything."

However, if filmmakers have thought ahead and printed up professionally made DVDs (through a company such as Breakthrough, for one example), they may be able to monetize their festival adventure. "Regional film festivals serve a role and they are great for those communities, but people should not just accept invitations to film festivals and invest in going unless they are thinking about how is it's going to help the film and how it's going to help sell DVDs," says Newman. "At the very least, filmmakers should collect the names and e-mail addresses of the people who are there so they can mail out a notice when then DVD does become available."

SO WHERE TO GET THE MONEY

Outside of friends and family and the mythical dot-com millionaire, documentary filmmakers often don't know where to look for seed money or urgent infusions of cash. In truth, the sources of significant financing are relatively few. "The funding strategies for these things are basically no-brainers," says documentary filmmaker Ric Burns, director of the PBS series *New York: A Documentary Film* and coproducer for his brother Ken's *The Civil War*. "You move up the learning curve rather swiftly in terms of where you're going to be able to get the money because there are very few streams to fund these films. There's the federal government, either through institutions like the National Endowment for the Humanities or the National Endowment for the Arts, there's money from the government through PBS, then there's private foundation money and money from corporations. There's also corporate underwriting and then of course there's money from individuals. And that's it. So for any given project, you can determine where you should look pretty quickly. It's extremely difficult to get the money, but it's not confusing. It becomes quite clear relatively early on."

What blocks many documentarians from reaching their goal is that they don't ever make a list of logical funding sources that match the tone or subject matter of their projects. As a result, most will spend years writing proposals that no one ever sees and/or end up courting the wrong organizations. "For instance, you shouldn't go to the Sloan Foundation for a film you want to do about Andy Warhol, but you may well go to the Sloan Foundation for a documentary about breast cancer," adds Ric Burns, who codirected an episode of the 2009 PBS series *We Shall Remain*, an American Express project focusing on Native American history. "So you can pretty easily match the funding source to the topic and the content of the project. It seems bewildering to people at the outset, like: 'How the hell would I get *this* funded?' But if you talk to a documentary filmmaker who's actually in the game, within an hour you'd get a very clear sense of how to go about doing it."

Other sources of financing include branded consumer-product manufacturers that are opening up to the idea of sponsoring documentaries as a way to reach targeted audiences. Vans, the casual sneakers made famous by Sean Penn in the Amy Heckerling 1982 hit *Fast Times at Ridgemont High*, financed *Dogtown and Z-Boys* in 2000. "A lot more corporations are following the BMW Films model and doing more and more with it," says *American Teen* director Nanette Burstein. "I think a lot of it has to do with TiVo: they're really worried about how people are going to be paying for programming. If people aren't going to watch advertising, but they have to have a way of getting their product out there, then they're going to do it. And the surprising thing is that a lot of companies like Nike don't want you to try to make a giant ad out of it, they want you to make a good film. So you have the freedom to actually make a good film. It's almost like the PBS model of having a corporate sponsor and just having their name associated with a program that doesn't feature the product."

Similarly, cable networks are also now looking to distinguish themselves in a 500- to 1,000-channel universe with branded documentary content. "They all want to do something special," Burstein continues. "Today VH1, A&E, Discovery, HBO, and others have all gotten into financing documentaries. I think now more than ever there are new sources of financing to go to. Sure, they want you to do more traditional projects, but they also want to win awards, and their executives are increasingly open to backing edgier material. They want the kind of attention they won't get from run-of-the-mill programs. They may not be guaranteed the same ratings they're used to, but they'll be written up in all sorts of newspapers for pushing the envelope."

Kopple agrees that cable networks are increasingly a source of documentary financing. "There's Showtime, there's HBO, there's Court TV, there's A&E, there's the Discovery Channel, there's Sundance Channel, there's IFC, and all of those networks allow you to show your film theatrically," she says. "I think financing is getting broader and broader. There's now a World Documentary Fund created by a partnership of the National Film Board of Canada, the U.K. Film Council, and the British Broadcasting Corporation dedicated to producing feature-length documentaries for theatrical release. There are people all over the world who understand what a nonfiction film is all about and who will help you."

SAVING FOR A SECOND CUT

Today, many documentary filmmakers believe they can make the *March of the Penguins* of poodles or *March of the Piranhas*. But the theatrical failture of *Arctic Tale* in 2007, a G-rated, kid-friendly documentary that had a *huge* push from Starbucks, proved that it is much harder to make March of the Anything than most people realize. The film bombed, grossing less than $1 million theatrically. But when *March of the Penguins* debuted at Sundance in 2005, nobody knew it would eventually become a runaway blockbuster and an Oscar winner for Best Documentary. After all, the film was originally in French with voice-overs enunciating what the penguins on-screen were thinking. Former Warner Independent Pictures president Mark Gill, who launched The Film Department with former Bob Yari executive Neil Sacker in 2007, saw it differently. While other specialized film distributors were shaking their heads, laughing unintentionally, or even walking out of the original cut, Gill was quietly reassembling the film in his head and thinking of an entirely different approach.

"What I could see clearly was that there could be a really involving emotional narrative in the story of one penguin family if you simplified it, rewrote it, rescored it, and recut it," he recalls. "I saw that that there was the basis for an emotional story about sacrifice for the greater good of family. What I could see, and this was the virtue of having spent five years recutting movies for Harvey Weinstein, was the potential of what *March of the Penguins* could be, not what it actually was in the screening. So the reason we thought it had a shot theatrically was that we were moved by its potential, while everybody else was walking out of the movie."

As Gill remembers it, the original voice-over—which used actors Romane Bohringer, Charles Berling, and Jules Sitruk to say what the animals were supposedly thinking, along the lines of *Happy Feet* or *Surf's Up*—was actually the least of its problems. "The score of what was then *The Emperor's Journey* was what we jokingly called a 'Eurothump on Ice,' with a Björk wannabe that just totally yanked you out of the movie and made it much harder to connect emotionally to the animals. It was also a story that was originally told from four points of view: there were the voices of the mother penguin, the father penguin, the baby penguin, and the omniscient point of view. Far more important, though, that first edit didn't have much of a traditional narrative and was much more poetic. After we bought it we added a ton of facts so the audience would have a perspective on what was happening with the penguins. We spent about $600,000 to reedit it, rescore it with *Confessions of a Dangerous Mind* composer Alex Wurman, and of course revoice it with Morgan Freeman, so our total investment was about $1.6 million."

The fact that a nature documentary could go from a laughable walk-out to one of the highest-grossing indie-film acquisitions of all time speaks to the value of hiring a different editor to recut and even reimagine an innovative second pass. It is true that, typically, filmmakers only get one bite at the apple with distributors, but documentary films might warrant an additional cut created by someone who is new to the project or has no emotional stake in its outcome. While creating dueling versions—as was the case on the DVD release of Lodge Kerrigan's *Keane*, which includes a second version created by the film's producer Steven Soderbergh—may not be economically possible, budgeting for an alternate edit may bring a fresh or innovative perspective to the director and/or producer.

In many ways, the same could be said for documentary filmmaking as an art form or exercise. "There's no career path in documentary film, none whatsoever, which is both a blessing and a curse," says Ken Burns. "It's a curse because you can't always figure out the right path to take, but it's a blessing because you get to find your own way. The best advice of course is don't give up, because if you know that making documentaries is what you really want to do, then— more than any other type of filmmaking—you'll get there."

15. Out of the Theater

BITTORRENT, NETFLIX, AND AMAZON

*n the old days, filmmakers who couldn't get their shorts, features, or docs into festivals often spent thousands of dollars creating professionally mastered calling-card DVDs, with custom four-color inserts tucked into each jewel case. These discs, duplicated from expensive glass masters and configured with elegant DVD menus usually had the director's contact information professionally etched into each disc so the talent agents, producers, and studio execs who received them would know who to call after being dazzled by the extraordinary talent on display. Filmmakers justified the expense with the hope that betting the farm would lead to a big fat check or a three-picture deal just minutes after the DVD stopped spinning. This daydream inspired poor filmmakers with the same goal but fewer resources to spend days watching the turquoise burn-in-progress line creep across their computer screens as they created homemade Apple iDVDs with their contact information scrawled out by hand in big blue Sharpie.*

Today, however, intrepid filmmakers hoping to get their work in

front of the "right" people can bypass the DVD route by posting their material to websites such as YouTube and Joost, and e-mailing the URL to whoever might take a look. Although the length of each video is often capped and the image quality is less than iMovie HD can export, the ability to get material in front of people has never been better. As a result, the marketplace for calling-card shorts and indie feature films is expected to expand, especially as many digital televisions come equipped with standard Ethernet ports. Indeed, as hosting charges and buffering times shrink, online video sites may become the hot new launchpads for indie-film talent, providing an alternative to the festival cycle, with its application essays, fees, first and second rounds, and fast-approaching deadlines. Ultrafast Wi-Fi and new mobile WiMAX connections coupled with the ability to quickly download content to subnotebooks and the next generation of 4G handhelds will democratize film distribution further and revolutionize the specialized sector the way MiniDV and Final Cut Pro once did. In the not-too-distant future, text blogging and v-logging may give way to homemade Webisodes or shorts that push the Lonelygirl15 concept to new heights and allow indie filmmakers to recoup their production costs and even earn profits from micropayments through PayPal, iTunes, or Amazon. As digital televisions and flat-screen monitors increasingly ship with HDMI ports and connections to Slingboxes and AppleTV-like PVRs, the desktop will increasingly become the nexus of where entertainment content is consumed. The secret to succeeding in this new environment will be identifying the new film grammar to tell stories on smartphones and devices similar to the next-generation Sony PSP or the Archos 605, storytelling for content aggregators such as LaughOrDie, iFilm, AtomFilms, or perhaps even an art-house multiplex in Second Life or its successors. The Christopher Nolans and Kimberly Peirces of tomorrow are likely to be discovered via PlayStation Home and Amazon Video On Demand with more content downloaded and consumed at a doctor's office, in line at the post office, hurtling toward Union Square on a number 4 express train, or stuck in traffic on the 405. While the Angelika, Landmark, and Sunset 5 were once the venues of choice, mobile premieres on 3G and 4G iPhones may soon be a viable alternative, as filmmakers learn to tailor their shorts, docs, and narrative films for a wealth of new gadgets and as-yet-unreleased devices.

Although many of today's $150, 14-megapixel cameras can record more than an hour of 1080i or 720p video with fuzzy sound, these cameras may soon include SMPTE time code and Bluetooth-linked wireless-microphone capability that could allow them to shoot a low-budget version of *Cloverfield* for $25,000 rather than $25 million. This future, which started with Casio still cameras that came with a YouTube capture mode, is bound to create an explosion of short and feature filmmaking that will mirror the blogging craze kicked off by the new software. Whereas blogging, IMing, and text messaging were once the province of teenagers and the digerati, these activities are now as common as uploading "I was there" concert video from a cell phone. Today, using Keynote or iMovie to marry music to slide shows of a family trip is less exotic than owning a home server or creating an avatar on the Nintendo Wii. The era of Web 3.0, of hand-held filmmaking with high-end digital still cameras equipped with 32-gigabyte Memory Sticks or 16-gigabyte SD cards, is bound to bring about a new kind of storytelling and not all of it bad.

It's a really exciting time to be an independent filmmaker. "HD cameras that traditionally cost $80,000 or more are now less than $2,000 and can be rented for about $300 per day," says BitTorrent president and cofounder Ashwin Navin. "Many of the newer models have ready interfaces such as flash cards or built-in hard drives to allow filmmakers to capture HD video and copy it easily to a PC for editing. The barriers to publication and distribution are already gone as far as I'm concerned, since filmmakers have been building audiences and connecting with people directly through all the means they have available, whether it's YouTube or Bit-Torrent or MySpace."

Video sites such as Yahoo! Video and AtomFilms have long given filmmakers a forum to showcase their shorts without having to be accepted by increasingly exclusive traditional festivals. And as data-hosting costs drop and broadband speeds catch up to the 100Mbps fiber-to-the-home empowered networks in South Korea and Japan, more sites offering filmmakers a chance to showcase full-on feature films will spring up.

"I think YouTube and similar streaming sites represent a great opportunity for aspiring filmmakers to distribute their films," says *The Wrestler* director Darren Aronofsky. "Filmmakers used to have to follow the festival cycle and wait for their applications and films to be approved, but today you can create something and get it out there immediately, and if it's good, people will watch it and tell their friends to watch it. And every once in a while you see something really clever and cool that breaks out, like the music video with the guys walking on the treadmills, and it's great. There are things online that might have never gotten that much exposure and now a creative filmmaker has created a viable band through OK Go's 'Here It Goes Again,' and the song's online popularity. Videos like that are going to be seen by a much larger online audience than if they only get a few screenings at a film festival that not everybody can attend."

New set-top boxes, rental download options, and fiber-optic broadband to the home have created an environment where this may be possible with features. "I think the real promise of the Internet is that independent filmmakers will be able to get full-length feature films in front of people. Bandwidth is getting cheaper and the costs of production are going down," says Ted Sarandos, chief content officer of

Netflix, which began streaming films from its site in July 2007. "All the barriers to entry are coming down. So someday you may only have to have talent to get your film distributed, whereas you have to have talent, luck, money, and connections to get your film distributed. Down the road, it might just be that talent is enough to carry the day."

Accelerating this trend are hardware improvements that continue to make things easier for novice filmmakers who have not attended film school. "HD cameras with flash memory cards or internal hard drives are now able to transfer video files just like copying Word or PowerPoint documents from one hard drive to another," says Navin. "The ability to create music and video and to edit and manipulate media with tools anyone can get at a really low cost has been tremendously democratizing and empowering. And as a result creativity is coming from places that it didn't come from or which were totally unexposed in the past. Just spend half an hour on YouTube and you'll see some things that are really phenomenal in their uniqueness and in the way that people have taken advantage of this new format."

While Sundance and other leading festivals often mandate that filmmakers not show their films anywhere prior to their festival premieres, many directors and producers are now considering skipping the festival circuit altogether and looking to the Web for a shot at making a name for themselves.

"We used to submit stuff to film festivals and we had some shorts play at festivals, but the Web was really where we got things going and how we managed to be able to quit our day jobs. Matt [Sloan] worked at a bookstore and I worked at a metal shop. Now we're going to finance additional episodes of *Chad Vader* with one of the many offers we've gotten from online entertainment sites," says filmmaker Aaron Yonda. Short films and videos are in demand from everyone, but right now the best-paying ones are places like Super Deluxe or Heavy. Advertisers have asked us to do a lot of work, too. We've done videos for Canon, International Truck, and some local companies as well. And we've been getting a ton of offers since the October 15, 2007, *New York Times* article. Not just for ads, people are asking us for feature scripts, TV-show pitches, etc. We're hoping to turn our online success into a multi-platform career."

Indeed, the popularity of applications such as BitTorrent, Pando, and Perenity, and streaming sites such as YouTube and Joost have changed the way independent films are distributed and even defined. "In a way, 'Star Wars Kid' and its many revisions and adaptations or even a clip of David Hasselhoff drunk on the floor of his house eating a hamburger is a type of filmmaking," says *Eternal Sunshine of the Spotless Mind* producer Anthony Bregman. "A lot of what you see on sites like YouTube is a kind of 'accidental filmmaking' or filmmaking that does not involve creating storyboards, planning out every shot, or making and composing it in a traditional way, and that is having a parallel impact on narrative. It's also changing our definition of what filmmaking is."

The impact on narrative is evident in the public's ability to understand and embrace an increasingly episodic style of filmmaking, be it a documentary-style assortment of individual clips such as *Jackass Number Two* or the mélange of set pieces that was *Pirates of the Caribbean: At World's End*. "I think *Borat* and films like it really come out of this new tradition of seeing these kind of short clips on the Internet," says Bregman. "I think it creates a stylistic difference in terms of what films are supposed to do—like, are all films supposed to tell stories in three acts with clear character arcs? Or can you make a substantial film that revolves around the engaging presentation of entertaining images and scenes? I think the pacing and form of *Borat* was something that was partially created on the Internet and which will continue to have a huge impact on narrative. You could argue that *Napoleon Dynamite* was really enhanced by the Internet since people had more of an appreciation for a quirky, loose dramatic style closer to reality television and viral clips and more tolerance for that kind of storytelling."

Even as technological innovation opens new sales channels and makes Chris Anderson's long tail theory more efficient, many filmmakers still cling to the the old ways, ignoring more innovative sales options, and shell out $50,000 to $100,000 for a 35mm blowup they think will secure a nationwide theatrical release after screening at a leading festival. Indeed, because that exact fantasy is often hanging in the balance, many indie filmmakers are crestfallen when they don't make it into a festival or when their festival entry is not picked up for distribution. Some are so bent on getting a theatrical deal that they lose sight of the fact that they might garner more attention and financial upside by actually considering a straight-to-DVD deal or cable premiere on Showtime.

"Filmmakers need to realize there are now a lot of places they can put their films to get them seen," says Byrd, president of New York–based IFP. "There's iFilm, there's AtomFilms, IFC has its media lab, there's Jaman, which offers high-definition films from around the world and 'a film festival that never ends,' and there are direct-to-DVD deals with Netflix, whose Red Envelope Entertainment has purchased more than a hundred independent films, including Mark and Jay Duplass's *The Puffy Chair*, as of 2008. There are actually more options than ever for filmmakers to get their work out in front of people, if they think outside of the box and do a little research about alternative options." In 2008, Red Envelope discontinued the business of buying all rights and releasing films in theaters and selling to television. However, the company continues to license the rights to produce DVDs and to stream movies such as *Elegy* to its subscribers directly from producers.

"You're still going to get independent films coming out of Sundance and kids whose careers are launched because they got some attention or buzz at a major festival," says Aronofsky, whose low-budget *Pi* premiered at the Eccles at Sundance in 1998 and received a standing ovation. "And feature-length film is still probably the premier way that people enjoy narrative entertainment. But over the next few years I think we'll continue to see a number of exciting developments for filmmakers as a result of opportunities emerging from online distribution."

There are now at least three generations of young adults who are totally at ease downloading ringtones and other content and receiving their entertainment via Hulu or Xbox LIVE rather than by television, a trend that some blame for the downturn in theatrical box office grosses of many specialized films in 2008 and 2009. "Young people experience and share entertainment content and information in a different way than their parents did," says Sony Pictures Classics copresident Tom Bernard. "The people right now under thirty are the so-called new brain generation: their brains work differently than anybody's have ever worked in terms of how they get information and the way they process it. They don't need newspapers, they don't talk on the phone in the conventional way that even their older siblings did. They have Skype, Facebook widgets, iChat, and electronic tools that get them their information as soon as it's available. They get their news from Yahoo!'s front-page rather than CNN. What all this has done is taught young people to multitask and process vast amounts of information in really quick flashes."

SHOOTING FOR ONLINE

Prosumer independent filmmaking has evolved from non-digital Hi8 in the mid-'80s that lacked time code and whose image quality degraded with every playback, to the MiniDV of the mid-'90s to today's consumer HD cameras and those that even record in QuickTime or AVI on half-size DVDs. Going forward there may be DV cameras that transfer their massive HD files via high-speed 3G and 4G broadband directly to a faraway edit bay so that editing and postproduction can run in parallel to production for indie filmmakers as it does for mainstream Hollywood projects.

While all this technological innovation makes older filmmakers jealous, shooting for the Internet does require some special attention and methods that filmmakers need to consider. "One thing you have to realize is that on the Internet, people watching your clip are going to miss a lot of the more subtle things," explains Yonda. "You have to consider depth of field, take into account what might be lost that's not in the foreground, and then pull focus accordingly. Sometimes it's facial expressions that don't register or the little things that are going on in the background that are lost on the Internet audience, so it's much more than just an aspect-ratio issue and the fact that you're essentially shooting for television given the shape of the YouTube player window."

When filming for the Internet, a number of immediate technical considerations come into play that sometimes run counter to the increasing sophistication of even the most basic digital cameras, such as frame rate, file size, and sound quality. Shooting for the Internet also requires a new perspective in the way that a live sitcom requires a different grammar of frame lines, reaction shots, close-ups, and cuts than a traditional indie-film shot list. "When we're shooting *Chad Vader* episodes we try to shoot with the idea that it will someday play on a bigger screen," says Yonda. "Sometimes we do have a live screening using a projector and we'll notice that a subtle gesture, something which is lost on most Internet viewers, will get a big laugh."

Yonda references a scene in the third episode's credit sequence in which staggering shoppers were positioned far back in the frame. "When you're watching it online, it's such a small screen and the quality is often so bad that people can't really tell the shoppers are supposed to be zombies," explains Yonda. "It's kind of a subtle zombie thing, but that's one example where if we had realized that they weren't going to read or register with viewers, we would have made it more obvious in the acting or easier for the audience to get. When you watch it on the big screen you can tell, but when it's online it's lost on most people."

Sometimes the conventions of a certain genre give online filmmakers a leg up. "Since we're shooting comedy, people are a little little more forgiving when it comes to the visuals," Yonda says. "Not much of what we do relies on the visuals per se and a lot of what we do, such as Chad waving his light saber, can be seen well enough so you get it. But we try to do good quality work. People surfing YouTube are willing to watch things that sometimes look pretty rough, so it doesn't have to be perfect, but we still try to constantly improve our lighting and sound and make it as good as we can."

Ironically, as the image quality of video sites remains relatively blurry, the equipment that is readily available to filmmakers even from big-box stores is getting remarkably advanced, leading to a widening gulf between file sizes that are permitted and the giant file sizes of full-res shorts and features. The first episodes of *Chad Vader* were shot using a Panasonic AG-DVX100A and edited with Final Cut Pro on an old-school G5 and then bashed down from five gigabytes to under one hundred megabytes for YouTube.

The light-saber effects in *Chad Vader* were far easier to accomplish given that a lightsaber plug-in for Final Cut Pro exists on the Internet and the glowing blades' iconic humming can be cloned from *The Force Unleashed* for Xbox 360 or PlayStation 3. Far more complicated was simply lighting their central character so he didn't show up as a dark blob on-screen, the classic problem going back to 1977.

"The problem with shooting the Vader suit is you need a lot of bright lighting so you can see the contours and folds of the cape and the lines of the mask that make it so iconic," explains Yonda. "That's hard to do when you're shooting with overhead fluorescents and the challenge becomes how do you light Chad to make sure you can see his face and get this sort of big reflective look that they have in the *Star Wars* films, and not overlight everyone who is standing nearby or talking to him.' "

The answer is to use a lattice of flags and scrims and make sure that the lights are aimed precisely and not bleeding over into the faces of other actors. But one of the lighting elements Yonda's team was not able to change were the overhead lights in the location, a working grocery store on the outskirts of Madison, Wisconsin.

"I think if we wanted to make the lighting look really great we'd have to bring in all of our own lights and actually turn off all the existing fluorescent lights," explains Yonda. "But we just don't have the ability to do that in the grocery store so we're sort of always fighting the location as far as light goes. You pretty much have the same lighting issues that you have shooting for any film or video. Although I guess one way to look at it is that a lot of people don't typically light for video on the Internet, especially when they're just posting a video of their cat being attacked by a turtle, or their video blog. So any additional lighting at all is a step up for most Internet video. It's hard to make any shot lit by fluorescent lights look ideal since they wash out the colors and automatically make things look a little less filmic."

Things often get even more complex when shooting special effects, since lighting for green screen is not something most aspiring filmmakers can learn from repeated viewings of director's commentaries of *Sin City 2*, *300*, or *Beowulf*.

"You have to have someone who knows green-screen lighting and can make sure that the light is evenly distributed so it will look good when you composite it together," explains Yonda. "And don't stand too close to the green because it reflects onto clothing if you're too close."

SOME RULES STILL APPLY

Whether they are debuting their films on a Web page or a giant screen at the Ziegfeld in New York City, coherent and compelling storytelling needs to be the most important goal. "Having access to cheap, high-quality digital-video devices to shoot and edit is wonderful, but it still requires a lot of creativity to figure out how to tell a story on a new platform," says Miles Beckett, who with Ramesh Flinders cocreated and codirected the YouTube sensation *Lonelygirl15*, the webcam musings of a home-schooled teenage girl named Bree. Millions of early YouTube fans believed her postings were legitimate before it was revealed that her video diary entries were scripted and produced by aspiring filmmakers. "Content needs to be tailored to the platform and *Lonelygirl15* was a show perfectly designed to be watched sitting at a desk in front of your computer. It was no accident that each video was short, interactive, and shot and edited to work well on tiny video screens."

The admonition should be heeded by aspiring documentary filmmakers who are thinking of debuting their material online. "The rapid proliferation of DV cameras and offline editing tools has democratized everything, but owning the latest MacPro doesn't automatically make you a good storyteller," says filmmaker Ken Burns. "Whether you're a documentary filmmaker or a feature filmmaker, you still have be able to tell a story well and it's a really tough thing to do; otherwise everyone would be able to do it."

Indeed, regardless of the exhibition medium, many of the basic requirements of independent filmmaking still apply to Web-based shorts. Internet filmmakers, thinking their projects are simply too short to require subplots, offscreen dialogue, voice-over narration, or even b-roll, often fail to shoot enough coverage to be able to stitch their story lines together should a narrative gap or story hole appear during the edit.

"Sometimes we just shoot each character saying 'yes,' 'no,' 'maybe,' 'okay' to someone within their eye line, just basic dialogue like that so we'll be covered in case we have to throw in a reaction shot or a reaction line somewhere," explains Yonda. "You don't always know what you're going to be missing until you get into the editing bay, especially if you use improvisation on the set like we often do. So you always want to have a lot of basic reaction shots of each character looking up, looking down, looking left, and looking right, smiling, frowning, listening, and just thinking, and reaction lines you can use in a jam. That way you can loop in any kind of offscreen dialogue later and create what looks like a conversation, either to fill a plot hole or to give yourself more freedom in the edit to go with improvised lines or to use different takes."

This coverage exercise, while seemingly tedious, can save the day when an actor delivers the first part of his or her line well but a second part without the same level of emotion or characterization. "A lot of people don't shoot this kind of coverage, but reaction shots give you an out if you end up needing to cut two takes together. If someone's dialogue is off," says Yonda, "you can loop in a better line reading from another take that sounds better and have it said off camera during the reaction shot. That way you don't have to lose the whole take or bring everyone back for ADR."

PREPARING FOR SUCCESS

Although many filmmakers would like their Web clips to be popular, most are not ready for the ferocity of interest that can spring from being featured on YouTube's home page or mentioned on ABC World News's daily list of "Top Rising Searches." The ability to forward URLs to dozens of friends with a single click and to create a critical mass around a particular clip by posting it to Facebook can turn filmmakers into Web stars almost overnight.

"On July 4, 2006, we had a *Lonelygirl15* episode entitled 'My Parents Suck' get 500,000 views in 48 hours. Prior to that, our videos were only getting around 50,000 views. That's when Greg Goodfried and I realized there was a possibility to continue the show on the Internet and skip the low-budget indie-film version we had planned. What we didn't realize when we started was the huge opportunity on the Internet because audience expectations are so undefined and the market is still largely wide open. There's room to try things like new characters and plotlines, have fans interact with the characters, mix mediums of video and text, and have a one-to-one relationship with the audience that you don't get with television. And it's possible to do it inexpensively. In 2007 we launched a new show on Bebo, the biggest social network in the United Kingdom at the time. We worked with them because we felt we could achieve more interactivity by using their social-networking features."

With the literally millions and millions of videos populating YouTube and other sites, it is hard for any one filmmaker to break out of the pack by design, but when it does happen, most filmmakers are not prepared to monetize their sudden Internet popularity.

"My advice would be to be prepared for success," says experimental filmmaker and early Internet video star Ahree Lee. "My short became a hit almost instantaneously, which was something I was not expecting. I showed *Me* to an acquisitions manager at AtomFilms on May 18, 2006, and he accepted it on the spot. It was officially acquired on July 18, 2006, after I signed the contracts and legal clearances and sent them the official DVD. I had a dentist's appointment the day that my short launched on August 8, 2006, because they had given me less than a day's notice, e-mailing at 5 p.m. on August 7 to let me know, and by the time I came back from the dentist, someone had swiped an older, incomplete version that was on my website and posted it to YouTube illegally. But that's when it really took off."

Before Lee knew it, the blogosphere was abuzz with chatter about her film *Me* and about Lee herself. "It immediately got really popular and big and then all of a sudden, I realized that there were literally millions of people who were watching this film. I saw all these comments on YouTube and on AtomFilms and it started to freak me out a little bit because I was wondering if I was going to start being followed or recognized on the street."

Interest in *Me* accelerated further after the mainstream press picked up on the story. "I was written up in *Wired* and the *Los Angeles Times* and *The New York Times* and then featured on ABC's World News webcast, which showed a good portion of the clip," she recalls. "ABC picked up on it really quickly, within a week of when it launched on AtomFilms.

And apparently *The Today Show* showed it as well, which I had no idea until my husband's cousin called to say he had seen me on NBC."

One of the people who saw Ahree Lee's YouTube video was Brooklyn-based fashion and lifestyle photographer Noah Kalina, who would go on to become a Web sensation in his own right with a similar photograph-a-day short film. *Everyday* became a huge hit and was specifically parodied on an episode of *The Simpsons*, in which Homer ages thirty-nine years in one minute while his eyes maintain the same dull expression, mirroring the haunting look on Kalina's face throughout his shifting haircuts, backgrounds, and shirt collars. "I had actually started taking pictures of myself every day since January 11, 2000, and then I saw Ahree's video in August of 2006 and realized that that was the form the project could take," Kalina recalls. "The original camera I used was actually a video camera that could take still photos, so they were each just one megapixel to start with. This was back in 2000, after all. I experimented with different frame rates and then ended up running it at seven shots per second for a total of 2,356 shots during the course of the video."

Musician Carly Comando, of the band Slingshot Dakota, created the wistful and elegiac piano line that is the heart of the piece and one that provided much of its locomotive momentum. "Carly was my girlfriend at the time, and after I made the video she watched it with me and just made the song from that," Kalina explains. "It's a really powerful score and the music is really what makes it work. When I first heard it I thought it was perfect because it went really well with what I had done."

Fans of *Everyday* debated online how Kalina had managed to get his eyes dead center in the frame so that his expression never changes or how he had managed to string the shots together using Adobe Premiere or some other software. "Actually, just like the Microsoft ads that say 'I'm a PC,' I made *Everyday* on a PC using Windows MovieMaker," says Kalina. "I've kind of always been a PC guy, although now I use Macs. [*Everyday*] was actually surprisingly simple to do. There was no editing involved and it was really just about laying down the audio track," Kalina continues. "I use cameras that have flip screens to shoot each image—I'm still working on the next version—so I can see myself and just put my nose in the center of the frame. That way I didn't have to use a computer program to align the photos up, but the assembly was a challenge. I had to do it year by year and then combine them, because when I tried to do all six years at once it was too much for my computer to handle. What kind of sucks is that the version on YouTube compresses it so badly for the first minute and is just really pixilated and poor quality because of their compression. I uploaded it to a site called Vimeo [www.vimeo.com] because the quality of the compression there was much better, but that site doesn't have nearly as many viewers.

"Carly and I thought only one hundred people would watch the video, so I didn't think of making mugs or T-shirts or hats or anything," Kalina says with a laugh. "I did have some limited-edition DVDs that were being sold through a gallery in New York, but it was really nothing to speak of. I didn't really consider myself a filmmaker so I didn't think of making *Everyday* available for sale on iTunes or on CD-ROM for people to buy, not until way after the fact."

Everyday started to gather tremendous interest in 2006 until it had more than four million page views on YouTube and became a cultural touchstone, reaching eleven million page views in 2009. Kalina, who maintains a photography site at www.noahkalina.com, was invited to the 2006 VH1 Video Awards and was named the number 14 Internet

Superstar by the network, but Kalina did not prepare for his 5:45 minutes of fame in terms of doing anything to monetize his creation.

"I think if I were a filmmaker I might have been able to do more with it, but right now I'm just doing my thing as a photographer," says Kalina. "Carly still sells the sheet music and sells the song on iTunes—she licensed it to the NBA and to *The Simpsons* obviously—but *The Simpsons* called her to license the song and didn't call me, which is fine. It's still flattering, and the fact that they used Carly's song I think speaks to our version and the power of her composition."

What frustrated Lee was that she also hadn't thought of ways to monetize her short should it become a hit. "A lot of people were saying, 'Wow, this music is great. Where can I get it?'" continues Lee. "I called my husband and said, 'You better put together a MySpace page right away, because all these people are asking about your music and want to buy it.' If we had realized how popular my film would be and how many people would be interested in his music, we could have set up a way for them to buy it before the film launched. Unfortunately it took two months to get the music out on iTunes and other online music stores. So the lesson is that you should really prepare for success, which I certainly didn't do. I wasn't even thinking that it was going to become popular, so all I had done to prepare was to add some stuff to my website, but I hadn't even switched the video that was on my website to the version that was up on AtomFilms yet, because I figured I had time to do it later. Success is not something a lot of people think is actually going to happen to them."

KEEP WEB SHORTS SHORT

Even though everyone has heard the adage "less is more," many student filmmakers still insist on writing and shooting interminable narrative shorts that few people are actually going to watch online or anywhere else. "In 1993 when I was getting ready to make my first feature as a grad student at USC, I would see these students ahead of me that were making ambitious twenty-minute shorts," recalls Slamdance co-founder Dan Mirvish. "Most of them were bad, but even those that were really good didn't get a lot of traction. These students would go into meetings with agents and producers and hear something like: 'This is really great. Let us know when you've got a feature to show us.' So the takeaway was: 'Screw the shorts world, I'm going to make a feature.' But the problem now—in this YouTube-focused environment— is you make a feature and the executives say, 'That's great, but if it was a short we could really pay attention to the whole thing,' since executives' and agents' attention spans are about nil these days. So it becomes a chicken-or-the-egg type question."

While there is some debate whether or not development executives sit around trolling YouTube on OLED screens looking for the next big thing, what frustrates many independent filmmakers is that what often plays on YouTube, simply stays on YouTube. "A lot of festival programmers I talk to will say, 'That looks like a cool thing for the Web but it doesn't really work for a festival,' and I say, 'Uh, yeah it does!' " explains Mirvish. "A clip might be a huge hit online and programmers may not see it as a festival thing, but they need to open their eyes a little more. Is something good for festivals? Well, does it make people laugh, and is it short? Yeah. Then it works as a festival short. And part of the reason is the length. If it's under three minutes that means you can program it before a feature."

One thing is fairly certain, however, from a consensus of filmmakers and festival programmers: brevity is better when it comes to short films. "The film-school students I knew making twenty-minute short films would literally spend $120,000, which is more than their tuition for a full year at USC, but the problem is, at that length they're really hard to get into festivals," explains Mirvish. "Long shorts make a nice showcase for the director of photography, but they don't really do anyone else much good. Which is why filmmakers are now starting to realize that three minutes really is the magic number for short films. And guess what? That's the magic number for festivals, too, because it means they can be programmed before a feature."

Even so, filmmakers continue to make long short films that rarely convert into deals. The lack of traction often surprises many student filmmakers, who look at film school as a golden ticket but who end up rolling calls as an assistant to a film executive, as does the fact that so many glossy three-minute short films in the $30,000 range may not get them directing jobs. "Getting into a festival is one dream, but I think the bigger, more usual dream is that they're going to get an agent, get a distribution deal, or get their career jump-started," says Howard Cohen, a former agent at United Talent Agency who cofounded *Super Size Me* distributor Roadside Attractions with *Lovely and Amazing* producer Eric d'Arbeloff in 2003. "Plenty of people think that, but the norm is that filmmakers usually don't get an agent at a big agency until they've made at least one movie. Some of the people attending Sundance have agents because either it's not their first film or somehow they had a connection, or they were once a commercial director, or they were a screenwriter who had an agent as a writer. There are many different scenarios, but even at a major festival like Sundance it's probably fifty-fifty in terms of people who don't have agents versus people who do."

Historically, there were four reasons filmmakers made short films: to learn how to handle equipment, to have a live-fire experience fighting the chaotic dynamics of a real film set, to serve as a calling card for the director's talent, or to act as a trailer for a film the director would like to get financed. Indeed, many shorts have evolved into successful feature films, such as *Half Nelson*, *Bottle Rocket*, *Boys Don't Cry*, and *Napoleon Dynamite*. "We showed Jared Hess's film *Peluca* at Slamdance a few years ago, and I was at the screening where producers approached him and said, 'Do you have a feature script based on this Napoleon character?' " recalls Mirvish, who has shot four festival shorts, including one that premiered at the HBO Comedy Arts Festival in Aspen in 2007. "And he said, 'Yeah, I've got it right here,' and six months later they were shooting," recalls Mirvish. "But what's interesting now is that people are making shorts, they're putting them up online at a time when you've got television executives watching YouTube, looking for the next new thing."

CREATING INTERNET PILOTS

While many filmmakers used to think that a short film and a feature-film screenplay were the magic combo toward landing studio rewrite work or getting feature-film directing assignments, smart filmmakers are increasingly presenting their short films as television pilots, since the "creator" fees for television series can be extremely lucrative.

While the presidents and top executives of major independent-film distributors have not yet turned to the Web to discover new directors, cable television executives are beginning to think outside the box and looking to YouTube and other online sites. "I can't imagine shooting a feature or pitching a television pilot the 'traditional way' right now," explains Beckett.

"It used to be that if you were talking about creating a series or a pilot, there were only four major networks you could pitch and they were a closed club," explains Mirvish. "Filmmakers didn't make Net pilots as recently as six years ago because there was no one to show them to and because of a certain snobbery in the independent-film world where people would say, 'I'm a filmmaker. I don't do television.' But what they forget is that Robert Altman started in television directing *Alfred Hitchcock Presents* and *Bonanza* and that a lot of their indie-film heroes have been doing television for years after their successes in the indie-film world. It all started with *Homicide*, the first show that I think actively went after a lot of indie filmmakers. Part of that was that the show was produced by Barry Levinson, who got his start in independent film, and the style of that show. *New Jersey Drive* director Nick Gomez, now a director of Showtime's hit *Dexter*, did a few episodes and that kind of opened the door for others."

Today, the smartest filmmakers are making shorts that could be considered television and Internet pilots, since it has become an area of opportunity. Indeed, the sitcom *It's Always Sunny in Philadelphia* was essentially a Net pilot shot on a standard-definition DV camera that made its way to FX. Today, network executives understand the idea of Adult Swim or funnyordie.com and that there are many more places for filmmakers to go with short films.

Of course, for a short film to be considered for a Web pilot or a television pilot, filmmakers should avoid the temptation to be overly controversial or shocking simply for the sake of keeping it real.

"You don't want to kill off all your main characters at the end or do something that might make the story completely unpalatable for television executives," says Mirvish. "They won't be able to see what the short could be with a different ending or without the scene of everyone getting shot at the end. Creative executives often don't have the patience to be creative—they don't have the vision to see what a short could be or the time to watch an alternate ending on a DVD—so if you kill off your characters at the end, it's going to be hard to explain to a television executive that 'Well, they're not *really* dead.' "

GOING STRAIGHT TO INTERNET

As more studio-produced content beyond trailers and "exclusive clips" migrate to iTunes, MovieWeb, Movielink, BitTorrent, and other online venues, filmmakers are starting to embrace the once-pejorative implications of going straight to video or straight to the Internet. Indeed, in today's competitive environment, with dozens of options competing for a share of consumers' entertainment dollar, indie filmmakers may someday reach a wider audience with an online or direct-to-DVD push than with a theatrical release in only a handful of cities. Although the Internet is not yet a commercially viable distribution platform and is still largely a marketing vehicle, filmmakers who don't consider the idea of an Amazon CreateSpace debut or a direct-to-Netflix release probably don't understand the economics and competitive dynamics of the current market and are likely to be wasting their investors' money by taking an elitist perspective.

"Let's say you have a release in one or two theaters on each coast that are the size of Film Forum in New York," explains Sarandos. "At the level you probably won't be able to afford a big marketing expenditure to support television spots, but at the same time you need your film to be a big hit during its opening weekend so you can keep the screens. The problem is, even a monster hit would not do enough business per screen for the producer's cut to be anywhere near the $30,000 it would cost to meet the house floor and

be profitable in each theater. There are just not enough seats
in each house and not enough hours in the day to make back
what even the smallest distributor releasing your film would
have to spend. What you're hoping for is that the movie will
somehow be big enough that they'll keep it for several weeks
and you would only pay the big fees up front. But most filmmakers with a limited release never recoup expenses because
audiences don't always discover their films in the first or second week and movies can't be held over with empty seats in
an art-house theater until audiences come around."

Netflix, however, utilizes systems that inherently help create a critical mass of support behind difficult indie films by
emphasizing customer reviews and recommendations. "If I
have a film like *Born Into Brothels*, I can make a list of comparable movies and try to get a sense of the size of the market
for the project," explains Sarandos. "Our customer information is proprietary, but it allows me to say that of the 1.8 million people who rented *City of God* from us, 900,000 of them
said they loved it by ranking it highly. Then I can do the
other part of the analysis and see that we had 2.4 million
people who rented *Hotel Rwanda* from us, and of the 2.4 million, 1.6 million of them said they loved it. Then of the
1.6 million who loved *Hotel Rwanda*, there's 400,000 people
who also loved *City of God* and who have rented five or more
documentaries, and those are the people that we're going to
target directly with our ad message for *Born Into Brothels*."

While theater chains and specialized film distributors are
not able to make targeted recommendations for upcoming releases even to their most satisfied customers, Netflix's
two billion computerized recommendations get increasingly
accurate with its members' rankings, allowing Netflix to recommend new releases that they would enjoy. As a result,
filmmakers who distribute their films directly to Netflix and
increasingly via Amazon's CreateSpace can make money

with a smaller hit than with a theatrical release that requires the cost of prints and advertising and studio overhead to be recouped before the producers see a check for overages.

"The economics of releasing a film nationally are really tough because the studios have to recoup the marketing costs: all of the awareness-building, all of the television ads, radio spots, everything we don't have to spend since we make recommendations directly to our members' Netflix home pages," explains Sarandos. "If you look at the two business models, the likelihood of a filmmaker making money with us is better because the old economics of distributing a film don't work any better today than they used to. In fact, in many ways they're actually worse because the media that specialized distributors have to buy is much more expensive. Just look at the struggle that Harvey's had in the last few years. When Harvey Weinstein first came up with this, there was no competition. Nobody was doing it any better. But now the market for the classic old Miramax-type film is incredibly competitive, especially for the top tier of those good films. Today you have Fox Searchlight, Focus Features, and other really skilled marketers who are making a lot of their own productions and spending heavily to support those efforts."

In 2006, Sarandos launched Red Envelope Entertainment, with a budget to acquire films at leading festivals. Sarandos says Red Envelope should not be considered a distributor of last resort but rather an innovative company willing to take risks with films that have a few strong or clear comparables. "Our distribution threshold can be very low because our cost to market a film is almost nothing. Our automated systems can put films in front of the right audience that will give it a shot and accept it without our having to buy expensive bill-boards and television spots to reach them. I guarantee you that the producers of the Maggie Gyllenhaal film *Sherry-*

Baby, which has been rented and streamed more than 700,000 times through Netflix, made more going with us than the producers of *Half Nelson* did from their theatrical release even with an Academy Award nomination. Which is why we were at Sundance that year competing with Harvey and THINKFilm and others for *SherryBaby* and the film's producers went with us." Netflix feels it has a competitive advantage the studios and Blockbuster do not have: it knows how to push videos to its membership of 8.4 million subscribers. Among the titles on Netflix, *Crash* has hit the high side in 2008 with 3 million rentals.

Sarandos's next step is to try to transform Netflix into the YouTube of movie rentals, as broadband speeds increase, hosting costs drop, and the standard definition DVD platform wanes. Netflix has roughly 12,000 titles available for free streaming out of its total 100,000 DVD titles, as part of the standard Netflix membership. "We actually save money on the streaming service because we don't have to pay postage or the cost of printing DVDs," says Sarandos. "What I'd like to see long range is the ability for a filmmaker to be able to upload a movie just like he or she would on YouTube. And if enough people watch it and rate it highly, we would then cut a deal to acquire the rights to the film and make DVDs and distribute it more broadly under a Netflix-branded banner."

Netflix, along with today's studio-supported BitTorrent, Amazon's On Demand service, and future websites utilizing Microsoft's planned Avalanche software may someday be the leading venues for breaking new talent.

"These days there are fewer distributors buying and distributing films that are smaller or coming out of left field, and that's not because of the Internet but more because the economics of specialized distribution have changed," says Bregman. "Many distributors have been shut down and the rest are owned by bigger companies. They are no longer looking for a movie that will only make $2 million at the box office, whereas ten to fifteen years ago the $2.7 million *Half Nelson* made would be considered a hit. It was great: you would make a movie for $500,000, it would make $2 million or so at the box office, and everyone was happy. Today, that is not a hit for anybody: a movie that makes $2 million, no matter what the budget, is considered to be a failure because the companies that are behind it are now dependent on making big specialized movies like *Good Night, and Good Luck* that make $10 million at least.

"In part it's because of the ways the remaining companies are structured: the executives are highly paid, the companies have so many people working for them and have to pay a large support staff—and because specialized divisions are in many cases expected to bring in more than $100 million per year from a dozen or fewer films," continues Bregman, who in 2008 produced the Charlie Kaufman–directed *Synecdoche, New York*. "As a result the bar has been raised so that what qualifies as a solid hit in the independent or specialized sphere has shifted significantly. Now you have independently produced films like *Napoleon Dynamite* that make $45 million theatrically or films like *Little Miss Sunshine* that make $60 million, and that skews the perspective of specialized-film distributors."

These huge numbers and certainly *Juno*'s $146 million theatrical gross have distorted acquisitions executives' opinions on what they're willing to take a risk on releasing, and made stars and bankable elements such as a high concept or director pedigree almost a requirement, leaving the future of ultra-low-budget debut films in the mold of *Clerks*, *El Mariachi*, or *She's Gotta Have It* in doubt.

As a result the Internet is looking more and more like a democratizing alternative for films passed over by acquisitions executives. "Once people figure out how to better monetize the playing of clips, the Web will take some of the difficulty out of distribution," says Bregman. "Anybody who wants to get something distributed, anybody who has something that's good, whether it's ninety seconds or ninety minutes long, will be able to put it up online somewhere so everybody can have access to it and its success will be dependent on how many people click on it to see it."

THE CAROUSEL OF PROGRESS

While U.S. theatrical box office grosses fell roughly 1 percent in 2008 and moviegoing declined 5 percent to roughly 1.3 billion tickets at U.S. theaters, aspiring indie filmmakers have reason to be optimistic. Despite the global downturn, the implosion of high-profile hedge funds, the shuttering of several leading indie-film distributors, and record unemployment figures among investment bankers who can no longer readily invest in first or second films, there are many trends taking shape that will create exciting opportunities for indie filmmakers in the near term. Clever new entertainment devices and Web 3.0 innovations are coming together to allow unaffiliated content creators (and independent video game designers) to reach enormous global audiences in 2010 and beyond.

Filmmakers can already purchase $300 Blu-ray DVD burners from AMEX and Sony that enable them to showcase and sell their films on high-definition discs just in time for the latest HD adoption wave, while the Web continues to provide more avenues for getting standard definition and HD content in front of consumers than ever before. In 2008 Netflix partnered with TiVo and Microsoft's Xbox LIVE to stream movies, Amazon's Video On Demand made movies available through TiVo, and Blockbuster began offering online movie rentals as well.

LG, Sony, Panasonic, Vizio, and others developed IP-enabled TVs to allow consumers to watch Web video without additional hardware, Pinnacle introduced its PCTV HD Pro Stick, while Apple boosted its selection of HD podcasts, movies, and TV shows. Hulu, a joint project of NBC Universal Inc. and News Corp., continued to catch on with a mix of ad-supported film and television content, while the new Adobe Media Player introduced audiences to PlayValue and other cool shows from OnNetworks.com.

In June 2008, the management consulting firm PricewaterhouseCoopers projected that the U.S. entertainment and media market would expand at a compound annual growth rate of 4.8 percent, reaching $759 billion in 2012. The PwC report also projected that the international growth rate for media and entertainment consumption would expand at a compound annual growth rate of 6.6 percent, reaching $2.2 trillion in 2012. This trend line was supported by Hollywood studios' record overseas theatrical grosses of $9.9 billion in 2008, up 4 percent from their $9.5 billion international theatrical gross in 2007. And as audiences overseas become more habituated to moviegoing, technology adoption will make it easier to deliver film content to their homes. The BRIC nations comprising Brazil, Russia, India, and China are expected to add more than 800 million new PCs by 2015, and the Asia-Pacific nations are projected to add still another 200 million PCs by 2015, according to Forrester Research.

Sorting and monetizing indie-film content on a global scale may still prove to be a challenge, but one bridge to increasingly tech-savvy audiences abroad could be real-time language translation software, a Holy Grail of computing, that would allow streaming content to be presented in each country's own language. While it may sound like science fiction, teams at Google, Microsoft, MIT, and Carnegie Mellon have long been looking into statistical algorithms for translating speech in real time. Google Mobile App for the iPhone can already provide voice-activated search results, but an even bigger opportunity will result from real-time language translation in nonmilitary applications.

Toward this end, translation softare developers from around the world gathered in Hawaii for the eighth biennial conference of the Association for Machine Translation in the Americas in late 2008, to discuss the rapid translation of spoken and typed chat communciation. A breakthrough in this area would allow nonnative speakers to enjoy overseas boradcasts and purchase films from a global database that could then be viewed in a person's native tongue the way DVDs regularly include multiple language tracks.

Another approach to translating independent films for audiences overseas may soon come from digital speech software developers such as Cepstral.com or NaturalSoft, whose downloadable software can already turn a dialogue continuity list—the written transcript of a film's final dialogue track—into English, either with accents or without. Someday soon, independent filmmakers will be able to use next-generation text-to-speech software to create alternate language tracks for streaming abroad, allowing filmmakers to aggregate billions of consumers and remain independent from idea inception to production to global distribution. Digital storefronts put up by Amazon, BitTorrent.com, or iTunes may someday host or mirror feature-length indie films and leverage the fallow processing power of millions of connected PCs (or next-gen video game consoles) to translate movie dialogue into multiple languages on the fly for streaming all over the world.

Until then, indie filmmakers can self-distribute DVDs

following the example of Sally Cruikshank's FunOnMars
.com and look forward to a day when AirCell broadband-
enabled airlines give passengers the ability to stream content
from Netflix, SnagFilms.com, and other film-related sites.
New Pay-Per-View libraries piped into headrest screens on
Boeing 787 Dreamliners and Airbus A380s will present still
another opportunity for tomorrow's indie filmmakers to
showcase and monetize their work.

With so many exciting possibilities taking shape, filmmakers should be wary of signing away their films' digital distribution or exhibition rights in perpetuity and recognize that
their work—however raw—may have real value that new
technology may unlock. As with many decisions in the indie-
film world, consulting a qualified attorney (and perhaps two
or three) about where traps and pitfalls may be hidden is a
smart place to start. Of course, however things ultimately
shake out and whoever becomes the next Tyler Perry, Barbara Kopple, Kasi Lemmons, Chris Eyre, Rebecca Miller, or
Robert Rodriguez, the best time to get started making an
independent film is not tomorrow, not next week, and not
next year, "maybe when the economy gets a little better," but
today.

Appendix I

INDEPENDENT-FILM BUDGETS

INDEPENDENT-FILM BUDGET: $75,000

Category Description

Above-the-Line Expenses

Story and Script	$1,500
Director	$1,500
Producers	$1,500
Casting Director	$500
Lead Actors	$1,000
Supporting Cast	$500
Day Players	$500
Other Casting Costs	$700
Transportation	$1,500
Fund-raising Effort	$2,000
Legal Consultation	$4,000
Above-the-Line Total	$15,200

Production Expenses

Cinematographer	$2,500
First Assistant Cinematographer	$500
Camera Package	$1,600
Second Camera	$1,000
Production Sound	$4,000
Vehicle Rentals	$3,000
Vehicle Insurance	$500
Production Designer	$1,200
Other Art Direction	$2,600
Wardrobe and Makeup	$3,000
Lighting Package	$5,000
Set Construction	$1,000
Set Operations	$10,000
Production Staff	$4,000
Bank Charges	$50
Miscellaneous Expenses	$2,000
Production Insurance	$5,000
Still Frames and Polaroids	$150
Production Total	$47,100

Postproduction Expenses

Editor	$5,500
Postproduction	$3,000
Editing Package	$500
Postproduction Sound	$500
Miscellaneous Expenses	$200
Composer	$1,000
Music	$2,000
Postproduction Total	$12,700
Grand Total	**$75,000**

INDEPENDENT-FILM BUDGET: $1.2 MILLION

Category Description

Above-the-Line Expenses

Story and Script	$50,000
Director	$50,000
Producers	$100,000
Cast and Casting Costs	$50,000
Fund-raising Effort	$20,000
Legal Consultation	$30,000
Above-the-Line Total	$300,000

Production Expenses

Art Department	$50,000
	$10,000
Set Operations	$35,000
Set Decoration	$8,000
Props	$10,000
Wardrobe	$8,000
Hair and Makeup	$5,000
Lighting	$7,000
Camera	$40,000
Sound	$30,000
Trucks and Vehicles	$10,000
Transportation	$50,000
Locations	$50,000
Film and Lab	$25,000
Tests	$500
Production Total	$338,500

Postproduction Expenses

Editing	$50,000
Music	$25,000
Score	$15,000
Post Sound	$50,000
Film and Lab	$160,000
Main and End Titles	$10,000
Reserve	$10,000
Unforeseen Costs	$40,000
Postproduction Total	$360,000

Other Expenses

Administration	$5,000
Insurance: 3 percent	$29,955
Contingency: 10 percent	$99,850
Self-Distribution Reserve	$100,000
Other Expenses Total	$234,805
Grand Total	**$1,233,305**

INDEPENDENT-FILM BUDGET: $5 MILLION

Category Description

Above-the-Line Expenses

Story	$50,000
Writing	$100,000
Producers	$200,000

Director	$100,000
Cast	$600,000
Cast Contractuals	$75,000
Travel and Living	$90,000
Fund-raising Effort	$50,000
Legal Consultation	$60,000
Above-the-Line Total	$1,325,000

Production Expenses

Background Actors	$70,000
Production Staff	$350,000
Camera	$170,000
Set Design	$70,000
Set Construction	$65,000
Set Operations	$110,000
Electrical	$150,000
Special Effects	$20,000
Set Dressing	$130,000
Props	$65,000
Animal and Trainer	$4,000
Wardrobe	$100,000
Makeup and Hairstylists	$50,000
Production Sound	$80,000
Transportation	$350,000
Location Expense	$200,000
Production Film and Lab	$175,000
Tests	$1,000
Production Total	$2,160,000

Postproduction Expenses

Editing	$200,000
Post Supervision	$40,000
Music	$60,000
Composer	$30,000
Postproduction Sound	$90,000
Titles	$15,000
Opticals, Mattes, Inserts	$6,000
Stock Footage	$4,000
Laboratory Processing	$25,000
Delivery Requirements	$20,000
Unforeseen Costs	$25,000
Extra Hard Drives	$5,000
Total Postproduction	$520,000

Other Expenses

Administrative Expenses	$15,000
Insurance: 3 percent	$120,150
Contingency: 10 percent	$400,500
Completion Bond: 3 percent	$120,150
Financing Costs: 6 percent	$240,300
Self-Distribution Reserve	$100,000
Other Costs Total	$996,100
Grand Total	**$5,001,100**

Appendix II

SAMPLE FORMAL AGENT / SCREENWRITER REPRESENTATION CONTRACT

This agreement is entered into this _____ day of _____, between _____ (hereinafter referred to as the "Author/Screenwriter"), located at _____, and (the person sending out the script on the Author/Screenwriter's behalf) _____ of company _____ (hereinafter referred to as the "Agent"), located at _____.

WHEREAS, the Agent acknowledges that the Author/Screenwriter is a writer of proven talents; and

WHEREAS, the Author/Screenwriter wishes to have an Agent represent him in marketing certain rights herein;

and

WHEREAS, the Agent is capable of marketing the writing created by the Author/Screenwriter;

and

WHEREAS, the Agent wishes to represent the Author/Screenwriter:

NOW, THEREFORE, in consideration of the foregoing premises and the mutual covenants hereinafter set forth and other valuable considerations, the parties agree as follows:

1. Agency. The Author/Screenwriter appoints the Agent to act as his representative for the Work:

   a) in the following geographical area—the World.
   b) for the following markets: Book publishing, motion picture, television, and subsidiary rights in serialization. As well as multimedia ventures related to projects represented by the

Agent, and on deals made by the Agent and agreed to by the Author/Screenwriter.

c) to be the Author/Screenwriter's Agent in the area and markets indicated for a period of undetermined months from the execution of this contract.

Any rights not granted to the Agent are reserved for the Author/Screenwriter.

2. Best Efforts. The Agent agrees to use his best efforts in submitting the Author/Screenwriter's work for the purpose of securing publication for the Author/Screenwriter. The Agent shall negotiate the terms of any publication contract that is offered, but the Author/Screenwriter may reject any contract if he finds the terms thereof unacceptable.

3. Term. This agreement shall take affect as of the date first set forth above, and remain in full force and effect for a term of undetermined months for marketing, unless terminated as provided in Paragraph 10, or superseded by a sale as specified in Paragraph 4. If the work is still being marketed and has not been canceled as specified in Paragraph 10, the contract automatically renews until such separation occurs.

4. Commissions. The Agent shall be entitled to a 15 percent commission for publishing work during the term of this Agreement and 10 percent on film, except that no commission shall be paid on work the Agent does not handle in the contract. However, it is understood that for any contracts negotiated the Agent shall continue to receive payments (commission on royalties, etc.) until the property is no longer for sale in any retail form. If terminated in conjunction with Paragraph 9, the Author/Screenwriter shall have the right to have payments, less agency fees, paid directly to them.

It is understood by both parties that no commissions shall be paid on publication or assignments rejected by the Author/Screenwriter or for which the Author/Screenwriter fails to receive payment, regardless of the reason payment is not made. Further, no commission shall be payable for any part of the billing that is due to expenses incurred by the Author/Screenwriter and reimbursed by the client (Publisher, Producer, or other buyer of the Author/Screenwriter's writings). In the event that a flat fee is paid by the client, the Agent's commission shall be payable only on the fee as reduced for expenses.

5. Sub-Agents. In the event sub-agents are used to secure other worldwide rights, the Agent will charge the Author/Screenwriter a 5 percent commission with sub-agent being paid separately. The Author/Screenwriter shall have the right to refuse sub-agent représentation and have offers negotiated by the Agent when possible.

6. Billing. The Agent shall be responsible for all billings.

7. Payments. The Agent shall make all payments due to the Author/Screenwriter within 30 days of receipt of any fees covered by this Agreement. Such payments due shall be deemed trust funds and shall not be intermingled with funds belonging to the Agent. Late payments shall be accompanied by interest calculated at the rate of 10 percent annually.

8. Accounting. The Agent shall send copies of statements of account received by the Agent to the Author/Screenwriter when rendered. If requested, the Agent shall also provide the Author/Screenwriter with semiannual accounting showing all income for the period. The clients' names and addresses, the fees paid, the dates of payment, the amounts on which the Agent's commissions are to be calculated, and the sums due less those amounts already paid will be handled by the Agent. The Agent shall also provide quarterly copies of all rejection letters and an accounting of monies paid out for manuscript mailings, telephone calls, or copies.

9. Inspection of the Books and Records. The Agent shall keep the books and records with respect to payments due at his place of business and permit the Author/Screenwriter to inspect these books and records during normal business hours on the giving of reasonable notice.

10. Termination. Either party giving thirty (30) days written notice to the other party may terminate this agreement. In the event of the bankruptcy or insolvency of the Agent, this Agreement shall also terminate. The rights and obligations under Paragraphs 5, 6, 7, and 8 shall survive termination, provided that in the event of termination the Author/Screenwriter shall have the right to have payments (less commissions) paid directly to the Author/Screenwriter rather than to the Agent as set forth in Paragraph 6.

11. Assignment. This Agreement shall not be assigned by either of the parties hereto. It shall be binding on and inure to the benefit

of successors, administrators, executors, or heirs of the Agent or Author/Screenwriter.

12. Postage and Copies. All copy and postage costs and will be accounted for in a log on a per submission basis, a copy of which the Author/Screenwriter shall receive as a billing for postage expenses, not to exceed actual costs. In the event the advance is equal to or greater than $10,000, and finalized within the first three months of the contract, the Author/Screenwriter shall be reimbursed fully for the marketing expenses.

13. Contact. All contact with editors, film producers, distribution companies, publishers must be made through the Agent until a deal has been made. Contact with buyers by the Author/Screenwriter without Agent mediation will result in cancellation of this Agreement.

14. Independent Contractor Status. Both parties agree that the Agent is acting as an independent contractor. This Agreement is not an employment contract; nor does it constitute a joint venture or partnership between the Author/Screenwriter and Agent.

15. Amendments and Merger. All amendments to this Agreement must be written. This Agreement incorporates the entire understanding of the parties.

16. Governing Law. The laws of the State of California shall govern this Agreement.

IN WITNESS WHEREOF, the parties have signed this Agreement as of the date set forth below.

Author/Screenwriter _____ Date _____

Agent _____ Date _____

Acknowledgments

This book could not have been possible without the encouragement and bottomless support of countless people, including:

Larry Aidem
David Albert
Rabbi Thomas Alpert
Robert Anderson
Tucker Austin
Dani Aznar
Andrew and Sarah Baehr
Matt Bai
Kim Bangash
Eunice and Jim Baros
Hope and Cara Baros
Irene and Bill Baros
Bruce Barr
Heidi Basile
Taylor Batten
Steven Beer
Tom Bernard
Julie Bernstein
Michael Biehn
Matt and Erika Bierman
Bryan Bilgore
Barry and Linda Blesser
Elliot Blumberg
Hannah Borum
Dave and Melinda
    Boxenbaum
Anthony Bregman
Megan Bruce
Dan Burrows
Michelle Byrd
Meir Calderone
Joe Cano
Noel Capon
Edward Carhart
Dr. Jim Cassiola
John and Meg Chamberin
Gloria Chapman
Mitchell and Walli Chefitz
Sarah Church
Dr. Bruce Churchill
Jodi Sternoff Cohen
Tim and Mandy Collins
William Cooper
Terry Corcoran
Sam Craig
Doug Creutz
Albie and Hillary Dahlberg
Julian D'Ambrosi

Craig Daniel
Rachel Deahl
Jess Dear
Carmen de Jesus
Gwarlann de Kerviler
Krystal Demaine
Stephanie Demos
David Doctor
Bob Doughtery
Meirav Eibushutz
Emmanuel Eleyae
Cassian Elwes
Gail Evans
Roxana Fariborz
Tammy Fastman
Bob and Brenda Feldman
Jessica Ferri
Adam Fields
Linda Fosburg
Joe and Jen Fox
John Frelinghuysen
Ron and Sherry Funt
Manny Garcia
Salvador Garcia-Ruiz
Jim Gianopulos
Laura Glenn and Eric Sorkin
Josh Goldberg
Betsy Goldman
Wendy Gordon
Tracy Grant
Micah Green
Emma Greer
Susanne Gross
Ted Gup
Yosh Han
Waleed Haram
Grant Hart
Patricia Hayes
Justine Henzell
John and Carla Hodulik
Wanda and Rev. George
    Holcombe
Ted Hope
Marcus Hu
Takuya Ito
Chere Jalali
Justin and Catherine
    Jefferies

Dr. Stuart Kammeny
Mike Katz
Melissa and Harry Keel
Omar Khudari
Abigail Kies
Michael Kirschenheiter
Geoff Kloske
Carin Knoop
Stephanie Kolin
Eva Kolodner
Steve Konicki
Hajime Kosai
Jennifer Krugman
Steve Kydd
Jennifer Lapidus
Rob La Franco
Bobo Lapidus
Hannah Lapidus
Horea Laptes
Rich Lara
David Lawrence, Jr.
Fr. Robert Lawton, S.J.
Annie Leahy
Betty Leu
Andy Levin
Owen Levin
John Lewis
Melanie Lipka
Lewis Lloyd
Denio Madera
Miriam Marcus
David Marlin
Melissa Martin
Rick Martin, MD
Robert Martin
Amy McCarthy
Gene Miller
Nicola Miner
Jerome Monstrone
Bob Mould
Jim Murray
Scott Neeson
Terry Nelson
Thao Nguyen
Eli Noam
Mike Noer
Greg Norton
Michael Now

Cory Oltz
Louise O'Riordan
Denise Oswald
Joe Ortiz
Sandy Padwe
Jonathan Paisner
Tim and Rebecca Panos
Kimberly Peirce
Jacie Peiser
Rabbi Rex Perimeter
Craig Phillips
Mark Piesanen
Laura Pinsky
Ken Pries
Christina Proenza
James Prusky
Jim Quinn
Tomaso Radaelli
Susan Radom
Michael Robinson
Jeff and Alison Rosenberg
Rob Rosenberg
Randall Rothenberg
Brad Rothchild
Alice Rowen
Dan and Coco Rowen
Emily Rueb
Bird Runningwater

Marc and Holly Ruxin
Sarah Ruxin
Dr. Steven Sabat
Ted Sarandos
Mary Beth Sasso
Cliff Schorer
Geoff Scott
Nina Shapiro and Alex
   Kentsis
Sharat Sharan
Paul Shea
Larry Sherman
Roxana Shershin
Joseph and Anat Shmulovich
Michali Shmulovich
Susan Short
Suhail Sikhtian
Kristen Silvi
Lowell Singer
Mary Jane Shalski
Ellen Sobolik
Penelope Spheeris
Mark Stolaroff
Elizabeth Stone
Kathy Styponias
Bruce and Cheryl Tall
Cliff Tall
Wyatt Tall

Betty Tanenbaum
Irina Tarses
Warren Thomas
Ken Thompson
Lance Totten
Peter and Wendy Trevesani
Katica Urbanc
Michael Vellinga
Sanjay and Monica Verma
Kathleen Walsh
Philippe Wamba
Hal Wanless
Carlos Watson
Paul Westerberg
Blake Wilkerson
Kristen Willard
Eugene Williams
Jody Wolfe
Jud and Liz Wolfe
Sean Wolfe
Eden Wurmfeld
Mitch Yankowitz
Eve Yohalem
Morgan Zalkin
Alyssa Zeller
Roy Zimmerman
and Quasar, the yellow
   Labrador

Index